So Cold A Sky

Upper Michigan Weather Stories

KARL BOHNAK

SO COLD A SKY

Upper Michigan Weather Stories

Karl Bohnak

Cover Design
Stacey Willey and Elizabeth Yelland
Edited
Rebecca Tavernini and Judy Johnson
Interior Layout
Stacey Willey and Elizabeth Yelland
Illustrations
Elizabeth Yelland

Copyright 2006
Karl Bohnak

Publisher
Cold Sky Publishing
Negaunee, Michigan

Print Consultant
Globe Printing, Inc.
Ishpeming, Michigan

Printer
Thomson-Shore
Dexter, Michigan

ISBN 0-9778189-0-X
Library of Congress Control Number
551.6/09774/9–dc22

First Printing April 2006
Second Printing July 2006

Bohnak, Karl, 1953-
So Cold a Sky: Upper Michigan Weather Stories / Karl Bohnak.
p. cm.
ISBN 0-9778189-0-X (pbk.)
1. Weather–History–Michigan–Upper Peninsula. 2. Climate–History–
Michigan–UpperPeninsula. 3. Upper Peninsula (Mich.)–History. I. Title.
QC857.U6B63 2006
551.6/09774/9–dc22

Cover Photo "Storm of 38" downtown Ishpeming Courtesy Superior View Studio

ACKNOWLEDGEMENTS

A project that covers this much territory (both geographically and temporally) requires cooperation and collaboration. I could not even have begun without help. For a number of years, this book was only an idea. It would have remained that way if not for my wife and partner, Liz. I thank her for her gentle urging and support. She was also behind the general design of this book. If this work were likened to a birthing, I thank David Hawthorne for inducing labor. I would also like to thank Christine Rosenberg who provided encouragement long ago.

Special appreciation goes out to my editor, Becky Tavernini. Her work cleaned up my work but kept its heart and soul intact. I am also grateful to Stacey Willey, who put in long hours in layout and design and to Judy Johnson for her meticulous proofing of the final draft.

I had a rough idea where I was headed when I began writing. These librarians and historians helped set a course and provided direction and resources as the work evolved:

Rosemary Michelin, the J.M. Longyear Library in Marquette as well as Kaye Hiebel, Marquette County History Museum; Elizabeth Delene, Bishop Baraga Archives; Lori Rose and Clara Mosenfelder, Delta County Historical Society; Janet Callow, Menominee County Historical Society; Barbara Bennett, Dickinson County Library; Joe Carlson, Carnegie Library in Ironwood; Ray Maurin, Gogebic County Historical Society; Bruce Johanson, Pat Simons and Vicky James, Ontonagon Historical Society; Joanne Josie Olson, Rockland Historical Museum; Denise Korman, Houghton County Historical Society; Nancy Bergman, Luce County Historical Society, Travis Freeman, WNBY Radio, Vonceil Le Duc, Schoolcraft County Historical Society and Susan James, Bayliss Library, Sault Ste. Marie. Special thanks goes to Myrna Ward of Kingsford and J. Ervin Bates of Mason for information they supplied, as well as Russ Magnaghi, professor of history at Northern Michigan University for his suggestions. I am also grateful to Regis Walling, past curator of the Bishop Baraga archives. The information she sent me some years ago provided a beginning.

I am also grateful to Jack Deo, Superior View Studio, Marquette, Tom Buchkoe, Marcia Mullins, Lyn Veeser, Art Maki, Gerry Gardner, John Mullins, Helen Micheau, Marko Movrich, Jim Koermer, Plymouth State University, Jerry Bielicki, Tom Hultquist and Don Rolfson, National Weather Service, Marquette, as well as Bob Johnson, Daily News, Iron Mountain/Kingsford and Howard Kiser, The Evening News in Sault Ste. Marie for their generosity in granting permission to use their images throughout this publication.

Special thanks is extended to all those who related their weather stories to me. Without your input, I would only have a collection of dry facts and figures. Your experiences provided insight and color to a subject and area of the country I am passionate about.

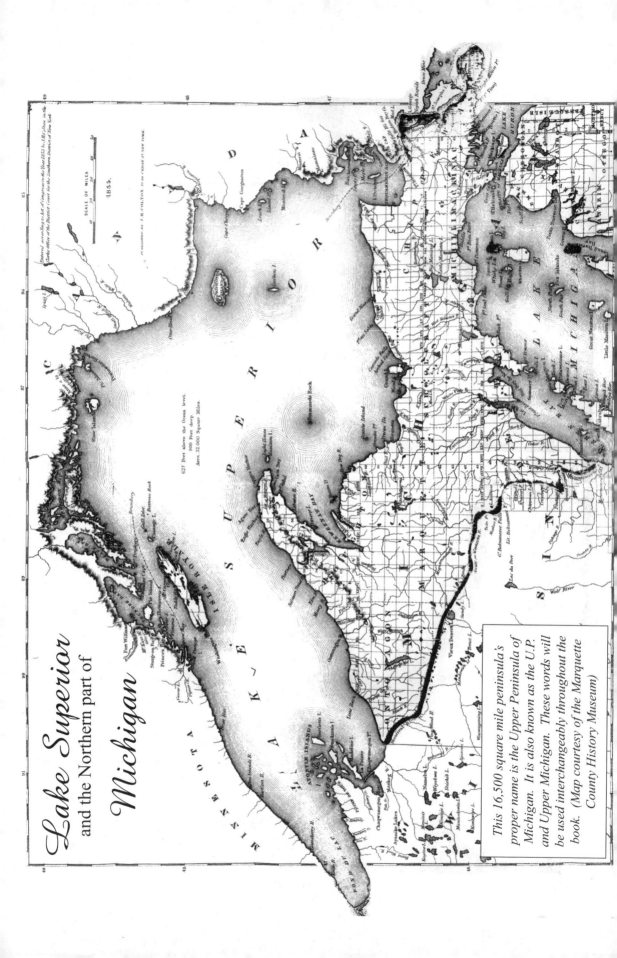

Lake Superior
and the Northern part of

Michigan

SCALE OF MILES
1854.

627 Feet above the Ocean level.
900 Feet deep.
Area 32.000 Square Miles.

This 16,500 square mile peninsula's proper name is the Upper Peninsula of Michigan. It is also known as the U.P. and Upper Michigan. These words will be used interchangeably throughout the book. (Map courtesy of the Marquette County History Museum)

"And we who have seen…[the Lake Superior region's]…development …may pause in wonder that so few and so feeble a people living under so cold a sky should have permitted to share so largely in changing the seat of empire, and enlarging the happiness of the world."

—Peter White's closing remarks during his address at the semi-centennial celebration of the opening of the Sault Locks, August 3, 1905

PROLOGUE

I grew up a snow fanatic in Milwaukee, Wisconsin. My first vivid memories of the weather go back to first grade during the winter of 1959-60. Milwaukee had an incredible snow year (for Milwaukee), accumulating a whopping 93.3", more than doubling the seasonal average. The total fell only a couple of storms short of the all-time record of 109.8" in 1885-86.

I remember being fascinated at how the sky would often be bright at night. What was the cause of this? My seven-year-old deductive powers came up with an answer to the mystery: The brightness came from the reflection of the street lights off the falling snow flakes, and further, I reasoned, the harder it snowed, the brighter it would be. I was enthralled and became a snow "freak." I longed for snowstorms. When a storm blew in, I would stay up all night watching it pile up. After the storm, I would help my father shovel our substantial driveway, and as I got older, I took over a good share of the shoveling duties. I loved piling snow on snow, trying to see how high I could grow the snow banks adjacent to the driveway entrance.

This love affair with snow also brought bitter disappointments. Most years had only average snow, which amounts to less than four feet, and some years had much less. I did not lose much sleep, either; even in a good year, there would only be a couple of big storms that got me excited enough to stay awake. More often than not, the storm would pass north of Milwaukee giving us a brief period of snow, sleet and then just rain. The local TV weatherman, my weather hero Bill Carlsen (I never met him in person but he talked to me every weeknight, grease pen in hand, standing in front of the glass covered map of the United States.), told me "If the wind comes around to the northeast, that means the storm will stay south of us and we'll get heavy snow." I watched the trees, the smokestacks and the flags, hoping for a sign that the wind was "backing" to the northeast. Most often, my hopes were dashed; the wind would "veer" from the east to the south as the storm passed north, dropping its heavy snow band on central or northern Wisconsin and the Upper Peninsula of Michigan.

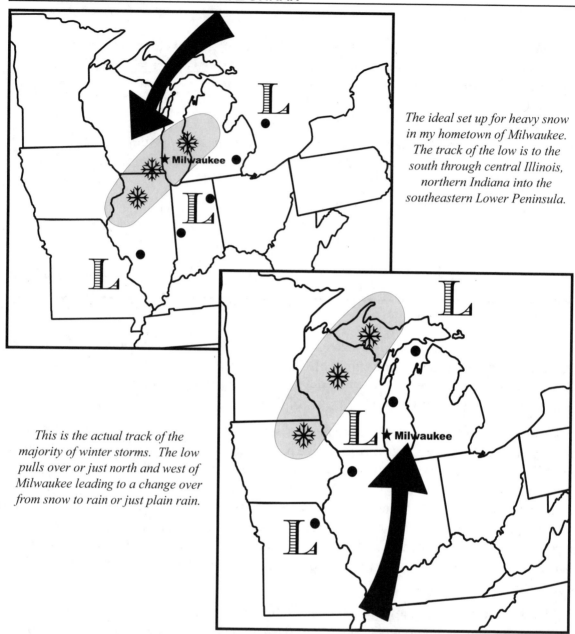

The ideal set up for heavy snow in my hometown of Milwaukee. The track of the low is to the south through central Illinois, northern Indiana into the southeastern Lower Peninsula.

This is the actual track of the majority of winter storms. The low pulls over or just north and west of Milwaukee leading to a change over from snow to rain or just plain rain.

There was one time when the wind swung to the northeast and started picking up with an ominous gray overcast, yet it only snowed a flake here and there. Ninety miles to the south, however, Chicagoans were living through a once-in-a-lifetime event: The blizzard of '67 brought two feet of snow and a week of paralysis there, while Milwaukee caught a mere dusting by comparison on the storm's northern fringe.

Then there was the time in early January 1971 when a mega storm developed in Texas and headed northeast, spreading a mantle of heavy snow from Kansas to Wisconsin. It began snowing heavily in Milwaukee early on Sunday morning, January 3. By early afternoon we had already accumulated a good six to eight inches and the forecast called for snow all night. I was very confident my high school Christmas vacation would be extended one more day. Then the temperature started to rise and by evening it began to rain. It rained all night accompanied by occasional lightning and thunder. By Monday morning, the streets were washed clean of all the snow and school started on schedule.

I began college with the goal of becoming a meteorologist. Mathematics was not my strong suit, however, and since meteorology, the physics of the atmosphere, involves a good deal of math, I was in trouble. I ended up settling for a degree in communications with the intention of one day going back to school for meteorology.

I began my career in broadcasting at a radio station in central New Hampshire. I moved there for, what else: snow. I was always impressed by and, at the same time, envious of the big nor'easters that roared up the east coast and buried New England. I was in New Hampshire during the winter of '78-'79, ironically, one of the snowiest winters this past century in the Midwest. Milwaukee ended up with a record snow cover of 30 inches at the end of January that year.

I eventually moved back to Wisconsin, got married and took a job at a radio station in Milwaukee. Then I got an opportunity to go back to school—I became unemployed. I got fired from my position at the Milwaukee radio station which I had only started a couple of months earlier. I went back to school and this time around I excelled in math. I took meteorology courses at the University of Wisconsin while working part time doing weekend weather at a TV station in Madison. I left school with the equivalent of a bachelor's degree in meteorology and through a mixture of persistence and good fortune landed a job at the station I grew up watching in Milwaukee.

I was never really satisfied with my stint at this station. First of all, I worked a spotty schedule broadcasting weather. The rest of the time I spent reporting; putting together feature stories that did not really interest me. Second, the snow situation was still a source of frustration. The storms still passed to the north on a regular basis, including the monster Thanksgiving weekend storm of 1985 (*examined in Part II of this book*), which moved just north of Milwaukee, burying a vast section of the Plains and Upper Lakes.

I searched for the "ultimate" job and location. At one point, I entertained the thought of moving to Burlington, Vermont to take a job as primary weather anchor at a small television station there. I would have had plenty of snow; however, I would have had to apply for food stamps to feed my family.

Finally, through a twist of fate, a good friend in the broadcasting field gave me a tip on a possible job opening at a TV station in Marquette, Michigan in the heart of the snowiest region in the Midwest. I loved the beauty of Upper Michigan. I had vacationed there, and at one point in the summer of 1980, I even drove up to check out the radio job scene in Marquette. I remember how long the drive seemed from the Wisconsin border through Bruce Crossing then east to Marquette. There was so much forest and so few people! To a kid growing up in the city of Milwaukee, northern Wisconsin was the forest. The U.P. was the wilderness!

The TV job opened up in Marquette and I started in April 1988. I have been a resident of Upper Michigan ever since. I now have snow and more snow as well as a gorgeous place to live with a rich, colorful history. One thing I noticed immediately when I began visiting with groups and organizations as part of my work on television, was the interest and pride Upper Michigan residents have in their history. Mention a big snowstorm and older residents will inevitably bring up the "Storm of '38." Just about everyone has a "storm story" to tell.

This book looks at some of those stories. Part I begins with the earliest recorded information on the region, compiled by the French Jesuit missionaries. To them, weather was merely an obstacle or advantage in their ultimate objective: the conversion of the natives to Christianity. Their legends and writings are examined and put into perspective by looking at what we know of the climate then compared to now.

The earliest Americans left tidbits of information that give us a glimpse at their way of life and the weather they encountered. This first section is really the early history of the region with weather and climate as a backdrop. I took some detours along the way; if a story or circumstance interested me, I included it, even if it did not deal explicitly with the weather. Some of these pioneers' feats were amazing; the obstacles they encountered and the conditions they endured are the stuff of legends.

A survey of more recent weather events is undertaken in Part II. The cold waves, snowstorms, gales, severe weather and even heat waves are chronicled. I tried to talk to as many Upper Michigan residents as possible to get their stories. It is their experiences that give the weather life. These accounts take weather events from charts, tables and statistics and breathe vitality into them. In this context, weather becomes part of the shared history of the U.P.—a region many feel is a very special place.

This is by no means an exhaustive study of all major storms and events. A few of the more notable or notorious occurrences are described. In some cases, a storm might be included because someone had a story or event connected with it that etched the date firmly in their minds. That, I believe is the point: we cannot separate the weather and environment from the milieu of our lives. This book is an attempt to honor that connection.

I have also sought to reach a wide audience. I have attempted to include enough weather facts, figures and maps to hold the interest of weather enthusiasts, while at the same time engage the reader who likes a good story about one of the more unique regions in the United States.

TABLE OF CONTENTS

PART I

CHAPTER 1
The First European Explorers in the Lake Superior Region

CHAPTER 2
Alexander Henry's Adventures in the Lake Superior Region

CHAPTER 3
Weather during the earliest american settlement: 1820s-1830s

CHAPTER 4
Weather of the Early Mining Boom: 1840s-1850s

CHAPTER 5
The Snowshoe Priest

PART II
Weather Events of the Modern Era:
1864 to present
CHAPTER 6
Cold Waves, Cold Winters

CHAPTER 7
Snowstorms, Snowy Winters

CHAPTER 8
Late Season Snows 1870s-1880s

CHAPTER 9
Floods

CHAPTER 10
Heat Waves, Hot Weather

CHAPTER 11
Severe Weather

CHAPTER 12
Fire Weather

CHAPTER 13
Autumn Gales

THE FIRST RECORDED STORIES
OF WEATHER IN THE REGION

The primary native people to inhabit the area were the Chippewa (popular adaptation of Ojibway or Ojibwa—these words will be used interchangeably). They passed down their history orally, though they also communicated through pictographs. Henry Rowe Schoolcraft, Indian Agent at Sault Ste. Marie, journeyed across Lake Superior to the Mississippi in 1831. At one point during the trip he was "astonished to perceive that... [figures drawn]...on the blazed side of a tree were read as easy as perfect gazettes" by his native guides. The author examines a drawing near the Agawa River on the eastern side of Lake Superior in Ontario. It depicts the frightful great-horned lynx or sea lion "Mishepeshu" who lurked under Lake Superior. This Manitou or spirit would stir the waters and drown people in sudden storms. Stories of this frightful creature were only told around fires in the lodges during winter, when Mishepeshu was securely locked beneath the ice.

PART I

CHAPTER 1

THE FIRST EUROPEAN EXPLORERS IN THE LAKE SUPERIOR REGION

"God speed you to Espirit," said the French cleric speaking in the tongue of the two Kiskokan Ottawas (Odawas) standing before him. The priest made a wide sign of the cross in the air as he spoke. "And take care of our young blackrobe." The speaker was Jesuit missionary Claude Jean Allouez. He was addressing the two Ottawas who would be acting as guides on a nearly five-hundred-mile canoe trip. Their charge, the blackrobe Allouez spoke of, was Father Jacques Marquette, a fellow Jesuit with a missionary zeal and an insatiable drive for exploration.

Allouez turned from the guides and glanced at the young priest who was carefully bundling his few belongings in preparation for the long journey ahead. He and the Ottawas would be traveling from the Sault or falls of St. Mary's to La Pointe on the west end of the largest of the inland seas; the one the natives of the region call Kitchi Gami, the Great Water. He would take over a mission Allouez had started two years earlier. At 32, Marquette was nearly the same age as Allouez, but he seemed younger.

Pere Allouez reflected on how he had felt that gushing idealism and sense of adventure once, too. Over time, the specter of reality had numbed some of his enthusiasm. The rugged, unforgiving harshness of the wilderness, the privation, the lack of responsiveness by the natives to God's word all took their toll and sapped some of his missionary zeal. He remembered how he had eagerly left Quebec only a few years back with plans to convert the tribes living along the great inland seas in the far west. He reflected on the long perilous journey of nearly two

Father Marquette
1637-1675

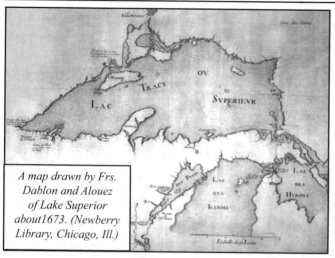

A map drawn by Frs. Dablon and Alouez of Lake Superior about1673. (Newberry Library, Chicago, Ill.)

thousand leagues to the "region of the Saguenay," the vast area that included the Great Water.

How he had suffered on that expedition! Fatigue, cold and hunger were his constant companions as he traveled with his reluctant native guides. He was amazed at how these people inured themselves to the privation. They could fast for days and still keep their strength. Yet even they had to resort to eating whatever they could to stay alive. Allouez remembered one particularly desperate time along the way when the party came upon a deer that had been dead for days. Everyone, including Allouez, consumed the rotten meat. He shuddered as the memory returned of the foul taste he carried in his mouth the rest of the day. The most despicable meal endured on his journey had to be the soup his guides made from a "certain moss that grows on rocks." The plant was always covered with spiders and caterpillars and when it was boiled it turned into a black, sticky broth. He reflected how the miserable fare did not impart life, but merely kept away death.

Allouez had borne the cross of his sufferings gladly, as did the other Jesuit missionaries before him. His predecessor, Pere Menard, had even given his life for the cause, disappearing mysteriously on a journey through the wilderness south of the Great Water in the summer of 1661. Allouez followed in the martyr's footsteps, establishing the mission where he was now sending his successor. He called the mission Espirit, the Mission of the Holy Ghost. His efforts at conversion fell far short of what he had originally hoped to achieve. The tribes of the region held fast to their aboriginal beliefs. While he was able to live peacefully among the natives and gain their trust while even baptizing a few of their children and dying elders, he had brought few souls into the fold of Christianity. This fact disappointed him. However, he put this unhappy feeling aside and marveled at the wonder of God's ways. A new missionary had come to pick up where he left off.

Jacques Marquette had already proven himself a capable missionary in his own right. While working with other Jesuits to establish the Sault mission, he had learned six native languages in just two years. He also developed a stoically optimistic philosophy concerning mission life in the New World wilderness: "One must not hope that he can avoid crosses in any of our missions," he wrote. "The best means to live there contentedly is not to fear them…and to expect…God's goodness."

Crosses in abundance were heaped on the shoulders of our young blackrobe from the start of his voyage to Espirit. Marquette bade his predecessor farewell and set off with the two guides in their birch bark canoe. After a strenuous paddle up the St. Marys River, the three travelers emerged onto Whitefish Bay, a large, relatively sheltered expanse of water on the eastern end of the Great Water, Lake Superior. Legend has it that before they even made it around Whitefish Point at the far northwest end of the end of the bay, they were hit with icy north winds laden with snow. A perilous journey along the south shore of Superior took nearly a month to complete.

Day after day in monotonous repetition, the voyagers fought wind, waves and then ice. Marquette may have learned the native languages of the region quickly, but he learned to follow the rhythmic swaying of his guides almost immediately. His life depended on it. As a big wave rolled its way from the open expanse of the angry lake they leaned their bodies landward to keep it from inundating their frail craft. The method worked but only to a point; water still constantly splashed into the

Marquette was accompanied by two Ottawa guides in his nearly month-long voyage along Lake Superior's south shore. The Jesuits, Marquette and Allouez, relied on the natives as their guides while traversing the region. (This image is from a bronze relief carving at the base of a Fr. Marquette statue in the City of Marquette.)

canoe drenching the priest's clothes, moccasins and the rest of his belongings. The great concentration that was needed to navigate among the pieces of jagged ice served to keep attention away from the discomfort. The effort expended while paddling and riding the swells created enough heat to keep Marquette from focusing on the unrelenting cold. It was when they found a safe place to land and stop for the night that the chill would set in.

Uncontrollable shivering would overtake the missionary once they reached the beach and put up for the night. The guides would find a spot to safely stash the canoe and then set up camp. The camp was often merely a spot on the beach out of the wind. If they were fortunate, they would scavange a few branches from the forest to provide a fire. The pine boughs also served as a crude bed. If the beleaguered party was extremely fortunate, a rabbit or other small game was snared to provide some nourishment. Some nights there was no fire, no food and no cushions and the missionary and his guides merely curled up wherever they could to spend a few hours in fitful sleep.

The wild beauty of this place was lost to our young blackrobe as he and his guides battled the wind, cold, snow and ice. The Pictured Rocks was only a place too steep and too dangerous to land their vessel; Grand Island merely a break from the icy north wind. Finally, "after a voyage of a

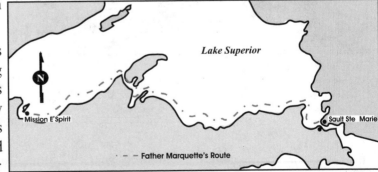

The route taken by Father Marquette and his native guides. Depending on the way his writings are interpreted, it was either a trip from the Sault to Espirit in August and September 1669 or from Espirit to the Sault in the spring of 1670.

What Caused the Little Ice Age?

Ascertaining a cause is difficult since weather observations were non-existent in the early part of the LIA and very sparse and primitive until the nineteenth century. Much of the evidence to support the existence of the LIA comes from indirect methods such as ice core analysis and tree ring measurements. Evidence also comes from unusual sources such as art. Paintings from Europe during this time often contain snow and ice scenes graphically demonstrating the degree of cold people lived with and to which they had become accustomed.

Art of the time graphically showed the degree of snow cover and cold during the Little Ice Age. (Peter Bruegel, the Elder "The Hunters in the Snow" housed at Kunsthistoricsches Museum Wien, Vienna reproduction from WebMuseum, Paris)

Scientists do know of two phenomena that appear to loom large as contributors to the cold, especially during the late seventeenth into the

month amid snow and ice, which blocked our passage," he later recounted, "and amid almost constant dangers of death" the weary trio arrived at their destination.

Here is where history becomes clouded. Marquette completed his harrowing journey and arrived at Mission Espirit on Madeline Island September 13, 1669. That would have meant he left the Sault and hit a snowstorm in the middle of August! The letter in which he wrote the account of his journey has been interpreted another way; the alternative view shared by some historians is that he was describing a voyage he took early that next spring back to the Sault.

Which interpretation is correct? Meteorologically there is nothing in the modern record which would indicate that such an extended period of wintry weather could occur in the late summer and early fall. The only two instances that come close over the last one hundred and thirty years is a wet, heavy snowfall that occurred during August in the early 1950s over a small area of northern Wisconsin. The other took place on August 8, 1872 when snow and slush "piled up to six inches in depth" on the decks of ships out on Lake Michigan with flurries reported at shore points the same day. These events were short-term anomalies, not a nearly one-month bout of winter occurring during late summer and early fall. It would be easy to dismiss this account as a popular legend until one looks at the backdrop of what was taking place in the rest of the world at this time. The latest research indicates the earth was locked in the depths of the Little Ice Age.

The Little Ice Age (LIA) was a period of great climate variability that included some brutally cold periods and lasted for several hundred years. Climatologists roughly place this wild period of weather between 1300 and 1900. In Europe, it followed a three-hundred-year interval of exceptionally mild weather called the Medieval Warm Period. During that time vineyards and winemaking flourished in England where even today it is too cold and wet to grow grapes. The warm, st... ...riod from about 1000 ...w the Vikings settle in ... while the Danes were ...celand.

...s began to change ...he worse as a series ...ought catastrophic ...Northern Europe. ...nd 1322 the "vast ...Northern Europe ...ion and death ...ear after year. ...bitter winters ...North Atlantic. ...nd became uninhabitable and the ...acuating Iceland. During the height ...e could climb the highest mountain ...pen water.

...inland, the Black Death ravaged ...eakened by malnutrition due to ...In some areas, over half the ...of the plague. As the weather ...he population of Europe looked ...ned that God's wrath was the ...e people found a scapegoat ...of witchcraft sprang up in ...the subsequent persecutions ...rians even claim the harsh ...pur migration to the New

v... Eu... col... dow... relat... hot s... much ... followi... the Old ... ice on L... ...ette made his harrowing ...approached its peak in ...anced daily due to the ...ast a kilometer farther ...lay. While there were ...tches that contained ...300 and 1900 was ...undred years or the ...t was happening in ...e idea of snow and ...ugust and early September

Maunder Minimum
(Graph To Show Sunspot Activity)

# of Sunspots — 150, 100, 50, 0

Year A.D. — 1600, 1650, 1700, 1750, 1800

1650 - 1710 NO SUNSPOTS

Between 1650 and 1710, few sunspots were observed. This appears to have been a contributor to the cold of the Little Ice Age, which reached its peak during these years.

early eighteenth century: sunspots and volcanic activity.

During the peak of the LIA, when Marquette made his miserable voyage on Lake Superior, very few sunspots were observed (sunspots were regularly counted shortly after the telescope was invented by Galileo in the early 1600s). This dearth of sunspots between 1645 and 1710 is called the "Maunder Minimum," named for the man who researched the phenomenon. In one thirty-year period during this time only fifty sunspots were observed. During the past one hundred years, a typical thirty-year period would yield forty to fifty **thousand** sunspots.

How might sunspots affect our climate? Sunspots are the measure of the sun's activity. The more sunspots on the sun, the more active it is; the fewer sunspots, the less active. Scientists are learning that very small fluctuations in solar output seem to result in noticeable changes in weather patterns hence, temperature changes on earth.

Some research indicates that high solar activity (large number of sunspots) leads to strong "zonal" or westerly flow in the mid-latitudes. In this pattern, cold air remains "bottled up" at high latitudes and will not hold over the continents. The fast westerly flow in the middle latitudes "scours out" the cold air. The winter of 2001-2002 occurred during a sunspot maximum. Fast westerly flow flooded the United States with mild air off the Pacific Ocean, resulting in one of the warmest winters on record. Conversely, in periods of low solar activity (lack of sunspots), the westerlies "relax" and cold air can easily and frequently move south into the middle latitudes.

Data also shows a large amount of volcanic activity during the latter seventeenth century into the early eighteenth century. Violent volcanic

remains an intriguing possibility.

If the unseasonable snowstorm occurred it was a singularity. The other Jesuits noted nothing unusual during their tenures in the Lake Superior wilderness. The harvesting of souls was the main concern of these missionaries and not the weather. The weather would be noted only if it was really unique or it hampered or aided travel.

Father Allouez recounted such an event in May 1667. On the 16th, Allouez left Madeline Island for Lake Nipigon. Like Marquette, he also left in a canoe with two native guides. On the 17th, they set out on a very dangerous twelve-hour paddle across the open lake. Allouez later recalled how "God assisted… [him]… very sensibly" in paddling with all his strength. He kept up with his Indian guides, paddling without stopping from morning until night. The "time of the calm" could give way to mountainous swells in a short period of time. If they did not reach the other shore before the waves started to build, the trio's canoe would be swamped and they would be doomed. The three made it across the lake safely, then retired for the night without eating.

The next day a forty-mile excursion across the open water of Lake Superior would have been impossible. A windswept rainstorm struck and the famished travelers had to be content with a "meager repast of Indian-corn and water" instead of fish. The wind and rain kept the guides from casting their nets. The following day the weather turned for the better and the voyagers made "eighteen leagues [around forty miles], rowing from daybreak until after sunset without stopping or disembarking".

They got word that Nipigon was still covered with ice so they did not leave Lake Superior until they got word that Nipigon's ice left on

Some research has shown that high sunspot activity contributes to fast zonal or westerly flow in the middle latitudes. These strong westerly winds "bottle up" the cold air in Canada leading to mild weather over the lower 48, including Upper Michigan. This and other factors led to one of the warmest winters on record in 2001-2002.

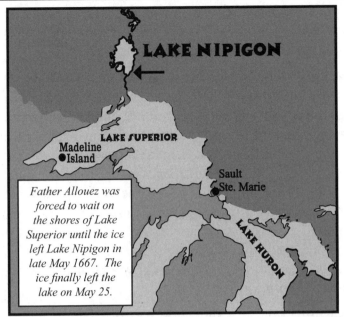

LAKE NIPIGON

LAKE SUPERIOR

Madeline
●Island

Sault
Ste. Marie

LAKE HURON

Father Allouez was forced to wait on the shores of Lake Superior until the ice left Lake Nipigon in late May 1667. The ice finally left the lake on May 25.

May 25. By modern climate standards, ice on Lake Nipigon in late May is unusual but not unprecedented. In 2003, after the coldest, longest winter in years, visible satellite pictures still showed ice on Lake Nipigon until May 16.

Allouez heard Indians talk of an exceptionally long, snowy winter in about 1664. He learned of this hard winter in conjunction with a tale that he found interesting enough to record. Allouez had baptized an old man on his deathbed and when the man died, contrary to normal burial custom, his family burned the body. When questioned why they reduced the body to ashes, they maintained that the father of this old man was a hare that walks on the snow in winter. Consequently the hare, the snow and the old man are from the same village. In other words they are considered relatives.

The Indians said that the hare once told his wife that he did not want his children to dwell in the bowels of the earth; that is to be buried. He felt that burial was not suitable for the relatives of the snow whose country of origin is the sky. Further, he proclaimed that if any of them were buried, he would pray

eruptions cool the atmosphere by throwing large amounts of debris into it; the debris can remain suspended up to several years after a major eruption. This "dust" filters sunlight and can cool the atmosphere significantly.

The most recent example of this cooling occurred in the early 1990s. Mt. Pinatubo erupted in the Phillipines in 1991. The dust ejected from the volcano circled the earth for the next year or two and contributed to one of Upper Michigan's coolest summers on record in 1992. New England's infamous "Year Without a Summer," in which significant snow fell in June, occurred in 1816 following the explosion of Mt. Tambora on an Indonesian Island the year before. Finally, the catastrophic eruption of Krakatoa in Indonesia in 1883 exacerbated Great Lakes cold in the middle 1800s (more on this in Part II). This combination of atmospheric anomalies may have led to an unseasonable

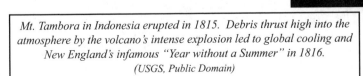

Mt. Tambora in Indonesia erupted in 1815. Debris thrust high into the atmosphere by the volcano's intense explosion led to global cooling and New England's infamous "Year without a Summer" in 1816.
(USGS, Public Domain)

snowstorm and cold wave in August and September 1669.

Father Allouez was told a story about a hard winter. The protagonist of the story was a hare that walks on snow in the winter. (Drawing by E. Yelland)

to his relative, the snow, to fall continuously and stay on the ground so that spring would not come. This he said would be punishment for not following his instructions.

It happened that three years earlier the old man's brother had died at the beginning of winter and was buried. Then the snow started to fall and kept on falling. It piled up to such an extent that winter hunting was impossible. Great numbers of tribal members died of hunger that season and the people despaired of ever seeing spring. The elders met to discuss what could be done in the face of this calamity and one of them remembered the story and what would happen if a member of that family was buried. Immediately the villagers disinterred the body and burned it. The Indians who related the story to Allouez maintained that as soon as the body was cremated the snow stopped and spring arrived.

Even in the midst of the Little Ice Age there were warm interludes. Father Marquette recalls how mild it was at Mackinac when he led a large group to the east in 1671. He spent the winter convincing four hundred to five hundred Indians to travel with him to Mackinac Island, where his superior, Father Dablon had set up the Mission of St. Ignatius. They left La Pointe on the west end of Lake Superior in a flotilla of 200 canoes, reaching Mackinac in the spring of 1671. The next winter did not truly set in at that location until after Christmas and then spring arrived in the middle of March.

Mild weather in the latter part of the winter of 1661 may have saved the life of Father Menard. He was staying as a guest of an Indian chief at the head of Keweenaw Bay near what is now L'Anse. As winter wore on, Menard felt compelled to criticize the chief for his intemperate habits. The chief did not appreciate Menard's counseling and banished him from the tribe. The unfortunate priest had to spend the remainder of the winter in a crude shelter made of branches and skins. Mild weather and the charity of a few women of the village helped him to survive the ordeal. In the summer of the same year he met his end under mysterious circumstances while bound for a mission on the north shore of Lake Michigan.

French Jesuit missionary activity in the Lake Superior region declined during the eighteenth century. By the mid-1700s, the French-Indian War brought the Upper Great Lakes under control of the British. Political boundaries in this isolated wilderness were not well defined. The British established a military outpost at Michilimackinac, at the present site of Mackinaw City, otherwise, the area for the most part, was ignored. British and French traders even managed to coexist in the Lake Superior region.

It was a Frenchman who told a young Brit named Alexander Henry about the wealth to be won in the fur trade of the west. The stories fired the imagination of Henry and he became determined to make his fortune in the fur trade of the Upper Great Lakes.

CHAPTER 2

The First Winter at Michilimackinac: 1761

Alexander Henry had big plans. At 21 years old he wanted to tap into the wealth of New France at the close of the French-Indian War. He left his home in New Jersey and headed north with the British Army in the summer of 1760. It was not long before tragedy struck; boats filled with supplies for his new life were wrecked in the St. Lawrence River. The determined young man pressed on. That chance meeting with the Frenchman who told him of the riches of the west gave him new hope and a new plan; he made his way to the Upper Great Lakes.

Henry traveled through the Lower Lakes up Lake St. Clair into Lake Huron and finally landed at the village of L'Arbre Croche near present day Harbor Springs. Maize was the chief product of the little trading post. Henry described this "Indian Corn" as the primary staple of the voyageurs who provided the main transportation to the region. The corn was prepared back in the village. First, it was boiled in strong lye to make the husks easier to remove. Then it was ground into meal and left to dry. This cornmeal was soft and friable like rice; perfect for a voyageur on the go.

Alexander Henry (1739-1824) spent some 15 years engaged in fur trading and mining in the Upper Great Lakes region.

"No other allowance is made of any kind, not even salt," wrote Henry about the voyageur's diet. "Bread is never thought of." Bread and meat were too bulky to carry on a canoe voyage that might last a year. The ration for each man was a quart of cornmeal a day; a month's supply consisted of a bushel with two pounds of prepared fat. Despite the monotonous, Spartan diet the men remained "healthy and capable of performing their heavy labor."

Henry ate what the Frenchmen ate as he traveled the Great Lakes. He also developed an understanding as to why these hardy men dominated trade in the Great Lakes wilderness. "The difficulty which would belong to an attempt to reconcile any other men than Canadians (Frenchmen) to this fare," he wrote, "seems to secure to them and their employers the monopoly of the fur trade."

The young Englishman settled at British occupied Michilimackinac during the winter of 1761-62. His chief amusements during his first long, cold season in the wilderness "consisted chiefly of shooting, hunting and fishing." Fish were incredibly abundant around the Straits of Mackinac. Each lake trout averaged "from ten to sixty pounds and upward" while whitefish were so numerous they were cut up and used as bait for trout. Because of high prices for meat and grain, Alexander Henry became a "very industrious" fisherman.

He bored twenty holes in the ice of the Straits where he set out as many baited lines which he checked every day. Often, he claimed, he came away with enough fish to feed one hundred men. While he caught a lot of trout, for him the real prize was the whitefish. He wrote: "Their flavor is perhaps above all comparison.... Those who live on them for months together preserve their relish to the end."

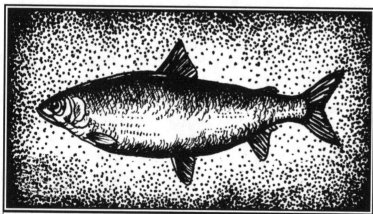

The delectable whitefish was incredibly abundant during Henry's time on Lake Superior. "Astonishing numbers" were taken by net through the ice. (Drawing by E. Yelland)

To catch this delectable creature he needed help. Whitefish were taken in nets which were set under the ice. Several holes were made and a line of sixty fathoms (360 feet) was braided through the holes with a pole. After the rope was strung through all the holes an assistant would grab the other end of the line and the net would be strung through and set with a system of stones to take it down. The three- to seven-pound fish would then swim up against the net entangling its gills. By this method "astonishing numbers" of fish were taken.

The winter of 1761-62 appears to have been a moderate one. Henry reported a fairly thick snow cover—around three feet at its deepest point just before spring break-up. The thaw occurred relatively early. On April 2 the ice left and navigation resumed. Immediately, Henry and the other inhabitants of Michilimackinac received rescue from their monotonous fish diet. Indians of the surrounding area began showing up with "large supplies of waterfowl."

A Trying Time in the Sault: The Winter of 1762-63

In mid-May, Alexander Henry left Michilimackinac in a canoe bound for Sault Ste. Marie. He and his party took four days traveling the "thirty leagues" (around 80 miles) to the French garrisoned entrance to Lake Superior. At this time, the fort, which comprised the entire village, contained only four houses. The nomadic Indians fished seasonally in St. Marys River and occupied "lodges…so rudely fashioned as to afford them but very inadequate protection against inclement skies." Henry quickly befriended Jean Baptiste Cadotte, the so-called "governor" of the French garrison, who merely served as a clerk, managing Indian trade for the government.

Cadotte's primary occupation was fur trading. As a young man he traveled throughout the Lake Superior region and became very popular among all the native tribes and clans. He married the daughter of an influential Ojibway chief; she worked side by side with him in the fur trade. Chippewa was the only language spoken in the Cadotte household and Henry's desire to learn it motivated him to winter in the Sault.

The summer of 1762 was "exceedingly hot" and Henry complained that the mosquitoes and black flies were so thick they made hunting unpleasant. However, aside from bugs, the place provided Henry and his hosts everything they needed: "pigeons were in great plenty; the stream supplied our drinking water and sickness was unknown." As at Michilimackinac, fish were also plentiful. During the first two weeks of October, Henry caught "upwards of five hundred" whitefish.

He prepared the fish for winter in the customary manner, drying them in pairs with their heads down. They were first frozen outside the night after catching them and then strung up on a pole for drying. Winter cold would preserve the fish "in a state perfectly fit for use even till the month of April."

Unfortunately, "a very serious misfortune" ruined the food supply just as winter began. On the morning of December 22, 1762, Henry "was awakened by the alarm of fire." The fort and all buildings but Cadotte's were ablaze. Henry became a hero. He came upon the house of the fort's commandant totally engulfed in flames. Determining that the commander was still inside, he broke the bedroom window, facilitating the man's escape. Henry also managed to save a small quantity of gunpowder a few moments before the blaze blew up all the rest of it. No one was able to save the food; most of the troop's provisions and a large quantity of the fish Henry had laid in for the winter was destroyed.

To prevent famine, it was decided to send the garrison back to Michilimackinac. This would be a difficult trip between seasons; if ice prevented the garrison from crossing the Straits of Mackinac, starvation would be inevitable. Fortunately, the winter proved mild during December 1762. The garrison was still able to take boats on the lake and the soldiers "happily reached Michilimackinac on the thirty-first day of the month." The very next day ice clogged the straits and surrounding area of northern Lake Huron and navigation ceased.

Back at Sault Ste. Marie, Henry, the commandant and all the rest were forced to take up residence in the small Cadotte house for the winter. Their only source of food came from hunting and fishing. A few hares and partridges were harvested from the surrounding woods,

MAPLE SUGARING WEATHER

In Henry's time, sap was collected in birch bark. Today, a system of tubing and pumps pulls the nectar into huge holding tanks where it is then pumped into stainless steel troughs for boiling. One thing that has not changed in over 200 years is maple syrup production's total dependency on the weather. Similar to the 1760s, present-day sugaring begins around or just before the equinox, approximately March 21.

"The rule of thumb here in our part of the U.P., on the Lake Superior side of the watershed, has been sometime shortly after the 20th," says Mike McCollum, owner and operator of the Rock River Sugar Bush. "South would be earlier, probably about a week or so."

Once the trees are tapped, the operation is at the complete mercy of the weather. "Some of the best years we've had," explains McCollum, "have been where you have a more moderate warm-up...where

Henry learned how to catch lake trout with spears through the ice. It must have been uncomfortable lying on one's stomach waiting for a fish to swim by a hole chopped in the ice. Seth Eastman "Spearing fish in winter" (The Newberry Library, Chicago.)

Today instead of birch bark, sap is gathered in a system of plastic tubing that flows into a central stainless-steel tank. It is then pumped into a vat for boiling.

Syrup is produced by precise temperature regulation and graded according to color and sweetness. The amount produced each year is still very dependant on weather. (Photos by E. Yelland)

while trout was taken from the St. Marys River. During the winter of 1763, Henry learned the native art of spearing trout through the ice.

Ice fishing using spears was quite an operation. First, a large hole two yards in circumference was cut. Then, a crude "cabin" two feet high was built out of small branches over the hole. The structure was covered with animal skins to block all light. The fisherman had to see fish "at a very considerable depth" and any light shining through the hole would make the surface opaque, hiding the fish from view.

Fishing this way must have been uncomfortable. The fisherman had to lie on his belly on the ice with his head under the "cabin." He lowered a barbed iron spear mounted on a ten foot wooden pole into the water. With his other hand, he let down a wooden fish decoy filled with lead. He lowered it about sixty feet; then waited patiently until a trout attacked. Then "by a dexterous jerk of the string" he instantly took the lure out of the fish's reach and brought it nearer the surface. With the spear in position, the fisherman waited again; this time when the fish lunged at the lure the spear was plunged into its back and then it was easily drawn through the large hole.

The tiny community

supported itself through hunting and spear fishing for almost two months. Then February 20, imagining the ice solid enough for safe passage to Michilimackinac, a party of seven men left Sault Ste. Marie and headed south. The party included Henry, the commandant, Jean Cadotte, two Indians and two voyageurs. The latter four men were "loaded with some parched maize, some fish, a few pieces of scorched pork, which had been saved from the fire, and a few loaves of bread made of flour…also partly burnt."

They traveled on snowshoes and the going was "slow, wearisome and disastrous." Henry found this mode of travel fatiguing, while the commandant had never walked on snowshoes before. They moved at a snail's pace, reaching Detour, the halfway point, after seven days. There, to their "mortification and dismay," they found the lake still open. Evidently, the winter of 1762-63 was a relatively mild one over the Upper Lakes. In a seasonally cold winter, ice would have covered the near shore of Lake Huron by late February.

The party was stuck. To make matters worse, their provisions were also running low. The only hope was to send the Indians and Voyageurs back to the Sault for more food. Henry, the commandant and Cadotte were left with about two pounds of pork and around three pounds of bread which would have to last until their "faithful servants" returned. Henry took the role of commissary, dividing the remaining provisions into four equal parts; one for each day he expected their swiftly moving servants to complete twice the distance they had covered in a week. True to form, the Indians and voyageurs returned about mid-morning on the fourth day. A late February cold snap settled in and they were able to walk on solid ice by day five.

More difficulties beset the travelers. After only a few miles the commandant's feet became so blistered by the snowshoes he could not go on. This forced the party to make little progress over the next three days. Now there was a renewed risk of starvation and this time they were too far from the Sault to travel back for more food. The only recourse was to send someone as quickly as possible to Fort Michilimackinac. Henry left his "fellow sufferers" with one of the voyageurs at daybreak the next day and arrived at the fort about three in the afternoon. The next morning a contingent of troops was swiftly sent to the rescue. On

spring comes in more normally. By that, I mean temperatures in the 40s during the day and 20s at night. The worst years are when it warms up into the 60s and 70s early in April and lasts for ten-day periods. That just absolutely shuts you down."

McCollum says cold nights "reset" the trees by stopping the sap flow. Then it starts over again the next day as it warms up. On the other hand, when it gets very warm and stays warm at night, the sap keeps flowing and soon the process of leaf formation begins—then the sap run is over.

"2003 was the best year we ever had," recalls McCollum. "Spring came in slow. Conditions were perfect." That year it warmed into the 60-degree range on a couple of days prior to the equinox, but then winter set back in with record cold in early April and only a slow warm-up afterwards.

"We tap about 4,500 trees," explains McCollum. "In 2003, our total sap production was 40,000 gallons of sap to produce in the neighborhood of 900 gallons of syrup." He says when spring comes in too fast the same number of taps yield a mere 125 gallons. "That's really significant," McCollum says with a chuckle.

the third day the commandant, Cadotte and the rest arrived safely at the fort after a tortuous nineteen-day journey.

Henry remained at Michilimackinac until March 10. He then set out for the Sault and with aid of some cold late winter weather took the most direct route straight north from the island

The entire village set up camp in maple stands near the beginning of spring. Sap was gathered in birch-bark "buckets" and was then boiled over a fire that was kept constantly stoked throughout the sugaring season. Seth Eastman "Indian sugar camp" (The Newberry Library, Chicago.)

across the ice to the "Bay of Boutchitaouy," now St. Martin's Bay. The journey to Upper Michigan's mainland was completed in only two days, but in the process, Henry was struck with "the snowshoe evil." His tendons became inflamed by the strain of snowshoeing and made it difficult to go on. He contemplated applying the recommended treatment for this malady: laying a piece of lighted "touchwood" on the tendon and leaving it there until the flesh burnt to the nerve. Even though he had seen the remedy work on others, Henry chose to forgo the experiment, electing to rest until his legs felt better. Eventually he healed and made it back to the foot of Lake Superior around mid-March.

The day after he arrived in the Sault, Henry accompanied the rest of the townspeople into the woods as maple sugaring season was at hand. The first several days were spent setting up the sugaring operation. Then for the next few weeks sap was gathered and turned into maple sugar or syrup. While the men did some hunting and fishing, most of the food supply was sugar from the maple tree. If there was any dispute about whether maple sugar could sustain a human, Henry put the argument to rest. He wrote that he had seen Indians live wholly off maple sugar and "and become fat."

On April 25, they returned to the fort in Sault Ste. Marie with "sixteen hundred weight of sugar" and 36 gallons of syrup. Several days later, "geese and ducks made their appearance," undeniable evidence the cold season of 1762-63 was over.

Life among the Chippewa: 1763-65

Alexander Henry befriended a Chippewa chief named Wawatam in 1762. The chief held Henry in high regard, declaring that on a vision quest years earlier he had dreamt of adopting an Englishman as a son, brother and friend. The first time he saw Henry, he recognized him as the one who the Great Spirit had shown him in his dream.

This friendship saved Henry's life. The next summer the tribes of the area attacked the Fort at Michilimackinac, massacring most of the English. Henry was spared though he was taken prisoner. He was later ransomed by Wawatam. He then lived with Wawatam's family in a Chippewa village near the fort.

The rest of the summer was a trying time for Henry. The only white man in the village and an Englishman besides, he endured "frequent insults" from the Chippewa who were not part of Wawatam's family. Food also became scarce; often they went twenty four hours or more without eating. When in the morning it was determined that there would be no food for the day, the custom was for everyone to blacken their faces with grease and charcoal, then exhibit a cheerful attitude, "as if in the midst of plenty."

Finally, the food situation became intolerable and they migrated north to the Bay of Boutchitaouy (St. Martin's Bay) on the shore of what is now Upper Michigan. There they found plenty of fish and wild fowl. On about August 20, Wawatam proposed going to his family's wintering ground. This proposal brought the "greatest joy" to Henry since the Chippewa separated into family units during the winter for convenience and for better chances of survival during short food supplies. Now he would be exclusively with his adopted family and away from the insults and abuse of the others.

Wawatam's family migrated south to the "River Aux Sables" near present day Ludington. On their way, they took many wild fowl and beaver. Henry later wrote that he enjoyed a personal freedom he had not felt for some time and became "as expert in the Indian pursuits as the Indians themselves." As fall wore on, he adjusted as best he could to life among the Chippewa. He reflected on how, if his mind had not entertained a lingering hope of one day returning to his former life, he could have enjoyed as much happiness in this as in any other situation.

On December 20 the family left on a hunting excursion. Packs were prepared by the women and Henry noticed he carried the lightest pack, while the women carried "the largest and heaviest" ones. They marched about twenty miles the first day and set up camp late in the day. Henry was tired from hiking and did not hunt. Wawatam did and killed a "stag" (deer) not far from camp. The next day they moved camp to where the stag was felled. The next two days were employed in drying the meat by cutting it into slices the size of steaks, then smoking them over the fire. On December 23, they broke camp and hiked through the woods until about mid afternoon.

While the women were busy erecting and

ADJUSTING TO THE CULTURE

Henry did have frustrations. One of them revolved around the taciturnity of his companions. He found the topics of conversation limited, for the most part, to transactions of the day. The men would discuss aspects of the day's hunt; otherwise they would sit in silence. Henry would have loved to pass the time talking politics or philosophy, but he realized these subjects were "utterly unknown" to the Chippewa. So he also sat quietly and took up smoking tobacco. Henry became attached to smoking as it was his principal recreation during the winter of 1763-64.

Another peculiarity of the Chippewa culture involved

Philosophy and politics were subjects "utterly unknown" to the Chippewa. Alexander Henry was frustrated by the taciturnity of his companions, so he took up smoking to relieve his boredom during his winter among Wawatam's clan in 1764-65. (Frank B. Mayer sketchbook, The Newberry Library, Chicago)

proper etiquette surrounding special events. On November 1, 1763 Henry came home from hunting and found the normal fire put out and the top of the lodge covered to exclude as much light as possible. He watched as a fire was made outside the lodge with a kettle hung over it to boil.

He supposed that a feast was being prepared. However, he did not ask what was going on; it would have displayed poor manners. Chippewa etiquette required "that the spectator should patiently wait the result."

As soon as night fell, Henry found his supposition correct; the whole family, including him, was invited into the lodge. He was asked not to speak; a feast was about to be given for the dead, who delight in uninterrupted silence. Everyone who entered was given a wooden dish and spoon and then sat down in the pitch dark lodge.

The master of the family, Wawatam, led the ceremony. He asked for everyone's dish in turn, placing two boiled ears of maize in each. After everyone was served, Wawatam began to speak. He called on his dead relatives and friends and beseeched them for assistance in the hunt and asked them to partake of the food which was prepared for them. After his discourse, which lasted about half an hour, the "feast" began.

The only noise Henry heard

preparing the lodges, Henry told Wawatam he was going to track down some fresh meat for supper. Wawatam answered that he would do the same and they both left camp heading in different directions.

Henry walked confidently through the bush, using the sun as his guide. He became distracted following the tracks of several animals and walked a considerable distance from camp. Suddenly, he realized it was near sunset; to make matters worse, the sky filled with clouds. "In this situation I walked as fast as I could," he said, "always supposing myself to be approaching our encampment." Soon it became dark and he began running into trees.

A sense of panic gripped Henry—he was lost in a strange country and in danger from other, likely hostile, Indians. He made a fire with the flint of his gun and curled up on the ground close to it and tried to get some sleep. It began to rain and poured all night. At the first light of day he awoke, cold and wet. Not knowing where to go, he set off into the woods, "sometimes walking and sometimes running, unknowing where to go, bewildered, and like a madman."

Toward evening he reached the shore of a lake so large he "could scarcely discern the opposite shore." Filled with consternation, Henry assessed his situation; he had never heard of a lake in this part of the country. Now he felt more lost than ever. He resolved to backtrack, following his steps as closely as he could.

Heavy snow began falling as night came on. Henry was able to make a fire and then stripped a birch tree of its bark. He covered himself as best he could with the sheets of bark and curled up for another night on the cold, now snow-covered ground. All night he heard wolves wailing around him "acquainted with… [his]…misfortune." Finally, despite the unnerving howls, he fell asleep.

The rest gave Henry a new perspective. He wondered how he had yielded to the terror of being lost. His panic of the last day and a half now seemed to him surreal and unbelievable. Wawatam had taught him all the skills he needed in a difficult time like this. These skills now came to mind: the tops of pine trees generally lean toward the rising sun; moss grows towards the roots of trees on their north side and trees carry the most and largest limbs on their south sides.

Armed with this collected mind set, Henry resolved to use these marks and march back to Lake Michigan. He estimated he had about a sixty-mile hike through the half-foot of freshly fallen snow. Examining the tree tops, the moss and the branches he found a consensus among them and marched "with some degree of confidence." Finally, "to his inexpressible joy," the sun broke through the clouds and he had no further need to inspect the trees.

A little while later, while descending the side of a steep hill, he saw a herd of red deer approaching. Henry had been three days without food and now had a chance to bag himself a meal. He hid in the bushes and when a large deer came close, he raised his gun, aimed and squeezed the trigger—nothing—the gun was wet and misfired. Despite the commotion, the herd walked along without showing the slightest alarm. He reloaded, followed them and took aim a second time; no shot again—he realized the cock was gone! Now he had no means to procure food or build a fire.

"Of all the sufferings which I had experienced," he later recalled, "This seemed to me the most severe. I was in a strange country, and knew not how far I had to go. Despair…almost overpowered me." Henry collected himself again, realizing how often "the hands of…Providence" had saved him before. He searched for the gun piece he had lost and when a thorough search turned up nothing, he resigned himself to another wet, cold night in the woods without supper.

were the participants' teeth working on the cobs of maize. It was hard work as the maize "was not half boiled." It took Henry an hour to work through his share. When everyone finished eating, Wawatam gave another speech and the ceremony concluded. A new fire was kindled, pipes were smoked and the cobs or "spikes" of maize were carefully buried. Afterward, the whole family began to dance, while Wawatam sang and played a drum. The dancing and singing continued most of the night "to the great pleasure of the lodge."

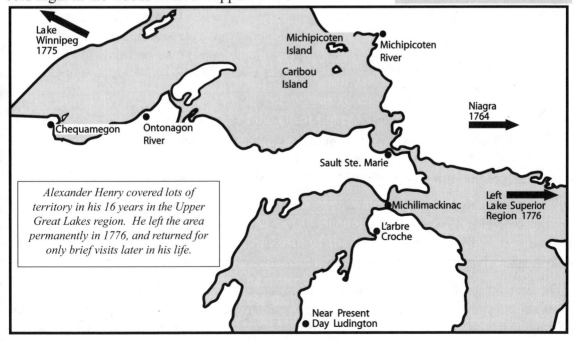

Alexander Henry covered lots of territory in his 16 years in the Upper Great Lakes region. He left the area permanently in 1776, and returned for only brief visits later in his life.

The sun was setting fast when he came upon a small lake which was entirely frozen over. Henry saw a beaver lodge in the middle of it, offering a faint hope of food. On further examination, he found the lodge already broken up. As he examined his surroundings, it suddenly occurred to him he had been here before. He looked around and spotted a tree he had cut down earlier that autumn. The lodge was abandoned because he had killed the beaver which occupied it. He was no longer lost! "An hour before I had thought myself the most miserable of men," he reflected, "and now I leaped for joy and called myself the happiest."

The Chippewa considered the female bear to be their grandmother, and they asked "a thousand pardons" for taking her life. They needed the fat from the animal, which they stored in porcupine skins. (Drawing by E. Yelland)

All night and the next day he walked up a rivulet, knowing the exact distance and location to camp. At sunset he reached home and was warmly greeted by Wawatam and his family who had given him up for lost after a long search in the woods. After a few days of rest, Henry felt strong enough and again "resumed the chase." Now that the snow lay on the ground, he felt secure knowing if he lost his way, all he had to do was follow his tracks back.

Sometime in January 1764, Henry found evidence of a bear on a huge pine tree. The tree was at least eighteen feet in circumference. Since there were no bear tracks around the tree, he assumed the bear was hibernating inside it. He communicated his findings back at the lodge. At first the women opposed the idea of cutting the massive pine down with the small axes they had available in camp. However, since there was a great need in camp for bear fat to make oil, they acquiesced. It took nearly two days of constant labor from everyone in camp to chop down the tree. Finally, on the second day, the tree came down. A five hundred pound bear stumbled out of the trunk, and Henry shot it.

All the Chippewa in camp went up to the bear and begged "a thousand pardons" for taking her life. They considered the female bear their relation and grandmother, yet Henry observed that they had no trouble skinning the hide, and extricating the winter fat that was six inches deep in places. It took two people to carry back the fat and another four to haul the meat.

A feast and ceremony was held the next day. Wawatam again gave a speech. In this discourse he also honored dead friends and relations while deploring the necessity of men to destroy their friends. He went on to say the killing of their friend and grandmother was unavoidable; that "without doing so, they could by no means subsist."

The bear fat was melted down, and the oil filled six porcupine skins. A part of the bear meat not consumed during the feast was cut into strips, fire dried, and placed in the skins containing the oil. Henry remarked that the meat "remained in perfect preservation until the middle of… summer."

The Chippewa called February the "moon of the crusted snow." The top layer of snow, through alternate thawing and freezing, could bear the weight of a man or at least dogs and greatly aided in the pursuit of hoofed animals like deer. A deer or stag, as Henry called it, would break through the crust, cutting its legs and thereby slowing it down. The wounded deer became easy prey; as many as a dozen would be taken in just two hours. "By this means," recalled Henry, "we were soon put in the possession of four thousand weight of dried venison."

With the arrival of March came the labor of transporting this huge quantity of meat along with all the rest of their wealth back north. The venison, furs and "peltries" were carried to market at Mackinac. Just to get their load to Lake Michigan required a march of about seventy miles through the woods. To do this, the women prepared the packs and the men took off with them at daybreak. They hiked under the weight of their loads until mid afternoon, then stopped and erected a scaffold where they deposited their bundles. They then walked back to camp and repeated the process with new loads the next day. This was done day after day until all was transferred to the first stage. Then the lodge was moved to the first stage where the "same patient toil" took their goods to the second stage, and so on, until they were fairly close to the lake.

The next phase in their journey north involved making maple sugar. The women were in charge of this labor, while the men cut firewood, hunted and fished. Their lodge was soon joined by several other lodges of families who wintered on jointly shared land. According to Chippewa custom, each family had a tract of land on which it was their exclusive right to hunt. Since these people were all part of the same family, Henry observed that he was "treated very civilly by all the lodges."

As the season grew gradually into spring, the Chippewa feared "a speedy attack from the English," who were expected to avenge the attack on Fort Michilimackinac. The basis of this apprehension grew out of the dreams of the elderly women in camp. Henry tried to persuade the people that nothing of the kind would happen, but he could not subdue their fears.

In late April, the family embarked for the fort. First they stopped at Grand Traverse Bay where they met a large party of Indians. These Indians also feared going the distance to Mackinac, lest they should be destroyed by the British. Councils were held and Henry complained of constant questioning from the united bands on what he knew about an impending attack.

They believed that he was gifted with a foreknowledge of events; that he could, through dreams, know what was going on at a distance. The more he protested his ignorance, the more suspicious they became of him. Finally, to ease their fears, Henry proclaimed that he knew there was no enemy waiting for them and that they could proceed to Mackinac safely. Further, he proclaimed that if his countrymen returned to Fort Michilimackinac, he would recommend that no harm come to the united bands gathered in Traverse Bay. Buoyed by these statements, the Indians left for the fort. On the first leg of their journey to L'Arbre Croche, they hit a heavy thundershower. The next day, informed by travelers that all was quiet at Mackinac, they sailed again with confidence and arrived safely at the fort.

In early May, a band of Indians arrived from Saginaw Bay to muster as many recruits as they could for more war on the English. The situation, once again, did not look good for Henry: "I was soon informed that as I was the only Englishman in the place they proposed to kill me in order to give their friends a mess of English broth to raise their courage."

Henry asked that Wawatam take him to Sault Ste. Marie. There he could take shelter with Jean Cadotte and live among the Lake Superior Chippewa who, through the influence of Cadotte and his powerful native wife, never joined the war in the first place. Wawatam complied, leaving that night with his entire lodge for Point St. Ignace on the north side of the strait. They then proceeded slowly toward Lake Superior, fishing and hunting along the way.

On the morning they were going to sail the last leg for the Sault, Wawatam's wife complained of being ill. She also reported bad dreams in which they were all destroyed on their arrival at the Sault. Based on this, they would proceed no farther. Henry's fate now seemed sealed; a return to Michilimackinac meant execution, while staying where they were, on a direct route from Lake Huron to the fort, meant almost equal danger.

Henry felt trapped. He climbed as far as he could up a tall tree and kept watch; hoping to spot unfriendly canoes as soon as possible and then hide himself. On the second day of his vigil, not long after settling in his watch tower, he spotted a sail coming from the fort.

The sail was a white one, much larger than ones employed by area Indians. "I therefore indulged a hope," he wrote, "that it might be a Canadian canoe on its voyage to Montreal." Maybe they could take him back east and he would finally be safe.

His confidence continued to grow; surely this was a Canadian canoe. The rhythmic paddling convinced him it could be none other than voyageurs handling the boat. He got down from his perch and reported the news to Wawatam. His "brother and father" congratulated him on his good fortune and while they were smoking a pipe together a boy walked into their lodge. He reported that the canoe carried Madame Cadotte from Sault Ste. Marie. Henry's hopes of an escape to Montreal evaporated; however, at least he could get to friendlier territory at the foot of Lake Superior.

Marianne Cadotte "cheerfully acceded" to Henry's request for a ride to the Sault. He bade an emotional farewell to his family and left in the Cadotte canoe. Now removed from the Chippewa's society, he disguised himself as a Canadian, donning a blanket coat and a handkerchief around his head. The disguise worked—to a point. The next morning, they were overtaken by a flotilla of Indian canoes. Soon they were surrounded, and before long, one of the Indians challenged Henry—declaring he looked like an Englishman. One of the other Indians agreed and Henry pretended not to understand. Madame Cadotte came to his rescue, assuring them Henry was a Canadian on his first voyage from Montreal.

The next day Henry landed safely in Sault Ste. Marie, where he experienced a "generous welcome" from Jean Cadotte. Henry enjoyed five days of tranquility, but the danger had not passed; the next day a report came that a canoe of warriors had arrived from Mackinac asking about him. At the same time a "good chief" of the village sent an urgent message that

Henry should hide until it was ascertained what these strangers wanted.

The Indians came to recruit the Chippewa of the Sault in their war against the English. Luckily, the leader of the band was a close relation to Cadotte's wife. He admitted there were designs against Henry; but added the plans would be abandoned if they displeased the well respected Cadotte. The peaceful chiefs of the Sault also came to Henry's aid, declaring any actions taken against him would be avenged. They told the Indians to go back where they came from; that the young men of the village were not foolish enough to join them.

At the same time a canoe arrived from Niagara. These strangers brought news that the English wished to broker a peace; that now was the time to seize this opportunity or be destroyed. They invited all the region's Indians, those from Mackinac as well as the Sault to come to Niagara for a feast.

"The tenor of this speech," related Henry, "greatly alarmed the Indians of the Sault." They agreed to send twenty deputies to Niagara. "This was a project highly interesting to me," he recounted, "since it offered me the means of leaving the country." He asked and received permission to accompany them.

The various tribes and nations of the Upper Great Lakes brokered a peace with the English. Tranquility again reigned from Detroit to Sault Ste. Marie. In this atmosphere, Alexander Henry returned to his fur trading business, spending the winter of 1764-65 at the Sault.

Winter at Chequamegon: 1765-66

Alexander Henry accompanied Cadotte and a band of traders, voyageurs and Indians to the western end of Lake Superior in the summer of 1765. Now a partner with Cadotte in the fur trading business, Henry fully engaged himself in this endeavor with the "Chippewa of Chagouemig." He distributed goods to them equivalent to three thousand beaver skins. The Chippewa then went on their hunt to secure the skins, while Henry settled into his new home.

Henry took up residence near present-day Bayfield, Wisconsin. He set up shop on the mainland just across from Madeline Island where Allouez and Marquette ministered to the tribes at La Pointe a century earlier. In six days "a very comfortable house" was built for the young fur trader. Now that he had a winter residence, he focused his attention on gathering enough food for the coming cold season. Henry "with the assistance of ... [his]... men" took two thousand trout and whitefish. He claimed some of the trout weighed as much as 50 pounds, while the whitefish commonly tipped the scales at between four and six pounds. The fish were dried in the open air and then either boiled or roasted. The cooking method provided the only variance in their diet; fish "without bread or salt" became their only source of food for the whole winter. Henry was surprised at how easily he adjusted to the monotonous fare. "I found less difficulty in reconciling myself to the privation," he wrote, "than I could have anticipated."

True winter set in by mid-December. On the 15th, the bay completely froze over and Henry took up his "former amusement of spearing trout." Sometimes he caught a hundred fish a day, each weighing an average of 20 pounds. He lived comfortably on the bay;

The Feast

The "sacrifice" began about an hour after dark. On the invitation list were Henry and four of his men. They joined the family, which consisted of two men and three women. The ten people sat down in the lodge and the feast began. The Chippewa of the Lake Superior region withstood times of famine and reveled in intervals of plenty. When there was plenty, nothing was held back or saved. "We were ten persons," wrote Henry, "upon whom it was incumbent to eat the whole bear." He received his dish loaded with "not less than ten pounds" of meat on it; his men were given twice that. The head of the household had an equal share along with the bear's head, breast, heart "with its surrounding fat," and all four feet. This astounding serving of meat was polished off in two hours!

Each member of the host family was done with their huge portions before Henry had even completed half. Henry's men also became stuffed and could not consume another mouthful. One of them had, what he thought, was a bright idea—he hid his leftover portion in the "girdle which he wore under his shirt." The next day he planned to eat the leftovers when he felt hungry again. Henry, on the other hand, wisely asked for assistance

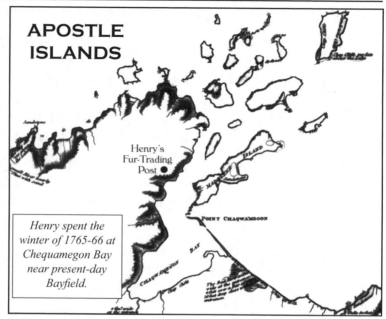

APOSTLE ISLANDS

Henry's Fur-Trading Post ●

Henry spent the winter of 1765-66 at Chequamegon Bay near present-day Bayfield.

POINT CHAQWAMEGON

the mainland's woods sheltered him somewhat from the northwest winds, while Madeline Island protected him from the east and northeast gales.

Henry experienced only one business transaction which threatened to turn ugly. The first hunting party returned with furs and demanded rum. He refused them liquor and the party talked of pillaging the place until they found some. At the threat of violence, Henry's men took off, but he stood up to the hunting party, scaring them off with a gun. The party backed off and his men returned, promising to never behave with such cowardice again. Henry buried the liquor he had and the rest of the winter passed without incident.

Finally March came and by mid-month a sure sign of spring arrived—the beginning of the sugaring season. Most of the residents of Chequamenon Bay came out of hibernation and left for the sugar bush. Later in the month Henry proposed a hunting excursion to some resident Chippewa. They "readily agreed" and a short while into the hunt spotted what they claimed were "footsteps of a bear" made in the beginning of winter just after the first snow. Henry was amazed by the discovery, remarking that he would "have passed over the same ground without acquiring any such information." The subtle dents or hollows the Indians found were barely distinguishable to him, but he trusted his companions' "long habits of close observation in the forest." The hunting party hiked a short distance and sure enough, following the traces led to a tree "at the root of which was a bear."

The bear was killed and since Henry proposed the hunt, by custom he was the owner of all the game. However, the head of the Chippewa family which comprised the hunting party "begged to have the bear." He wanted to make a feast to the "Great Spirit" in thanksgiving for preserving his family through the long winter. Henry consented and preparation for the feast began.

Ice left Chequamenon Bay on April 20, 1766—an average date for break up, indicating an overall moderate winter. Henry noted the arrival of several canoes filled with women and children. The men in their tribe had gone to war against the Sioux. Henry stayed and waited for the spring shipment of furs. When that business was completed he headed east to spend the next winter at Sault Ste. Marie.

1766-67: Famine at the Sault

Fish were so abundant in Lake Superior and its tributaries that a ready food supply was seldom a concern. The autumn of 1766 was a demoralizing exception; the fishery failed. To make matters worse, winter set in early, which made it impossible to obtain assistance from the fort at Michilimackinac. Five men were sent away to fend for themselves "at a distant post," but even they were driven back by hunger the day before Christmas. The situation became desperate. News arrived at the Sault of a possible fish supply to the north at Fishing Cove or Oak Bay about 30 miles to the north at the present day Goulais River. Alexander Henry immediately headed north with several men, packing only a pint of maize for each person.

Over the next couple of weeks Henry and his men had spotty success feeding themselves. At times they caught fish "with great facility," at other times they went to bed hungry. Eventually, a band of Chippewa, also suffering from starvation, joined them in the quest for food. A couple of days later a lone, young Indian came out of the woods. He explained that he left his family behind; that they were starving and too weak to travel. "The appearance of the youth was frightful," recounted Henry. "And from his squalid figure there issued a stench which none of us could support."

"His arrival struck our camp with horror and uneasiness," he wrote. Later, the Chippewa camping with Henry's party pulled him aside and voiced their concerns; they suspected that the youth had been eating human flesh and that he had probably devoured the family he pretended to leave behind. The young man was questioned, but he denied the charges. His denials did not sit well and only served "to increase the presumption against him."

with his uneaten portion. He explained that the Indians "cheerfully" jumped at the chance to help, "eating what I had found too much with as much apparent ease as if their stomachs had been previously empty."

The feast was brought to an end with a prayer and thanksgiving. As the guests began filing out of the lodge, the "poor fellow" who hid away his uneaten portion got up and walked past two dogs, which, "guided by the scent" of bear meat, grabbed at the man's girdle and tore the "treasure" to the ground. The Chippewa were astonished by "this profane attempt to steal away" a portion of the offering to the Great Spirit. Further, they felt the dogs were led by inspiration of the Great Spirit to frustrate this blasphemous act. The Indians confiscated the meat, roasted it in the fire and consumed every last bit of it.

The state of Michigan operates a state park at the site of Fort Michilimackinac complete with colonial reenactments. (Courtesy of Mackinac State Historic Parks)

Several Chippewa in the group decided to follow the youth's tracks and investigate. They returned the next day with human remains. When shown the evidence, the young man confessed. He explained that he was with his uncle, aunt and their four children. His uncle had missed several opportunities to bag game and became despondent. The uncle asked his wife to kill him; that it was the Great Spirit's wish that he die. When his wife refused, the youth and one of the man's older sons agreed to murder him. According to the youth's testimony, they "accomplished their detestable purpose" to prevent the man from murdering them. They then devoured the man's body but it was not long before famine closed in on them again. The rest of the family was taken one by one. Finally, the youth preyed upon his cousin.

The Chippewa in camp were horrified. They expressed their belief to Henry that once a man has tasted human flesh he would not be satisfied by any other. While Henry was skeptical of their claims, the young man's behavior seemed to justify their worry. "He ate with relish nothing that was given him," remembers Henry, "But…fixed his eyes continually on the children." Several times while gazing at them Henry heard the youth remark "How fat they are." This behavior alarmed the men enough that they resolved to kill him before he preyed upon their children. The next day the execution was accomplished with the single stroke of an axe aimed at the back of the young man's head.

Soon after this sordid affair the fish supply at Oak Bay also failed. Henry and his men returned to the Sault, hoping that some provisions might have arrived. They found the same desperate situation they had left. With no other option open to them but starvation, they headed south for Michilimackinac with only a day's supply of food.

Happily, at their first camp along the St. Marys River they hit the jackpot. An hour's fishing produced seven trout, each from ten to twenty pounds. Later they came upon two Chippewa lodges. The inhabitants had fish and shared them generously. The next day Henry shot a caribou. They ate off the animal for two days. On the seventh day of their journey they arrived at Michilimackinac "where… [their]…difficulties ended."

At Michipicoten: 1767-68

The wanderlust in Alexander Henry led him over a hundred miles north of the Sault late in 1767. He set off with several men in a canoe and gazed at the "great capes" at the mouth of Lake Superior. Heading north he surveyed the rugged shore that makes up the eastern side of the lake: "I observed the banks to be low and stony and in some places running a league back to the feet of a ridge of mountains." He chose Michipicoten Bay as his wintering grounds (not far from present day Wawa). There he explored the steep ridges or "mountains" just inland from the lake. Some of the summits were topped with sugar maple, but Henry explained that most of them were draped with spruce and pine; the lowlands with birch and poplar. Occasionally he saw a few caribou, while hares and partridges supplied his Sunday dinner. By Christmas Day 1767, the bay was entirely ice covered.

At the beginning of April, Henry headed into the hills to make maple sugar. He built a "house in a hollow dug out of snow." The winter of 1767-68 must have been snowy; he claimed the house was seven feet high, yet lower than the top of the snow cover! On April 24, Henry began manufacturing sugar. He reported a thick fog below him toward lake level on the 28th. But the high ridge at sugar camp "all was calm, and from the top of the mountain not a cloud" could be seen all the way to the horizon.

The next day, Henry observed a most unusual phenomenon: he descended the high ridge down into the valley where he found a half-foot of freshly fallen snow. He learned that the snow had been accompanied by strong winds, while it remained calm and clear at his mountain-top location. Henry concluded that he had been making sugar "above the clouds."

On the mountain Henry and his men ate nothing but maple sugar. He explained that "each man consumed a pound a day, desired no other food, and was visibly nourished by it." Sugaring operations concluded on May 12 and Henry returned to the banks of the river where he saw so many waterfowl that "a day's subsistence for fifty men could be shot daily by one" man. This super gathering of birds lasted less than a week; one day the waters of the river and bay were completely covered with waterfowl, the next day they were "left naked" as the birds continued their migration north.

Henry continued his fur trading business while at Michipicoten. On May 20 a party of Chippewa came in from their winter's hunt. Over the next several days Henry reported with satisfaction that all those he had advanced goods to returned to pay their debts in furs. Out of two thousand skins only thirty were left unpaid. Those thirty were from a Chippewa who died during the winter. Even then his family brought all the furs he had in his possession at the time of death. They even offered to pay the rest owed by him, believing their dead relative would not rest in peace until his debts were paid.

Later that spring, Henry took a trip south to Michilimackinac where he began investigating another business enterprise—mining. He met with Alexander Baxter, an Englishman who came to the wilderness on reports of rich mineral resources in the Lake Superior region. Henry discussed his "mineralogical observations" and showed Baxter some of the specimens he found. This piqued the Englishman's interest and he talked of a partnership with Henry, which "was soon…formed for working the mines of Lake Superior."

But Henry's fur trading business needed attention and for that reason he prepared to spend another winter at Michipicoten. He arrived back there in early fall 1768, just before the Chippewa left on their hunt. They were supplied by Henry's store of goods and in no time were "at the chase" to secure the furs they owed.

In October Henry had time on his hands so he decided to "indulge himself" with a voyage to Sault Ste. Marie. He took along three Canadians as well as a young Chippewa woman who wished to see some relatives there. The party of five cast off in a canoe and headed south. They each carried only a quart of maize apiece because it was only a couple of days of strong paddling south to the Sault and they planned to fish along the way.

The plan went awry. The party made it south to Nanibojou, an island near present day Lake Superior Provincial Park. They set their net, planning to retrieve a large catch of fish the next morning. That night a violent storm arose. It blew for three days, making it impossible to check the net. They rationed their small cache of maize during the storm, nearly finishing it over the three days. When the storm abated on the evening of the third day, they went to check the net. It was gone!

A return to Michipicoten was impossible because of a strong headwind, so the party floated south for Sault Ste. Marie. The next evening "the wind came around and blew a gale all night." This storm lasted nine days. The waves were so high and broke so violently that it was impossible to take a canoe out. They were marooned.

Their food ran out. They finished the maize the evening the storm abated, figuring they would make the Sault with a good paddle the next day. With each passing stormy day, the specter of hunger closed in on them. Henry went back into the wooded ridges to hunt the first and second days. He walked many miles but came back empty-handed. The next day he was too weak to walk more than a few hundred yards without stopping to rest. He returned that evening "with no more than two snowbirds."

One of the Canadians greeted Henry with a grisly proposition: the other two men proposed killing the young woman and eating her. Henry could not believe what he was hearing but on questioning the two he realized they were dead serious. Further, he found them "much dissatisfied" at his opposition to their scheme.

The next morning Henry was able to struggle up a "lofty mountain." On top of it he found a very high rock covered with edible lichen the Chippewa called "waac" (*probably the same "moss" that Allouez subsisted on, See page 2*). Henry descended the precipice as quickly as possible and fetched the rest of his party. The Chippewa woman knew how to prepare the "soup." She boiled it down to "mucilage," a slimy broth "as thick as the white of an egg." In no time, they had a hearty meal; and while the sludge was "bitter and disagreeable," Henry was so overjoyed at finding the lichen that he ate it with "much appetite and pleasure."

As for the rest of the party, the lichen saved the woman's life. Henry was certain that the Canadians would have "unquestionably" killed and eaten her. One of the men confided that he was not a novice to cannibalism; that he had wintered in the Northwest and had at one point resorted to eating human flesh.

On the evening of the ninth day the wind finally calmed and the canoe was launched. It was a struggle to move forward because of their weakened state. They paddled all night, while constantly nodding off to sleep. "Whenever my eyes were closed," Henry wrote, "I dreamed of tempting food."

The next morning the party met up with two canoes of Chippewa heading back north after a trip to the Sault. Henry explained their situation and was offered "as many fish" as he would accept. Immediately, they set up camp made a fire and "relished... [themselves]...with a plentiful breakfast." That night they arrived at Sault Ste. Marie after two weeks of misery and starvation. Henry explained that the privation had serious health effects on everyone in the party, but after a few days of recovery they returned safely to Michipicoten.

Mining the Lake Superior Region: 1769-1774

Henry began exploring for precious minerals soon after the ice left Lake Superior in the spring of 1769. Spring into early summer is the time of calm on Lake Superior. The icy water creates its own atmosphere; a thin sheet of cold air develops above the lake. This layer of cold air is like molasses; it is dense and heavy and does not move easily. Thus, the winds are light and, the lake is most often calm at this time of year.

Henry took advantage of this calm by visiting Michipicoten Island. He paddled the "twelve leagues" from Michipicoten Bay to the island with two Chippewa guides. Informed that the island contained "shiny rocks and stones of rare description," he was disappointed by what he observed. "I found it one solid rock," he wrote. "On examining the surface I saw nothing remarkable." His inspection revealed large veins of "transparent spar" and a mass of rock at the south end of the island that appeared to contain iron ore.

Undaunted, Henry heard legends among the Chippewa of an island south of Michipicoten Island that they said was covered by "a heavy yellow sand." This piqued the adventurer's interest. Could this yellow sand be gold? There were no firsthand reports from this island in the open waters of Lake Superior but Indian legend said the yellow sand was guarded by giant serpents. That was all the knowledge he had regarding this mysterious jewel in the lake.

Henry kept this image of a gold-covered island on the back burner. Travel to this mystic place would require a more substantial water craft. Henry worked with his partner, Alexander Baxter, and eventually secured funding for construction of a forty-ton sloop. The ship was built on a safe harbor near the Sault and launched as soon as the ice left Lake Superior in early May 1771. Henry and his crew of adventurers set sail, promising "to make… [their]… fortunes in defiance of the serpents."

After two days of searching, the island was spotted through a looking glass and in the early afternoon of the third day they landed on one of the island's beaches. Henry later wrote a bit tongue-in-cheek: "I was the first to land, carrying with me my loaded gun and resolved to meet with courage the guardians of the gold. [However]…no immediate attack was feared."

There was no yellow sand at this spot, but Henry did spot caribou tracks on the sand adjacent to the woods that met the beach. A short distance into the woods, he came upon three of the animals. They

Henry came to the mysterious island looking for gold but found an abundance of stunted caribou. The island was named in honor of this member of the reindeer family and still bears its name today. (Drawing by E. Yelland)

MICHIPICOTEN ISLAND

See map on page 17 for shoreline in relation to islands

CARIBOU ISLAND

also noticed him "with much apparent surprise." He fired at one and killed it then tracked the other two for about a mile, where he killed a second. The next day, he shot three more. During their stay on the island the party bagged thirteen caribou. Henry found the tops of antlers protruding from the earth at various places throughout the island. He supposed that the lack of food, or more likely the lack of predators, allowed these animals to die of old age.

The explorers dried the caribou meat while exploring the island for precious metal. They found no gold, nor for that matter, any yellow sand. There were no giant serpents either. However, a number of hawks "guarded" the island. Henry wrote that they "appeared angry at our intrusion, pecking at us and keeping us in continual alarm for our faces." One of them even took Henry's cap off his head.

Had the serpents disguised themselves as hawks? Had the demons changed this magical place from a gold-covered jewel to a very normal looking island about twelve miles in diameter, containing many small lakes, stunted trees and an abundance of equally stunted caribou? Henry consoled himself with this "romance" as they sailed away from Caribou Island after four days of fruitless exploration. They sailed back to the mainland in eighteen hours with nothing but a large supply of dried caribou meat.

Henry's nascent mining company continued exploring the shore of Lake Superior in the summer of 1771. He and his cohorts covered lots of territory, reaching the Ontonagon River late that summer. There they found boulders of mass copper; though their real objective was silver. The area looked promising enough that a winter shelter was erected for the miners, while provisions were procured from the Sault. When the mining camp was set up and in order, Henry returned to Sault Ste. Marie for the winter.

Another boatload of supplies was sent from the Sault to Ontonagon in the spring of 1772. The boat came back, and to Henry's surprise, so did the miners. They abandoned the project after penetrating into the side of a hill some forty feet. The clay they bored into seemed stiff and solid so they dug into the hill without shoring the hole with supports. When the spring thaw came, their excavation site caved in. To continue their search and re-dig the hole would have cost too much, so the project was abandoned.

One more search was made in a promising vein of copper on the north shore of Lake Superior that following August. With great difficulty, a thirty-foot hole was gouged out of solid rock. After a year's labor, the miners met with more frustration; a four foot vein of copper at the surface contracted to four inches at thirty feet. "Under these circumstances we desisted," wrote Henry, "and carried the miners back to the Sault."

Alexander Henry left the mining business in 1774 when his financial backers in England pulled their support. He kept active in the "Indian trade" and applied himself to it "with more assiduity than ever" after the mining venture failed. Henry journeyed to Lake Winnipeg in the summer of 1775 and left the Lake Superior region for good the following year on the day the Declaration of Independence was signed, July 4, 1776.

His allegiance remained with Great Britain and he made several voyages to England during the Revolution. While he made numerous trips to the Lake Superior wilderness in later life, he set up his base of operations in Montreal. He became a wholesale fur trader, preferring to send his hired clerks into the wilderness to do the things he used to do. In 1809, he began writing about his exciting adventures in the Upper Great Lakes wilderness. In 1824 Alexander Henry, the Englishman who set out to make his fortune in the wilds of the Northwest as a young man, befriended Frenchmen and Indians and narrowly escaped death on a number of occasions, died peacefully in his bed of old age.

Cabin Fever: A Winter in the Wilderness, 1812-13

During the Revolution and into the early 1800s, the Lake Superior region remained a lonely outpost, inhabited by Ojibwa, a few Englishmen and French Canadians. One of these hardy Frenchmen was a man named Edouard Sansavaine. "Old Edward," as he was known in later life, was a fellow with an iron constitution; he survived brutal cold on the shores of Hudson Bay, near starvation and a number of bouts with bad whiskey and still lived to at least 90 years old.

In his later years he told the story of how he drifted down from Hudson Bay to the Lake Superior region in about 1810. Some time later, Edward's circumstances brought him work as a servant for a fur trader and the man's Indian wife. The couple kept a crude residence near the Brule River, deep in the forest of what is now the border between Wisconsin and Upper Michigan. They traded for fur and some food with the tribes in the area. Then the War of 1812 began. The native men left the region to fight with the British while their wives, children and old men left for the rice lakes of Wisconsin.

Sansavaine and his employers found themselves isolated and alone with winter fast approaching. No one was left to trade with, for beaver tail, rice or corn. Fish from the Brule River was their only food source. Sansavaine began to stock up on suckers he netted in the river. The fishing wasn't very good that season and winter arrived earlier than expected. The meager fish supply was stored in wooden troughs and the long wait for spring began.

One often hears the term "cabin fever" during an Upper Peninsula winter. Old Edward and his companions undoubtedly had a major bout of the ailment. Imagine three people occupying a little shack, alone in a thick forest buried in snow, much deeper than in years past, with no escape or diversion and a short food supply. That's *cabin fever*. As the winter wore on and the frozen fish pile dwindled, Sansavaine's master put him on a ration of one sucker a day. "I begin starve," Old Edward related in broken English. "I tink of noting but feesh, feesh all the time. At night I dream about heem... I say, I moost have some of dem soockers or I die."

Old Edward and his two employers spent the winter of 1812 isolated deep in the wilderness along the Brule River, probably somewhere in present-day Iron County. (Drawing by E. Yelland)

The hunger pangs became too much for Sansavaine and one night he slipped into the fur trader's room, where the raw, frozen fish were kept in one of the hand-hewn wooden troughs. He began feasting on the raw fish and his master was roused out of sleep. Old Edward had a mind to kill the stingy fur trader but it wasn't to be. The fur trader's wife helped defend her husband and Sansavaine, by his own admission was "whip bad." The next morning, the fur trader relented and gave Old Edward "plenty soockers. "Den I got better and was content," he recalled. Somehow the three survived the harsh winter of 1812-13—but just barely. According to Sansavaine, "…We were most like dead mens when spring came."

The conclusion of the War of 1812 saw clear geographical boundaries set between British controlled Canada and the new United States. The Lake Superior region became an American territory and as the nineteenth century advanced, irrevocable change came to the northern wilderness.

Chapter 3

Schoolcraft Heads Northwest

Not long after Old Edward and his companions suffered through their winter of hunger and isolation, the Americans began to arrive. At first, only a few would travel to so remote an area. The region was likened in its isolation to the North Pole and the "wild Siberian end of the world." Even the well informed thought of the Upper Peninsula the way the Sahara Desert is thought of today—a large expanse of territory containing little or nothing of value. That view gradually changed as sketchy information trickled back east of vast mineral resources near Lake Superior. These stories caught the attention of Washington, and in 1822 an Act of Congress established an Indian Agency at the strategic location of Sault Ste. Marie. President Monroe immediately sent the nomination of Henry Rowe Schoolcraft, an ethnologist and mineralogist, to head the Agency and Congress voted him in on May 8, 1822. Less than two months later, Schoolcraft was heading northwest to set up the first permanent American settlement in the Lake Superior region.

Schoolcraft's party traveled through the Great Lakes from New York to Detroit. As soon as he set foot in Michigan territory he "was attacked with fever and augue." Fever at that time was treated with mercury and Schoolcraft urged his doctor to administer "renewed doses" of the toxic element. The fever disappeared but the treatment "completely prostrated...[his]...strength" and paralyzed his cheek. After convalescing for several days, he set off north, recovering enough to enjoy a voyage of "pleasant excitement" through

Henry Rowe Schoolcraft, 1793-1864 was part of the first permanent American settlement in Upper Michigan. (Courtesy Marquette County History Museum)

Lake Huron up to Mackinac and then through the Straits of St. Mary.

Schoolcraft's party arrived in Sault Ste. Marie on July 5, 1822. The contingent was accompanied by a number of soldiers led by Colonel Hugh Brady, whose name was eventually given to the fort that guarded the east entrance to Lake Superior for many years. Brady took possession of the old Nolin House and a number of buildings once occupied by the North West Fur Company. The troops immediately began repairing the buildings "to fence out," as Schoolcraft put it, "as much as possible, the winds and snows of a severe winter. A winter," he added, "which every one dreads the approach of, and the severity of which was perhaps magnified in proportion as it was unknown."

As summer wore on, Schoolcraft settled into his new home and got to know some of the long-time residents of the old fur trading post and mission. One of them was John Johnston, an Irishman who "pushed his way to the foot of Lake Superior about 1793." Johnston took a native wife, a daughter of one of the most revered chiefs in the region. The couple eventually had eight children and built one of the most regal structures in the Sault, part of which is a museum today.

Their allegiance was with the British and two of Johnston's sons served in the British navy during the War of 1812. The Johnstons knew which way the political winds were blowing at the conclusion of the conflict and they extended their hands to the Americans. Two years earlier, Mrs. Johnston was credited with saving the lives of General Cass and his party (which included Schoolcraft) when they journeyed to the Sault to broker a peace with area tribes. She met in feverish, secret meetings with the leaders of a war party bent on attacking Cass's group. Her influence averted disaster and the U.S. government later rewarded her and her descendants with large tracts of land.

Schoolcraft developed a close friendship with Johnston. His journal contains a number of passages praising the man for his generosity and refinement. "He is the soul of hospitality, honor, friendship and love," Schoolcraft wrote years later. "And no one I have ever known has a more forgiving and truly gentle and high minded spirit." Johnston soon became Schoolcraft's father-in-law. Henry Rowe married the patriarch's eldest daughter, Jane, the next year.

John Johnston "pushed his way to the foot of Lake Superior in 1793" with his wife Susan (Ozhahguscodaywayquay), a Chippewa princess from a prominent Lake Superior tribe. They had eight children and became an important family in the Sault Ste. Marie region. (John from the collection of the Chippewa County Historical Society, Sault Ste. Marie, Michigan; Susan from the collection of the Marquette County History Museum)

The First Winter: 1822-23

On November 1, Schoolcraft wrote, "we have snow, cold and chilly winds." He observed an early lake-effect event noting "huge piles of clouds hanging over Lake Superior." A hint of developing isolation and loneliness also came through as he closed the day's entry with the comment that "the rest of the United States is a far off land to us." By the 20th the transformation was complete. "We are now shut out from the world," he penned. "Nature… shows her teeth in ice and snows." Schoolcraft had plenty of time to philosophize as winter set in and on the 25th he noted that the Sault "is a capital place, in the dead of winter, for stripping poetic theories of their covering."

He probably grabbed a thick coat and huddled around the fire on December 1 as the region "plunged into the depths of boreal winter." His quarters were as comfortable as one could hope for in the far northern reaches of the Michigan territory. His home and office was a building thirty-six-feet square made of large squared timbers joined with mortar and whitewash. In the center was a large Montreal stove that accepted three-foot logs.

On December 4, Schoolcraft observed "the weather has been intensely cold for the last three days." Shortly after, the sense of loneliness again crept into his writing. "Snow covers everything," he penned. "We are shut out from the world, and thrown entirely on our own resources. I doubt, if we were in Siberia…we could be so completely isolated."

The weather of December 1822 exhibited the typical variability associated with an Upper Michigan winter. After a bitter start, a thaw set in on the 5th and the mild weather lasted eight or nine days. During this time nearly all the snow cover "was carried off by rains or at least the heat of the sun." The weather was so mild that Schoolcraft sat in his office "without fire, for about two hours" on the 13th. Finally on the 15th, the wind "veered around to a northerly point" and winter set back in. The cold was consistent enough so the St. Marys River froze during the night of the 22nd. Schoolcraft made good use of the winter isolation by plunging headlong into his study of the Chippewa language.

The Indian agent would go out to dinner each late afternoon and return home after dark. On December 26, Schoolcraft returned to find that his dog "Ponty" had chewed up a sheet of paper containing native grammar that he had been working on for days. Schoolcraft was beside himself. He thought of whipping the dog but realized that his retaliation would serve no purpose. He looked at the small pile of shredded paper on the floor and sighed, despairing that he "scarcely had the courage to begin the labor anew." There was no alternative but to gather up the pieces, soak them in warm water, rearrange and attach them together so the list "could be intelligibly read." He stayed up well into the night pursuing this labor he had imposed on himself, noting that if it had "been imposed by another, I would have been ready to pronounce him a madman."

The New Year was preceded by dancing at the home of one of the officers of the fort "till the hour of separation, which was a few minutes before twelve. And thus closed the year eighteen hundred and twenty-two." 1823 began with a mail "express" to Detroit via Mackinac carrying almost one hundred letters from the lonely outpost. "We divert ourselves by writing," noted Schoolcraft. "…[And in]…our insulated situation…cling with a death grasp…to our friends and correspondents."

The weather that early January was bitter. "The thermometer has stood at 25 below zero a few days during the season," observed Schoolcraft. "I noticed it at 10 below this morning.". Despite the cold, he received a visit from a Canadian, who crossed the river on snowshoes, testifying to the fact that frigid weather had lasted long enough for the river to freeze thickly.

Schoolcraft learned that the Chippewa "turn up the fore point" of their snowshoes for less resistance in walking. (Diocese of Marquette Archives)

The snowshoes the visitor wore were of Chippewa design. It was pointed out to Schoolcraft that there were differences in the construction of snowshoes among the Indian tribes. The Cree "make a square point in front, tapering away gradually to the heel." The Chippewa, on the other hand, "form theirs with acute points fore and aft, resembling two inverted sections of a circle." The "Chippewyans," he was told, "turn up the fore point, so that it may offer less resistance in walking." Male and female designs also differed. In the female shoe "the netting is more nicely wrought and colored, and often ornamented, particularly those worn by girls, with tassels of color worsted."

As the winter wore on, Schoolcraft worked diligently on Indian vocabulary and study. He became so devoted in his pursuit that he admitted to "have almost grudged the time…devoted to eating and sleeping." Visitors were a continual problem for him. Schoolcraft lamented that he "gained but little by their visits." One made him "waste the whole morning…on trifling subjects." Another "a gourmand," was only interested "in subjects connected with gratification of the palate." And still another exhibited "such lounging habits that he remained two and a half hours with me." Schoolcraft promised himself that he would "try to recollect, when I go to see others, that although I may have leisure, perhaps they are engaged in something of consequence."

The resolution did not keep him from socializing or attending gatherings to which he was invited. At one, Schoolcraft dined with a party of sixteen and "first tasted the flesh of the cariboo, which is a fine flavored venison." That night his party could have used a designated driver. So many toasts were drunk that "in coming home in the cariole, we all missed the balizes, and got completely upset and pitched in the snow."

The cold January of 1823 wore on and led Schoolcraft to write: "A pinching cold winter wears away slowly. The whole village seems to me like so many prescient beavers, in a vast snow-bank, who cut away snow and make paths, every morning, from one lodge to another." Soon, though, the "express" returned after three and a half weeks with the mail. The post contained New York papers for Schoolcraft that dated back to November 11. That fact led him to grumble, "We are now more than two and a half months behind the current news of the day."

February brought the lowest temperature of the winter when on the 4th Schoolcraft

An artist conception of the Sault Ste. Marie area, circa 1838. Fort Brady, Schoolcraft's first home in the Sault, is on the left, or U.S.-side of the river. (The Newberry Library, Chicago)

recorded a 28 below zero reading at one o'clock in the morning. Daylight saw the thermometer only rise to 4 above. A mysterious event accompanied the extreme cold that day. "A loud meteoric report" was heard around noon. Schoolcraft thought it issued "from the explosion of some aerial body" and "seemed to proceed from the south-west." A prolonged rumbling sound accompanied the blast but the source of the sound was never traced and Schoolcraft made no more mention of it.

A party of men from British-occupied Drummond Island came for a visit on February 7. The Brits trudged the 45 miles on snowshoes and were given a rousing welcome by the snowbound villagers. A social call from distant travelers was a cause for celebration during the winter. The partying lasted a week, which seemed to wear on the studious Schoolcraft. When the visitors finally headed back to their island, he wrote, "time devoted to public dinners and suppers, routs and parties, is little better than time thrown away." A week later, Schoolcraft had devoted enough time studying and writing to allow himself a little leisure: "The commanding officer gave a party in honor of Washington's birthday" complete with dancing. The revelry lasted until two the next morning.

It wasn't until March 26 that Schoolcraft noted "winter…[is showing]…signs of relaxing its iron grasp, although the quantity of snow on the ground is still very great, and the streams appear to be as fast locked in the embraces of frost as if it were the slumber of ages." He noted sleighs and dog trains leaving the village regularly for the woods since about March 10. It was maple-sugaring time and the whole town seemed to be involved in the enterprise. "Few of the resident inhabitants are left," observed Schoolcraft. "Many buildings are entirely deserted and closed."

He took a nine-mile jaunt into the woods on snowshoes to visit one of the camps. There he found a large, temporary building surrounded with piles of split wood to boil the sap. Schoolcraft sampled some of the "candy" and headed back to town. On the way back, he nearly fell through the river, an indication that the long winter of 1822-23 was beginning to wind down.

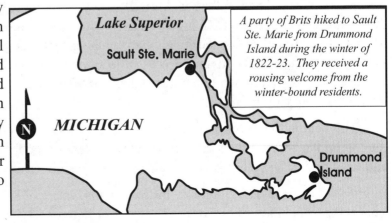

A party of Brits hiked to Sault Ste. Marie from Drummond Island during the winter of 1822-23. They received a rousing welcome from the winter-bound residents.

Spring's arrival was a slow process in 1823. On April 1 he penned, "The ice and snow begin to be burthensome to the eye." He recorded a Chippewa allegory of winter and spring, personified by an old man and a young man. They lived at opposite ends of the world and both boasted of their powers. "Winter blew his breath and the streams were covered with ice. Spring blew his breath and the land was covered with flowers." Every year the old man is eventually conquered "and vanishes into thin air." In Upper Michigan during many years, old man winter is not so much conquered—he just grudgingly gives up and fades away.

According to a Chippewa allegory, the old man of winter blows his breath and the streams are covered with ice. (Drawing by E. Yelland)

As April advanced and winter held on, Schoolcraft speculated that certain species of birds extended their migrations farther south during severe winters. He arrived at this theory after an Indian boy shot an unusual "yellow and cinereous" bird with an arrow at one of the sugar camps. The boy brought the bird to Schoolcraft who felt it was a member of the grosbeak species. The Chippewa, he learned, called it "Pas hun damo" or a bird with stoutness of bill, able to break surfaces. The bird was sent off to New York where it was determined to be, as Schoolcraft conjectured, an evening grosbeak.

Horse trains were still able to cross the river on April 8. Schoolcraft noted that "the night temperature is still quite wintry," however, the rising angle of the April sun could "be sensibly felt during the middle and after part of the day." The river could still be crossed on the 11th but by the 12th the ice was so bad "that no persons have ventured to cross." The sound of the Rapids of St. Mary became a little deeper and louder each day and bare ground began to appear, but the snow still lay deep in the woods. On the 14th, Schoolcraft spotted a robin and gray ducks appeared in the rapids two days later. Large bare spots were carved out by the sun and on April 19 "the first canoe crossed the river…although ice still… [lined]…each shore…for several hundred yards in width." Characteristic of Upper Michigan weather, the ascent to spring took a slide backwards on the 22nd with a late-season snowstorm.

Schoolcraft remembered that on April 28 a few years back he was served cucumbers at a dinner in the Washington, D.C. area. "What a contrast in climate," he mused. "Here…heaps of snow are still seen in shaded situations, and the ice still disfigures the bays." However, the warm season inexorably advanced with little signs to encourage the winter-weary denizen. At the end of the month, whitefish were taken out of the river, which according to Schoolcraft was rare so early in the season.

Ice still held in the lower part of the river and straits on May 1. However, the bay opposite the fort on the northwest shore was completely clear of ice for the first time in "four months and ten days." The yellow sparrow also took up residence again in the woods.

The land warms up considerably faster than the waters of Lake Superior during the spring. This is the foundation of one of the U.P.'s most famous (or infamous) local effects: the lake breeze. Schoolcraft discovered this phenomenon during early May 1823 when he observed, "sudden changes of temperature…very much governed by the course and changes of the wind." The chill of Lake Superior would be felt whenever the wind shifted to the west or northwest, which likely occurred most afternoons during April and May.

Schoolcraft and the rest of the inhabitants of Sault Ste. Marie, however, directed their eyes to the east where soon the first boat would arrive to deliver them from their winter "incarceration." It took until May 15 for the first vessel to navigate through the Straits of St. Marys to the Sault. The boat contained provisions and a "carnival" of letters. Schoolcraft spent the rest of the day "Reading, reading, reading, big and small, scraps and all."

The first winter of American occupation in the Lake Superior region was finally over. If there were any doubts that the warm season had arrived, they were put to rest by the mild days, the blooming wild cherry trees and the mosquito. Schoolcraft noted the appearance of the pesky creature on May 30; right about on the schedule kept by the 21st century version of the bloodthirsty parasite.

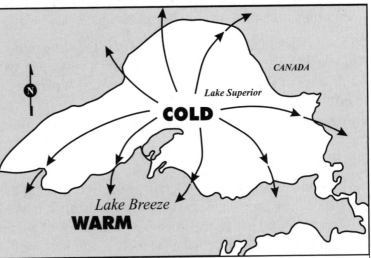

Cold air is generated just above the water of Lake Superior, which retain its winter chill well into spring. This heavy dense cold air pushes out over the land adjacent to the shore on most days through spring and early summer.

Winter of 1823-24

The winter of 1823-24 passed with no comment by Schoolcraft until it was almost over. On March 31 he declared, "The season has been severe." The long winter months were spent huddled by the fire "while the tempest howled around us." Schoolcraft busied himself attending to his new bride, Jane, the daughter of his dear friend John Johnston, and his growing body of Indian lexicon and legend. Occasionally he would brave "the clear winter evenings, to gaze upon the splendid display of the Aurora Borealis." Sometimes he tied on the snowshoes "and ventured over drifts of snow, whose depth rendered them impassable to the horse."

Schoolcraft's assertion that the winter had been severe was probably based on an early beginning and a cold end to the season. The records from Fort Howard, near the site of what is now Green Bay and the nearest observation point to the Sault, indicated the arrival of the first cold wave in the middle of November 1823. On November 17 the Fox River froze over and at Fort Crawford, near present day Prairie Du Chein, the temperature fell to zero.

December, however, began very warm and ended on a normal note. January 1824 was a very mild and open month along the Mississippi and while it would not have been near as warm at the Sault, we can assume the same general weather pattern would have affected the region. The first real cold wave struck at the end of the month, yielding a below zero day at Fort Crawford on the 31st. February and March were wintry months with below zero readings at the start of a number of days through the middle of March.

Marooned by an Early Autumn Storm

Schoolcraft took an extended journey in the summer of 1825 to settle territorial disputes among the tribes in the Wisconsin territory and Upper Mississippi Valley. He and his party left Mackinac Island on July 1. They sailed through the Straits into Lake Michigan, and after encountering disagreeable head winds and fog, reached Green Bay on the 4th. The party stayed in Green Bay for over a week and then began their journey up the Fox River. They crossed over the famous Fox and Wisconsin portage and descended the Wisconsin River safely to Prairie Du Chein.

Schoolcraft found a "very large number of the various tribes assembled." He asserted, "No such gathering of the tribes had ever before occurred". The banks of the Mississippi were lined with tents and wigwams "for miles above and below the town."

The trip back to the Sault was made along the same route they had traveled on the way out. Schoolcraft wanted to go back straight north by way of the Chippewa River then along the south shore of Lake Superior, but abandoned that plan because he could find no one willing to take him that way. A year earlier an American trader named Finley and three Canadian voyageurs were murdered by a Chippewa war party along his proposed route back. The lingering fear caused by the incident was still strong and Americans avoided travel through that area.

By the end of August, Schoolcraft's party was drifting down the Fox River. He described the waterway as "serpentine, almost without parallel; it winds about like a string that doubles and redoubles and its channel is choked with fields of wild rice." A heavy shower at three in the morning on the 27th delayed the party's departure until sunrise. The day turned out to be hot "beyond any experience on the journey."

Schoolcraft was suffering from homesickness when he wrote, to his wife, "Why should I relate to you our dull progress through fields of rice—through intricate channels, and amidst myriads of ducks and wild water fowl?" The heat rendered him pensive, apathetic and listless. "My thoughts are employed on home. A thousand phantoms passed through my head. I tried to imagine how you were employed at this moment, whether busy, or sick in your own room. It would require a volume to trace my wandering thoughts. Let it suffice that another day is nearly gone, and it has lessened the distance which separated us, about seventy miles."

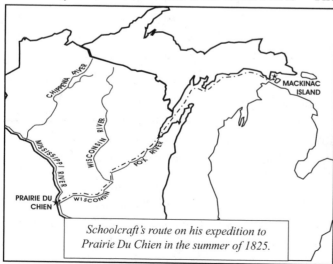

Schoolcraft's route on his expedition to Prairie Du Chein in the summer of 1825.

His party camped that night near a large village of "Winnebagoes and Menomonies." The Indians begged Schoolcraft for food. He gave most of the bread, hard biscuit, pork and tobacco he had purchased to present to the Chippewa in northwest Wisconsin and Upper Michigan had he traveled the Chippewa River route. The Indians were grateful and Schoolcraft later wrote, "Never, I believe, was a more appropriate distribution made."

The homesick traveler made it to Mackinac in early September. On Monday morning, the 5th, only a good day's journey lay between him and reunion with his wife, Jane, and his young son, Willy. Schoolcraft rose at seven, had breakfast and spent time ordering provisions for the Indian Agency. After lunch he went to his camp, anxious to set out for home. He arrived to find two of his men "ill with fever and augue" and three others "much intoxicated." To add to his woes, "the atmosphere was very cloudy and threatening."

Schoolcraft decided to wait until the weather looked more agreeable and ordered his men to be ready at two the next morning. The party finally set out from Mackinac at half past six after a thick fog had lifted. They reached Goose Island in a light head wind in about three hours, then made it to Outard Point, "But could go no further from the increased violence of the wind." An early autumn gale was settling over the Upper Great Lakes.

The evening of the 6th saw Schoolcraft camped on Outard Point waiting for the regular diurnal drop in the wind. "I expected the wind would fall with the sun," he wrote, "but, alas! It blows stronger than ever." He had no recourse but to wait. "I feel solitary. The loud dashing of the waves on shore, and the darkness and dreariness of all... conspire to give a saddened train to my reflections."

He attempted to divert himself with a walk along the shore. As he strolled along the beach he amused himself, as he put it, "with the reflection that I should, perhaps, meet you coming from an opposite direction on the beach, and I half fancied that, perhaps, it would actually take place." Schoolcraft returned from his imagined reunion with his wife "fatigued and half sick," resigned to the fact that it would take longer than anticipated to get home.

Heavy rain and gale force winds pummeled the party all night into the next morning. The rain was driven right through Schoolcraft's tent. Soaked and shivering, he looked out and beheld "a wide vista of white foaming surge as far as the eye could reach." The storm continued to increase, forcing his party to move their tents and belongings back among the stunted, scrub trees of the little island. Schoolcraft termed it "a real equinoxial storm." "My ears were stunned," he noted, "with the incessant roaring of the water and the loud murmuring of the wind among the foliage." All he could do was sit in his tent, wrapped in a cloak to keep out the damp, chilly air. The tempestuous scene brought out the poet in him:

Outard Point
What narrowed pleasures well the bosom here,
A shore most sterile, and a clime severe,
Where every shrub seems stinted in its size,
"Where genius sickens and where fancy dies."

If to the lake I cast my longing view,
The curling waves their noisy way pursue;
That noise reminds me of my prison-strand,
Those waves I most admire, but cannot stand.

If to the shore I cast my anxious eye,
There broken rocks and sand commingled lie,
Mixed with the wrecks of shells and weeds and wood,
Crushed by the storm and driven by the flood.

E'en fishes there, high cast upon the shore,
Yet pant with life and stain the rocks with gore...

You get the idea. Schoolcraft was trapped and could do nothing about it except try to keep dry. About two in the afternoon on the 7th, he set out to view the "angry vista" and catch some hopeful sign that the tempest was winding down. He returned disheartened. "It seemed as if the lake was convulsed to its bottom," he wrote.

An hour later, a transient glimmer of sunshine appeared and buoyed his hopes. The wind also seemed to die down a bit and Schoolcraft ordered his party to prepare for departure. The canoe was moved inland to a quiet bay and as it was being loaded, "a most portentous cloud gathered in the west, and the wind arose more fierce than before." Reconciled to his fate, Schoolcraft pitched his tent, sat down and waited and waited some more. "Up to a late hour at night," he recounted, "the elemental war continued, and, committing myself to the Divine mercy, I put out my candle and retired to my pallet."

The next morning the stranded traveler pushed his way through the "spruce and brambles" of his encampment to get a view of the open lake. Nothing much had changed. "Lake Huron...still...[had]...the pouts." Schoolcraft did notice the wind had shifted. The waves were now coming directly from the west. It was a sign that the storm had passed off to the northeast and would eventually clear the area entirely. He did not want to take the time for that to happen. He devised a risky plan to cast off with a "close-reefed" sail into the wind and waves to Point Detour. His voyageur guides thought the plan too hazardous. However, "their habitual sense of obedience" led them to comply. At ten in the morning they set off, "not without imminent

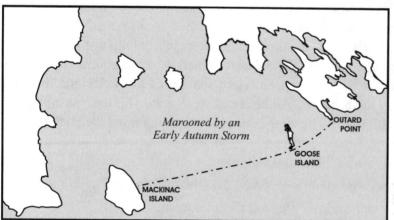

Schoolcraft and his voyageur guides set out in his small sailed vessel from Mackinac Island early on the morning of September 6, 1825. They made it to Goose Island in a light headwind but became stranded on Outard Point (now Point Fuyards) as an early autumn storm lashed Lake Huron.

hazard" and made their way to the Capes of St. Marys.

The party "literally went 'on the wings of the wind.' We had reefed our sail to less than four feet," recounted Schoolcraft, "and I put an extra man with the steersman. I do not think myself to have ever run such hazards. I was tossed up and down like Sancho Panza on the blanket." After three hours and twenty minutes of this punishment, the crew took shelter behind the small Isle St. Vital. The party had lunch and "put out before the gale" again. They arrived safely at De Tour and sailed into St. Marys Straits.

The beleaguered crew came upon the anchored schooner *Harriet* soon after entering the protected water. A passenger on the *Harriet* had just visited the Johnstons two days earlier and told Schoolcraft all was well on the home front. The captain of the vessel presented them with some whitefish. "The delicious fish is always a treat to me," wrote Schoolcraft, "but was never more so than on the present occasion."

The tired, wet and cold traveler set up camp on an island opposite St. Joseph's Island. He warmed himself by the fire and reflected on the good news he received about his family. "I feel quite re-invigorated," he penned just before retiring for the night. The next day the crew sped the last forty miles to the Sault and Schoolcraft made his way to his beloved "Elmwood" estate. He neglected to make an entry in his journal on September 9, 1825. "The excitement of getting back and finding all well drove away almost all other thoughts."

Death of a Child and another Trip South

Tragedy visited Elmwood in 1827. On March 13 of that year, Schoolcraft's three-year-old son died. The winter as a whole had been exceptionally mild. Fort Snelling reported temperatures nearly eight degrees above normal in both January and February. "The month of March was more than usually changeable in its temperature," observed Schoolcraft, "with disagreeable rains and much humidity, which nearly carried away the heavy amount of snow on the ground." He felt that the mild, damp weather fostered "cold and croup" in little William Henry. The illness claimed its victim quickly. The despondent father still seemed to hear the boy's "silver, playful voice…ring through the house when… [his body]…lay a placid corpse". Schoolcraft poured out his grief in his journal a few days later:

"Who was it nestled on my breast,

And on my cheek sweet kisses prest,

And in whose smile I felt so blest?

Sweet Willy

After a difficult spring, Schoolcraft got the order from General Cass to make a trip south. A treaty setting territorial boundaries between Indian tribes of the region was set for ratification later that summer. Schoolcraft took the opportunity to get Mrs. Schoolcraft out of the house on a visit to Green Bay, "as a means of diverting her mind from the scene of our recent calamity."

The couple packed their bags and set out on the steamer *Henry Clay* June 8, 1827. They "had a pleasant voyage until into the bay," when "an obstinate head wind tossed us up and down like a cork on the sea." Schoolcraft recalled how the retching of the waves brought a plague of seasickness over the crowded vessel: "Every being…bearing a stomach which had not been seasoned to such tossings…was prostrate." Mercifully the *Clay* stuck in the mud at the head of Green Bay and the passengers disembarked on small boats to a little settlement nearby. The Indian Agent left his wife in Green Bay and drifted down the Fox, traveling to Butte Des Morts near present day Oshkosh. The treaty was eventually approved by the tribes and signed at that site on August 11, 1827.

Heroics on the Ice

A series of mild winters visited the Upper Midwest during the late 1820s into the 1830s. A thaw in late March 1829 led to a near fatal accident on the ice of the Straits. John Agnew, the Inspector of Customs, was traveling back by dog train from Mackinac on the channel when he encountered "faulty and rotten" ice. He tried to avoid the bad places but fell in the ice along with his dogs and sled. "The struggle to get out only involved him worse," chronicled Schoolcraft, "and, overcome by fatigue and false footings he at length gave over the strife, and …as a last resort, uttered a yell."

A Chippewa named Magisaunikwa happened to be camping in the woods nearby. "With the ever ready ear of the aborigines," he caught the sound of Agnew's call for help. Magisaunikwa set out on the dangerous ice to aid the man who had already "relinquished the struggle, and resigned himself to his fate." The Indian applied all skills his people had developed for such emergencies and eventually pulled the unconscious Agnew from the icy water. He put the body of the inspector on a sled and drew it to his lodge. He revived the lifeless Agnew by the fire, "applied dry clothing, prepared a kind of tea" and kept "unremitting" watch over the man until the danger had passed. "I invested… [Magisaunikwa]…with a silver medal for the act," wrote Schoolcraft, "and gave him a chief's flag, with goods and cutlery…to the value above fifty dollars."

Warm Winters: 1828-31

Despite the relative warmth of the winter of 1828-29, Schoolcraft still observed patches of snow along the banks of the St. Marys as he left home for Detroit on April 27. He also encountered "fields of ice" in Muddy Lake. "It was not until entering the St. Clair," he noted, "and passing down beyond the chilling influences of Lake Huron, that spring began to show striking evidence of her rapid advances." Finally on reaching Detroit, Schoolcraft noticed how far along the blossoms had developed on the fruit trees. The scene "betokened a quite different and benign climate," he wrote. "The difference in latitude, in this journey, is a full four degrees. This fact, which it is difficult to realize from the mere inspection of maps, and reading of books…is important…to bear in mind, in setting a just value on the country and its agricultural advantages."

The striking climate change when going from north to south is no different today. But today, with modern transportation, the change is more immediate. Areas around Detroit see spring come about a month earlier than areas in the northern U.P. around places like

Marquette or the Sault. At the same time, winter's advance in northern Upper Michigan is about a month ahead of Detroit's.

The winter of 1829-30 was notably warm. December 1829 ended as one of the warmest in the early frontier period. At Fort Snelling the mercury stayed in the 40s and 50s most days from the 15th through much of Christmas week. February saw many days in the 40s and 50s, too, with only one major snowstorm on the last day of the month. March came in over three degrees above average. The Mississippi and St. Peters (now the Minnesota) Rivers broke up on the 20th of the month and were clear of ice by the 25th. The warm March of 1830 set the stage for James Schoolcraft's *Perilous Trip on the Ice* featured in his brother Henry's journal.

James left the Sault "on the ice with a train" about April 1. He later wrote his older brother Henry from Mackinac, "We were seven days from the Sault to the Point, at which place we arrived in a cold rain storm, half starved, lame and tired." He declared, "I am sure mortals never suffered more than us. After leaving the Sault, disappointment, hunger, and fatigue, were our constant companions."

James' party found the ice on Muddy Lake in better shape than the slushy rotten covering on Lake Huron. "After leaving Detour," he recounted, "we were obliged to coast, and that too over piles of snow, mountains of ice, and innumerable rocks." At one point, they were forced to portage across a cedar swamp, which was thawed because of the mild weather. James had to drive his dog, Jack, about a mile through the water with the sled in tow. Later they had to "round all those long points on Huron," afraid if they cut straight across the lake, they would fall through bad ice.

Jack fell through the ice three times. "It was with great difficulty we succeeded in getting him out." James explained that "all our harness… [was lost]… in the Lake." They had to improvise with "an old bag, a portage collar, and a small piece of rope-yarn." Jack went without eating for three days, "except what he could pick up on the shore." "Take it all in all," James asserted, "I think it rather a severe trip."

The next winter was also exceptionally mild. Schoolcraft spent much of the season in Detroit but kept in contact with family and friends by letter. On December 6, 1830 he received a letter from his wife. She wrote, "The weather has remained very fine, till within two days, when we had, for the first time, a *sprinkling* of snow. Such a season has never been heard in this country—not a particle of ice has…formed anywhere."

Later that winter Schoolcraft started an entry with the title *Temperature at the Foot of Lake Superior.* A friend wrote, "The weather has been very mild indeed,

The Minnesota territory. Fort Ripley, just southwest of present-day Brainerd, was the nearest weather-observing point with a similar latitude to Upper Michigan during the 1820s-1830s.

The French Canadians handed down the voyaging tradition from father to son for over one hundred and fifty years. The men became guides and hired themselves out to "bourgeois" like Schoolcraft. They were a rugged, cheerful breed known for their strength and endurance. Indian ethnographer Johann G. Kohl described how his voyageur guide tied his blue woolen knapsack up and "hung the whole on his back...while fastening... [a]...broad band...round his head." The voyageurs "carry with their foreheads and backs, like our oxen drag with their heads." The weight rested only partly on the back.

The weight a voyageur carried through the woods "with a light and elastic step" was huge. The ordinary weight carried by each man was at least one hundred and fifty pounds. The voyageur tradition honored a man

here, until within a few days." He went on to say that there had not been enough snow to cover the stubble in the fields. "Severe weather commenced" on the January 23, however. At nine that morning the temperature fell to 11 degrees below zero with below zero readings the next three mornings.

Outside of that late January cold spell, the overall impression of the winter was one of warmth. Schoolcraft's received a letter from his brother-in-law George on March 8, 1831. "The weather has been uncommonly mild the whole winter," he wrote. "The southern shore of the lake from Whitefish Point to Ance Kewywenon (L'Anse) presents a scene of open lake, not any ice forming to enable the poor Indians to spear fish." This winter sounds reminiscent of a number of winters during the 1990s when little if any ice formed along Lake Superior's Upper Michigan shore.

Summer Expedition West: 1831

The next summer, Schoolcraft set out west from the Sault along the south shore of Lake Superior. "The purpose of the mission was to vaccinate the Indians for smallpox and… learn as much as possible… [about their]…culture, customs and history." He invited a young, talented professor he admired named Douglass Houghton along on the trip. While Schoolcraft studied the Indians, Houghton would "gather information on the Natural History of the region."

They set out from Iroquois Point at the east entrance to Lake Superior's Whitefish Bay with a small detachment of troops on June 27, 1831. They sped quickly and easily along the south shore of the mighty lake with voyageurs powering their large canoes. Schoolcraft looked out on the vista as they drifted along and was inspired to write one of the more cogent descriptions of the beauty and immensity of Lake Superior:

"He who, for the first time, lifts his eyes upon this expanse, is amazed and delighted at its magnitude. Vastness is the term by which it is, more than any other, described. Clouds robed in sunshine, hanging in fleecy or nebular masses above-a bright, pure illimitable plain of water-blue mountains, or dim islands in the distance—a shore of green foliage on the one hand—a waste of waters on the other. These are the prominent objects on which the eye rests. We are diverted by the flight of birds, as on the ocean. Sometimes there is a smoke on the shore. Sometimes an Indian trader returns with the avails of his winter's traffic. A gathering storm or threatening wind arises. All at once the voyageurs burst out into one of their simple and melodious boat-songs, and the gazing at the vastness is relieved and sympathy at once awakened in gayety."

Schoolcraft displayed a prophetic sense of what lay ahead for the region. "The sources of a busy commerce lie concealed, and but half concealed, in its rocks." He also gazed landward and observed that the "forests are not without timber to swell the objects of a future commerce."

The first day they made it to just the other side of the "long and bleak peninsula of Whitefish Point" where they camped for the night. The next day they glided "forty miles along a shore exclusively sandy" and camped for the night at Grand Marais. Schoolcraft noted the place was "a striking inlet in the coast" which had grown considerably since the last time he saw it on a trip with General Cass eleven years before. He attributed the growth of the inlet to "the force of the north-west storms." The phenomenon "exhibits striking proof of lake action," he declared.

The expert paddlers made impressive time the next day. The party quickly skimmed past the high sand dunes of Grand Sable then "the storm-beaten" Pictured Rocks to Grand Island where they put up for the night. On July 1, the expedition made another forty to fifty miles camping at the Dead River on the north side of present day Marquette.

In the Marquette area the party "examined the bay behind this peninsula." The bay is now called Middle Bay and the peninsula Presque Isle. He observed that the bay "appeared to be capable of admitting large vessels." It never did become a harbor owing to its exposure to northwest gales. The lee side of Presque Isle, protected from the northwest wind, eventually became a docking place for vessels; the Upper Harbor still serves as Marquette's industrial dock today.

Schoolcraft and his companions climbed the rock knob the Indians called "Totosh" (Chippewa for breast, now Sugarloaf). As he gazed upon the landscape, Schoolcraft noted "the lower saddle-shaped mountain…named "The

who carried more as a hero. "Unluckily," wrote Kohl, "these heroic porters overwork themselves in their zeal, grow old prematurely, suffer in the chest, and bring on peculiar diseases."

The voyageur's paddling exploits were also the stuff of legend. Kohl was told the story of the annual voyage of Sir George Simpson, the governor of the Hudson Bay Territories. "The great gentleman," wrote Kohl "is always in a terrible hurry." His canoe was exceptionally long and "remarkably pretty" with a crew of twenty or twenty-four voyageurs manning it. They cut a path through the water "as a bird the air." They would keep a steady eight mile-an-hour clip; a pace the steamers of the day could barely maintain.

The men paddled eighteen to twenty hours per day. When they reached camp in the evening, they would wrap themselves in their blankets and sleep four or five hours. "Young men," related Kohl, "who try it for the first time, are so excited that they neither sleep nor eat."

At sunrise, a signal was given and the cycle was repeated. If the party came upon a portage, the operation was performed with "the greatest order and energy." A command was given and the paddles were "unshipped." Each man knew the packages he was to carry and trotted quickly over the portage. Ten men dragged

Voyageurs working a canoe up a rapid. (W.H. Bartlett; S. Bradshaw; London, 1841, The Newberry Library, Chicago)

Cradle Top" (now Hogsback) by local Indians. He noted that the granite hills to the west reminded him of "the rolling appearance of the sea in violent motion."

The expedition moved on to the Keweenaw where he observed that "the northwest coast of the peninsula is greatly serrated and broken, abounding in little bays and inlets." The rugged appearance of the coast was "proof," he stated, "of the terrible action of the storms of this rugged shore." The proof can still be seen today. McLain State Park, situated on the shore that Schoolcraft described, has lost considerable shoreline in recent years to the ravages of the perpetual northwest gales.

A few days later, Schoolcraft described an incident he termed of "singular vivacity." The expedition hit a downpour just off the tip of the Keweenaw Peninsula. "Rain literally fell in sheets," Schoolcraft recounted. "There was no escape, and our philosophy was to sit still and bear it. The shower was so great that it obscured objects at a short distance." "All at once," he related in amazement, "the men struck up a cheerful boat song, which they continued, paddling with renewed energy, till the shower abated. I believe no people under the sun would have thought of such a resource."

Henry Rowe Schoolcraft left Sault Ste. Marie permanently in May of 1833. He was reassigned to Mackinac Island where he stayed until 1841. Here, isolation in the winter was even more complete. He was now "shut out from the world by a long expanse of coasts, which cannot be navigated in the winter." Part of his diversion, he resolved, would "consist in notices of… (Mackinac Island's)…meteorology, the changes of winds and currents in the straits," and so on. On December 2 he observed, "Mild weather had characterized the season."

This was in keeping with the warm winters over the last several years in the Upper Midwest. Schoolcraft stated the current warm season had been predicted by some because of the "remarkable meteoric display" in November.

the canoe out of the water swung it on command over their shoulders and quickly bounded down the path with it. In ten minutes' time all gear was back in the water and the governor's party was again dashing through the waves.

Schoolcraft also marveled at his voyageurs' feats. They ascended the summit that separates Lake Superior from the Upper Mississippi Valley: "The exertion was incredible," wrote Schoolcraft. "I expected every day some of the men to give out…but…they gloried in feats under which ordinary men would have fainted. To carry a horse load over a portage path which a horse could not walk, is an exploit which none but a Canadian Voyageur would sigh for the accomplishment of."

Farther south in Wisconsin, after a particularly grueling

Spectacular Meteor Shower: November 1833

The "remarkable display of the meteorites" was observed at various points across the United States during the early morning of November 13, 1833. Schoolcraft described the phenomenon as "radiating balls, streams of fire or falling stars from the zenith into the lake."

On the east coast, "those who were up at four saw the grandest site." There were three distinct lights in the night sky besides the usual array of stars. There were "shooting points of light" that emanated from a center point and cascaded to the horizon, "resembling a thick shower of luminous snow." Then there were "luminous bodies which hung dimly in the air." Finally, the most spectacular sight was the "falling fireballs, some which burst, while others went out of sight." They were so bright that even the smallest object could be seen as the meteors lit the night sky. One of the fireballs was reportedly larger than the moon; another was "like a serpent coiling itself up," while others resembled "square tables" or "pruning hooks." The ones that burst left "trains of light behind them, some tinged with… prismatic colours."

Schoolcraft's brother-in-law, William Johnston, was in northern Minnesota "on the sources of the Mississippi" at the time and concurred that the event was nothing short of wonderful. "The weather," Johnston wrote, "is still very pleasant, with very little frost at night. About two or three in the morning one of the men came and awoke me. 'Come and see a strange sight,' he said. We went to the door, where we saw every now and then, stars shooting or falling. The center from whence they first appeared to the eye was, to us, nearly in a direct line above our heads—from whence they went in all directions, to all points of the compass." He related that he and his companion went into the house, sat down and smoked their pipes, shaking their heads in astonishment at what they had seen.

They decided to take one last look before retiring. "What a sight it was!" exclaimed Johnston. "The whole heaven appeared to be lit with falling stars, and we could now more plainly see…the center from whence they would shoot. The night was calm, the air clear, nothing to disturb the stillness, but the hushed breathings of the men. The stars were accompanied with a rustling noise, and, though they appeared to fall as fast and as thick as hail, above them, now and then,

trip of 42 miles over rapids and portages, Schoolcraft described what happened after they set up camp for the night. He explained how the voyageurs "ate prodigiously and then lay down and slept with the nightmare. Poor fellows, they screamed out in their sleep. But they were up and ready at five o'clock the next morning with paddle and song."

The French Canadians' feats of endurance extended to snowshoes, too. The story goes that a man named La Branche bet James Schoolcraft that he could walk on snowshoes from Sault Ste. Marie to Mackinaw and back in thirty hours. The distance between the two settlements is about 50 miles, as the crow flies. Through the forests and ice-covered swamps, then over the hopefully frozen water, it had to be considerably farther. La Branche accomplished the feat, with two hours to spare. He supposedly remained just outside of the Sault at a promontory called Coalpit hill so that he could walk into Schoolcraft's place of business at exactly thirty hours. He feared that if he came any sooner, he would lose the bet! After he collected on the bet he was said to have celebrated his success by dancing the night away in a local saloon.

This decade-long period of predominantly warm winters can be favorably compared to the warm winters of the 1990s. The 90s saw exceptionally mild winters in '90-'91, '94-'95 and '97-'98. There was a long, bitter stretch from Christmas 1993 to the middle of February 1994, but a mild late winter and early spring followed. The long, cold and snowy winter of 1995-96 was a glaring exception (See Snowstorms, Snowy Winters, page 195).

This comparison brings up an interesting question. Is our climate changing? More to the point, is our climate changing because of man's activities? Unfortunately, this question usually turns into a political debate. Politics aside, close examinations of the records extending back to pioneer days are inconclusive regarding man's contribution to climate change. There have always been weather extremes: bitter cold, torrid heat, droughts and floods. Dire claims that a specific warm spell, drought or flood is "proof" of global warming due to anthropogenic causes are not good science.

we could see some of the fixed stars, shining as bright as ever. I can compare it nothing more comprehensive than a hail storm. The sight was grand beyond description." Johnston watched the heavenly display until "the bright streaks of day" appeared and "the light of the sun caused them to disappear."

Schoolcraft was reassigned to Mackinac Island in 1833. The island would soon become a "refuge for the opulent or invalids in the summer." (Courtesy of the Diocese of Marquette Archives)

The heavenly phenomenon was the Leonid Meteor shower, probably the most spectacular of modern times. At Fort Snelling, a diarist noted the "shooting stars were seen early in the morning and continued flying in every direction until daylight. They were extremely brilliant and very much alarmed the Indians."

The prediction of warmth following the meteor shower held true with December ending up the warmest twelfth month in Fort Snelling's record; a remarkable 14.8 degrees above the long term average. The coldest reading until the day after Christmas was a balmy 14 above zero.

The Open Winter of 1833-34

As testimony to the exceptional warmth, the Indians of the region were making maple sugar across the Upper Great Lakes. Schoolcraft got a piece of maple candy from an Indian in late December "as proof of the mildness of the weather." Just as in Minnesota, colder air settled over Mackinac Island the last several days of December. During the first part of January 1834, more average winter weather was observed with "snow-blustering cold" on January 8 and 11. By the 13th, deep snowdrifts made for difficult travel on the island.

Travel was also impeded on the water surrounding Mackinac due to the unseasonable warmth. The harbor and straits remained mostly ice-free until the last few days of December. Then as the weather finally grew colder, floating ice became a problem. On January 6 Schoolcraft wrote, "Indians, detained by floating ice since New Year's, got over to Pt. St. Ignace." By the 14th, ice completely filled the channel between Bois Blanc and the main harbor, though the outer channel remained open.

A thaw occurred on January 16 with rain that continued all evening. Schoolcraft was out visiting late that day and recalled that he "got a complete wetting" on the way home. On the 17th, he noted that the rain "much diminished the quantity of snow; bare ground is to be seen in some spots." In the wake of the rainstorm, Schoolcraft observed the air was "murky, and surcharged with moisture, rendering it disagreeable to be out of doors."

Fort Snelling also had rain and a thaw on the 16th but by the 17th winter began closing in again. Colder air did not reach Mackinac until the 18th, when Schoolcraft reported a "depression of the atmospheric temperature." The ice made "walking slippery and the snow crusted and hard." He was told the crusted snow "was fatal to wild hoofed animals, which at every step are subject to break through, and cut their ankles." This fact was good news for the Indians who "successfully pursue and take the moose and reindeer" when the snow is crusted over by a thaw and subsequent freezing.

The last part of January 1834 saw the only true bitter period of the winter. Arctic air began flowing over the open waters of the Great Lakes on the 19th and led to snow. The snow was attended by a west wind, which made the day "very blustering and boisterous." The wind was "so strong as to blow some persons down." The next day the temperature stood at only 2 degrees above zero at 8 in the morning. By the 24th the temperature at the fort had fallen to 5 below, while in Minnesota the lowest reading of 32 below was reached, attesting to the moderating influence of the Great Lakes.

Schoolcraft was an astute observer of lake-effect. He noted "the air…became colder than the water of the lake, producing an interchange of temperature, and the striking phenomenon of rising vapor." He went on to explain, "The open waters gave out their latent heat, like a boiling pot." Schoolcraft stated he observed this spectacle "in the basin of the Upper Lakes, some days every winter." The mechanism he described occurs only when the air flowing over the water is cold enough to lead to evaporation. It is this process that leads to heavy snows on the lee shores of the Great Lakes during the fall and winter months.

NIMMI

The deer, named "Nimmi," grew to full size and became a pet and companion at the Schoolcraft estate. "Its motions were most graceful," he wrote. "It was perfectly tame. It would walk into the hall

On his travels to Wisconsin, Schoolcraft brought back a young deer who became a tenant of the family's grounds and gardens. (Drawing by E. Yelland)

and dining-room, when the door was open, and was once observed to step up, gracefully and take bread from the table. It perambulated the garden walks. It would, when the back-gate was shut, jump over a six feet picket fence, with the ease and lightness of a bird."

He added that, "some of its instincts were remarkable. At night it would choose its place of lying down invariably to the leeward of an object, which sheltered it from the prevailing wind. One of its most remarkable instincts," he felt, "was developed with respect to the ladies. On one occasion, while an unattended lady was walking up the avenue from my front gate to the door, through the garden grounds, the animal approached from behind, in the gentlest manner possible, and placed his fore feet on her shoulders. This happened more than once."

Nimmi had a propensity for eating plum leaves and was eventually banished from the Schoolcraft garden. Nimmi was then allowed to roam freely on the island. The deer's free ranging eventually led to its demise. He got into another islander's fruit trees and that "vicious person broke one of its legs." An injury of this sort is fatal to deer and his master was persuaded to have Nimmi shot; so ended the life of the three-year-old "inmate" of the Schoolcraft estate.

"Poor Nimmi, some are hanged for being thieves,

But thou, poor beast! wast killed for eating leaves. "

An example of the "striking phenomenon of rising vapor" which Schoolcraft observed often during the winter. This is the evaporation off the lake that eventually leads to lake-effect snow that buries areas downwind each winter. (Photo by Don Rolfson, NWS, Marquette)

Schoolcraft probably saw no "rising vapor" off Lake Huron for much of the rest of the winter. After the cold start on the 24th the temperature began to moderate. By the last day of January 1834 he wrote, "The sun shone clear; no snow; no high winds, but a serene and pleasant atmosphere." February was exceptionally mild. Even when it cooled down briefly on the 7th, the temperature only slipped to 26 degrees. After snow and a brief cool-down on the 16th and 17th, the weather turned even warmer. Rain began on the 19th accompanied by spring-like thunder on the 20th. In Minnesota, February 1834 was the warmest second month of the pioneer era, averaging an incredible sixteen degrees above normal.

March came in like a lamb. On the 1st it was "so mild and warm" that a good deal of snow melted. What snow was left became "soft and sloppy" on the 4th. The ice became "dangerous to cross" on the 5th. Schoolcraft wrote in amazement, "The lake west has been, in fact, fast and solidly frozen, so as to be crossed with trains, but twelve days!" the whole winter. The first vessel dropped anchor in the harbor on March 14. Its appearance, he recalled, caused "all hearts to be gay at the termination of our wintry exclusion from the world." The "incarceration" lasted only two and a half months this time, compared to four and a half months during his first winter at the Sault in 1823.

A cold, snowy period the last third of the month reminded islanders that winter usually lasts into spring. A "boisterous" northeast storm dropped twelve to fourteen inches of snow on March 20, the largest single fall of the season. It stayed cold for several days after the storm but by the end of the month, lamb-like weather again prevailed. On the last day of March 1834, Schoolcraft recorded a "clear and sunny" day.

The remaining ice surrounding the island was "completely broken up by an easterly wind."

The fourth month of 1834 brought true spring weather to the Upper Lakes. The harbor was completely free of ice on April 2. Schoolcraft began to prepare hotbeds and flower boxes on the 4th. On the 9th the schooner *White Pigeon* came from Detroit with a mail delivery. At the same time a group of Indian families came up from their "wintering places." They came, observed Schoolcraft, "as if from a cemetery. They seem almost as lean and hungry as their dogs." By the 14th he announced, "spring advances rapidly." Two days later, a party of Beaver Island Indians reported that the Straits were completely clear of ice. That bit of news led Schoolcraft to declare, "We are once more united to the commercial world, on the great chain of lakes above and below us."

The opening of navigation brought disaster to the schooner *Nancy Dousman* on April 22. The vessel "arrived…from below" on the previous morning in a northeast wind accompanied by snow. A couple of inches fell along with freezing temperatures that put "a sad check to vegetation." The next morning the wind developed into a gale and the *Nancy Dousman* was wrecked with no apparent injuries or loss of life, but its cargo was saved. The incident was "proof," asserted Schoolcraft, "that the harbor is no refuge from a north-easter."

The "cold and backward" weather continued the next several days with periodic rain, some sleet and snow flurries. Then the last five days of the month "the atmosphere… regained its equilibrium fully" with mild, sunny days and clear nights. The area Indians began freely moving to the island and Schoolcraft busied himself in his garden, sowing radishes and other early seeds. On May 1, he pronounced "the winter…gone and past." He took his children on a stroll up the cliffs of the island to gather wildflowers; more evidence the *Young Man of Spring* had blown his warm breath over the Upper Lakes early in 1834.

Schoolcraft ignored mention of the weather during the next winter. There were apparently no outstanding events during the winter of 1834-35 worthy of mention. It was another mild winter in keeping with most of the cold seasons of the past decade. However, February 1835 was very cold in Minnesota at Fort Snelling, but the rest of the winter was

A FOREIGNER'S PERSPECTIVE

English travel writer G. W. Featherstonhaugh gave a more grim assessment of the "sad fate of the Indians." He was traveling through the region in 1835 and reflected on how their way of life had changed. He observed that before the white man came there was enough game to feed and clothe the population, which remained at a steady state "from causes inherent to the conditions of the aborigines." Over time, the white man taught the Indian to substitute blankets for furs and to want whiskey, firearms and tobacco. "To acquire these," wrote Featherstonhaugh, "the Indian…must kill all the animals he meets with, not to subsist upon…but to carry the skins to the trader to discharge his debts."

Game was becoming scarce because of this practice and it would not be long before the traders would abandon them. "This state of things," observed Featherstonhaugh, "would cause their immediate extinction, but for the policy of the American government." He went on to explain how the policy worked: the government "under the form of a treaty-bargain" would seize Indian lands and the Indian would be driven away "to a more distant region." Featherstonhaugh felt that there was no alternative for the native people of the Great Lakes. ✳

RARE GENEROSITY

It was about this time an incident of "rare generosity," as ethnographer Kohl put it, occurred in the snowbound wilderness of the Upper Great Lakes. An "educated American" and his two companions found themselves completely out of provisions while on a journey through the forest. The snow was so deep it made travel difficult and hunting impossible. The party marched for three days without food and was rapidly running out of energy and hope. "At length," Kohl was told, "they discovered an Indian lodge, entered it, and begged some food." The Indians had none. The men were told that the inhabitants of the lodge had fasted as many weeks as they had days. "The deep snow has prevented us from killing anything," said one of the elders, "our two sons have gone out to day, but they will return, as usual, with empty hands." It was suggested that the American and his companions check with Indians that lived about twenty miles to the north. Disheartened and tortured by hunger, the three set out on a march through the drifts to try their luck with the distant neighbors.

They struggled about four or five miles through the thick, white, icy mantle when they heard a voice from behind. They saw an Indian hurrying after them on snowshoes. "Come back," said the Indian.

consistently warm with another early spring.

While the question of man affecting the climate did not enter Schoolcraft's mind, he did reflect on another contemporary issue: land speculation. "An opinion rose that… [Mackinac Island]…must become a favorite watering place, or refuge for the opulent or invalids during the summer," he wrote in August 1835. "Lots were eagerly bought up from Detroit and Chicago." Schoolcraft himself took a steamer to Green Bay on the 17th where he attended the first land sale in the Wisconsin Territory. He purchased several parcels and also procured a pet—a young fawn, which he took back "to be a tenant of…[his]…garden and grounds."

1835: A Change in the Weather and a Way of Life

By Halloween 1835 the native tribes were ready to cede a portion of their vast holdings in the Upper Lakes. "Game had failed in the greater part of it," observed Schoolcraft, "and they had no other method of raising funds to pay their large outstanding credits to the…traders." Profound changes were occurring for the Indians and Schoolcraft saw this as "an interval of transition between the hunter and agricultural state."

Area tribal members prepared to visit the "Great Father" in Washington to negotiate the land deal and Schoolcraft decided to make the trip east himself. Changes were also occurring in the weather. In sharp contrast to the last several years, winter set in quickly during the fall of 1835. Travel writer G. W. Featherstonhaugh endured a sleet storm in northern Minnesota on October 3. That evening, he later wrote, "It became excessively cold, and a sharp wind, accompanied with frozen sleet, set in from the North East. This soon became so thick, that I could scarcely look up, much more see anything." The poor traveler's "feet and hands were so cold that… [he]…had scarcely any power over them." He and the horse carrying his belongings were completely covered "with a glaze of ice." A few mornings later, Featherstonhaugh rose at dawn and found the spring water in his tent frozen across the pail.

On October 22nd, a half-foot of snow fell at Fort Snelling. Cold weather accompanied the early snowstorm. "The day I left Fort Snelling," wrote a friend to Schoolcraft, "the thermometer was very low…in fact, it was quite winter, and all were of the opinion…that ice would form and drive… [on the river]…in a few days."

Schoolcraft left Mackinac for Washington by way of Detroit then New York on November 9. He left aboard a schooner "on the eve…of a great tempest, which rendered that season memorable in the history of wrecks on the Great Lakes."

The boat had barely cleared the lighthouse of Mackinac harbor when the wind increased to a gale. "We soon went on furiously," recalled Schoolcraft. "Sails were reefed, and every preparation was made to keep on our way, but the wind did not admit of it." The navigator, Captain Ward, was an experienced Great Lakes master but even his efforts to keep them moving while hugging the shore were futile. In great peril he ordered the schooner anchored "under the highlands of Sauble."

Johann Georg Kohl (1808-1878), German travel writer lived among the Chippewa during the summer of 1855. (From the book "Kitchi-Gami" published by the Minnesota Historical Society)

"Here we pitched terribly," recounted Schoolcraft, "and were momentarily in peril of being cast on shore." One of the men, feverishly working the ship, fell overboard, passed under the vessel and was lost. The situation seemed hopeless to the Indian Agent. "It was thought our poor little craft must go to the bottom; it seemed like a chip on the ocean contending against the powers of the Almighty. It seemed as if, agreeable to Indian fable, Ishkwonameka himself was raising a tempest mountain high for some sinister purposes of his own."

Captain Ward, never faltered in the face of the gale, the rocky shore or the loss of one of his crewmen and eventually triumphed. "For a day and a night he struggled against the elements, and finally entered the straits of Fort Gratiot." The storm-tossed Schoolcraft eventually made it safely to Detroit.

After his experience on Lake Huron, Schoolcraft, knowing boating conditions would probably get worse as November wore on, lost no time in making his way "over the stormy Erie to Buffalo." He got to New York City in mid-December during one of the most spectacular cold

"Our sons have returned. They shot a deer and brought it home. We now have a supply, come and join us." The travelers turned back and "were stuffed with food even though the deer was small and the family large."

"Voyageurs curse and growl when times are bad and food is scarce," wrote Kohl, "while the Indian laughs and jests." Further, Kohl was told the Indian squaw never complains when her husband comes home empty-handed from the hunt. "When he enters…[the lodge]…she pretends as if she did not notice." But she sees at once in the way he comes in, the color of his hands, if there are drops of blood on his shirt, whether there is a deer outside in the snow. "If he brings home nothing," wrote Kohl, "she sets supper before him." She and the children go without so the man of the house, the hunter, will have enough strength for hunting the next day.

A voyageur told Kohl that among the Indians of the Upper Lakes "a man is always welcome. If the weather is bad, or your feet sore, you can live with them for eight or ten days, choose the best piece of meat, and dare not speak about payment."

waves in the history of the Northeast.

A "great fire" occurred in New York during the bitter cold wave. He stayed at the Atlantic Hotel, "immediately west of the great scene of conflagration." "The cold was so bitter while the fire raged," he wrote, "that I could not long endure the open air, which seemed to be surcharged with oxygen." His journey took him to Philadelphia on the 19th and to his final destination, the nation's capital on December 21.

Schoolcraft stayed in Washington until the following spring. The winter of 1835-36 along the Eastern Seaboard was a "standout" winter of the first half of the nineteenth century. Besides the unprecedented cold blast in December, there were two great snowstorms in January and a prolonged cold spell in February. By the end of the second month of 1836, all harbors along the Atlantic coast except two were locked in ice. There was said to be snow on the ground at the Harvard Yard at Cambridge from November 23 until April 1. Farther south at Philadelphia, horses and sleds were crossing the Delaware on March 5. The iceboat *Pennsylvania* cut through one- to-two-foot-thick ice on March 17. Finally on the 18th, a fleet of seventy vessels, some anchored in lower Delaware Bay for ninety days, made their way to the city.

In the Northwest, the winter was also memorable. It became known as the "starving time" in Lower Michigan along the Grand Valley. The winter was not extremely cold, but it started early and hung on late. Scanty provisions, typical in a pioneer economy, were nearly exhausted as the backward spring of 1836 wore on.

Farther north at the Sault, James Schoolcraft reported an exceptionally harsh February. "The month has been remarkably cold," he wrote his brother in Washington, "the thermometer having ranged from 13, 23 to 38 below zero. Snow we have in great abundance." The intrepid missionary Fredric Baraga reported from La Pointe: "The winter of 1835-36 was very long and severe. As late as June 7th large blocks of ice were to be seen along the lakeshore." Farther west in Minnesota, one of Schoolcraft's correspondents observed, "The…winter has been severe—the depth of snow greater, by far, than has fallen for several years. Feb. 1 the mercury fell to 40 degrees below zero…the mercury…fell nearly into the ball."

The tribes of the region ceded a huge portion of their territory to the United States in 1836. The land encompassed an area "lying in the Lower Peninsula of Michigan north of the Grand River and west of Thunder Bay; and on the Upper Peninsula, extending from Drummond Island to Detour, through the Straits of St. Mary, west to the Chocolate River (now the Chocolay), and thence south to Green Bay." The selling price was $2 million or about 12 1/2 cents an acre. Schoolcraft was present in Washington when the final treaty was agreed upon on March 28, 1836. He noted with surprise at the end of the day that his birthday had slipped by without his remembering it.

The Chippewa, in the treaty of La Pointe, formally ceded the rest of Upper Michigan in 1842. Now nothing stood in the way of American settlement. Shortly afterward, the land was surveyed and prospectors flooded the Lake Superior region. The great mining boom of the 1840s had begun.

CHAPTER 4

WEATHER OF THE EARLY MINING BOOM: 1840s-1850s

The Discovery of Iron Ore

"How would they survey this country without my compass?" The "excitement of the old gentleman" was contagious. "What could be done here without my compass?" The morning of September 19, 1844 dawned clear and sunny, providing a perfect setting to demonstrate the value of the solar compass invented by "the old gentleman", surveyor William Austin Burt. He was only 52-years-old, but by mid-nineteenth century standards he was elderly. Half a century later, life expectancy still hovered under 60.

As the survey party commissioned by State Geologist Douglass Houghton struggled up a hill south of Teal Lake on the northwest side of present-day Negaunee, the compassman with them hollered, "Come and see a variation which will beat them all." The men gathered around the compassman and watched in amazement as the magnetic needle—a surveying party carried magnetic compasses with them in addition to the solar compass— bounced a few degrees south of west. "Boys, look around and see what you can find," exhorted Burt. The men spread out on the lead surveyor's command and came back with the ore specimens that gave birth to the iron industry of the Lake Superior region.

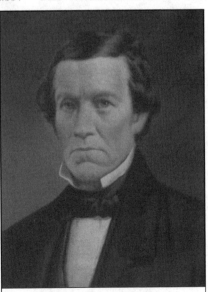

William Burt, 1792-1858, was Michigan's preeminent surveyor. His surveying party discovered iron ore near Negaunee in 1844, which led to the opening of the first iron mine in the Lake Superior region a few years later. (From the collection of the Marquette County History Museum)

THE SOLAR COMPASS

William Austin Burt (1792-1858) had been a deputy surveyor for the U.S. government since 1833. While surveying lands in the Wisconsin territory during the

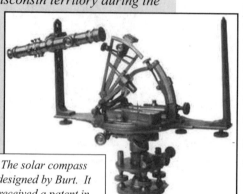

The solar compass designed by Burt. It received a patent in 1836 and became an essential surveying tool in the Upper Michigan wilderness. (Courtesy of Michigan History)

fall of 1834, he encountered a dilemma—the preexisting township lines did not line up with his newly surveyed lines. Burt found that mineral attractions in the area deflected the needle of the magnetic compass just enough to produce errors. In addition, existing township lines ran by the true meridian; the magnetic compass used to set the lines pointed to magnetic north, which could be up to 1,200 kilometers away from the North Pole. Other surveyors put up with the errors, but not Burt. He was determined to solve the problem.

He applied the science of astronomy to the art of surveying. Burt determined that if the surveyor knew the

The next day the solar compass was useless. Burt recorded an all day rain with cloudy skies in his diary entry for September 20. On the 21st, he wrote, "snow fell in the forepart of the day 3-6 inches deep."

Burt's encounter with early winter only reinforced the perception that the Upper Peninsula was a cold, hostile environment. A few years later, Philo Everett, who made the first mining claim in the "Iron Mountains" west of Marquette, complained how hard it was finding men willing to work in the rugged wilderness of the Lake Superior region. "I found it difficult to hire men," he later recalled, "because they were afraid of suffering with the cold, believing they would freeze to death in that cold region."

That fear was misplaced but not unfounded. There would always be enough wood from the thick forest for building fires to keep warm. Food was another story. The natives of the region had a hard enough time feeding themselves during the winter. The pioneer settlers had to rely almost solely on provisions shipped in during the preceding summer or fall. These stores had to last during the long months when navigation on Lake Superior was impossible. If the last boat with winter supplies failed to arrive, starvation would follow. This sequence of events is clearly revealed in the tragic story of Charlie and Angelique Mott.

Philo Everett, 1807-1892, began the first mining venture on the Marquette range. He complained how difficult it was finding men willing to work in the rugged northern wilderness. (Courtesy of Freshwater Press)

The Mott Tragedy

The Motts, Charlie and Angelique, lived in La Pointe near the mission established by Father Baraga in 1835. Charlie was of English descent, while Angelique was a full-blooded Chippewa. In the summer of 1843, some businessmen from

Detroit ("big bugs," as Angelique described them) sailed up to Lake Superior on the schooner *Algonquin*, looking for copper. These entrepreneurs invited Charlie and Angelique to accompany them on a trip to Isle Royale. The couple agreed to go with the men and when they arrived, Angelique wandered alone along one of the island's deserted beaches while the men explored the interior of the island. On her walk, she came upon a shiny object in the water. It was a chunk of float copper.

She told the party of her find and they became excited. The businessmen offered a salary of thirty dollars a month to the Motts if they would stay on the island through the summer to guard the claim. The Motts agreed and they made their way to the Sault to lay in a good supply of provisions. There they encountered one of the businessmen, a man named Cyrus Mendenhall. He told them he had plenty of what they needed at La Pointe; there was no need to incur the expense of hauling so much across the lake.

"When we got to La Pointe," Angelique recalled, "we

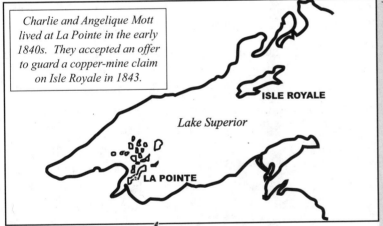

Charlie and Angelique Mott lived at La Pointe in the early 1840s. They accepted an offer to guard a copper-mine claim on Isle Royale in 1843.

ISLE ROYALE

Lake Superior

LA POINTE

found that this was not so." All they could gather was a half-barrel of flour, which they borrowed from the mission, six pounds of half-rancid butter that smelled bad and was white like lard, and a few beans. "I didn't want to go to the island until we had something more to live on," she said, "and I told Charlie so, but Mendenhall over-persuaded him." He promised the Motts a bateau with provisions in a few weeks. Then in three months he would personally come to take them back to the mainland before winter set in.

"So very much against my will," said Angelique, "we

location of the sun in relation to his position on the earth, he could get an accurate reading of direction and location apart from magnetic fluctuations. Burt designed his solar compass, had a prototype built and began testing it in the field. His device was patented in early 1836. It proved highly successful and was first recommended, then adopted, by the federal government for its surveys.

The solar compass had its limits. To use it, a surveyor had to sight it on the sun. A dark, cloudy day rendered it useless. Even on a clear day, the Upper Michigan wilderness posed challenges. "The thick forest prevents the rays of the sun falling on the Solar Compass in many places," complained Burt. "And in the early or later part of the day, high hills and knobs sometimes intervene between the instrument and the sun."

The difficult terrain of the Lake Superior region also challenged the surveying teams. In 1840, Burt ran the principal meridian across the Straits of Mackinac to Lake Superior. He found the territory above the Straits the toughest work he ever attempted. The swamps and heavy brush proved fatal to clothing. Burt wrote his wife that his "Coat and Pantiloons are most gone." He asked his wife to make him another outfit out of the "strongest kind of bedticking" she could find.

William Austin Burt, pioneer and inventor, was the leading surveyor in Michigan. He pushed west with his men and reached the Chocolay River in 1842. After the Chippewa ceded the rest of their land to the U.S. that year, the remainder of the peninsula was surveyed over the next several years. The Michigan survey was essentially completed in 1851.

went to Isle Royale on the first of July." For a while all was well. The supplies never arrived, but they had a bark canoe and a net so they caught fish. Then disaster struck. Toward the end of summer a storm carried away their canoe and a short time later the net fell apart and became useless. The meager provisions they brought over from the mainland eventually ran out and the pair resorted to eating bark, roots and bitter berries—anything that appeared edible. The miserable forest fare only seemed to make their hunger worse. "Hunger is an awful thing," Angelique later explained. "It eats you up so inside, and you feel so all gone, as if you must go crazy. If you could only see the holes I made around the cabin in digging for something to eat you would think it must have been some wild beast."

Outside of foraging for food, their main activity was searching the distant horizon for the boat that Mendenhall promised would bring them back to the mainland before winter set in. "Oh, how we watched and watched and watched, but…no vessel ever came to take us away; neither Mendenhall's nor any other." Their fate seemed sealed: abandonment, starvation and eventually death. "I tell you," she said, "such a thought was hard to bear indeed."

They kept track of every day spent on the island, and Angelique recalled that it was five days before Christmas when every bit of food was gone. At the same time, the snow piled into huge drifts around the cabin and bitter cold rendered the ground "hard as a stone," preventing foraging. Angelique remembered how they "drew… [their]…belts tighter and tighter." "You can't cheat hunger," she said. "You can't fill up that inward craving that gnaws within you like a wolf."

Charlie suffered most intensely from the privation. He developed a fever, which grew worse with time until he "went clear out of his head." One day he jumped out of his bed and grabbed a butcher knife and began sharpening it

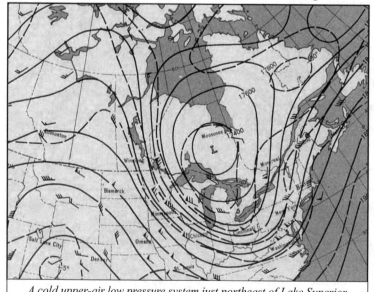

A cold upper-air low pressure system just northeast of Lake Superior brought Sault Ste. Marie its heaviest early-season snow on record on September 20, 1956. (NOAA Central Library Data Imaging Project)

on a whetstone. As he scrapped the knife across the stone, he declared how tired he was of being hungry. He muttered through his delirium he would kill himself a sheep and cook it up. "He… [then]…glared at me," recounted Angelique, "as if he thought nobody could read his purpose but himself. I saw that *I* was the sheep he intended to kill and eat."

Angelique, fearing for her life, kept vigil day and night, not allowing sleep to come, expecting her husband to pounce on her at any moment. Gradually Charlie's hallucinations stopped, she wrested the knife from him and he became "as kind as ever." She then sat at his bedside trying to hide her tears, as she watched her mate's life pass gradually from his body. "I thought of our hard lot, and saw him sink away and dry up until there was nothing left of him but skin and bones. At last he died so easily that I couldn't tell just when the breath did leave his body."

Now Angelique was alone on a deserted snow and wind-swept island with the bulk of winter still ahead of her. While the winter of 1843-44 was relatively mild, records show a cold January and first half of February. Fort Snelling at the confluence of the Mississippi and St. Peters Rivers reported most mornings below zero during the first month of 1844. The cold continued into the first half of February before rather mild weather settled in through March.

Angelique faced more troubles besides the cold and her unrelenting hunger. First, she was not able to bury Charlie. All the land around her was either rock or frozen as hard as rock. She sat with the body for three days, later explaining that, "it seemed almost like company" to her. She knew, however, that if she kept a fire, the body would soon spoil. Not willing to dispose of Charlie's body in the snow, she decided to leave the cabin herself. Angelique used the skills she learned from her native background and built a lodge. It was difficult work in her weakened condition; made even harder by the pain of a severe arm sprain she suffered while

This is the type of lodge Angelique Mott likely built during her winter of isolation on Isle Royale in 1844. (Courtesy Bayliss Public Library, Judge Joseph H. Steere Room, Sault Ste. Marie, Michigan)

SEPTEMBER SNOWS

The beginning of fall normally brings the return of unsettled, gloomy conditions to the Lake Superior Region. Modern day records show a peak of sunny days during July. The cloudiest months are normally November and December, but September also has its share of clouds. September, on average, is the wettest month of the year as the upper level "jet stream" that steers precipitation-producing storms sinks south out of Canada into the Upper Lakes.

But how common are September snowfalls like the one Burt encountered? They are unusual but not unprecedented. A heavy snowstorm brought out the plows on September 22, 1996 as over six inches piled up in the Ironwood area. An upper level low with its attendant cold pool brought just the right ingredients together over the far western end of the peninsula, while farther east a drizzly rain fell, mixed with only a few snowflakes.

On September 27, 1993 an exceptionally cold air mass helped produce a quick two inches of snow which led to slippery driving

in the higher elevations around Marquette. The most exceptional September snowstorm in recent times brought over five inches of wet snow to the city of Marquette on September 23, 1974. Snow at "lake-level" so early in the year is rare. The temperature of the lake reaches its summer peak in August and is still close to those warm values in late September. It took an unusually cold air mass combined with a wind off the land to produce that much accumulating snow in Marquette so early in the season.

On September 20, 1956, Sault Ste. Marie collected 2.7". A disturbance rotating around an unseasonably deep upper-air low just to the east provided the energy for the snowfall. The anomalously cold air mass associated with the low overcame the warmth of Lake Superior, despite the fact that the wind was cutting in off the lake. It was the Sault's largest recorded September snowfall.

nursing and lifting Charlie before he died.

She completed the task, built a fire and left her hut only occasionally to peer into the cabin for a look at her dead husband. "Oh that fire," she remembered. "You don't know what company it was. It seemed alive just like a person with you, as if it could almost talk, and many a time, but for its bright and cheerful blaze that put some spirits in me, I think I would have just died." At one point, she almost lost the lodge to her flaming, inanimate friend. "I built too big a fire," she explained, "but I had plenty of snow handy and saved what I had built with so much labor."

Angelique's biggest dilemma arrived as the depths of winter slowly ground by and her empty stomach continued its perpetual torment. She did not fear being alone because she had her fire. Occasionally the night sky turned almost as bright as day from the north horizon to nearly the zenith as northern lights danced across the heavens. "I was used to the dancing spirits," she said, "and was not afraid of them." She was not afraid of Matchi Manitou, the Bad Spirit of her ancestors. Father Baraga at La Pointe had converted Angelique to Christianity. "I believed there was a Christ," she asserted, "and that He would carry me through if I prayed to Him." What she feared most was herself.

"Sometimes I was so hungry, so very hungry, and the hunger raged so in my veins that I was tempted, O, how terribly I was tempted to take Charlie and make soup of him." Angelique feared she would fall into delirium as Charlie had and that she would come to her senses and find herself devouring her dead husband. "When the dreadful thought came over me, or I wished to die and die quick, rather than suffer any longer," she recalled, "then I would pray; and it always seemed to me after praying hard something would turn up, or I would think of something that I had not thought of before and have new strength given me to fight it out still longer."

At one particular low point when all hope seemed gone, Angelique stepped outside her lodge one morning and noticed rabbit tracks for the first time. The tracks "almost took my breath away," she said, "and made my blood run through my veins like fire." She immediately pulled out a lock of her hair and fashioned a braided snare out of it. As she set the snare, she prayed she would "catch a fat one and catch him quick."

Her prayer was answered; she caught a rabbit that very day. Ravenous, tortured by hunger and nourished by nothing but bark for the last several weeks, she tore away the skin of the animal and ate it raw. It was nearly a week before she caught another one, and this pattern went on for many weeks. "The thing seemed so very strange to me," she remembered, "that though I had torn half the hair out of my head to make snares, never once during the whole winter did I catch two rabbits at one time."

Time hung on the shoulders of the last living inhabitant of Isle Royale like an oppressive weight. "It seemed as if the old moon would never wear out," she recalled, "and the new one never come." At first she tried to sleep as much as she could, welcoming unconsciousness to waking misery. Later she developed insomnia and found that sitting for any length of time led to a debilitating stiffness that left her feeling unable to move. Her remedy for the affliction was to walk "like a bear in a cage." "I found myself walking all the time. It was easier to walk than do anything else."

Early in March she found a canoe that had washed up on shore before the ice set in. She repaired it and fashioned part of the sail from the vessel into a net. Soon the songbirds returned and Angelique knew spring was close at hand. "I felt I was saved", she said. Eventually, more explorers would come to the island and discover her.

One morning in May she had great luck fishing; she caught four mullets. As she was cooking them for breakfast she heard a blast from a gun. "I fell back almost fainting," she remembered. And then there was another blast. She began to run toward the shore but her knees crumbled beneath her. There was another gun blast and she picked herself up and made it to the beach just in time to meet a boat as it reached shore.

The very first man off the vessel was the wretched Mendenhall. He extended his hand to Angelique and she reluctantly held out her thin, bony hand to his. He asked where Charlie was. "I told him he was asleep," she said, "and that he could go up to the cabin and see for himself." All the men ran up together and saw that Charlie was dead. They removed his clothes and shoes inspecting his body for mortal wounds. They convinced themselves that he died of starvation and Angelique had no part in his death.

Angelique then walked into the room and Mendenhall began to cry, declaring that he had sent a bateau with provisions, wondering why it never arrived. The other men later told her his story was all a lie. "I was too glad to get back… to do anything", she said. "I thought his own conscience ought to punish him more than I could do."

Angelique lived another thirty years in the Upper Peninsula. She spent some time in Marquette where she became a servant in the household of Marquette founder Amos Harlow. Later she migrated to Sault Ste. Marie where her incredible strength and endurance became legend. She once wagered a Frenchman that she could carry a barrel of pork to the top of an adjoining hill and back. She performed the feat with ease and offered to carry the barrel up again with the Frenchman on it.

An Easier Life on Isle Royale

A few years after the Mott tragedy, an unknown author penned this poem at the height of winter on the island:

"Here on this lonesome spot, (confound this place,)

I wish I ne'er had seen its dismal face;

When Winter comes, the frighten'd Sun retires,

We sit in rags, and shiver round the fires.

The only breakfast for us every morn,

Is Cold Pork, Slap Jacks, or a mess of Corn;

The tempest howls, yet I must go to work,

Although I'm shivering like a frozen Turk.

At night return and after gorging slaw,

Lie down and slumber on a nest of straw."

The author consumed a monotonous fare, but the verse hints there was plenty of it. The poet endured the bleak existence of island life the winter of 1847 in a substantial two-story structure. Mining captain C.C. Douglass and his wife Ruth occupied the same house during the winter of 1848-49. Ruth kept a journal during 1848 and wrote on December 19 "I was very much amused last evening at perusing… [the above poem]…which I found penciled upon the blank leaf of a book under date of March 2nd, 1847, Isle Royale."

In the summer of 1848, Ruth's husband was asked to move to the island to oversee a mining project for the Isle Royale and Ohio Mining Company. Mr. Douglass made a remark that while he was used to backwoods living, he never thought he would be "banished to a desolate island." Ruth agreed to accompany him, but the next day she wrote, "There is nothing said about going to Isle Royale to day, I abstain from mentioning it in hopes it may blow over." Her secret wish was dashed as company officials were "determined to prevail on C. C. to…see if he will go." Two weeks later, the couple "Sailed from Detroit…bound for Isle Royale Lake Superior."

As their boat approached the "bold rocky cliffs" of the Island on August 30, Ruth felt, "The view…was any thing but a favorable one for me at least, as there was nothing to be seen but barren rocks and a small growth of evergreen and birch timber." She wrote, "I was happily disappointed at the appearance of our temporary home." The next day she busied herself "house cleaning, and making an effort to get settled in our new log Cabin." The mining superintendent's home which they occupied was "very large and quite convenient, having eight large rooms on the first floor."

The Douglass's life on Isle Royale could not have been more different from the Mott's. Historian Robert L. Root, Jr. shows evidence that Ruth had a house servant who took care of cooking and cleaning chores. Her journaling indicates she lived a life of leisure with plenty of time for reading, knitting and strolling along the rugged trails and beaches of the island when weather permitted. On September 8, even though the weather was "cool…and the wind quite fresh and chilly" she "bundled in cloak and hood" and went on a fishing trip with her husband. She "had one bite, but lost it."

They then sailed down the harbor about two-and-a-half miles to the Siscowit Mining Company location. There they visited a graveyard there where they learned of the recent Mott tragedy. She explained there were only three graves in it. "One of them," she wrote, "is a man that starved to death on this Island in the month of March A.D. 1844." She went on to recount the tragic tale she was told in which "his wife was the only person remaining on this Island, and she supported herself by ensnaring Rabbits."

A month later with fall advancing, "The sail vessel *Algonquin* appeared at Rock Harbor bringing us our winter supplies." Mild weather lingered after the *Algonquin* visit. October 11 was judged "very fine" by Mrs. Douglass. "One would hardly expect such weather on Lake Superior at this season of the year," she wrote. Despite the mild spell, a director of the mining company, a Mr. Giddings, appeared "quite uneasy…about going home." Apparently the poor gentleman was told about the fate of the Motts, because by the 16th when the weather turned "very cold with a very strong wind," Ruth observed "Mr. Giddings is almost crazy for fear we shall not have a vessel in time to take him home." A few days later a steamer arrived and Giddings wasted no time in boarding the vessel bound for the cities of the Lower Great Lakes.

Ruth observed the first snowflakes of the season on October 21. Ten days later on Halloween she noted the beginning of a "severe North East snowstorm." The storm continued into the next day accompanied by very high winds. By November 4, as another "very severe snowstorm with high winds" blew in, Ruth proclaimed, "Winter has fairly commenced." She also speculated the *Algonquin* would probably not return until next spring. Ruth judged the thought of being isolated on the island for six months "a gloomy idea," but resolved to "submit without murmuring" with the same graceful optimism and sense of duty that brought her to Isle Royale three months earlier.

The early start to winter continued on the 6th. Ruth ventured out on a "clear and pleasant" morning to tally the pre-dawn snowfall along with that of the storms during the past six days and came up with an "average depth…of sixteen inches." The next day, Ruth's journal entry contained a tinge of despair. "I have been waiting all day to have it stop snowing before I opened my journal," she wrote, "but there is no more prospect of it ceasing now than there was early this morning. I never before saw the Winter commence in any place, as it has done here at this time."

The wintry period reached its climax with an early morning temperature of 9 degrees on the 8th. Ruth noted six inches of new snow the day before—Election Day. "No elections… [were]…made here," wrote Ruth. "I for one think it is quite doubtful whether the inhabitants of Isle Royale know who to hurrah for, before next spring." (Zachary Taylor, a southern slaveholder and Whig, became the Twelfth President of the United States, narrowly defeating Democrat Lewis Cass, the former governor of the Michigan Territory.)

The weather turned dramatically over the next couple of days. "It is thawing very fast," observed Ruth on the 11th. Some rain fell accompanied by a south wind. Two days later the snow was "melting off fast" and the south wind blew in "the long looked for" *Algonquin*. The vessel contained "a well-filled mail, and sundry other comforts for winter." Unfavorable wind kept the captain from sailing the next day and allowed Ruth an opportunity to dispatch some last minute correspondence. "I do not know how, when or where to stop," she penned. "I want to say so much. It appears to me as though it was the last opportunity I should have of sending any communication…this winter."

Fine weather continued into the third week of November 1848. "It is a delightful morning," declared Ruth on the 20th. She had just returned from her longest walk yet on the island. She noted piles of snow here and there and proclaimed "the air calm…and salubrious." "Indeed it appears to be spring", she added. While the mild weather gave her a chance to get out and exercise, it also brought her an odd feeling of homesickness. "I think a great deal more about home when the weather is pleasant," she recorded in her November 21 entry, "than I do in a dark and cloudy, or stormy day."

Sad thoughts of home left the next day. November 22 was dark and rainy. Ruth occupied herself with sewing and reading and she found "no time to get lonely." The 24th was a snowy, blustery day. Along with the snow, high winds buffeted the island toward the end of the month. "Settled winter," as Ruth termed it, had begun.

Early December brought a mass of Arctic air over the island. While the thermometer sank to 4 degrees above zero early on the 4th, there was still no ice in their bay. "The winter, thus far, has been more open than I anticipated," wrote Ruth. The next day she was "quite surprised…on arising to see the bay frozen over." She explained that the island fishermen had set their nets the evening before and had to go out and break the ice in order to pull them in.

A boat tried to enter the harbor on December 6 but was turned back by ice that extended "more than a half a mile" into the lake. The next day the snow was falling "thick and fast" and by the 8th was two feet deep. "I endeavor to keep from thinking or even looking on the dark side of the picture," wrote Ruth. "Did I allow myself to meditate on the situation in which we are now placed and all the circumstances connected there with I should be miserable enough." On the 11th, Ruth's spirits were buoyed by a visit from some neighbors on the other side of the bay. "Winter has not settled upon us so stern yet," asserted Ruth, "as to prevent our neighbors from visiting us occasionally."

Mr. Douglass took his first walk on snowshoes across the bay December 12. He came home late in the afternoon exhausted. The deep, powdery snow made for "very hard walking." The next day Ruth wrote her husband was "quite lame" due to the previous day's exertion. The weather was described as "pleasant" and by the 15th Ruth proclaimed it "a lovely day." She went on to add, "I little expected to see such weather as this, in the middle of December on Lake Superior."

By the 18th, severe winter conditions set in when "a very boisterous…storm commenced in the east and passed around to the south." Ruth measured six inches of snow "in a short time" from the storm. The next day was pronounced "the coldest through the day, of any previous this winter." Bitter cold continued, freezing the bay "nearly out to the Passage Islands," with a morning low of 12 below zero on the 21st. The temperature then only "rose to 2 degrees below zero where it remained during the day."

A close call occurred on the ice the day before when a distant neighbor, Mr. Veale, crossed over new ice on the bay for a visit. That evening, "thinking to try the strength of the old ice," Ruth recounted, "he broke through." Somehow, he managed to pull himself out but "was so wet and frightened" that he returned to the Douglass's where he spent the night.

On December 25 Ruth's entry began: "Christmas has come, with pleasant winter weather, and snow sufficient for good sleighing, but unfortunately for us, we have neither roads nor teams." The Douglasses made the best of it and traveled by foot, instead. Mr. Douglass persuaded his wife to take a walk on the ice December 27. Ruth had been cooped up for a number of days due to the cold and snow. She found the excursion exhilarating. "I am too fond of exercise in the open air," she wrote, "to stay in the house long." They walked on the ice "for some distance" but were turned back by the cold.

Ruth's journaling stopped at the end of the year and there is no information on what happened on the island during the heart of winter. It was likely a long and tedious one. The winter of 1848-49 was labeled a "severely cold and snowy" one in Minnesota. Fort Snelling had consistent cold through February 1849. It was also considered the snowiest winter at that location in over a decade. Spring brought river flooding in early April, with the first steamboat arriving at the prairie settlement April 9. On Lake Superior, the opening of navigation would probably have been delayed an extra three or four weeks to early May. That means the islanders were isolated for nearly six months in the winter of 1848-49.

The Douglasses eventually migrated to the western Upper Peninsula copper mines in the rugged highlands southeast of Ontonagon. There, Ruth gave birth to a son, Edgerton, on May 27, 1850. Two weeks later, Methodist missionary John Pitezel endured a rough canoe ride on a "heavy sea" and reached Ontonagon late on the afternoon of June 11, where he was surprised "to learn that the wife of Mr. C. C. Douglass was a corps (sic) in the house. She was confined," he recounted, "a few days ago several miles back in the woods, on a location. Was brought from the location on a bier in a bed by hand but no help could be obtained." Ruth likely succumbed to complications due to childbirth. She was a few months shy of her twenty-sixth birthday.

Early Copper Country Weather

Adventurers and speculators were drawn to the Lake Superior frontier by Houghton's favorable reports of copper deposits in the region. Hundreds and perhaps thousands explored the area around the Keweenaw Peninsula between 1843 and 1849, most without success. "At that early day," wrote historian and pioneer John Forster, "miners groped much in the dark." He described one instance where he and C. C. Douglass hiking at night along a trail through the wilderness west of what is now Baraga, came upon a clearing. Two log houses were "reposing in the moonlight," but there were no occupants; the place was utterly deserted. They stayed the night in one of the houses which they found swept neat and clean along with a bed made up and ready for sleeping.

THE DEATH OF DOUGLASS HOUGHTON

In 1845, State Geologist Douglass Houghton died while boating on the west side of the Keweenaw Peninsula. Warned of an impending storm, Houghton decided to press on anyway. On October 13, 1845, Dr. Houghton, along with three voyageurs, hit the sudden northwest gale and snowstorm while canoeing from Copper Harbor to Eagle River.

His voyageur guides wanted to put ashore at a sandy beach, but Houghton, anxious to arrive at his destination, ordered them to keep going. Their craft was swamped about a mile and a half north of Eagle River. Two of his companions were "hurled by the waves upon the rocks, ten feet above the usual level of the waters." These men lived. Another voyageur named Pequette was found dead with a few pieces of the boat.

Houghton apparently foundered before he could be swept to shore. His body was recovered the next spring. Michigan's first State Geologist was 36 years old at the time of the accident. He went down with a large body of knowledge concerning the geology and minerals of the region. William Burt eventually finished the unpublished geological works begun by Houghton. ✳

Douglass Houghton, 1809-1845, was Michigan's first State Geologist. (Courtesy of Freshwater Press)

The next morning they discovered that considerable copper mining had been done there: "A trap knob, standing out in an otherwise level country, was the foundation of the mine. Of course, it was a mistake. A little geological knowledge would have prevented the undertaking in the first place. This knob was far removed from the mineral range." The vast majority or early miners went home back east with nothing more than memories of pioneering on the rugged Keweenaw frontier.

One of these early explorers was John Hays, a druggist from Pittsburgh. He left for the long trip up the Great Lakes the same summer the Motts were stranded on Isle Royale. Hayes made the trip "primarily to regain his health and incidentally to inquire into the mineral deposits." With the financial backing of a Pittsburgh doctor, he made his way to the frontier outpost of Copper Harbor on the busy schooner *Algonquin*. There he met another eastern speculator who took him to several promising mining locations in the area. Hays struck up a deal with the speculator to buy into the sites and headed back east to get final approval from his financial backer. In the spring of 1844, he left Pittsburgh again for Lake Superior with a crew of eight laborers and a geologist.

The little schooner *Algonquin* dropped off the Hays party at Copper Harbor in early summer. That September it became the only supply vessel sailing Lake Superior when the brig *John Jacob Astor* succumbed to a violent storm on the night of the 19th. The brig had come to Copper Harbor with a load of government supplies for the newly established Fort Wilkins. That night it anchored in the harbor when the storm blew in. The Captain of the *Astor*, Ben Stannard, decided to ride out the gale; if the crew pulled up anchor, the ship would drift into the rocks (Ben's brother, Charles, discovered what was to be named Stannard Rock, a mile-long reef 50 miles offshore from Marquette while captaining the *Astor* in August 1835.). As the storm increased, the anchor gave out and the brig smashed into the rocks anyway. The crew saved the cargo and themselves but the *John Jacob Astor* was pounded to kindling by the mountainous waves. It was the first documented shipwreck on Lake Superior. The miners and soldiers then became solely dependent on the *Algonquin* for provisions.

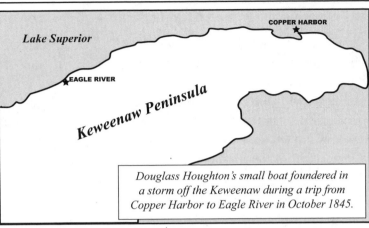

Douglass Houghton's small boat foundered in a storm off the Keweenaw during a trip from Copper Harbor to Eagle River in October 1845.

Hays later credited the kindness of the fort commander, Captain Clary, with saving his nascent mining operation. His crew put down a shaft near Lake Fanny Hoe near the fort and struck a vein containing eighty-six percent pure copper. Hays's crew built two log structures, one to house the workers, the other to store supplies. Late that summer, the financial backers of the new mining company came to visit the mining site. Hays gave them a list of provisions that his crew would need to take them through the winter. The backers ordered the supplies too late to be shipped that fall. Clary provided the provisions, which Hays returned when his supplies finally arrived in the spring of 1845. The commander's aid kept one of the first commercial mining operations going through the winter of 1844-45.

Hays set off on a hazardous boat ride from Copper Harbor to Eagle River in the middle of November 1844. He and two companions launched a small Mackinaw boat and had completed over two-thirds of the 30 mile trip when they were hit by a sudden squall. They took shelter in a natural harbor about six miles from Eagle River. On November 18 the party hiked to the Eagle River area where Hays discovered what was to become the Cliff mine. It became the first historic mine to yield pure native copper in the United States. Hays's discovery would have been impossible had winter set in early that year. Fortunately for the metallurgic world, the start to winter was mild. Out west at Fort Snelling, the first substantial snow held off until November 16-17. Ice commenced floating on the Mississippi and St. Peters on November 19. The system that brought snow and a taste of winter to Minnesota probably moved east and buffeted the Hays party with the sudden squall. Navigation ceased for the winter on Minnesota rivers November 24, 1844 as the mercury dropped to 4 below zero.

Long Winter Journeys

Hays was excited by his discovery of a large body of Copper near Eagle River. He wanted to share the news with his partners back east in Pittsburgh, but could find no one willing to undertake the long, dangerous overland journey. Finally he decided to make the trip himself. With the help of missionary Pitezel, he obtained two Chippewa guides and set off on snowshoes from the Methodist mission at Keweenaw Bay on December 18, 1844. The trio's camping outfit consisted of blankets, cooking utensils, two axes, a gun and a dog. Their only provisions were a supply of flour and pork, along with tea and sugar. This Spartan diet was supplemented with an occasional partridge or rabbit they shot along the way.

The party moved south. "Some days," recounted Hays, "…we made…very good time; then again it would become very fatiguing on account of having to cut our way through the underbrush." At night they cleared away snow and his guides constructed a crude, temporary wigwam made of pine boughs and bark. They made some bread for the next day's meals, then wrapped themselves in blankets in the wigwam near a fire made of birch bark and logs. In ten days they reached within fifty miles of the mouth of the Menominee River. "On account of the hard country we had to go through," explained Hays, "the underbrush and heavy snow—often on our hand and knees—and cumbersome snow shoes, made it impossible for us to make more than twenty miles in a day."

As they crossed the Menominee, Hays lost his dog. "The ice at one place in the river had given way," recalled Hays, "and he jumped to swim across. The current proved too strong and it carried him under and we never saw him again." Later that evening they found an Indian trail, followed it for short time and came upon the "Great Falls" (probably present-day Pier's Gorge). They spotted an Indian camp there, but his guides were "somewhat timid" in approaching the strangers. "They were all intoxicated," according to Hays, "and were certainly a hard-looking lot of red men." But hunger overcame their fear and the trio approached the revelers and told them of their plight. They were invited to dinner that "consisted of boiled sturgeon and flour mixed with it, making it into a kind of soup or paste." The fish stew was "not very palatable," said Hays, "but we were in prime condition to do it justice." He then purchased some flour, venison and fish from the Indians and "left them next morning at daybreak, all sound asleep from their night's debauch."

Farther down the river, the trio met a white family from Maine engaged in hauling logs for a sawmill they were building. The family invited them to stay for dinner. "It was appreciated," Hays said, "for it was the first good meal we had partaken of since we left L'Anse Bay." He also noted that the Indians in the area kept "a large quantity of fish [sturgeon] piled up like cord wood and frozen hard.". It was their main source of food for the winter.

John Hays, a Pittsburgh druggist, was one of the eastern speculators who prospected in the Copper Country during the mid-to-late 1840s. He undertook a winter journey through the Great Lakes wilderness in early 1845. (Courtesy of Freshwater Press)

Hays settled with his Indian guides, paying them a dollar a day from the time they left L'Anse to the time they returned. He also set up an agreement where they would meet him at the same outpost the following March. Hays then traveled by sleigh, stage and foot down the Menominee, to Green Bay then south through the Wisconsin Territory to Chicago. He made it to the town of Marshall in the Lower Peninsula where he took a strap railroad to Detroit. There he met with Douglass Houghton and showed him some copper specimens he had brought from the mines he was working. Houghton was "astonished and interested" in Hays's project. On

January 10, 1845, after a three-week journey, Hays arrived in Pittsburgh. There he met with his partners who "were surprised and much elated" by the news. Six weeks later, Hays set off for the Michigan wilderness and met his guides at the appointed spot. They arrived in Copper Harbor on March 21, 1845.

There were others who "traversed the unbroken forests" in the dead of winter. One of them was Keweenaw pioneer John Senter, who traveled on snowshoes from Copper Harbor to Green Bay and back five times. During the middle 1850s, in the midst of the coldest winters of the early mining boom, a rich vein of copper was discovered in one of the mines of the district. Senter and his associates wanted to immediately buy shares in the mine while the price was low. If they sent their order by mail to the East Coast, it would take several weeks to get there. By that time others would find out about the discovery and the stock price would go up. Senter decided to hike to the nearest telegraph station in Appleton, Wisconsin and wire in the order to buy.

Clad in mackinaws and furs with a stout pair of Chippewa snowshoes strapped to his moccasins, the intrepid pioneer set out on the nearly three-hundred mile journey. He carried a compass, gun, matches and a small cache of provisions. As he left he had to slog through four feet of snow, with the thermometer hovering well below zero. Despite the harsh conditions the trip was safely made in two weeks. The message to buy flashed over the wires from Appleton and "laid the foundations of several large fortunes."

Bitten Almost Blind and Parboiled

Summer exploring and traveling through the Upper Michigan wilderness during the early Copper Boom held its own unique challenges. Explorer George McGill left Ontonagon in the early summer of 1852 bound for the Adventure Mine deep in the woods east of town. He followed an old Indian trail and found the going "almost impassable" due to the thick woods. "It was perfectly wild," he wrote. "Wild as the wild man ever was before a continent was discovered. The woods presented a continual mass of tall thick pines, huge cedars, and the most noble of maples."

Then there were the insects. Naturalist Louis Agassiz explored the Lake Superior basin in the summer of 1848 and wrote "Neither the love of the picturesque…nor the interests of science could tempt us into the woods, so terrible were the black flies." He described how his party stayed along the Lake Superior shoreline under protection of "smudges"—smoky fires designed to keep the bloodthirsty creatures away. One unfortunate scientist in the party dared to take an excursion up river into the woods looking for water plants. He returned a "frightful spectacle." The man had blood-red rings around his eyes; his face was bloody and covered with punctures. Agassiz said the next morning "his head and neck were swollen as if from an attack of erysipelas" (an acute skin disease characterized by fever and intense inflammation).

Cornelius Shaw, who helped start a mine on Isle Royale in the summer of 1847, kept a journal of his experiences. The daily entries were peppered with complaints about biting insects. On June 11 black flies were "troublesome." On the 13th his "face swelled from the bite of sand flies." On June 22 he found a vein of copper but was driven from the woods by "black flies & almost blind when I got home by their bite." On the 25th his suffering reached a peak as the fly bites were "so bad" that he was almost blind and his face was "one complete sore."

Along with the thick woods, biting flies and mosquitoes, a sojourner might get caught in a summer thunderstorm. Pioneer John Forster was once exploring the ridges south of Huron Bay during the summer when he heard the "distant bellowing of thunder". Occupied with his work, he ignored the coming storm too long. It rapidly grew dark with the storm's approach, so he hurried down from the rocky highlands to the lowlands. There he had stashed his pack of camping blankets and provisions under a dry cedar, which he was planning to use for a campfire. It was too late; he later wrote in the third person: "The storm burst upon him in all its grandeur and wetness. He was speedily drenched to the skin."

Forster had no choice but to "sit it out till morning." He spent an uncomfortable night with no fire in the midst of a cedar swamp that showed an appreciable rise in water levels as the rain continued to pour down, accompanied by "the glare of lightning and the crashing of thunder." The next morning, Forster "fortified his courage" with a breakfast of raw pork and hardtack. He then strapped on his wet pack, "which weighed somewhat less than a ton," and headed along a section line for the Lake Superior shore, about ten miles away.

The journey through the hot, steamy forest and thicket was made difficult and irritating because of the wet vegetation. "One became not only drenched, but parboiled, like a red lobster," wrote Forster years later. On finally reaching Lake Superior, he walked straight into the icy water with his clothes on and took a swim.

Caught in a Wet, Early Snow

In late fall 1846, Forster, accompanied by a Scotsman named Reid and a party of voyageurs was sent to explore a tract of land about twenty miles west of the Sturgeon River in what is now southern Houghton County. The party who employed them had bought the land on the recommendation that it contained mineral deposits. The explorers found the claim of mineral deposits false: "For several days Reid and I made a diligent survey of the ground, looking in vain for... [a]...vein of mineral or even an outcrop of trap-rock. The country was level, well wooded...but the underlying rocks were covered by a deep drift of sand and clay. The tract was evidently not on the mineral range and it would be a loss of time to look for copper there." However, the men had to complete a thorough survey of the land so a complete map could be made. "Otherwise new suspicions would arise" concerning the parcel's value.

Before the survey was finished, it snowed about two feet one night. Then prospecting became a "preposterous" and "disagreeable" task. Camping in the wet snow became most unpleasant. Their rude hut constructed out of hemlock boughs became weighted down with snow and the fire built close by to warm them melted the snow on the hut, which ran into their bedding, soaking everything.

"As soon as possible we beat a retreat," explained Forster. But in their haste they miscalculated time and found themselves in a dense cedar swamp at nightfall. It was too dark to keep moving so the party was forced to bed down in the swamp. A nighttime thaw added to the misery; in the morning they were saturated with melted snow. After an excruciating night in pools of water, a huge fire had to be built to dry the drenched woolen blankets; they could not be packed wet. Finally at noon they set out for their boat at the mouth of the Sturgeon River.

Hiking through the soggy snow was "difficult and exhausting." In a short time Forster "gave out" and fell behind Reid and the voyageurs. His problems were compounded by the heavy cowhide boots he was wearing; they chafed his ankles so badly "that walking became absolute torture." Forster sat on a log and painfully removed his boots. He then bandaged the sores on his feet with strips of silk handkerchiefs supplemented with cut-up strips of his freshly dried blanket fashioned into makeshift moccasins. Throwing his heavy, wet boots over his shoulder he resumed his march, following the trail made by the rest of the party.

He finally caught up with Reid and the Frenchmen and found them waiting for him at the boat. The voyageurs had voted to leave Forster "to his fate in the woods" but Reid forced them to stay and wait. The haggard explorers floated for a few hours and finally reached safe and comfortable lodging where they filed their report and took time to recover from a most uncomfortable expedition between seasons.

Dangerous Trip between Seasons

Travel between the boating season and hard winter could be perilous as well as uncomfortable. Charles T. Harvey, the engineer who oversaw the building of the first locks at Sault Ste. Marie in 1855, headed west that same year, eager to expedite overland travel by rail across the Upper Peninsula wilderness. In mid-November, Harvey visited Ontonagon, then the largest village on the Peninsula, working on land grants for eventual railroad construction. He intended to take the last steamer of the season east, but "it passed in the night of the 19th." The landlord of the hotel Harvey was staying at "whether by accident or

design" failed to wake him in time and he was left stranded in the town with no more boats expected until next spring.

He was in a quandary: "To the south intervened four hundred miles of wilderness. Eastward, an overland trip of sixty miles to the head of Keweenaw Bay and about one hundred forty miles of lake coasting would enable me to reach Marquette." Harvey chose the latter route but had to wait, because the trip to Keweenaw Bay was riddled with impassable swamps. They could not be traversed on snowshoes until they froze over sufficiently.

Winter made a late start in 1855 and kept Harvey in Ontonagon more than two weeks. Finally, at the beginning of December, a mail carrier arrived in Ontonagon from the east and reported the swamps frozen. On December 3, Harvey headed east accompanied by the mail carrier, two voyageurs

Charles T. Harvey, 1829-1912, was a self-taught civil engineer. He oversaw the building of the first locks at the Sault. (From the collection of the Marquette County History Museum)

SOUTHVIEW TOWN ONTONAGON
LAKE SUPERIOR, MICH.

Ontonagon at the time of Harvey's visit in 1855. He stayed at the four-story Bigelow House, the most prominent building in the center of the picture. (Courtesy Clarke Historical Library, Central Michigan University)

engaged to carry packs, and a business partner, E.C. Hungerford. The party loaded provisions, blankets (they decided against carrying a heavy canvas tent) and a "train dog" into a two-horse sleigh and headed east up the road to the Minnesota Mine then to the Toltec Mine where the road ended. At that point, the team was turned back and the men camped for the night.

The next morning, each man strapped on snowshoes, the dog was hitched to a sledge and the party set off into "the forest primeval." The mail carrier led them through "various unfrozen streams and morasses," which hindered their progress and made for a long trip. They spent two nights camping under the stars and on the afternoon of the third day "the blue waters of Keweenaw Bay came in sight." That night was spent at the Methodist Indian Mission, and the following day plans for the next and longest leg of the journey were made.

"The air was mild, the water calm, and the sky serene," recalled Harvey. The party was faced with two travel options: take the overland route to Marquette, which would require at least six days of "very hard traveling" or go by boat. The placid weather led them to choose the latter option and a small Mackinaw was purchased and made ready for the one-hundred-mile journey.

The next morning, four men (the mail carrier went on to Marquette on foot the night before) and the dog were packed into the "row boat" along with the sledge and provisions for three days. The Mackinaw, fully loaded, had only eight inches of "freeboard" above the water and the sharp, wedge-shaped ends made the craft unsteady, like a canoe. However, the weather was still mild and quiet and they made good time skirting along the glassy surface on the east end of the bay heading north. That night they camped at the tip of Point Abbaye, the strip of land separating Keweenaw Bay from Huron Bay. After a quick breakfast, they cast off on a dangerous, 12- to 15-mile stretch over open water.

The voyageurs rowed, with Hungerford stationed in the front as lookout and Harvey serving as steersman with a short oar or paddle. The dog sat in between the oarsmen. "Our progress was slow," Harvey recalled, "not more than three miles an hour." By midday they were still miles from land. There was no wind, "but a heavy 'dead swell' of increasing broad crestless billowy waves" broadsided the fragile craft from 150 miles of open lake to the northeast. The swells were an ominous sign of an impending gale. "The oarsmen were urged to the utmost," Harvey later wrote, "and at intervals Hungerford and the writer took their places." As they frantically labored to reach the safety of the main shoreline to the southeast, "the sky became overcast with a murky haziness." Far off to the northeast Harvey spotted whitecaps from the approaching storm.

"There was yet a mile or more to the point we were aiming for, when the wind reached us," recounted Harvey. "The size of the 'white caps' grew rapidly larger, and 'ere long began to come over into our 'cockle shell' boat." Fortunately, they kept the vessel afloat by bailing and finally reached a rocky point along the shore in what is now extreme northern Baraga County. Quickly the men hauled the boat a safe distance from the angry lake. Harvey remembered how close they came to disaster: "A few minutes delay would have sufficed for the waves to fill the boat, and thus ended our lives."

As night approached, the gale increased until the spray from the waves went over the tops of nearby trees. Three times during the night they moved the boat farther away from the raging waves, which Harvey

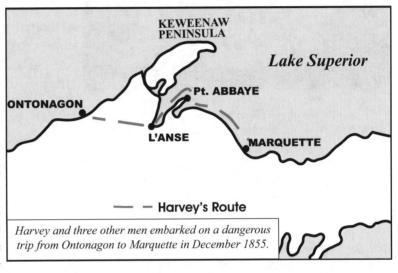

Harvey and three other men embarked on a dangerous trip from Ontonagon to Marquette in December 1855.

felt rivaled those found on the ocean. The following morning the cold, wet party beheld a sight that "was grand beyond description." Their landing point extended into the lake and received the full force of the waves whipped by the nor'easter.

"The concussion of the waves on the shore sounded like a battle cannonade," wrote Harvey, "and shook the ground like earthquakes." Luckily, the wind was not extremely cold and it actually began to subside. Then heavy snow began falling. The snow "covered the ground about two feet deep," recalled Harvey, "and… [also]… ourselves…as we lay the third night, 'camped out' in our blankets."

The fourth day the snow and wind ceased, the sun shone and the lake calmed down. The party's provisions were exhausted and they began eating the dog's food, which consisted of fried cakes, made of half tallow and half cornmeal. They realized their situation was desperate, so they chose to cast off for Marquette as soon as possible while the weather held. That afternoon they launched their Mackinaw and headed along the shore of what is now far northern Marquette County.

"The daylight soon passed," remembered Harvey, "and a night of inky darkness came on, so dark at times that we could hardly distinguish each other in the boat. But the surf along the shore was loud and continuous, thus enabling us to follow its contour with certainty hour after hour."

Suddenly, an apparition seemed to rise out of the depths of the cold, black water straight ahead of them. To Harvey, it seemed to resemble "a colossal human head with flowing white

In the middle of the night in a small mackinaw on Lake Superior, Harvey beheld an apparition that he thought resembled "a colossal human head with flowing white hair." (Drawing by E. Yelland)

hair muttering dire threats." He snapped out of his momentary confusion and sprang to action, shouting to the oarsmen to back stroke while he made similar quick motions with his steering paddle. They barely avoided a rock outcropping that extended a foot or two out of the water. The apparition he saw was the spray of the surf against a rocky reef.

Hungerford, who had passed along the same coast in daylight, concluded they had encountered the dangerous "Sauks-Head Reef." The party had another difficult decision before them; the rock formation extended far out into the lake, but landing on the main shore was too risky, owing to the rocky cliffs and inky blackness of midnight. They felt the only alternative was to turn the boat around so the roar of the surf would be at their back. They had to "outflank" the reef by heading toward the open lake.

In his anxiety to avoid the reef, Harvey steered the vessel on the same course for about a half hour. Suddenly it occurred to him that he might have led them too far out into the "trackless waste of waters." A cold shudder passed over him as he ordered the oarsmen to cease paddling. Harvey listened: "No sound could be heard, and for a moment…[my]… heart stood still". Were they lost out in the open lake? He leaned over and brought his ear close to the water and in time noticed "a faint sound like the buzzing of a fly." He turned the boat toward the sound and the voyageurs rowed at full speed. In a few minutes Harvey repeated the ear test. "To …[my]…inexpressible joy, the sound was more distinct" and they continued until the surf again became a distinct roar and steadfast guide.

The danger was not past, however. About one in the morning it turned very cold and an hour later ice began forming on the oars, steering paddle and the sides of the boat. The craft began to lower in the water and it became evident they would founder before daylight. The only hope lay in attempting a risky landing in the pitch dark. The shoreline was faced with huge, perpendicular cliffs rising straight out of the water sometimes to a height of one hundred feet. As the sound of the surf got closer, Harvey shouted "Brace up boys, for we will be on Earth or in Heaven in the next few minutes!" No sooner had he spoken when he felt his paddle hit a sandy bottom. A moment later, the boat slid up a sandy beach. They had landed safely.

They noticed the woods came very close to the water, and after disembarking they groped among the trees until they found a white birch with shaggy bark. They pulled off some of the bark and gathered a collection of moss off other trees. Snowshoes were then used to clear a spot to make a fire. Harvey, cold, wet and exhausted, rifled through the provisions looking for matches. He found the matchbox and realized there was only one match left!

There was a single chance to get a fire going to ameliorate the unrelenting cold. Hungerford was appointed "district fire lighter" because he had "a remarkably steady hand." He took the last damp match, struck it and carefully cupped his hand around the tiny flame while he eased it over to the heap of moss. Success! The moss caught fire and spread to the birch bark and soon there was a roaring fire. The Frenchmen, who were all but paralyzed by the cold, had remained sitting in the boat. They were helped out of the Mackinaw and led to the fire to thaw out. Harvey pulled out a small amount of food he had saved for an emergency and the tired, drained travelers consumed the small ration, rolled themselves up in their blankets in the snow by the dying fire and fell fast asleep.

The men woke up to bright sunshine. They quickly packed up and launched the boat, and as they drifted from their haven, Harvey surveyed their landing site: "On both sides of our mooring place were frowning cliffs—but a small stream…had worn a gulch and created the cove where we landed." Had the craft floated a hundred feet left or right, it would have been dashed to pieces against the rocky precipice. Harvey looked south and recognized "the bold headland of Presque Isle" (now a Marquette city park) about ten miles away. The travelers, buoyed by the site, rowed at full speed toward the landmark. At about three in the afternoon on December 13, ten days after leaving Ontonagon, they disembarked at the small hamlet of Marquette.

Harvey later found out that the Methodist missionary at L'Anse had sent a letter to Marquette's Postmaster explaining how a party of four led by Charles T. Harvey had left his mission in a boat just before a great storm set in. He stated how it seemed impossible that anyone could have survived the gale and suggested a search be mounted along the lakeshore for the travelers' bodies.

Harvey rested in Marquette, but was determined to go south to Green Bay, then Chicago and finally Washington D.C. to plead Upper Michigan's case for railroad land grants. He had to wait some more: this time for Green Bay to freeze enough to carry a horse-drawn sleigh. Fortunately for the determined Harvey, steady cold settled in after midmonth. At Minnesota reporting stations, the temperature finally went below zero for the first time on December 17. Then perfect ice making weather ensued. Below zero readings were reported all day on December 23 and 24 and also from the 26th through the 29th. Steady cold continued into January and by the end of the month, word came of good solid ice on Green Bay. A sleigh path opened between the iron mines west of Marquette and the Escanaba River lumber camps and Harvey hitched a ride south on a on a two-horse sleigh driven by Dr. Morgan Hewitt, one of Marquette's founders. In three days, the team reached the mills near the mouth of the Escanaba River. Now, only 120 miles of ice lay between them and Green Bay.

The sleigh hardly penetrated the icy expanse of the bay when near disaster struck. Harvey was at the reins when the horses plunged through the ice. A fissure in the solid ice pack developed and became covered with a thin, camouflaging film of ice and snow. One moment the team was gliding along at a brisk pace, the next moment "all to be seen was their heads…held up by the pole end, resting on the opposite edge of ice."

THE U.P.'S FIRST MURDER MYSTERY

The Schoolcraft shooting became Upper Michigan's first murder mystery, and weather played a part in the story. There were two main suspects in the case, a Lieutenant Tilden, who was stationed at Fort Brady in the Sault at the time of the murder, and John Tanner, the "bogie man" of Sault Ste. Marie.

Not long before the murder, Tilden and Schoolcraft were involved in a dispute. Tilden later talked about how "cold lead would settle it." A story circulated immediately after the shooting that two soldiers emerged from the woods near where Schoolcraft was gunned down after a "hunting" trip. The barrel of one of the soldier's guns was reportedly empty. Had Tilden hired these men to kill Schoolcraft? That lead was never followed up on. A short time later, the two men were standing with a group of other soldiers outside Fort Brady when a summer thundershower quickly sprang up. There was a stroke of lightning, an explosion and then a downpour. Immediately after the shock of the explosion the group realized that the lightning bolt had hit the two men suspected in the Schoolcraft shooting. No one else was harmed. The post doctor worked in vain to revive the men but pronounced them dead. Their secret, if they had one, went to their graves.

Fortunately, Harvey and Hewitt saw a sleigh approaching from the north. Amos Harlow, also one of Marquette's founders, was at the reins. With his help, the horses were hauled out on the south side of the fissure. They sustained no serious injury and the sleigh continued its glide across the frozen bay. The trip to Green Bay was completed in three days.

Harvey eventually made his way to Washington as an official "Northwest" delegate to Congress. He represented the interests of the nascent Upper Michigan railroad companies in acquiring federal land grants for railroad construction. His arrival in Washington caused quite a stir. "When I reached Washington," he recounted, "my snowshoes were strapped to my grips and attracted so much attention that I had to elbow my way through the crowd on the sidewalk to the entrance of the National Hotel."

Adventure, Murder and More Pioneer Tragedy

The Copper Boom of the middle-to-late 1840s kindled the imagination of many adventurers including a young man named Peter White. At fifteen years old, he ran away from his home in Green Bay in hopes of obtaining passage to the copper lands. He made his way to Mackinac Island and eventually boarded a steamer for the Sault in June of 1847. When Peter got off the boat, he encountered a great commotion in the small frontier town. He gravitated to a crowd of people and noticed they were standing around a body lying face down on the ground. The body was that of James Schoolcraft, Henry's younger brother. He had just been shot and killed under mysterious circumstances.

On June 10, 1847 Peter White had his chance to travel to the Copper Country. The schooner *Merchant* was going up to Portage Entry. Possibly as an omen of what was ahead or a stroke of good fortune, the captain of the schooner suffered a broken leg while disembarking from the vessel. Another shipmaster, Captain Brown, was asked to take over and as he was about to cast off, Peter asked if he might work as deckhand for passage across the lake. Peter was refused because the boat had a full crew and a heavy passenger list. The *Merchant* never made it to Portage Entry. She sank near Grand Island with all aboard.

Peter headed back south and worked a variety of jobs over the next couple of years. He worked as a deckhand on the schooner *Bella Hubbard,* then as a clerk in a store in Detroit. Eventually he made his way back north to Mackinac Island where he made a living as a laborer with the lighthouse service in the summer and as a store clerk in the winter.

Difficult Trip to the Iron Mines

In the spring of 1849, Robert J. Graveraet appeared on Mackinac Island looking for men to help develop the iron mines to the west. Peter White was urged to join the expedition, even though it meant taking a two-thirds cut in pay from 35 dollars a month plus board to only 12 dollars. The eighteen year old jumped at the chance and embarked on the journey northwest to the place that would become his lifelong home.

The house of Reverend Bingham, Baptist missionary at Sault Ste. Marie. He played a role in Upper Michigan's first murder mystery. (Courtesy Bayliss Public Library, Judge Joseph H. Steere Room, Sault Ste. Marie, Michigan)

The party left the island on the steamer *Tecumseh.* Years later, White recalled the "little…and…almost worthless" vessel "was not as fleet as the famous chief whose name she bore." He believed the Indian chief "could have beaten her best speed, on foot and through a thicket." *Tecumseh* left port on a "tempestuous April morning." The vessel plowed through heavy seas and after only a few miles, a mountainous wave tore off her yawl boat and washed most of the deck freight overboard. The captain swung the boat around and it limped into "the haven of safety…[it]…had left only a few hours before." Repairs

Peter White, 1830-1908, came to a small trading post on the south-central shore of Lake Superior in 1849 at the age of 18. He helped found the city of Marquette at the site, made his fortune through various enterprises and became a philanthropist in later life. (Courtesy of Peter White Library/ Freshwater Press)

The other suspect, John Tanner, was a "notorious and desperate character" with "strong passions and a violent temper." Tanner, a white man, was raised among Indians of the Red River country. He migrated to the Sault where he became an interpreter for Reverend Bingham, a Baptist missionary. Tanner originally married and had children with an Indian woman. When she died, he married a white woman from Sault Ste. Marie. His fits of rage were so intense that his new wife lived in constant fear for her life. Eventually with the help of Reverend Bingham and the Schoolcrafts, the woman escaped to her original home in Dearborn.

Tanner was outraged. He went downstate and tried to persuade his wife to return, but to no avail. He came back north and vowed to kill everyone he suspected of spiriting his wife away. Everyone in town feared him. John Tanner had a distinguished, striking appearance with a fine, long face and flowing white hair, parted in the middle and put back at his ears. When he went into one of his tirades, however, he assumed a frightful countenance. Mischievous children would be put in line by the mere threat that "Old Tanner, the bogie man" would get them if they did not behave.

Tanner's actions became more threatening and irrational. He quietly stole into Bingham's study one night, snuck up behind the Reverend, reached over his shoulder and wrung his nose with the intention of breaking it. He later approached Schoolcraft's sister-in-law and threatened to harm her children, shaking his fist and warning her to "Look out for the flowers in your garden." The madman also killed several valuable cattle belonging to Bingham and other residents of the community.

On Saturday night, July 4, 1846, the day before Schoolcraft was murdered, Tanner's house burned to the ground and he was never seen again, except once. An eyewitness reported seeing him seated on a log in a thicket not far from the Bingham house; gun in hand with a bundle at his side. A few hours later, Schoolcraft was shot through the heart and killed instantly as he sauntered in his garden at the old Johnston Estate.

The rest of the season became known as "The Tanner Summer." The fort sent a guard every night to the Baptist mission. People only left their homes at night if they were armed, in case they spotted Tanner. Every animal that died, old Tanner had killed;

were made on the steamer and she cast off again from Mackinac the next day.

Tecumseh carried more passengers than she had accommodations for, but the trip up through the Straits of St. Marys was scheduled to take only twelve hours. Schedules meant nothing on the frontier of the Upper Lakes. "The lively little steamer (lively with bed bugs)," remembered White, "finally got inside the Detour, and there met with solid ice, two to three feet thick." The party bound for the Iron Mountains came up against the remains of the long, hard winter of 1848-49.

"The boat was run about half her length into the ice," said White, "when some passengers debarked and ran up it in all directions." A suggestion was made to chop a canal through the ice with saws and axes. That idea was abandoned after it was realized the ice would probably melt faster than they could cut through it. The next day the steamer backed up and took another channel through the Straits. Instead of twelve hours, it took *ten days* for the little boat to hammer her way to the Sault. During the long, tortuous trip there was "a bread riot, an insurrection, and once the boat sank to her deck, full of water." *Tecumseh* might have gone down were it not for the skills of a strange old man the passengers and crew had christened "Old Saleratus." It turned out the eccentric fellow was a ship carpenter. After the boat was unloaded and bailed, the carpenter found the leak and repaired it with a new plank. *Tecumseh* and her cargo and crew finally limped into the Sault with the greater part of her journey still ahead.

"We succeeded in

Chief Charley Kawbawgam, C. 1800-1903, The full-blooded Chippewa spent his entire long life along the shores of Lake Superior, making Presque Isle his home from roughly 1880 until his death. He is buried there with his wife. (Courtesy of Marquette County History Museum)

crowding our large Mackinac barge up the rapids, or falls," recalled White, "and, embarking ourselves and provisions, set sail on Lake Superior for the Carp River Iron Region." It took eight days of "rowing, towing, poling and sailing" to reach Iron Bay, the present-day Marquette harbor. The first night, the party stayed at the "Cedar House of Charley Bawgam." The sea-weary men appreciated Bawgam's hospitality. White's most vivid memory of that first night centered on the food the Chippewa chief presented them. "He had fresh venison, wild ducks and geese, fresh fish, good bread and butter, coffee and tea, and splendid potatoes."

Bright and early the next morning the men set out for the iron hills some ten miles west of the lakeshore. Each man loaded a "pack-strap" with as much weight he felt he could comfortably carry. Peter White described his first hike to the iron mines: "I put up forty pounds and marched bravely up the hills with it for a distance of two miles, by which time I was about as good as used up. Graveraet came up, and, taking my pack on top of his, a much heavier one, marched on with both, as if mine was only the addition of a feather, while I trudged on behind and had hard work to keep up. Graveraet, seeing how fatigued I was, invited me to get on top of his load, saying he would carry me, too, and he could have done it, I believe; but I had too much pride to accept his offer."

After a stop for lunch, White felt renewed strength, took his pack back from Graveraet and marched the rest of the way to the mines. They stopped at the Jackson Forge a few miles east of present-day Negaunee. There they met Philo Everett and his associates. The party then hiked a few miles southwest to their destination near present-day Ishpeming. Captain Sam Moody and John Mann met them there. The two hardy prospectors had spent the severe winter of 1848-49 at that isolated wilderness location in an effort to keep possession of what looked like a promising location for an iron mine.

The next morning, White recalled how astonished he was when Moody asked him to accompany him to his garden to dig some potatoes for breakfast. It was only May, yet "we ascended a high hill…and on its pinnacle found half an acre partially cleared and planted to potatoes." Quickly Moody filled a pail with "large and perfectly sound potatoes". The

everything that was lost, Tanner had stole; everyone missing or late, Tanner had slain. All sorts of wild stories and rumors circulated in town.

The next year, some Red River Indians told the story of a mysterious white man with an Indian nature who appeared among them at the time of the wolf moon (January). He told wonderful stories and did strange things. A few moons later the man died. Was it Tanner? Did he kill Schoolcraft?

The mystery was never solved. Martha Tanner, John's daughter, lived out her long life on Mackinac Island. She maintained that Lieutenant Tilden confessed to the killing on his deathbed. Peter White believed Tilden had nothing to do with the crime. He felt that even if the soldier confessed, it was a case of deathbed delirium and nothing more. In his view, Tanner was the perpetrator. He kept a portrait of John Tanner hanging in his study. The piercing eyes and striking, virile face in the picture served as a reminder of his first eventful day in Upper Michigan so many years earlier.

young White did not realize that Moody had actually converted that piece of land into a crude root cellar. The amazed, young pioneer watched as the Captain also "harvested" parsnips and carrots, too.

Pioneering on Iron Bay

The next two months the men spent most of their time "fighting mosquitoes at night and the black flies through the day." White admitted, "Perhaps a small portion of it was given to denuding the iron hills of extraneous matter" in preparation for the mining ahead. On July 10, the party hiked back down the hill to meet their associate, Amos Harlow, who was due in from the East Coast. They arrived at the lakeshore before noon and discovered that Harlow had already landed "with quite a number of mechanics, some goods, lots of money, and…better than all," according to White, "we got a glimpse of some female faces." The event bolstered the settler's spirits. "We were all much excited and buoyant," remembered White, "with the hopes of a bright and dazzling future before us."

That same day, the men began construction of a dock. They began by cutting down trees and throwing them over the bank on to the lakeshore. Then under the direction of Captain Moody, they carried the whole trees into the water and "piled them in tiers, crosswise, until the pile was even with the surface of the water." The crew then wheeled sand and gravel on top of the structure and spent the next two days improving it by "corduroying the surface." At the end of the third day, the men "looked upon…[the dock]…with no little pride." Its east or outer end, recalled White, "was solid rock, and all inside of that was solid dirt, brush and leaves. We could not see why it should not stand as firm and as long as the adjacent beach itself."

The next morning the men arose and could not believe their eyes. The dock was gone! The action of waves had floated away and apparently sunk the makeshift structure they had crafted with so much care. Not a trace of it remained. "Not even a poplar leaf was left to mark the spot," said White. "The sand beach was as clean and smooth as if it had never been disturbed by the hand of man." After the initial shock wore off the mischievous, young Peter White took a stick and wrote in the smooth sand: "This is the spot where Capt. Moody built his dock." The captain was not amused. He stomped and trod upon the announcement and told White he would get his discharge at the end of the month. Fortunately, according to White, "he either forgave or forgot the affront. It was a long time before any one had the hardihood to attempt the building of another dock." During the rest of the summer, cargo steamers would anchor as far as two miles from shore. The freight and passengers were then landed in small boats. Cattle and other livestock were pitched overboard and forced to swim ashore.

In late October 1849, the stock of provisions in the little community on Lake Superior was very low. The last cargo vessel brought food in August. "Butter and luxuries of all kinds were wholly exhausted," recalled White. "Only a few barrels of pork and flour remained, and the danger of being put on very short rations was imminent." A guard was set up day and night at the warehouse where the food was kept to prevent looting.

As November began and the stockpile of provisions continued to dwindle, a group of

German immigrants hired in Wisconsin by Graveraet earlier that summer went on strike. "A large number of them started out of the country," said White. They planned on hiking along the lakeshore to Grand Island, forty miles east, and then through the interior to Bay De Noc on Lake Michigan. Only a few reached the island. Most of the others "lagged at different points along the beach." Their feet were sore, they were weary and hungry, and they would have probably died at the place they stopped if not for the return of their stronger comrades. The hikers who reached Grand Island learned that a "propeller", loaded with provisions, had landed at the nascent settlement the day after they left. With buoyant spirits, the workers returned to Marquette.

Tragedy visited the pioneer village as November 1849 ended and the first winter settled in. Amos Harlow heard of a new iron ore deposit near the mouth of the Carp River. He wanted to establish a claim on the deposit. To do that, a trip was necessary to the land office at Sault Ste. Marie. Four men volunteered for the dangerous journey. They set out in little more than a rowboat on November 27. Weeks later, the boat was found some distance down the shore. Two frozen bodies were found; one at each end of the vessel. The other two, apparently swept overboard by a late November gale, were recovered the next spring. The tragedy was compounded by the sad fact that there was no ore found near the mouth of the Carp River.

Legend of the Siscowit

Winter food supplies for the pioneer residents were adequate as 1849 came to a close. Grain and hay stores for livestock were not. Earlier that fall, Graveraet had brought a large number of horses from Chicago, arranging for feed to be brought up later. Weather disrupted that plan. "The schooners *Swallow* and *Siscowit*," remembered White, "with their cargoes of grain, were unable to make Marquette, owing to a storm, and ran to L'Anse, where they laid up for the winter." The feed shipments were critical if the livestock were to survive the long winter ahead. There was only one alternative—go to L'Anse and bring back the grain.

One person was up to this seemingly impossible task: Captain Moody. The man may not have been much of a dock builder, but he "had a heart of oak" and was a capable navigator. He immediately set out for L'Anse on snowshoes, accompanied by James Broadbent, "an old salt-water sailor." They arrived at Keweenaw Bay to find the two vessels stripped for winter and froze fast in the ice. This disheartening state of affairs did not stop Moody. He and his companion began to refit the *Siscowit* for the voyage to Marquette, "on the principle," as White put it, "that might makes right." They paid no attention whatever to the urgent protests of her owner, Capt. James Bendry. There was a village eighty miles down the lakeshore in urgent need of supplies; there were two of them and only one person standing in their way. For good measure, they held off Bendry with a shotgun. Later Moody commented on how much respect he had for Bendry's command of the English language. He recounted how Bendry, realizing he could not stop them "contented himself by firing upon them as picturesque a stream of profanity as ever emanated from human lips."

They took all the grain and corn off the *Swallow* and loaded it onto the *Siscowit*. Now there was the ice to contend with. To surmount that obstacle, Moody "employed a large number of Indians to cut a passage…between two and three miles long." The two sailors finally succeeded in floating the vessel, and began the perilous voyage to Marquette on Christmas

Eve, 1849. They employed every bit of courage and sailor's sense they could muster. All the while they were on the lake, a heavy snowstorm and northwest gale assaulted the small craft. They could not see land from the time the *Siscowit* floated free of Keweenaw Bay ice until it limped into Marquette Bay on Christmas Day. Its sails were frozen stiff and immovable and her deck was covered with ice a foot thick. The rejoicing townspeople unloaded the feed and other supplies into the warehouse. Then Moody ran the schooner into the Chocolay River where she lay until spring. The village was saved, but the story did not end happily for the *Siscowit*. "When, in coming out…[of the river in spring]," reported White, "she ran on the beach and went to pieces."

Will Winter Supplies Arrive?

The little settlement came close to disaster the next winter. In autumn of 1850, Marquette was "a small number of houses," recalled Mrs. Philo Everett, "scattered here and there among the pines, mostly built of logs, and one small store." From there "all the necessaries to sustain the little community were distributed—mostly in small allowances—so that none would fare better than his neighbors." Everyone depended on the success of the forge that would be making bloom iron as soon as the ore could be shipped down on sleighs from the hills to the west. Ore could not be moved over the rough trails during the summer. It took a deep snow cover, packed down hard over the thicket and rock, to make way for the horse-drawn sleighs with their heavy loads.

The little steamer *Napoleon* was chartered to bring food and supplies to the town. "As usual," recalled Everett, "[she]…attempted to do more than she was able to accomplish." *Napoleon* was over laden with freight for Marquette and other ports to the west. The captain of the steamer decided to pass by Marquette early in autumn and then come back with a full load from the Sault after it was too late to go farther up the lake. The days passed, and with no mail communication except by boat, there was a growing fear among the residents that they had been abandoned.

November came and went with its gales and snowstorms and still no boat. "Winter seemed closing in upon us," said Everett, "and all eyes and hearts ached in vainly looking so long and anxiously for the…[steamboat]. The first thing in the morning, and the last thing at night, was to cast a long look on the sea of waters, and turn away with a sickening fear that there was little hope that relief would ever reach us." All business halted. There was no use in working because everything depended on the arrival of supplies.

Marquette in 1850 was "a small number of houses scattered here and there among the pines." (Courtesy Superior View, Marquette, Michigan)

Winter settled severely on

the Upper Midwest in 1850. The St. Peters River in Minnesota froze over in early December with four consecutive mornings below zero. To the northeast, Everett reported a "cold and stormy" start to the twelfth month. "All hope seemed gone," she remembered. "At last it was decided to kill the horses, and divide the coarse feed left among the most needy families of women and children and send the men away through the wilderness."

The weather moderated a little at mid-month and faint hope was revived; maybe a boat could still reach them before the lake became unnavigable. On the morning of December 15, Mrs. Everett "fancied… faint smoke now and then through the haze." When she was convinced it was the smoke of a steamer she told her children to spread the word. They went about the village shouting "PROPELLER! PROPELLER!" Soon the rest of the townspeople took up the cry. "Men shouted and swung the remnants of hats, women tore off their aprons and waved them, and the little feet that were bare for the want of shoes that were on the boat, danced out in the cold." There was a man who exclaimed on hearing the news: "Now, if old Bill is not dead I can save him." Old Bill was his last horse. He had watched the rest of his "fine span" of horses starve to death. It is not known whether Old Bill was saved, but the timely arrival of food and supplies rescued the little frontier community and kept it going for another long winter.

A similar situation occurred in the Keweenaw four years earlier. In the fall of 1847, the vessel scheduled to bring winter supplies into Copper Harbor burned before it arrived. An inventory was taken at the area mining camps. Provisions were so low that it was decided to "send all single men out of the country" to fend for themselves. Just before they left, the steamer *Independence* arrived with their supplies. The boat had been laid up at the Sault but the people there who knew of the plight of the Copper Country settlers convinced the captain to risk the dangerous trip.

An early spring may have averted disaster in 1851. An inventory taken at mining camps from the Keweenaw Peninsula to Ontonagon in March 1851 showed precariously low food stores at all locations. The winter had started cold back in December but turned progressively warmer. In Minnesota, February ended nearly 5 degrees warmer than the long-term average. The frontier newspaper *Pioneer* commented: "We have had days like April—too fine, in fact, for February. The snow has nearly disappeared and the winter is dissolving into the lap of spring." March came in nearly 10 degrees above average. Ducks arrived in the North Country by the 10th. The rivers opened on the 21st. Farther northeast, food was being rationed but great suffering was averted. The unseasonably mild weather allowed a vessel to arrive early with needed supplies for Copper Country pioneers.

As late as the fall of 1856, Marquette and settlements to the west teetered on the brink of disaster when the propeller *B. L. Webb* burned en route between the Sault and Marquette. She was the first lake boat with a thirty-foot beam, designed especially for bulk freight and specifically for carrying iron ore. She never did carry any ore and when she caught fire in Waishkey Bay just west of the Sault, she sank, carrying to the bottom winter provisions and mining supplies for the struggling Lake Superior settlements. In Marquette, the loss caused shock and anxiety bordering on panic. The propeller contained feed for the community's horses as well as food for the human population. The horse feed was the most important, since there was little hay left and no means of obtaining any more until spring.

The owner of a shipping concern in the Sault came to the rescue. He ordered the propeller *General Taylor* to sail from Detroit to Marquette and west loaded with the same cargo that went down on the *Webb*. It was an expensive and hazardous undertaking for so late in the season. First, insurance could not be secured for either the vessel or cargo, and second, the crew would have to remain with the vessel on Lake Superior over the winter. Freight costs were double the usual rate, mounting to three dollars a barrel in Marquette and six dollars per barrel in Ontonagon. The residents of both towns were glad to pay the price for winter supplies and the trip went off without a hitch. The *General Taylor* laid up for the exceptionally harsh winter of 1856-57 in Ontonagon (See *Snowstorms, Snowy Winters*, Page 147).

Tales of Peter White

Most mining operations failed within the first few years of operation. Already in the spring of 1850, the first iron mine, the Jackson, "bust all up" and work at the mine and forge near Carp River was suspended. The workmen at the mine were not paid for the work they had done during the winter and now they were unemployed. "The men talked seriously," remembered Peter White, "of hanging and quartering" 'Czar' Jones, the company president. Jones, in fear of his life, asked White to serve as his guide on an overland trip through the wilderness to Escanaba.

The young adventurer had accompanied a couple of Indians through the nearly trackless forest to the Lake Michigan shore the summer before. White had suffered on a nearly week-long journey through thicket and swamp just to get to the mouth of the Escanaba. He vowed to never attempt a journey like that again. But after Jones raised his bid from one dollar to three dollars per day and promised to pay for sixteen days, White decided he could endure another trip south.

It took seven full days to reach what is now Escanaba. Most of the roughly 70-mile journey consisted of grown-over thicket and brambles through the forest or swamp with a layer of soft ice on top that when stepped on would break through. Jones asked constantly if they were lost. On the fourth day, White paused, wiped his brow and looked around with a thoroughly perplexed expression on his face. "I am lost," he said in a matter-of-fact way. Jones broke down. He dropped to his knees and wailed, "To pretend to be a guide and not know the way."

Actually, White had been unsuccessfully looking for the Escanaba River that whole day. A little while later he found it, but Jones no longer trusted his young guide. He went his own way, walking along the river. White called him back, but the frightened traveler would not listen. Finally, White caught up with Jones and broke the ice on the river to show him that he was traveling *upstream* back toward the north. Jones relented and followed White. Three days later they made it to Little Bay de Noc. White made the return trip to Marquette in only three days.

The little community barely hung on through 1851 as transportation difficulties and lack of capital led to a period of "woeful stagnation." Despite the bleak prospects, Marquette

County was organized and 21-year-old Peter White was appointed county clerk and register of deeds. The administrative positions naturally fell to the young man since he was one of the few in the area who could write. He also demonstrated a tenacious "can do" attitude and looked about 30 years old in his full black beard. The appointments may have been compensation for a difficult trip he made to the Keweenaw in the dead of winter the year before.

In January 1851, Marquette was part of Houghton County. The county seat at the time was Eagle River, far up the Keweenaw Peninsula in what is now Keweenaw County. Some Marquette businessmen needed certificate to certain legal documents, which meant a trip to the county seat. White volunteered for the trip and set out on snowshoes around New Year's Day 1851. He made his way to L'Anse then across the ice of Keweenaw Bay to Portage Entry where he met two men who accompanied him the rest of the way to Keweenaw Point.

As they were crossing Portage Lake, the party overtook Father Baraga and his guide. Baraga had established a Catholic mission at L'Anse in 1843. The cleric had gained a reputation as the "Snowshoe Priest" traveling throughout the sparsely populated Lake Superior region under the most difficult and dangerous conditions (*See "Chapter 5, page 3"*). Baraga at once surmised that White spoke Chippewa fluently. "He seemed delighted to meet me," recalled White over fifty years later. "In the course of our conversation, while walking on, he most

cordially invited me to call on him at the mission, and I cheerfully promised him that I would at the first opportunity." The two parties walked together for a few miles, but White's party wanted to go faster, so they separated and went ahead.

White finally arrived in Eagle River and attended to his business with Mr. Kelsey, the Houghton county clerk. Kelsey asked him when he would return to Marquette. When White replied "tomorrow," Kelsey

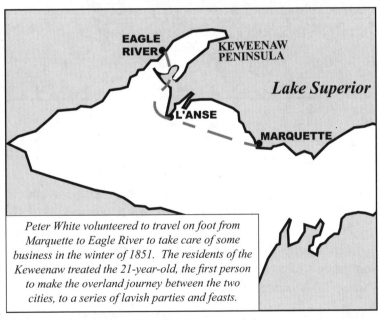

Peter White volunteered to travel on foot from Marquette to Eagle River to take care of some business in the winter of 1851. The residents of the Keweenaw treated the 21-year-old, the first person to make the overland journey between the two cities, to a series of lavish parties and feasts.

shot back: "Oh no, we never allow a winter visitor to depart under two weeks." He went on to explain that since the young traveler was the first person to ever journey overland from Marquette to Eagle River, a celebration was in order. Kelsey met with other townspeople and it was agreed that a big party would be thrown in White's honor.

White was suspicious of all the attention he was getting. He wondered if these strangers had some malicious plot in the works. "The thought occurred to me whether I had not better cut and run for home," remembered White. However, he decided that if he did and was

Father Frederic Baraga, the famous missionary to the Chippewa of the Lake Superior region, met Peter White for the first time on the trail to Eagle River in January 1851. (Courtesy of the Marquette County History Museum)

caught, they might be even harder on him. "I resolved to stay," recalled White, "and, if necessary, run the gauntlet, or fight for my liberty if cornered." He met a number of area residents who came to pay their respects, including John Senter, the entrepreneur who would later hike in the dead of winter to Green Bay. White watched everyone closely but could find no hint of a conspiracy.

He was invited to another party the next night, and when he protested that he had no clothes suitable for a formal party, White said, "I was forcibly taken into Senter's store and there compelled to put on an elegant suit of clothes." The next ten days he was wined and dined. White declared he "could not have been more civilly feasted and toasted had… [he]…been the President."

When he finally prepared to leave, he asked for and was given two cans of "elegant cove oysters" to take back to his "Carp River friends." He struggled through the snow to the Portage Entry and found the ice on the bay broken up. White was not in shape to go any farther anyway. "I was laid up for three days," he said, "with 'Le mal de Racket,' or snowshoe sickness." He stayed and recovered at the home of Ransom Sheldon, one of the Copper Country's prominent first settlers.

White mended sufficiently, and on January 18 set out through the woods toward Baraga's mission at L'Anse to pay the priest a visit. Not exactly sure of the route, he decided to keep the bay in sight. He soon found that plan unworkable because of the thick underbrush, so he "struck back for better walking." The mission was sixteen miles from Portage Entry but White felt he had walked thirty. To compound the hardship, he was traveling during one of the coldest periods of the winter of 1850-51.

Fort Snelling in Minnesota reported severe cold from January 16-18. The mercury failed to rise above 10 below zero on the afternoons of the 17th and 18th, so White was not embellishing when he explained, "It was very cold—twenty-two degrees below zero—and night was close at hand."

He crossed a little valley and mounted a small hill, looked back and caught the first glimpse of sun he had seen all day. The frozen hiker was shocked. He realized that to get to the mission he should have been traveling *toward* the setting sun. White turned in the direction of the sun, and in a short time came upon a single pair of snowshoe tracks. Buoyed by the thought that someone else had passed through the area recently, he followed the tracks. Before long, he crossed another pair and then another. "A little closer examination convinced me," explained White, "that they were all my own tracks, and that for hours I had been traveling on a circle, only enlarging it a little each time."

With darkness closing in rapidly, the dejected White resigned himself to spending the night under the stars in the bitter cold. All he had was a "good double blanket, matches and the two cans of oysters" from the Keweenaw. "I succeeded in starting a fire at the foot of a dead cedar that leaned into the forks of a hemlock," recalled White, "and, as fast as it burned to coal, it would slide down a little, and thus, my fire was replenished all night. I was much too excited to be either tired or hungry." He managed to catch a little sleep sitting in a sort of "snow chair" he fashioned with his body in the thick, fluffy cover. "I had lined… [the chair]…with balsam boughs, so that it was quite comfortable."

The next morning he broke all the blades of his knife opening one of the cans of oysters. "I boiled them in the can and tried to eat them," explained White, "but it was hard work; they wouldn't stay down." He was in a quandary: How would he find his way out of the forest and back on the trail? He decided to try to find then follow his tracks from the day before some twenty miles back to the Portage Entry.

As the tired, cold traveler set off on his exploration, he heard an Indian yell off to his left, then another to his right. He kept answering their yells and in about twenty minutes the two Indians closed in on him from opposite directions. "The priest sent us to find you," they said. Father Baraga

After his rescue, White spent time recovering from his night into the woods at the L'Anse mission (Assinins). This photo was taken in the late 1890s. (Courtesy of the Diocese of Marquette Archives)

had arrived at the Entry an hour after White had left the day before. He took a route that brought him to the mission well before dark and when White did not show up, he became concerned that the young wayfarer was either hurt or lost. So the next morning he sent out the search party as soon as it became light enough to see.

The Indians guided White to the mission and Baraga's house. "Father Baraga did me a good turn," said White years later, "and perhaps actually saved my life." He never forgot Baraga's kindness and concern. In about 1870, just after Baraga died, White championed the proposal to honor the cleric by renaming Marquette's Superior Street Baraga Avenue.

Winter Mail Carriers

Winter was a time of isolation for early Upper Michigan settlers. A. P. Swineford, owner and publisher of Marquette's Mining Journal during its earliest days, described what happened after the close of navigation: "For weeks upon weeks there were nothing but clouded skies and falling snow; no bright ray of sunshine darted through the noonday gloom; the days were short, and the nights proportionately long; Jack Frost reigning supremely, penetrated everywhere, hushing in silence the babbling brook and flashing lake, and smothered every voice of nature in a deep pall of snow; the deep forests, stripped of their summer apparel, and with lesser growths buried out of sight, presented a cold, bare melancholy picture, not at all conducive to buoyancy of spirits. Often, after a great snow-storm, accompanied by high winds, locomotion, even on snow-shoes, was impossible."

Communication with the outside world was no better than when Schoolcraft clung "with a death grasp" to his friends and correspondents thirty years earlier. A newspaper became community property in the early days of Marquette. It would be carefully wrapped and passed from household to household for cover-to-cover reading. Mail was eagerly anticipated but delivery was uncertain and disappointing.

Mail carriers traveled on snowshoes alongside a dogsled laden with mail through trackless wilderness thick with snow. The round trip from Green Bay to Copper Harbor via Marquette was a full 600 miles and took a month to complete. Usually, the carriers were recruited from the ranks of the voyageurs. Some of them were of French-Canadian and Chippewa extraction. The forest contained nothing that frightened these men. The dogs pulling the sleds were "mongrels, stout curs" capable of making up to four or five miles in an hour. They had to be fed at short intervals to keep their moods at a normal pitch. At times they would become wildly excited at the scent of wolves and become almost unmanageable. Bad roads or heavy loads would cause the teams to sulk and often stop in their tracks.

Swineford explained that a mail carrier adopted an efficient, simple way of lessening the load of his dogs: "He simply had to hang a bag or bags of mail matter upon a tree, and leave them, in most cases, to winter." The mail would remain undisturbed and when spring came, the winter-weary settlers had at least a half-bushel of letters to read.

Initially, the new village of Marquette was not on the regular winter mail route. Postmaster Amos Harlow, looking for reliable mail delivery during the long winter, thought of one person he could turn to—Peter White. The young man had proved his mettle, determination and reliability over and over during the settlement's first two-and-a-half years of existence.

Harlow secured $1,200 in pledges from the townspeople that would be paid to White after the trips were completed. White agreed to the proposal and left the next day accompanied by two Indian guides. The whole town saw them off.

Upper Michigan residents in the pioneer days relied on mail carriers, who traveled on foot over vast distances with sled dogs loaded with mail. (Courtesy Marquette County History Museum)

White left with a staggering load on his back. Hundreds of letters were written when the word spread that he would deliver the mail. The party headed west toward L'Anse where they met other carriers. Eventually a relay station was established in the woods. The station was a fork in a prominent tree along the trail where the mailbag would be hung then picked up by the next carrier in the relay to the Copper Country.

On the second trip White had a team of dogs and a sled to ease his burden. He controlled the lead dog by a string rein and used his staff as a brake, pushing it into the snow while holding the rein when he wanted to stop. Seven more trips were made during the winter of 1852. In his later years, Peter White would tell stories of these journeys, assuming the name "Pierre La Blanc" along with a French-Canadian dialect.

The mail runs may be rich in history but they did not enrich young "Pierre." Of the $1,200 in pledges, only three dollars were offered to White. Those three dollars came from Silas C. Smith who saw White on the street one day and handed him the money, explaining that it was the pledge he made before the mail runs began. White, to Smith's surprise, handed back the money without explanation. Later he told Smith he did not want just one person paying for all nine trips.

In the spring of 1852, the first vessel of the year arrived at Marquette carrying a thick and bulky envelope addressed to Peter White. It was stamped with the official seal of the United States and looked quite menacing to the young man. He delayed opening it, fearing what it might contain. However, the rest of the villagers had heard about it and badgered him until he finally opened it. He found, to his utter amazement, that he had been appointed postmaster of Carp River.

In late 1851, the general mail contractor in Green Bay examined his lists and noticed Philo Everett's resignation as Postmaster of Carp River. The contractor had heard a lot about Carp River. He thought of it as an important location in the rising iron country. What he had not heard was news of the Jackson Mine closure and the virtual abandonment of the settlement. He felt he needed to appoint a new postmaster, and since Peter White's father managed the contractor's office in Green Bay, Peter became the logical choice to fill the position—besides, White was the only person they knew in Upper Michigan except Marquette postmaster

Harlow. Eventually, Harlow stepped down and the Carp River and Marquette offices were consolidated with the versatile Peter White at the helm.

One Last Winter Mail Run

Over the next couple of years, the fame of the Iron Hills spread. The plank road leading from Marquette to the mines was converted into a strap railroad. The conversion took lots of labor and brought in many new faces. One thing had not changed—mail service to the northern outpost remained sporadic and unreliable. In early January 1854, the townspeople appealed to their postmaster to make another trip into the snow-covered wilderness to bring back word from the outside world.

Peter White yielded to their demands. He assembled an entourage of six Indians, three dog sleds and nine dogs, plunged into the woods at the mouth of the Carp River and headed south. The sleds were loaded down with a thousand letters ready to be posted. Only slow progress was made; the snow was soft and deep, the product of a transition from a mild December to a bitter January.

The first month of 1854 turned out to be one of the coldest of the frontier period in the Upper Midwest. Fort Ripley in central Minnesota registered below zero readings most of the month. "Quicksilver receded entirely into the ball" on January 22 as the temperature plunged to an estimated 48 below. The next day, a small quantity of mercury was placed in a cup and left outside. It reportedly froze solid in fifteen minutes.

This frigid backdrop tested the mettle of Peter White's group in their seven-day journey from Marquette to the Cedar River in present-day Menominee County, near the waters of Green Bay. As they slogged through the deep snows on the river, the party spotted what appeared to be five immense loads of hay slowly crawling toward them. It turned out to be five double teams loaded with seven tons of mail bound for the Lake Superior region. In addition, an immense quantity of mail still remained in Green Bay. White had two of his sleds loaded with mail and sent them north, while he proceeded south to Green Bay in the other sled.

The two-sled mail train arrived "after great tribulations, delays and troubles" in Marquette January 21. Some of the dog teams were dispatched ahead of the others with letter bags. The teams were met at the mouth of the Carp River by half the town, ravenous for word from friends, family and associates to the south and east. The little village shut down the next two days as the

The dogs in this photo had it much easier than the ones who hauled mountains of mail back to Marquette in January 1854. (Courtesy of the Marquette History Museum)

townspeople plunged themselves into a "riot of reading."

In Green Bay, Peter White found 24 bags of mail posted for delivery to the Lake Superior region. Each bag contained four bushels of letters. He also learned that mail was accumulating at the rate of six bushels a day. A series of heated confrontations took place between the postmasters of Marquette and Green Bay. Receiving no satisfaction in Green Bay, White then took a trip to the nearest telegraph station fifty-some-odd miles to the southwest in Fond du Lac. There he communicated his town's outrage to U.S. Senator Lewis Cass in Washington. Cass was bombarded over a two-day period with the force of White's words. Eventually, he became convinced that an insurrection was imminent in the northern peninsula of his state. Cass quickly set up a meeting between a special postal agent and his impetuous young constituent. White got what he wanted and was also given a $66 dollar bill for telegraph usage—a staggering sum in 1854.

When the special agent arrived from downstate, White immediately escorted him to the finest hotel in Green Bay for a dinner of oysters and champagne. Over the next few days, amid more wining and dining, it became apparent to the special agent that an emergency existed. He told White that he would immediately arrange for a set schedule of once-a-week delivery to Michigan's Upper Peninsula. After one more round of friendly persuasion from Marquette's charismatic postmaster, mail service was increased to three times weekly. White returned to Marquette a hero.

The Strap Railway and an Overland Trip to Lansing

A strap railroad from the Iron Hills west of Marquette to the lakeshore community went into operation in November 1855. The railroad consisted of strap iron placed on wooden rails. Flat-bottomed cars were equipped with small railroad-type wheels to run on the iron strap. It was an inefficient, dangerous and costly way to move ore to the lakefront.

Mules powered the cars, each having a capacity of four tons. When loaded, the cars would scrape against the wheels, cutting away a portion of the platform. A team could only make a trip a day, and thirty-five tons moved was considered a good day's work. The grades downhill to the lake were "frightful" and often the cars ran away, jumping the track on the

With hardships and trials of the early pioneer days behind him, Peter White relaxes with some friends at a rustic hunting camp near the turn of the century. White is second from right in photo. (Courtesy of Superior View, Marquette)

first curve. At the first sign of trouble, the driver would bail off the car into the soft sand on either side of the track; but the mules had no protection. More than once, an out-of-control car laden with ore mangled the mule team in its tumble down a hill. Mules cost $1,400 dollars apiece and the hay to feed the animals was as high as fifty dollars a ton. The track, too, was in constant need of repair.

It was quickly realized that the strap railroad was not the future for iron ore transport from the hills to the lake. At the same time the strap railway began operation, construction began on a steam railroad line from Marquette to the west. The next year, the U. S. Congress passed a land grant act to stimulate construction of railroads. The "Iron Horse" was where the future of transportation was heading. A number of mining companies consolidated efforts to build a railroad to the mines. Before the state doled out the federal land grants, the Upper Peninsula needed a representative familiar with the area and its unique situation. The most obvious candidate to fill the seat was Peter White. In 1855, he added real estate to his resume when the Cleveland Iron Company turned management of a sixty-four acre tract of land to the young entrepreneur.

In November 1856, 26 year-old White was elected representative and in the winter of 1857 he headed south to Lansing. It took fifteen days to complete the journey during the harshest winter of the early frontier period in the Upper Midwest. He traveled the first leg from Marquette to Escanaba on snowshoes. He then took a stage to Fond du Lac, Wisconsin, and walked from there around the south end of Lake Michigan to the State Capitol. When White took his seat at the first legislative meeting, he was heartily cheered by the entire assembly. Every member appreciated the tremendous obstacles that stood in the way of his being there.

Nothing stood in the way of Peter White and the rest of the pioneers of the early mining boom. A blinding snowstorm, bitter cold, a deep forest thicket or a half-frozen swamp would not stop them. Their stories demonstrate again and again the tenacity, resourcefulness, patience and faith of these remarkable people. Nowhere are these traits, particularly tenacity and faith, more evident than in the missionary work of Father Baraga.

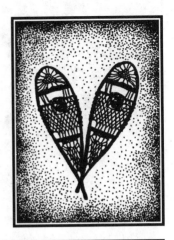

CHAPTER 5
THE SNOWSHOE PRIEST

The Exhausting Journey and Return of the Missions to Lake Superior

"After two days, extraordinary exertion and fatigue, I reached my journey's end. Often I sank in the snow exhausted, to rest up a little...I thought many times I could go no further."—Father Baraga 1833.

If pioneers wanted to get somewhere during an Upper Michigan winter, they used snowshoes. "In the absence of beaten roads or trails," wrote early pioneer John Forster, "snowshoeing was the only mode of locomotion in that new country." Traveling during the winter actually had advantages over the summer: "The thick underbrush and all fallen timber were buried under the snow, so that in a level country, a smooth, clean park-like plain lay before you."

Snowshoeing back then was not easy, even under the best conditions. "When the snow was packed, or crusted over, walking was a laborious effort although the gait was rapid", explained Forster. "But upon new fallen, or wet snow, the labor was multiplied many fold, as the heavy shoes, sinking into the soft deposit, would become loaded and icy, entailing exhausting and irritating fatigue. Men were often compelled to stop and rest, and if the toes of the feet, as they were apt, from tightening of the thongs by wet, became sore, then traveling became absolute torture." The indefatigable "Apostle of the Chippewa" trudged many hundreds of

Frederic Baraga (1797-1868) was drawn to missionary work as a young priest in his native Carniola (now Slovenia). He made his way to America in 1831 and spent most of the rest of his life in the Lake Superior region, ministering to the Chippewa and later, to the growing mining population of Upper Michigan. (Courtesy of the Diocese of Marquette Archives)

Chippewa students studying from a prayer book. Baraga quickly learned the native tongue and published his first Chippewa prayer book in 1832. (Courtesy of Superior View Studio)

miles on these "rackets" throughout the Upper Great Lakes during his almost forty years of ministry in Michigan, Wisconsin, Minnesota and Canada.

Baraga was drawn to missionary work while a young curate in his native Slovenia. He accepted an appointment to the Cincinnati diocese (which at the time encompassed a huge territory, including the Upper Great Lakes) in late 1830, finally arriving at his first mission, Arbre Croche, near the present site of downstate Harbor Springs in May 1831. The 33-year-old priest quickly learned the native language and published his first Indian prayer book in 1832. In July 1835, Baraga made his way to the Lake Superior region, where he would spend the rest of his life.

One hundred and sixty years had passed since a mission was operated at La Pointe, Madeline Island on the west end of Lake Superior. In fact, Father Baraga was the first missionary in the area since Father Marquette. Wars and revolution held back exploration and settlement and Baraga was pioneering all over again.

His journey from the Sault to La Pointe was more pleasant than Marquette's legendary voyage. It was taken in July and even then, the priest later wrote, "on the 7th of July ice to

An artist's perspective of La Pointe in the 1850s. Over 150 years elapsed between the early Jesuit Mission Espirit and the arrival of Baraga, who reestablished a mission at the site in 1835. (Courtesy of Wisconsin History Magazine)

the thickness of a knife-blade was found along the shore of Lake Superior." Summer ended pleasantly, however, with some hot days during August. Then winter set in early. On September 22, the first snow arrived and Baraga was completely unprepared. His winter clothes were to have been forwarded to him but they failed to arrive. It was a long, cold first winter in the Lake Superior region for the Snowshoe Priest. He reported ice still floating in Lake Superior as late as early June 1835.

After ministering to the Chippewa on the west end of Lake Superior, Baraga finally settled in the Upper Peninsula near what is now L'Anse in 1843. It was here that some of the priest's most famous winter journeys occurred.

All Night Walks and a Wet, Cold Night Spent in the Wilderness

"On one of my apostolic journeys this winter I was in great danger...of losing my life."—Father Baraga 1851

January 1851 was a mixed month with periods of alternating cold and warmth. The last few days of the month, temperatures failed to reach zero at Fort Snelling. At about this time, Baraga set out on snowshoes to visit area mines. The mining settlements were separated by many miles, which required walking long distances through deep snow. At the start of his journey, the snow was only about a foot deep. It then snowed heavily all day and all night. Baraga set out the next morning while the blizzard still raged. He had 30 miles to go to the next settlement, which meant a 10- to 12-hour walk under normal conditions. He labored through the deep drifts all day and as evening closed in, he realized he had only made it halfway!

"It was certainly terrifying...all alone in a dark, frightfully cold night, without a fire—tired to exhaustion! Now what was I to do? There was no other choice but to go on or freeze." Baraga realized he was 15 miles from shelter either way and had to keep moving. Stopping to rest would have meant falling asleep and dying of exposure. He stumbled and plodded through the bitter cold night, averaging just over a mile an hour. Finally, at seven the next morning, Baraga arrived at his destination. He had walked for 24 hours without rest.

In the fall of 1852, the missionary was touring the Ontonagon mining region when he lost the trail. A cold rain had turned to snow and Baraga had to spend the night in a dense forest "without fire, without blankets." The next morning "wet, hungry, cold and exhausted," the priest was discovered sitting on a log by a passing hunter. The hunter took him to his cabin, gave him a hot meal, dry clothing and a warm bed. The next day Baraga left for Rockland, but not before giving the man a crucifix he was wearing as a memento for saving his life.

HALLUCINATION

A voyageur described another all-night walk endured by Baraga during severe winter conditions. He was on the last leg of a two-month visit to area missions when he was faced with a choice: Stay at an abandoned hut for the night or proceed across frozen Keweenaw Bay to his home at the L'Anse mission.

"Everything seemed to advise him to...spend the night... [in]...the lonely hut," explained the voyageur nicknamed Petit Francois. "But his burning zeal urged him to continue his journey and face wind and storm." Baraga set out across the frozen expanse into the teeth of a strong wind. "The worst," according to Francois, "was that the snowshoes would not glide along properly, as the snow was very deep, granular, and shifting. A traveler will endure any fatigue so long as he sees he is advancing; but when you are working so with your feet, slipping and stumbling, and the snow sinks in like wool and piles up before you like the sand of the desert, and you try in vain to steer a zig-zag course to get out of the holes and drifts, oh! Then matters are really bad. The air is gloomy and thick...[and]... the whole atmosphere is filled with piercing ice needles."

Francois explained what happens to a traveler under these conditions: "You fall into a strange and feverish state; your head grows heavy, and your thoughts are confused." Eventually Baraga's eyes swelled shut in the face of the blinding snow and he stumbled on mechanically as if his legs moved by themselves. His only directional guide was the wind; when he started out he was moving straight into the wind toward his destination. As soon as he perceived one side of his face warmer than the other, he knew he was going the wrong way. Then he turned his "full face to the wind, which...[he]... cut through with the keel of... [his]...nose."

At sunrise, Francois opened the door to his cabin and was shocked to see the priest standing before him "covered with ice and snow, with swollen eyes, stiff hands, and wearied limbs." Baraga asked in a dazed, confused manner, "Where am I?" He did not recognize his friend Petit Francois "and almost doubted it was really the sunlight which glimmered through the foggy atmosphere." In his hallucinatory state he believed he had only spent a few minutes snowshoeing on the bay when in reality he had endured a 12 hour struggle.

"It was all to him as a dream," explained Petit Francois. "Such snow-storm dreams are followed close by death." For Baraga, it was God's hand and his own iron will that guided him through another perilous journey and enlarged the legend of the Snowshoe Priest.

Perils on the Ice and a Chance Meeting

In early March 1853, Baraga made his way down to Bay de Noc on a trip to Detroit to get his Ojibwa dictionary printed. From there he secured a ride on a sleigh to Green Bay on a bitter cold day. About nine miles from the city, the sled broke through the ice and Baraga "almost drowned." He wasn't hurt and his dictionary was saved, but undoubtedly it was a painfully cold ride the rest of the way to Green Bay.

On another occasion earlier the same year, a chance meeting with a small group of travelers may have saved Baraga's life. In January, he undertook a journey of 250 miles from L'Anse to near present-day Duluth to deliver medicine to a widow and her five sick children. A businessman named Benjamin Armstrong and his party were hiking along a trail outside of Ontonagon when they met the priest struggling through deep drifts.

"I am quite positive that he would have perished that night but for our meeting," Armstrong recalled. "His snowshoes had given out, and it would have been impossible for him to have proceeded far without them because of the deep snow. Our party made it comfortable for him that night and one of my men repaired his snowshoes." Some months later Armstrong said he ran into Baraga again. The missionary assured the businessman that the journey had been completed, the medicine delivered and the family was well and comfortable when he left. Curiously, the Bishop made no mention of this trip either in his diary or letters.

The determined missionary pressed on, even when it meant risking his life. On one occasion, Baraga chose to cross the ice of Lake Superior rather than undertake a long, tedious walk along the sandy beach. It was spring and the ice was "spongy and dangerous." He and a native guide set out across the ice. After traveling for some time they noticed that the chunk of ice they were on had broken off from the mainland and began drifting toward open water. The wind at the time was blowing offshore toward mid-lake. The guide became alarmed, but Baraga assured him that God would protect them. The priest calmly sang hymns in the Chippewa tongue and after a while, the wind shifted and blew in the direction toward which they were heading. They reached their destination that same day. "You see," said Baraga gleefully, "we have traveled far and yet worked but little."

The "Grandest" Traverse

The priest's astounding faith prevailed during a celebrated voyage across Lake Superior one summer. This journey was recounted by a voyageur to German ethnographer and travel writer Johann Kohl during his summer among the Chippewa in 1855.

Baraga was ministering to the Indians on one of the Apostle Islands when he got word that he was needed immediately at a mission on the northern shore of Lake Superior.

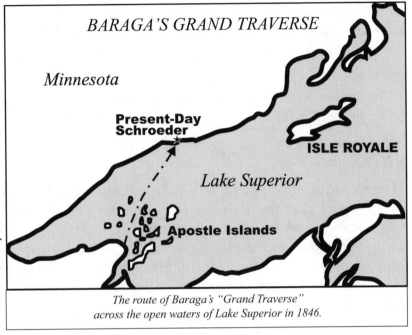

BARAGA'S GRAND TRAVERSE

Minnesota

Present-Day Schroeder

ISLE ROYALE

Lake Superior

Apostle Islands

The route of Baraga's "Grand Traverse" across the open waters of Lake Superior in 1846.

He was always ready to leave at a moment's notice, and this time was no different. He sought out a well known voyageur named Dubois and said, "I must cross the lake, direct from here to the northern shore. Hast thou a boat ready?"

"The boat is here," said Dubois, "but how can I venture to go with you straight across the lake? It is seventy miles and the weather does not look very promising. No one ever yet attempted this 'traverse' in small boats. Our passage to the north shore is made along the coast, and we usually employ eight days in it."

"Dubois that is too long," answered Baraga, "It cannot be. I repeat…I am called. I must go straight across the lake."

Baraga then took a seat in the little vessel, which was nothing more than a rowboat or large canoe, and waited patiently as the wide-eyed voyageur, shaking his head and muttering to himself, obediently packed his things. In a short time he was casting off with his intractably determined passenger on a perilous, foolhardy voyage across the open lake.

Indians and voyageurs rarely made trips of over 15 miles across open water. They would travel only from cape to cape so they could easily put their boats into shore at the first sign of rough weather. A passage of 25 miles was considered a "grand traverse" and this voyage of 70 miles was considered an impossibility. Nonetheless, Dubois paddled cheerfully along and "they were soon floating in their nutshell in the middle of the lake like a loon, without compass and out of sight of land."

Soon it became stormy. The south wind rose and the waves came up. Dubois expressed his concern, but Baraga calmly read from his prayer book, only occasionally lending a word of encouragement. The priest reiterated that he was called across the lake and that God would guide them safely to land.

"Their little bark danced like a feather on the waters" all night long. While the waves made for a frightening canoe ride in the middle of the night, the south wind at their back moved them along quickly. The next morning, Dubois caught a glimpse of the north shore. In the dim light of dawn, he barely recognized the long rows of dark rocks with a white strip at their base. The white indicated the "dashing surf of terribly excited waves."

"We are lost, your reverence," Dubois exclaimed. "It is impossible for me to keep the canoe balanced in those double and triple breakers."

"Paddle on, dear Dubois—straight on," returned Baraga. "We must get through, and a way will offer itself."

Dubois shrugged his shoulders, said his last prayers and paddled toward the rocky shore. As they approached the shore, the noise from the surf became so deafening they could no longer hear each other. Dubois slipped his jacket from his shoulders, preparing for a swim. All at once, a dark spot opened up in the white edge of the surf, which soon widened. At the same time, the violent heaving of the canoe relaxed. The vessel glided into the perfect safety of the broad mouth of a stream. Dubois did not see the stream mouth from a distance because the rocky cliffs concealed it.

"Did I not say, Dubois that I was called across, that I must go, and that thou wouldst be saved with me?" Baraga spoke to his guide as soon as they stepped on shore. "Let us pray!" The wet and cold travelers then went into the forest, cut down two trees and erected a cross as a sign of gratitude on the spot where they landed.

Later, a rich fur trader heard of the miraculous journey and at his own expense had a more substantial cross erected on a higher rock. The monument became known as "The Cross of Baraga's Traverse."

"Baraga is made of iron," wrote Kohl. "Nothing holds him back and he lives even in places where an Indian would die of starvation." The privations and hardship did take their toll in later life. In 1865, the bishop admitted as much: "Now I first feel the results of my former mission hardships and physical exertions. I was told long ago that I would feel it in my old age, but at that time I did not believe it. Now I believe it, because I feel it."

This cross marks the spot above where Baraga and Dubois landed safely after their all-night trip across Lake Superior in a canoe. (Courtesy of the Diocese of Marquette Archives)

The Resolution

Baraga began a daily diary just before his 55th birthday on June 27, 1852. About a month later, Rome approved the establishment of the diocese of Upper Michigan, appointing Baraga bishop of Sault Ste. Marie. He moved his permanent residence from L'Anse to the Sault but spent little time there. In 1853, he traveled to Cincinnati for his formal induction as bishop. Shortly afterward, he left for Europe, staying abroad until late summer 1854.

Baraga chronicled details of his meetings and travels in his diary. At first, little mention was made of the weather. In fact, for the first four years, writings were sporadic with gaps of several weeks or more between entries. It's as if the bishop didn't want to be bothered with mundane details. Toward the end of 1856 he made this resolution: "This has not been a real diary because I did not record something every day. From Nov 1 I intend to record something every day." On October 30th, he tersely noted, "*Superior*' shipwrecked." On the 1st he began a daily record that gives us a glimpse of the winter of 1856-57, the harshest winter in the early pioneer days of the Upper Midwest.

1856-57: "The Severest Winter Ever Known"

"An extremely snowy day" greeted people going to the polls on November 4. This full 24-hour storm led the Bishop to predict, "It seems we will have a snowy November." Over the next few days, in typical November fashion, it snowed and thawed with an all day fall that melted on contact November 15. A period of mild weather melted the existing snow cover by the 24th. Then on the 29th, an all-day storm put down a blanket of snow that would last well into spring.

On December 2, the day started "very nice and sunny, but only in the morning. In the afternoon it clouded over." These clouds heralded the arrival of a snowstorm that was already making news to the southwest. "The Severe Plains Storm of December 1856" encompassed a huge area from Kansas and Nebraska to Iowa, southern Minnesota and the western Great Lakes. One pioneer in Kansas wrote, "I have spent fifty-two winters in Kansas and have passed through many blizzards, but for the amount of snow, high wind and intense cold, I think none have equaled the one…[of]…December…[1856]."

This system was the classic 'panhandle hook' that developed off the Rockies, and then likely headed southeast to the Oklahoma-Texas panhandles where it then "hooked" northeastward. In Iowa, snow, strong winds and falling temperatures made it a storm remembered for decades. In 1913 a Des Moines newspaper devoted a column to its description. It was judged the area's worst storm, with drifts three- to five-feet deep. No mail was delivered for ten days. Dubuque had between 16 and 18 inches, though measurement was difficult because the snow "was swept through the streets by an angry wind with blinding velocity."

The storm then raged into Wisconsin on its trek northeastward. At Platteville, 14 inches of snow fell, accompanied by vivid lightning and heavy thunder. The temperature fell to 2 above. In Milwaukee "it was almost as wild a day as we have ever seen." Gale force winds piled up huge drifts in town and whipped up massive waves on Lake Michigan. An unknown number of vessels were still anchored in the bay, "but the storm was so thick that none could be fairly distinguished."

The northern reaches of the storm hit eastern Upper Michigan on the 3rd. Baraga noted that the day was "very stormy and cold." He was aware of at least one vessel left on the lake, which led him to write, "Poor people on the *General Taylor* (the vessel that saved the day with a last minute run to Marquette and Ontonagon a short time later) who are on Lake Superior." The storm then headed northeastward, likely parking itself over eastern Canada, sending bitter northwest winds across the unfrozen lake and dumping lake-effect snow on the Sault. On December 4, he wrote, "It snows very heavily." On the 5th: "It again snows heavily." The 6th also saw it "snowing very hard."

The rest of December was a true winter month. At Fort Ripley, in central Minnesota, the average temperature for the month was only 2.4 degrees. The lowest reading of 22 below zero came between the 12th and the 16th. Farther east, Bishop Baraga tried his hand at weather forecasting on the 14th when he wrote, "This evening is rather cold. It will be a cold night." It was a good forecast. On the 15th, his entry read, "indeed it was a very cold night."

January was a historically cold month. Fort Ripley's average temperature was a bitter 6.5 below zero. For fifteen days the temperature never topped zero, with a 40-below minimum on the 5th. A large part of the country experienced extreme cold. Readings as low as 50 below occurred in New Hampshire and Vermont, while New York City ended the month 11 degrees below average.

Bishop Baraga only mentioned the weather a couple of times during the rest of the winter. He seemed to be dealing with a bout of cabin fever on January 7 when he penned, "…filled the wood box. That is the most noteworthy that has occurred today. It is very cold. It will be a cold night." And on the 8th he appeared angry or bored: "Nothing! –It is foolishness to want to enter something everyday. Sometimes I really find nothing to enter." He left the Sault at mid-month for a trip to St. Ignace and Mackinac. On his way back home, he was forced to spend

Probable track of severe plains storm of 1856. It buried sections of the Kansas territory, Iowa and Wisconsin in an early-season blizzard. Baraga noted the storm's arrival at the Sault on December 3

the night outside on the 22ⁿᵈ. His entry for that day read: "Camped in a forest in a –40 F cold…I was in danger of freezing my face."

Harsh winter conditions continued the first half of February. The coldest temperatures recorded in early Minnesota history came on February 10 with a 50 below reading at Fort Ripley and a minus 56 reading nearby. The bitter cold finally broke the second half of February, with thawing weather on a number of days. To the east, Bishop Baraga did not even mention the weather in his diary until well into one of the most disagreeable springs ever experienced in the region.

"Bravo spring! O you delightful, charming month!—Month of Ice!" This tinge of sarcasm revealed Baraga's frustration on May 16 after he noted, "today it snowed again heavily." The backward nature of the spring of 1857 comes through the diary in an entry on May 8 when "finally this afternoon the first boat arrived [at Sault Ste. Marie], *Northstar*,

The steamer Northstar *was the first boat to arrive at Sault Ste. Marie during the backward spring of 1857. Baraga traveled frequently on the Northstar, a work-horse vessel during the early days following the building of the lock and canal in 1855. (Courtesy of Diocese of Marquette Archives)*

and right after it the second, *Illinois*." By the 10ᵗʰ, spring bowed to winter again as "it snowed heavily all day." On May 13 "the last little pile of snow…finally melted (only to be replaced by the May 16ᵗʰ storm)." But Baraga noted that the St. Marys River was "full of floating ice" even on May 21. At last, on May 23, it was warm enough so Bishop Baraga "*only* made a fire in the morning;" a sure sign that the long, cold winter of 1856-57 had finally ended. (*For more on this famous winter, see Snowstorms, Snowy Winters, page 147.*)

The Big Turnaround

The next winter saw a complete reversal of the bitter winter the year before. On October 19, 1857 it "snowed…for the first time but melted the next day." Winter set in by mid-November as "the church stoves heated for the first time." Then the mildest December in many years set in with no zero days reported out west in Minnesota. On New Year's Eve, Baraga noted, "…it does not freeze at all and is always calm. The river is as clear as summer; not a piece of ice on it." On January 5, he observed that there is "always fair weather, still no snow, nor is it windy; what snow there is almost melted." It turned "very slushy" on the 13ᵗʰ, which led the Bishop to write: "poor wayfarers." He was now almost 60 years old and he didn't travel as much during the winter. But he remembered how hard it was to get around when the snow was soft and heavy and thawing weather formed pools of water in the woods. "Soft" weather led to wet clothes and uncomfortable traveling.

Baraga's diary entries were peppered with sympathy for the "poor wayfarers" during times of "soft," thawing weather. These winter travelers enjoyed good solid ice and fresh snow in the late 1800s. (Courtesy of Marquette County History Museum)

Finally, in early February Baraga learned from the mail carriers that the ice was strong enough "at least for foot and dog." He left for Cincinnati by way of the north end of Georgian Bay for the Council of Bishops meeting, due to begin on the 12th. It had turned cold enough so there were no particular problems or dangers with taking a trip. However, he ran into the typical problems of pioneer travel during the winter when, on the 18th, he was forced to stay "in an Indian lodge, which was just a little better than outdoors." The next night he spent in an abandoned mail carrier's house without doors or windows. February was the only true winter month during the 1857-58 season. In Minnesota, February averaged almost eleven degrees lower than January with twelve mornings below zero. On February 28, Baraga observed that the canal between Cincinnati and Toledo was "frozen shut."

Spring arrived early in 1858. In Minnesota, wild ducks appeared on March 11. By the 18th, the Mississippi River was nearly clear of ice. Boats came up through Lake Pepin to St. Paul on the 25th, besting the previous spring's arrival time by five weeks. Baraga remained in Cincinnati during the spring for the Bishop's conference. However, he later made special note of the arrival in the Sault of the first steamboats on April 18, commenting, "…never have they come so early before."

The next winter started severe but turned mild. It rained in Sault Ste. Marie in the middle of winter on January 19, 1859. "The poor travelers!" wrote Baraga, "the ice is so weak the canal can be crossed only with danger. The risk did not seem to faze the old missionary. He ended the day's entry with the method he used to face the danger: "Alone I walked the ice." On February 19 it also rained. After a series of rainstorms, Baraga noted on March 10, "This is the mildest winter that I have seen in this country."

The end of March turned severe with a "terrible" snowstorm on the 29th and 30th. The Bishop felt that more snow fell on these two days than in the entire winter. On April 15, he devoted his whole entry to the weather, remarking on the severity of this "springwinter." "It snows nearly every day," he wrote. "The ice in the river, especially in Mud Lake is still thick and solid. I believe navigation will be late this year." It turned out to be a good prediction; the boats didn't arrive at the canal until May 3.

On May 15, Baraga finally left the Sault for a tour of the Ottawa missions. He had to wait because the ice remained on area lakes and rivers through the first part of May. The difficult journey was made even more unpleasant since some nights were spent camping on the shore of Lake Michigan. These spring nights in 1859 "were very cold." As late as June 13, Baraga complained of the cold: "On the return trip, in the night, which was stormy and cold, we had to disembark and spend the night on the shore." He related how he was forced to curl up on the cold sand, shivering all night. The following morning he "could barely speak and also could scarcely get up." He came down with a bad cold but joyfully arrived back home on June 17.

The next season started with a snow on September 14 that "disappeared quickly." The next few weeks Baraga waited patiently for "three new laborers" for his diocese. One of them, Father John Chebul, arrived with much "surprise" and "rejoicing" on October 13, 1859.

A Rough First Year in the Lake Superior Wilderness

Chebul, a fellow Slovenian, was born in Baraga's home province of Carniola 27 years to the day before his arrival at the Sault. He arrived at twilight at the door of the Bishop's "little house, a miserable, wooden cathedral." as Chebul called it, in "deep slushy mud and a sharp wind." The two men passed the evening in "pleasant conversation" and the next morning the young priest set off for his post, the "big mission of Minnesota [mine]," near Ontonagon.

His journey on the steamer *Mineral Rock* was a long and tedious eight day voyage over a stormy Lake Superior. Several times the boat was forced into a harbor or bay to wait out squally weather. Chebul admitted to sinking into a melancholy that he "could barely overcome" during the voyage. His courage was bolstered, however, with a pleasant visit with Reverend Thiele in Eagle Harbor on the 6th day of the trip. The missionary Thiele assured the young priest that he would quickly learn the languages missionary work in the Upper Michigan wilderness settlements required (in eight months Chebul mastered English and French).

A letter to his cousin illustrated the loneliness and isolation the young missionary felt during his first months in the rugged Lake Superior region. He held off on writing the letter for a year because he knew "that there will be more than five piles of grief spilled over" it. He described what it looked like to him as he surveyed the landscape: "a horror overcomes me as I look from some heights—upon the black ground…there is no hill – no mountain – no snow peaks… [only]…terrifying forest without end, without limits…."

Father John Chebul (1832-1898) came from Baraga's native Slovenia and arrived in the Lake Superior region on his 27th birthday in 1859. He had a difficult first year in Upper Michigan, but then spent most of the rest of his life in the region. (Courtesy of the Diocese of Marquette Archives)

Father Chebul's first winter in the Lake Superior wilderness was quite an initiation. It was one of the

Chebul, traveling on snowshoes in a blizzard, was saved by the unexpected arrival of a horse-drawn sleigh, probably similar to the one pictured, after he fell into the state of semi-consciousness in December 1859. (Courtesy of Superior View)

coldest Decembers in the early Upper Midwest frontier period. Fort Snelling in Minnesota had 15 days during the month with zero or lower. Fort Ripley to the north had a mercury thermometer congeal at 40-below on December 7. Chebul wrote of his suffering during that December: "First, a piece of my ear fell off—on December 4, 1859. Secondly, my soul already had a peek into eternity." This brush with death occurred on a December 21 and 22 trip through the backcountry.

Chebul visited a mine 22 miles from Ontonagon, said mass and set off for Ontonagon in a heavy snowstorm with "a dangerous north wind." He waded eight miles through the drifts and spent the night in an unoccupied cabin. As the priest slept, it continued to snow and the wind "did not whistle, it howled," he later recounted. "The cabin did not shake, it crackled." The next morning he set out and waded through the first five miles "rather easily." The next eight miles became a nightmare as fatigue overcame the young missionary. "I began to move the snow in front of me, 3 feet high, and then sat down and rested." As he rested in the below-zero-cold, his sweaty clothes froze solid which made moving nearly impossible. During the next hour he "scarcely made 50 steps." With snow up to his chin, Chebul pushed himself forward but his cold, tired limbs became useless against the mountain of white. The young priest did what Baraga had feared doing during his harrowing all-night walk nearly a decade before; he fell asleep. He tried to struggle up and move forward, but all his strength had given out. At that point he commended his "soul to God" and dozed off again.

Suddenly, the semi-conscious traveler heard human voices. It seemed impossible that someone would be on this deep-woods trail during a storm, but there was. He was saved! An American agent and his wife were riding by sleigh to Ontonagon on special business. Chebul called for help.

The man, "although a protestant," took pity on the priest and invited him into the sled. The poor horse had struggled before with just the agent and his wife but now with the priest aboard, it became an even greater exertion to wade through the drifts. The agent's wife apparently had more compassion for the horse than for the priest and bade her husband to order Chebul to walk alongside the sleigh. "The man, though unwilling," ordered the exhausted priest out. Chebul obeyed, stepped out, collapsed and remained lying face down in the snow.

At this point the man ignored his wife, got out, and helped the exhausted, frozen clergyman back into the rig. The agent then tried to wade through the mountainous drifts alongside the sleigh. He, too, found the going most difficult, so he also got back in. The "poor animal had to pull all three to the first human habitation" where Chebul got out, thanked his rescuers, thawed out and rested.

Bishop Baraga transferred Father Chebul to La Pointe (Madeline Island) in May 1860. Chebul spent twelve years at the west end of Lake Superior, did some traveling, and spent the rest of his working life in the Indian missions of Wisconsin. He became famous throughout the Upper Great Lakes for his dedication and endurance. Chebul could walk 60 to 70 miles at a time on snowshoes. Indians and trappers would know when he was on the trail by the bloody tracks his feet left in the snow.

Another "Tramp" for the "Old Mission Bishop"

During Chebul's first winter on the west end of the U.P., the indomitable Snowshoe Priest made yet another long winter journey to missions in Mackinac and St. Ignace. He had promised to confirm some fishermen, who would be gone during the spring and summer when he usually visited the area. Baraga seemed less than enthusiastic about another long tramp on snowshoes. He complained that he was out of practice and "already somewhat stiff," and because of past hardships, he was prone to feel the cold more. "Marching throughout the day is still tolerable," he explained, "but when it comes to the evening, to spend the night under the open sky in this northerly climate that does not go well. If on these winter journeys I could come every evening to a house, then they would not be difficult for me. But in this desolate country one must travel many days before he again comes to a house."

Nevertheless, the bishop kept his word and set out on "this dangerous march" on February 6. "God grant me a successful journey," he wrote. "I feel that my loins are a little tired; I don't know if it is fear, or a reality." The first day went well as Baraga's two companion-guides walked ahead, trampling down the snow a bit to make it easier for the "old mission bishop" to walk. They made 20 miles the first day and stayed in an old Indian lodge, which, while it didn't have a door, was warmer than staying under only "the dusky, gray heavenly arches over us."

The next day started with "a frugal breakfast that…consisted of tea and bread". The second day's tramp went well until evening when Baraga "felt a terrible fatigue, so that I could scarcely keep on my feet." They stopped to camp and his companions scraped the area clean of snow and chopped a few pine boughs that served as their beds under the open sky. A big fire helped to take the chill out of the night and warm some melted snow-water for tea. After a prayer, the bishop retired to his "cold bed and slept only a little from time to time." On the third day, Baraga was already feeling tired at noon when they stepped out on the "deeply frozen-over Lake Huron" for the last fifteen miles of the journey. They had walked only a short distance "when an extremely welcome scene came before…[their]…eyes". The people of Pointe St. Ignace and Mackinac, anticipating the bishop's arrival, sent "more than twenty nicely decorated sleds" to meet him. After expressing his gratitude and giving his blessing "with deep emotion," the entourage transported the weary travelers at "the fastest pace" over the ice to Pointe St. Ignace.

Baraga stayed in old, abandoned cabins and Indian lodges during his winter treks. If there was no shelter available, he and his guides would wrap themselves in blankets and sleep out under the stars. (Courtesy of Superior View Studio)

The eight-day stay at the mission was a huge success for Baraga. He confirmed 172 persons at Mackinac and St. Ignace. No outstanding weather events took place the first few days, though it was "a very cold day after a cold night" on the 16th. After the cold spell, a major change in the weather pattern took place. On February 22 "it *rained* (!!!) and stormed all night and all day; it was by no means a traveling day," chronicled Baraga. However, the weather improved the next day and he began his trip back home. Baraga wrote that he "endured two days and two cold and very unpleasant nights" on his return to the Sault but arrived with "great satisfaction" on the 25th: "Thanks be to God! I am very well."

1860: A Warm Spring and Extended Fall

The spring of 1860 turned out to be one of the mildest in early pioneer history. March 5 was described as a "beautiful spring day" in Stillwater, Minnesota. It reached a balmy 66 degrees at Fort Ripley on the 16th. Farther east, Bishop Baraga exclaimed it was "a wonderful nice day!" on March 31. "March has its twisted tail," he penned. "This year it twisted for the better. – Would that every spring this would happen." Despite the warmth and a series of summer-like days during April, the bishop still waited "with yearning, a boat from above, on Lake Superior" as late April 26.

Baraga left for a trip to the Copper Country on the steamer *Lady Elgin* May 1. He noted that it had snowed a little the night before: "a nice white beginning of beautiful spring." As the steamer made its way to Whitefish Point, it "met immense fields of floating ice extending on all sides as far as the eye could see." The trip was delayed by about twenty hours "until the wind drove the ice ahead." He lamented the harshness of the Lake Superior climate even in the midst of a warm spring when he compared the region to Russia: "St. Petersburg is already free of ice by this time in April."

That next fall the *Lady Elgin* went missing during a mid-September storm with more than 300 lives lost. Overall, autumn was mild in 1860. Baraga noted many calm, nice days all the way through the middle of November. Winter set in, as usual, by the end of November with snow from time to time and a very cold and stormy day on the 24th. The bishop could gauge church attendance by the severity of the weather, and on Sunday, November 25 he counted "very few people in church." He noted that the five-year-old canal, "the very costly gate, the largest gate in the world is useless this year, it cannot be closed" because it is "frozen hard." Four days later two boats managed to pass through the canal, heading south as winter closed in.

The winter of 1861 was a near normal season with a cold January. On New Year's Day, the river was not yet frozen, and according to the bishop it was "not cold at all, but much snow." By the 3rd the river was "frozen over hard." On the 12th, Baraga recorded a temperature of 40 below zero.

The January thaw held off until mid-February in 1861. It was a very cold night the day after Baraga bought a pair of snowshoes. He was very pleased with the deal he got. They only cost him three dollars and they were judged "very strong, not at all expensive." By the 10th the weather had warmed up considerably so that the bishop felt it would rain soon. It did so the next morning, moving him to feel sympathy, as always, for "the poor travelers."

A Most Difficult Journey

Baraga again joined the ranks of the travelers on April 1, 1861. He was to attend another Council of Bishops in Cincinnati on April 28. The bishop decided to walk to Mackinac rather than risk waiting for a boat to arrive at the Sault: "If I waited for the opening of navigation here, I would yet be in my own residence on the 28th of April." He hoped the ice would be gone at Mackinac Island "where the winds have great sway, and break and drive away the ice, sooner than it can melt in our quiet St. Marys river." The ice had not melted and the "old Indian Missionary inured to such inconveniences" rode across the Straits on a horse, "which on the way back fell in a crack in the ice and there perished."

The accident may have been an omen for the difficulties that lay ahead for the 63-year-old bishop. It took him five days over "good and bad, but predominantly muddy roads to reach Lake Huron where he came to "a small beginning of a town...named Alpena." He had not felt well for the past few days and retired to bed where he stayed for several days.

Baraga was never the same after this difficult march. On subsequent journeys he would often suffer chest pains along with great fatigue. He recovered sufficiently to continue the journey. However, even though "the ice had been driven out by the wind" no boat arrived. The wait became unbearable for the restless bishop.

Father Jacker, one of Baraga's caretakers during his last years, noted how difficult it was for the bishop to wait. "The good old man had not the patience of a saint at

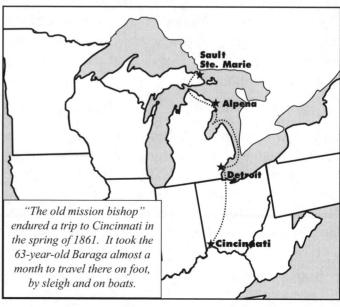

"The old mission bishop" endured a trip to Cincinnati in the spring of 1861. It took the 63-year-old Baraga almost a month to travel there on foot, by sleigh and on boats.

Father Edward Jacker (1827-1887) took care of Bishop Baraga during his final days in Marquette. (Courtesy of the Diocese of Marquette Archives)

such occasions," he wrote some years later. "It was the energy of his will always bent on the thing before him. His mind, at such times, must have been in the state of a healthy stomach to which food is denied: a terrible gnawing! He was no contemplative."

This "gnawing" clearly comes through in his entries during the following days. On the 15th he penned: "Still no boat. Spent the entire day in a cold little room, in great boredom waiting for the news that a boat is coming." On the 17th he again spent the day in oppressive waiting: "sat all day in my cloak. Until now have never known what boredom was, as I do here." By the 18th the situation became critical, as he described it as "one of the saddest days in my life." The weather did not help lift his spirits as it was "a dusky, stormy day; it snows and storms terribly."

Finally on the 19th he boarded a "fishboat" with the assurance he would arrive soon at Saginaw. The vessel only made it to a small town 38 miles away where a contrary wind caused another delay. The other passengers chose to walk to Sable River, 18 miles away. Baraga alone had to stay, admitting he was not able to walk "a distance of one mile" anymore. After more days of waiting, he finally set out to find another boat. He had barely walked a half-mile when he felt "such a tightness and oppressiveness" in his chest that he was forced to turned back. Later that day, the *City of Cleveland* arrived and Baraga sailed to Detroit. He arrived at Cincinnati with one day to spare before the Council began. It had taken him almost four weeks to make the journey.

Late the next summer on a mission trip downstate, Baraga became ill after a tedious voyage by boat that involved "continuous rowing" and an overnight camp under the stars. After an all-day, "unpleasant journey" he arrived at his destination that evening, sick. He then spent the next two days in bed and arose on the next day still feeling weak. He later confided that this entire summer was spent with pressure and discomfort in his chest whenever he "walked only a short distance." It was another reminder of the toll his missionary hardships had wrought and a sign that the end was near.

1861-62: A Slow Start Leads to "Good Solid Winter"

The next year saw a mild beginning to the winter season. The end of November did bring a bitter day to Fort Ripley, Minnesota. On the 30th, the post reported its coldest November temperature at 25 below zero. The same day at the Sault Baraga reported "it is snowing rather hard." The day before, the *General Taylor* passed through the unfrozen canal and became the last boat through the locks in 1861. The heavy snowfall and lack of ice coincident with the Minnesota cold illustrates the warming influence of Lake Superior during the fall and early winter.

Warmth was not just confined to the lakeshore during December. The twelfth month came in much above average in Minnesota after a chilly start. By December 6, Baraga reported "all the snow melted" at the Sault. Rain fell on the 9th, and he pronounced it "a beautiful summer day" on the 12th. The last day of 1861 the Bishop commented on the "very mild weather" and lamented "there is almost no ice on the river."

1862 started stormy, cold and windy. Baraga gave thanks for the cold and wanted more. "Would that it were very cold, so we can get some ice," he wrote. He got his wish. The next two months saw "good solid winter." In Minnesota, temperatures averaged well below average during January. February turned even colder. Fort Ripley had readings below zero every morning between the 13th and 20th with a nadir of minus 43 on the 14th.

Baraga made two mission trips during this cold February. He felt obliged to make the first visit to an Indian Mission at St. Martin's Bay, near present-day Hessel, because he was the only priest in the area who could speak the language. He departed with a guide on February 5, an unusually "mild, still day" during this otherwise frigid month. They had "scarcely gone a mile" when he was overtaken by the now familiar "heaviness and pressure" in his chest: "I thought I would have to fall. I recommended myself to God and walked on. The pressure gradually decreased and finally disappeared entirely. Although for several successive days I went over very difficult roads, I, nevertheless, felt no difficulty anymore."

His return trip went smoothly. On the 11th he "marched all day, well and comfortable." The next day, two mail carriers overtook Baraga and his guide and "went on ahead to the Sault, making an excellent trail" that made for a quick homecoming.

The second trip began on February 20. The old bishop got up early and "confidently set out" for Goulais Bay north of the Sault. He carried with him the nagging fear that the "pressure on the chest" would again return. But, "thanks be to God," he later wrote, "I walked all day easily and rapidly over hill and valley." The revitalized missionary covered approximately 20 miles in seven hours. He stayed several days at Goulais Bay, giving instruction and announcing "the word of God in a poor hut." He promised the small community a church the next spring and returned home on the 26th. The next day Baraga noted "this is a stormy and very cold day. Thanks be to God I am here and not on the trail."

March of 1862 began like a lamb with mild weather, and Baraga reported nice days throughout the month. On the 29th, however, he observed "windy, unfriendly weather" and the month ended with "hail," or more likely sleet, on the 30th. April was quite mild but "always windy." Baraga lived in the elements during his legendary travels and had a keen sense and intuitive feel for the weather. He knew that spring and fall were transition seasons that brought changeable, often wild weather to the Lake Superior region. He put the windy weather of April 1862 in perspective, noting that the wind was a product of "equinoctial storms by observation."

The mild April weather brought tragedy on the 12th. A resident of Sugar Island, "the 17-year-old son of St. Cyr, drowned coming across weak ice" that afternoon. The next several days brought rain and mud. By the 18th it was "terribly dirty and muddy every where." The warm weather brought a relatively early start to navigation; on the 27th, despite snow and rain, "the first boat came up" and the Sault emerged from its winter slumber.

Baraga lamented the isolation of winter at Sault Ste. Marie. He admired "the charming little town" of Marquette where transportation by stage and railroad came much earlier than at the Sault. (Image courtesy of the Diocese of Marquette Archives)

The winter isolation of Sault Ste. Marie frustrated Bishop Baraga. He admired the progress in winter transportation farther west in the mining districts of Upper Michigan. There communication was "very much facilitated" by stagecoaches and railroads. "On the other hand," he lamented, "in Sault Ste. Marie one is entirely locked in for five or six months in a prison of ice and snow." The Sault still depended on mail delivered by sled as late as the early 1860s. In late January 1862 Baraga commented there was "still no mail, although…[it has been]…hourly awaited for the last 5 days." He looked west to Marquette, "a charming little town on Lake Superior" which he noted was "still small, [but] increasing very much. This summer about forty new homes are being built." The Sault was no longer the center of commerce and communication on the peninsula and Baraga knew a move was imminent. He settled in Marquette in 1866 where he stayed until his death in 1868.

1862-63: The Last Winter of the Diary—A Remarkably Warm Start

"*Misere!*—A gloomy day; it was hardly or scarcely day all day." Baraga's entry November 1, 1862 revealed one of the trademarks of the eleventh month in Upper Michigan; the days get shorter and seasonal shifts in temperature bring more cloudy days than any other month except December.

On the 4th the Bishop left on a late-season trip to Ontonagon. He boarded the *Northern Light* at the Sault and the vessel only made it to Whitefish Point, where remained the next 36 hours. The trip consumed most of the month, with stops in Marquette, Hancock, Copper Harbor and the mining district around Ontonagon. The voyage back was delayed at Copper Harbor by stormy weather on November 22. On the 24th, *Northern Light* docked in Marquette all day loading iron ore and pig iron. The boats of the day were all-purpose vessels, tooled for carrying passengers and hauling raw materials. In the evening as they were about to cast off, a storm arose and they remained in the bay. The gale continued all the next. "The ship rolled very much," wrote Baraga, "which made me very sea sick." Finally, after another delay in Waishking Bay at the far eastern end of the lake, Baraga arrived home on November 27.

December began with snow, and then a thaw set in. It rained all day on the 13th and Baraga noted the snow was almost entirely melted by the 15th. Just before Christmas he lamented,

"It does not want to snow, although we wish for snow." Snow held off right through New Year's Eve day when Baraga penned, "beautiful weather! The old 1862 makes a nice exit."

The "open" winter continued into early 1863. A diarist in Minnesota wrote on January 1: "We have had two rains this winter lately, a thing altogether unusual for Minnesota. Ground still bare and ice on lake still unsafe. Weather mild." To the northeast, Baraga noted "very mild and windstill weather" the same day. It took until January 17 for the ice on the river to become firm enough to cross with a horse. Some snow fell, but Baraga complained the amount "was much too little for our desires." Toward the end of the month a stretch of mild weather opened up the St. Marys River again.

February 1863 exhibited more normal winter conditions. The month began cold and stormy. On the 2nd Baraga wrote: "Thanks be to God...it snows heavily." That night was judged the coldest night of the winter. Out west in Minnesota, it reached only 14 below for a high on February 2 at Fort Ripley. The morning of the 3rd a bitter 43 below was recorded. At the Sault, the rest of the month turned variable with alternating periods of cold and mild weather.

Baraga "assumed the occupations of a simple priest for the entire winter" in 1863. The former pastor at Sault Ste. Marie, "an Irish priest,...began to show an inclination for strong drink" during the latter part of 1862. Baraga, a strict teetotaler, "in order to avoid a scandal which could have occurred," dismissed the priest in November just before the close of navigation. The Bishop then found himself "alone for all the functions of the holy ministry." Word on a replacement pastor did not come. On February 9 Baraga wrote: "When there is no more navigation, then there is no more communication in this country." The added duties brought "a little misery" to the aging prelate. He described a difficult winter journey in a letter to a benefactor: "The other day I was called to a sick person seven leagues [about 17 miles] from here, across ice and snow, in piercing cold."

March 1863 continued the variable trend set the month before. At mid-month, the weather turned milder and the approaching vernal equinox signaled "sugar time." The last several days of the month turned unpleasant with stormy, cold days. Baraga proclaimed the night of March 28 "the coldest...of the winter, in my opinion." And the night of April 1st

John Bouche served as a guide to Baraga during his early days in the Lake Superior region. (Courtesy of the Diocese of Marquette Archives)

he judged the windiest of the entire winter. Baraga speculated on the reason for the blustery weather and concluded: "The March moon is still with us, that is it."

April 5, 1863 was Easter Sunday, "a nice, mild, windstill day." Adjectives like "uncommonly" and "unusually" were peppered throughout the pages of the bishop's diary

Bishop Baraga, weathered and worn, after more than 30 years of privation and hardship in the Lake Superior wilderness. This photo was taken in 1867, a year before his death at age 71. (Courtesy of Diocese of Marquette Archives)

during the rest of the month to describe the mild, placid state of spring 1863.

"Boredom" was another word that cropped up a couple of times. Baraga was waiting for the first boat of the season, which was slow in arriving despite the "splendid spring." On April 21 he noted that the ice and snow was all gone and "the boats could have come a few days ago if they had known what we now know." On April 28, the *Mineral Rock* finally arrived and by evening three more boats pulled into the Sault, signaling the beginning of the shipping season and an end to winter's isolation.

The diary entries ended in the summer of 1863 (Baraga reportedly kept the journal going until September 1866 but those volumes are lost). His last entry on July 16 ended, appropriately, with a comment on the weather: "Very cool, yes, cold. This morning I made a fire in the stove, in spite of July."

Father Baraga labored in the Lake Superior region for over three decades. During this time, Upper Michigan went from an isolated wilderness to a booming mining and lumber region, feeding raw materials to the insatiable appetites of cities and industry to the south. The end of the Pioneering Era can be arguably set at the Civil War. Baraga lamented the "terrible" war and the toll it took on this country. While he noted the hardships visited on his parishioners due to the war, he admitted: "In this diocese, so remote, there is less to see and hear in this regard than in the southern parts of this country."

PART II

CHAPTER 6

COLD WAVES, COLD WINTERS

Nestled in forests and in close proximity to the warming influence of the Great Lakes, Upper Michigan residents generally escape the brutal cold and wind felt on the Prairies and Plains to the west. On the other hand, we get our share of chill during a normal winter. Below zero readings can occur from late November to early April, and in some of the harsher cold seasons, there are long stretches where the temperature stays below freezing.

This section examines some of the memorable cold seasons and cold days and how this extreme weather affects our people and infrastructure. The patterns that lead to extreme U.P. cold will also be illustrated.

Cold New Year's Day of 1864

January 1, 1864 was long remembered as "The Cold New Year's Day," from the Rockies to the Appalachians, including Upper Michigan. The arctic blast brought "the greatest combination of cold, snow and blow" in the Middle West's recorded history. Two deep low-pressure systems tracked from the Southern Plains to the Great Lakes the last four days of December 1863, dumping heavy snow to the northwest of their centers. After the first storm passed, arctic air bottled up in western Canada made a move southeast into the Northern Plains as far east as Minnesota. The second storm moved on a similar path, developing a raging snowstorm with gale force winds from Iowa and Missouri into the Western Great Lakes and Upper Michigan. This low center passed over Alpena just after midnight New Year's Eve. As the storm pulled quickly into Canada, the dam burst; frigid air surged east and southward on gale-force northwest to westerly winds.

Temperatures remained below zero all New Year's Day from Minnesota to Ohio and from the Canadian border to Tennessee. St. Paul, Minnesota never had a colder day. The temperatures at 7 a.m., 2 p.m. and 9 p.m., respectively, were: 35 below, 25 below and 28 below. In Milwaukee, at the same times, the observed readings were: 27 below, 23 below and 23 below. The low temperature for the day was a record 30 degrees below zero. Chicago had its all-time low temperature of 25 below. It dropped to 10 degrees below as far south as Memphis, Tennessee.

Up north on the shores of Lake Superior it was judged "about the coldest… day… that had been experienced." The daytime high in Marquette was 18 degrees below zero with a low of 31 below. The mines to the west reported readings as cold as 35 degrees below.

The Cold Winter of 1875

Most years from the late 1860s through the 1880s featured long, cold winters. One of the longest was 1872-1873, which featured the famous "ice blockade". This is Marquette harbor in June 1873. (Courtesy of Superior View, Marquette)

In general, the winters of the 1870s and 1880s were unusually severe (*there is one glaring exception later in this chapter, page 119*). A daily stagecoach line was set up across the ice from Marquette to Bay Furnace (near present day Christmas); it operated during a number of years for up to three months at a time. The coldest winter of this period began in late December 1874.

The fall of 1874 was exceptionally mild. The temperature reached 71 degrees in Marquette on October 25. After a cooling trend brought a little snow on the 29th, more warmth developed in November, with high temperatures in the 60s from the 6th through the 8th. The mild spell culminated in a gale that tore away the front of Sam Risdon's residence in Marquette. Risdon had "to move his family and household goods to other quarters."

By the third week of November, winter had set in; there was enough snow in Ishpeming and Negaunee for "splendid" sleighing. In Marquette, the relatively warm water of Lake Superior delayed this winter activity, prompting a reporter in Ishpeming to quip "the city by the lake beats us on mud." Finally, a "delightful, old fashioned snowstorm" hit the area November 23 through 25; piling drifts around Marquette from five- to six-feet-deep. In Escanaba, the first substantial snow held off until the 29th.

By mid December, Ishpeming had a snow depth of at least two feet. *The Mining Journal* reported no snow in Green Bay, but the river and harbor was "frozen as solid as a granite quarry." The article went on to boast that in Marquette "we are still shipping ore from our docks, our harbor is as free from ice as in mid-summer, and it is more than probable that navigation will remain open till the middle of January." A swipe was then taken at Green Bay's paper: "Now let us hear from the *Advocate* about 'those long, tedious Lake Superior winters.'" The writer was unwittingly prophesizing what lay ahead the next few months for Upper Michigan residents.

The first brutally cold day occurred December 29. The early morning temperature in Marquette dropped to 10 degrees below zero with mid-afternoon readings barely rising above zero. Negaunee checked in with a morning low of 23 below, while Green Bay reported 20 below. The ice conditions on Lake Superior changed dramatically by the end of the month. Around the New Year, the propeller *Chaffe* was reported fast in the ice as she attempted to leave Grand Island harbor. A week later, the ship was still stuck about a mile from shore, as the coldest weather yet was about to settle in.

The propeller Chaffe became stuck in the ice as the cold intensified around New Year's Day 1875. (Courtesy of Marquette History Museum)

Saturday, January 9 brought a genuine zero day with the afternoon reading in Marquette marking only 10 below. A west wind gusting as high as 32 miles-an-hour accompanied the cold. Negaunee reported a "great many people" with frozen ears, fingers and toes as the temperature fell to 26 below that morning. In Ishpeming, nearly every water pipe "froze solid," a condition that only spread and worsened as winter wore on.

As the January cold spell continued, Upper Michigan residents settled in and made the best of it. Old man Satterlee, a Marquette grocer, offered a reward of $3.75 to anyone who would show him a mosquito. It was so cold, the loafers at his store "didn't pretend to go home for dinner, but just sat around the stove nibbling chunks of cold whisky." A reporter in Marquette wrote: "Up at Ishpeming they hang their thermometers up by the stove at night—to keep them from freezing." He went on to describe the preferred beverage of the mining community: "Whisky, straight and solid...."

The cold enveloped the rest of the Midwest in January 1875. In Green Bay it was so cold "the frost...pulled all the nails out of the best buildings in the city." In Missouri, "thermometers...were...busted all to smash by congealed mercury," implying the temperature reached the freezing mark of mercury—forty below zero.

By the third week in January Marquette Bay was "closed with ice." The closure was at least a month earlier than in any other year since the city was settled. In the 1800s, up until the time electricity came into wide use, the only way to have ice during the summer was to "harvest" it from area lakes and rivers during the late winter. The ice was cut out in large cubes then stored in an icehouse, covered in sawdust for insulation and pulled out when needed. In 1875 the harvest began two months earlier than usual. On January 23, the ice in Marquette Bay was "twenty inches thick, blue and transparent."

Ice formed incessantly during January as the first month of 1875 came in with an average temperature of 5.9 degrees, some 10 degrees below the recently established average. On 20 of 31 days the temperature fell below zero in Marquette. In Escanaba, the cold was consistent and unyielding, prompting a newspaper writer to complain that "the January thaw this year… was…a fraud and delusion."

In early February, the cold eased slightly as a great snowstorm pummeled the Upper Great Lakes. Snow fell heavily in Marquette from the evening of February 2 to the forenoon of February 4 accompanied by sustained northerly winds of 25 to 30 miles per hour. The snow piled into huge drifts, rendering streets and sidewalks nearly impassable. Train traffic came to a virtual standstill over all of the Upper Peninsula, as well as over most of the Western Great Lakes.

In Escanaba, the storm was judged the worst in years. As in Marquette, snow commenced on the 2nd and "continued all day and night and the following day and night," accompanied by a raging wind. The daily stage across the ice at Fayette left early on the morning of the 3rd, on a trip to Escanaba that would normally take between four and five hours. It finally reached its destination at 10 a.m. the following day. The stage was forced to stop at a farm on the Stonington Peninsula after the horses became so fatigued battling the wind and snow of the storm that it became impossible to drive them through.

Feb 3, 1875: Low pressure moved from the Kansas City area 24 hours earlier to near Rockford, IL. To its northwest, a raging blizzard engulfed parts of Iowa into Upper Michigan.
(NOAA Central Library Data Imaging Project)

The storm was a classic system that moved northeastward from the Southern Plains across the Lower Peninsula. Reports received via telegraph indicated a warm, gentle rain at Grand Haven with a strong southerly wind during the day on the 4th. The wind direction and precipitation type indicated that Grand Haven in southwestern Lower Michigan was in the "warm sector" of the low-pressure system. The storm passed north of the town later in the afternoon, followed by "a terrific gale of cold, blustering wind" from the southwest accompanied by blinding snow. The center of low pressure moved over Lake Michigan, and then headed northeastward for the Straits. As the storm deepened, winds reached 65 miles an hour at Grand Haven.

Northwest of the storm's track, a raging blizzard paralyzed the region from Iowa to Upper Michigan. Near Dubuque, an Iowa Central train became "stuck fast in a snowdrift." Thirty passengers on the train were stranded "without food or fire." In Ripon, Wisconsin, no trains arrived or left for three days. Ten-foot drifts shut down all business. In the wake of the storm, bitter cold air rushed into the central Wisconsin community on gusty northwesterly winds, dropping the temperature to 20 degrees below zero.

Snow measurements were not taken in any organized fashion in 1875. Strong winds accompanying the snow would have made measurement difficult, but the editor of Marquette's paper judged the storm "the worst we have known during our residence on Lake Superior."

Around Whitefish Point the storm was described as "fearful." Two miles inland from the point, at a settlement called Little Lake, residents had to raise flagpoles at their homes so they could find their way back after a trip to the neighbors. A resident was said to have "lost" his house after being gone "for an hour or so" during the storm. He passed "within two rods" of the house without noticing it. After a careful search in the drifts he located the roof of the structure and dug his way in. He found his wife in the dark, "badly frightened." They decided to evacuate their home and stay with neighbors, "concluding that if they were to be buried alive... [at least]...they would have company." At the conclusion of the blizzard, the snow at that location was six feet deep on the level.

The coldest weather of this bitter winter followed the storm. In Marquette, temperatures on the morning of February 9 ranged between 24 and 30 below zero. The cold across the rest of the Peninsula was unprecedented. L'Anse hit 35 below, Menominee 37 below, Houghton minus 38 and Escanaba an incredible 40 below zero. Michigamme was even colder. The mercury in a thermometer there congealed at minus 42. Negaunee reported "the lowest... [temperature]... ever known" there at 43 below, while Ishpeming checked in with minus 48. The nadir was reached in Champion, where Dr. Trest's

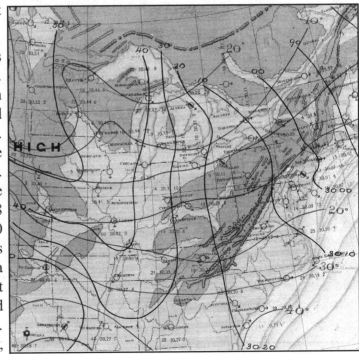

Arctic high pressure crested in the Plains on February 9, 1875. Note the 20 below zero isotherm to south of most of the U.P. Temperatures around 50 below zero were observed over portions of the central interior at sunrise. (NOAA Central Library Data Imaging Project)

Fireman of the late 1800s. The intense cold of 1875 led to frozen fire hydrants and near disaster in Marquette. (Drawing by E. Yelland)

spirit thermometer reached 51 degrees below zero and another "veracious inhabitant" close by got to minus 54!

Despite the intense cold, the daylight of the 9th was described as "remarkably pleasant": "There was no wind stirring, the atmosphere was dry, and the sun shone brightly, making the trees sparkle as if their branches were decked with millions upon millions of diamonds." An immense arctic high-pressure system likely crested over the Upper Lakes during the night of the 8th and lingered over the region the following day. The system brought bone dry, dense air with it, promoting clear skies and virtually no wind.

The cold raised havoc with Upper Michigan's 19th century infrastructure and led to inconvenience and near tragedy. Covered wells in Ishpeming as deep as sixty feet were frozen solid. In Negaunee, a large number of wells were so frozen it was "almost impossible to get any water out of them." Escanaba also reported many of the wells in town "frozen up." Settlements throughout the peninsula reported potatoes and other vegetables frozen in their root cellars. The liveryman in Ishpeming froze both cheeks and his nose one day driving his route to a mine a few miles away. In Marquette, a fire broke out in a school building on Washington Street. Firemen soon realized that nearly every fireplug in the city was frozen solid. After a frantic search, a working plug was found a couple of blocks away on Main Street. A thousand feet of hose was run from the plug to the fire, keeping the blaze from becoming a conflagration. The school building, however, was a total loss.

February 1875 became the coldest second month in Marquette's recorded history with a mean temperature of 1.8 degrees, more than 14 degrees below the long-term average. Out of any winter month on record, only January 1912 was colder. By mid-month, the ice in Marquette Bay was 31 inches thick. Duluth newspapers proposed building a railroad across the ice there, while the Marquette paper mocked the idea and marveled at "what awful long drunks those fellows...must be in the habit of indulging in."

Just as in January, the February cold covered a large portion of the country and northern Europe. It was reportedly so cold in Detroit that horses were frozen standing up. In Lansing, ice on the Grand River was five feet deep. Engineers began blasting ice out of the river in Chicago, while the Great Salt Lake in Utah froze over: "an event here to unknown, even to the oldest inhabitant's father." Across the Atlantic in Sweden, the temperature tumbled to an incredible 60 degrees below zero.

March began in the Upper Peninsula with a moderate snowstorm and below zero readings on the mornings of the 2nd and 3rd. Then a mild spell set in. "Patches of sidewalk" began to ppear, and the early March sun melted nearly all the snow on area roofs. Temperatures rose above freezing most afternoons from March 8 through13. The warm spell greatly improved the roads around Marquette, while Ishpeming's streets were "lined with the gay and the young" pent up so long by the cold. In Negaunee, the relaxation of the cold brought out a "champion lager drinker" who downed forty glasses of beer at a local tavern inside of three hours.

Milder weather brought out residents cooped up so long by the harsh winter of 1875. Among them was a champion beer drinker in Negaunee. These men raise a glass for the camera at an Upper Michigan saloon near the turn of the century. (Courtesy of Superior View)

"Another great snowstorm" commenced on Sunday evening the 14th and continued through the 16th. The drifts piled up by the storm "caused great inconvenience to pedestrians and teams" all over the mining districts of Upper Michigan. In Marquette, it began with wet, heavy snow and temperatures around freezing and ended in gale-force winds and readings near zero.

The mid-March storm dashed the hopes of an early breakup and prompted a request from the editor of Marquette's *Mining Journal* for "poems, sweet poems on the gentle springtime." The invitation was followed by the real reason for the request: "Our coal bin is getting low." One of the paper's reporters, in the flowery tradition of 19th century journalism, wrote: "Mournfully, oh so mournfully the cold west wind is sighing and coughing its last requiem over the waning winter; solemnly, oh so solemnly, do our people await the coming of the mud and slush of the approaching springtime."

In Marquette, the final below zero reading occurred on the first day of spring. The solemn wait for mud and slush ended the last five days of March as persistent southerly winds brought the first genuine taste of spring. Readings in the 40s and 50s culminated in thunder and lightning on April 1; a sign that the winter of 1875, one of the most severe ever recorded in Upper Michigan, was coming to an end.

1877-78: The Warmest Winter

This winter is included in this section because it was such an enigma and anomaly; an extraordinarily warm season amidst equally cold ones. Sometimes a mild winter will turn cold late; this one began warm and ended even warmer.

A significant player in this incredible season appears to have been El Nino. The SOI index, a measure of sea level pressure in the equatorial Pacific, showed a strong El Nino signature from September 1877 through March 1878. A strong El Nino correlates with warm, dry winter weather over the north-central portion of the United States, including

The Suffering of the Birds

The extended, severe cold of 1875 had far-reaching impact on wildlife, too. As an example, in the Baltimore area, thousands of crows died of starvation or froze to death, while hundreds of others were found blind, unable to navigate and find food. "A sort of fierce cannibalism" caused the blindness, where the starving birds picked at each other's eyes at night while on their roosts.

Wild ducks in the area were captured, "stupefied and starving." Robins wintering in the region exhausted all the food in outlying areas and converged on the city. They reportedly stripped holly trees of all their berries. In one instance, "there was a robin on a holly tree for almost every berry it bore."

In frozen Baltimore Harbor, a large number of crows and seagulls were seen commingling, "moved by one common impulse—the desire to find food." It was concluded that the crows, unable to find food on land, were driven by starvation to the refuge of the harbor.

(Photo by E. Yelland)

Upper Michigan. In a strong El Nino, a split occurs in the jet stream or storm track; one segment travels through the southern United States with stormy weather, while another segment is directed through central or northern Canada, keeping cold air bottled up to its north.

Snow cover is usually established for the winter over most of the U.P. during the latter part of November. The average date of permanent winter snow cover in the hills west of Marquette is around November 21. On this date in 1877, "a drizzling rain storm set in and lasted all day." The event was deemed a "most remarkable circumstance" for so late in the fall. Lake Angeline in Ishpeming was not yet frozen on November 24. It had been many years since the lake had been open so late in the season.

In Negaunee, a "driving snowstorm raged all day" on Thanksgiving Day, November 29. The snow fell so thickly at times it hindered a shooting match held in town that day. There likely was not much snow accumulation because in Ishpeming, they wanted more. "Come on, ye snowstorms!" wrote a reporter. "Two feet, three feet, ten feet—cover us up with snow, only don't let us see that outrageous hematite mud again for six months to come."

Despite the appeal, the mud reappeared again as December wore on. Complaints were registered in Negaunee that "sleighing was a decided failure" during the third week of the month. In many cases, wagons were brought back out for transportation. Even after Christmas, a dog sled race had to be cancelled in Ishpeming because, it was noted, "mud is a poor stuff for dogs to run through."

Out west in Ontonagon, lighthouse keeper Tom Stripe reported "No Snow, Warm Weather" on December 27. On the 30th he crossed the Ontonagon River in a boat because he observed no ice in the river and "no sine [sic] of snow."

December ended with an average temperature of 35.2 degrees, an incredible 12.3 degrees above normal.

Some genuine winter weather was felt as the new year began. The temperature dipped to 16 below zero in

Ishpeming one morning the second week of January. However, the lack of snow seriously hampered work at the Jackson Mine near Negaunee. Work had to be entirely suspended because of poor sleighing—a good snow cover was needed for hauling ore. The skating rink finally opened in that town in early January, but as the weather turned mild again, it was thought the rink might be forced to close.

On Lake Superior, "fishing boats were plying on Marquette Bay" at the end of the third week of January "attending to business with as little danger or obstruction as in mid summer." There was not enough snow in the city to afford comfortable sleighing. The pond in the cemetery, which was used for skating, remained unusable; the ice on it had "never been over an inch thick" all winter.

The Mining Journal claims a correspondent sent in a butterfly he had caught seven miles north of L'Anse on January 20. One source maintains that lilac bushes were budding in Marquette. By the end of the month, a reporter in Negaunee declared "storm doors are more ornamental than useful this winter." January ended in Marquette with an average temperature at 24.8 degrees, almost 9 degrees above average.

The Ontonagon lighthouse built in 1866. During late December 1877, the scene probably looked similar to this as incredibly mild weather prevailed. (Courtesy of the Ontonagon Historical Society)

In early February, the sleighing in Negaunee remained "just about so-so." In Marquette, there was speculation that ice would have to be transported in for next summer's use; no where in the vicinity was ice thick enough to begin the all-important ice harvest. The question was asked, "Is this the continuation of last fall or the beginning of next summer?"

There was a "light April shower" February 7 in Ishpeming. At the same time, plans were made for a sleigh ride and surprise party at Humboldt on February 15. It promised to be a grand affair. However, gentlemen would only be allowed to take along one bottle of whiskey apiece. The whole event hinged on snow; so it probably was cancelled. Two days before the party, a reporter in Marquette wrote: "Here it is the 13th day of February, and we sit in our den with a straw hat on, handkerchief around our neck to

The ladies of Ishpeming planned a sleighing party for the February 15, 1878. It was probably cancelled due to lack of snow. (Courtesy of Superior View)

keep off the sun's rays which reach us through the window. Outside, the earth is bare as in summer, parasols over the heads of our fair ones are many…rowboats are bounding o'er the waters of the bay." Sleighing was "completely ruined" in Negaunee and rubbish piles, usually buried in snow until late March or April, were completely bare and tinder dry.

Over other parts of the U.P., it was the same story. John Longyear traveled Menominee country as an agent for the Keweenaw Canal Company. He called the winter of 1877-78 the "Snowless Winter." "Almost no snow fell during the season," he recalled. "Lumbermen were put to great expense and inconvenience thereby, as they depended on snow to help move the logs." He reminisced about a trip through the south central U.P. between the Paint and Michigamme rivers. There was "just a sprinkle of snow on the ground" in the region during February, "just enough to make it white."

Daniel Ward Powell was logging in the Huron Mountains near Ives Lake back in the winter of 1878. He claims that horse manure sprouted oats that winter. Dan Hornbogen of Marquette, Powell's great-great grandson, researched the germination temperature of oats. "I…found for oats to germinate," he says, "it requires something like two weeks above 32 degrees." That sort of temperature regime was possible, especially during mid and late February of 1878.

In early March, a comparison was made between this winter and the winter of 1829-30. That winter was said to have been a "warmer one than the present, not a flake of snow falling until February 2nd." But, there was no permanent settlement in the Marquette area back in 1829-30. However, evidence provided by the writings of Henry Rowe Schoolcraft, who lived in the Sault (see "Warm Winters: 1828-31", page 42), supports the favorable comparison between these winters.

Lumbermen needed snow to move logs out of the woods. It was in short supply during the winter of 1877-78. (Courtesy of Superior View)

On March 9, a report came from Munising that the harbor and bay there were completely free of ice. "Steamboats can make excursions there now," the account continued, "and the passengers picnic in the woods the same as if it 'twas summer." In Marquette cattle, sheep and geese were already grazing in the pastures around town at the beginning of March. Women were "going around without their flannels" and men "without their undershirts."

In Ishpeming, "king mud" reigned supreme the beginning of March 1878. More snow likely fell in the hills west of Marquette before the big meltdown and that fact made for sloppier conditions than in the Queen City by the lake. Negaunee even reported a few traces of snow lingering on the hillsides. Those few patches of snow did not have a chance; they could not survive the warmest March ever recorded in the area. Marquette registered an astounding average temperature of 40.3 degrees, more than 16 degrees above normal.

This anomalous warmth brought the spring season in a month or more ahead of schedule. Navigation began on the bays of Lake Superior earlier than ever in 1878. Boats began moving between Houghton and L'Anse by mid-March. In Ishpeming, the "swamp frogs," or peepers, could be heard before St. Patrick's Day. Trees began to show buds in Negaunee and farmers began plowing their fields. "More lovely weather is scarcely within reach of the imagination," wrote a correspondent in Marquette. "Such an early spring is not within the collection [sic] of our oldest inhabitant."

The legend of the St. Patrick's Day storm was already alive back in the 1870s. In fact, the "first snowfall…in some weeks" occurred on the night of the 16th. It kept alive the myth of "the infernal blizzard that invariably accompanies" the March holiday. The "blizzard" hardly lived up to its name, however; it snowed and froze just enough to put a light coating on the ground that lasted through the morning of the 17th.

More signs of spring provided evidence of the unprecedented warmth. "The chirp of robins, bluebirds and woodpeckers" was heard after mid-month. On the big lake, the largest haul of whitefish in some time was taken out of Marquette Bay. Four-hundred-fifty pounds of the delectable fish were caught with a gill net just off Shot Point. It was considered a remarkable occurrence for so early in the season.

In Ontonagon, lighthouse keeper Stripe lit the lamp in the lighthouse on April 1, a very early date in the 1870s. The first steamer came into port the next day.

Comparisons can be

THE ST. PATTY'S DAY STORM

"There is always a St. Patty's Day storm." This matter-of-fact statement will often be heard when the subject of U.P. weather comes up; it is one of our more enduring weather myths. Evidence shows this supposed phenomenon is just that; a myth. In over 50 years, starting from 1949, there has been only one St. Patrick's Day with a bona fide snowstorm; that was in 1965. If you adopt the liberal view that a St. Patty's day storm can be either early or late, and include the entire month of March, the statistics are still much less than impressive.

First, we must define the term "snowstorm." For our purposes, it is characterized as a heavy fall of snow over a relatively short period of time, i.e. a 24 hour period. All data comes from National Weather

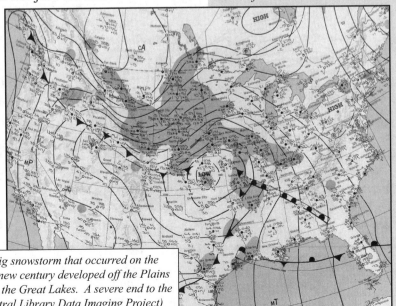

March 17, 1965. The only big snowstorm that occurred on the holiday between 1949 and the new century developed off the Plains and headed northeastward into the Great Lakes. A severe end to the month followed. (NOAA Central Library Data Imaging Project)

The aftermath of a "St. Patty's Day Storm" in Escanaba, 1919. (Courtesy of Delta County Historical Society)

made with this winter and other mild, open winters, but they all fall short in some way. For example, the winter of 1931-32 began very warm; December 1931 ended over nine degrees above average, while the next January wound up just over 11 degrees higher than the long-term norm. However, the latter part of winter cooled, with March actually coming in a bit below average. The winter of 1986-87 proved an exceedingly mild season with a warm March. However, there were a couple of late snowstorms, the heaviest of which edged into the first couple days of April 1987. Over 130 years of records show that the winter of 1877-78 stands alone for both its warmth and lack of snow.

Service (NWS) records in the Marquette area beginning in 1949. A "heavy fall of snow" is delineated in this way: nine inches or more in a 24-hour period in the city of Marquette at lake level, and 12 inches or more at the Negaunee Township site in the higher elevation west of town where snowfalls are usually heavier (The NWS moved their offices and hence, their observation point, from the city "up the hill" to Negaunee Township in 1979.).

For the entire month of March, only 11 heavy snowstorms occurred in the 30 years from 1949 to 1978; a paltry 37%. From 1979 on, the percentage rose to just over 50, higher, but still hardly worthy of the description "always."

Cold Years of the Mid-1880s

The mid-1880s were cold years, exacerbated by the explosion of Krakatoa in 1883. Krakatoa is a volcano located on a small island in Indonesia off the west coast of Java. After 200 years of inactivity, the volcano came to life in May 1883, culminating in a series of four catastrophic explosions in late August. The last of the explosions was heard 3,000 miles away. The total energy released during the cataclysm was equivalent to 200 megatons of TNT. By way of comparison, the atomic blast at Hiroshima released energy equivalent to 20 *kilotons* of TNT. Therefore, the Krakatoa blast was 100 times greater than Hiroshima!

The ash released from the volcano rose 50 miles into the atmosphere and plunged the area within a 50 mile radius of the crater into darkness for three days. The estimated 11 cubic miles of debris ejected into the stratosphere began circling the earth; it would do so for the next few years. The "volcanic dust veil" acted as a solar radiation filter, lessening the amount of sunlight reaching the earth. The veil reduced global temperature an estimated 1.2 degrees Celsius. It also led to spectacular sunsets in higher latitude locations, including Upper Michigan.

Newspaper articles in January 1884 and again in October 1884 mentioned the "extraordinary sunset phenomena caused by...volcanic dust." The October mention noted, "The sunsets have been as red for the past week as they were during the latter part of last winter." In mid-November, a reporter noted that "the sunrises have been worth seeing...the last three or four mornings."

The dust also helped lower temperatures. In Marquette, temperatures in 22 of 24 months were below normal following the eruption. The greatest departures from normal occurred during the winter months.

January 1884 came in more than 6 degrees below the long-term average. In late January that year, the temperature plunged to 47 degrees below zero in Republic. The Ishpeming reporter observed that "the atmosphere was almost frozen solid" on January 24, 1884. At the month's end, an observer in Marquette declared: "The first twenty-six days of January will bear comparison for steady cold with any period of equal length of which there is any record."

Krakatoa volcano just before the big explosion in 1883. Its effect on climate around the world, including Upper Michigan, lasted for at least two years. (Courtesy of Dr. George Pararas-Carayannis; http://www.drgeorgepc.com/)

February was even colder: over 7 degrees below average. In Ishpeming the thermometer registered a bone-chilling 34 degrees below zero February 28. March began cold but then an extended warm spell settled in. It rained all day on March 11. The rain turned area roads into a quagmire of mud and water, ruining sleighing. By the end of March, Escanaba reported "some of the pleasantest weather that was ever turned out." At Sault Ste. Marie, the mild weather gave the winter-bound residents visions of "the smoke from some incoming steamer" about ready to come around the bend. This was only illusion, however. Despite the "soft weather," The *Menominee Daily Herald* stated the ice on Green Bay was "as solid as the Rock of Gibraltar" the third week of March.

The relative warmth brought out wheeled vehicles. "Everything was running on wheels" in Negaunee from March 20 to April 14, 1884. Then a two-day snowstorm brought out the runners until the last week of April. After the storm, it was a disagreeable spring.

The light keeper at Ontonagon claimed "the entire length of April was a reverse of March" at his location. He noted cold, wintry weather deep into the fourth month. On April 26, a south to southwest wind finally moved the ice "off shore a short distance for the first time." However, the cold spring weather continued, and on the first day of May he could still observe ice on the lake "as far as the eye can see." He recorded ice along the shore in Ontonagon as late as May 19.

A diarist in Negaunee chronicled the more notable cold events of spring 1884: "April 28th,

Cold and Snow; May 2nd, slight snow flurry; May 13th and 15th, snow flurrys; May 27th Pretty cold, ice formed and overcoats worn with comfort."

Summer 1884 was generally cool with only June a little warmer than average. "A cold and drizzling rain" ruined July 4th festivities. The next morning "a visible snow flurry" was seen in the air at Negaunee. Fall brought "a great amount of wet weather." In Ishpeming, the excess rain brought concerns that the potato crop would rot in the fields. August, September and October each brought around five inches of rain.

In 1884, winter set in early. On November 7 the first sleigh bells of the season were heard in Negaunee. Much of Upper Michigan endured an extended stormy period from Friday, November 21 through the weekend. It snowed a couple of inches in Marquette Friday night, then warm southeast winds led to a drizzly rain all day Saturday. The wind shifted northwesterly at night and the rain changed to snow. Sunday morning "found a blizzard in full progress," complete with heavy snow and huge drifts. The brunt of the storm was felt from Seney westward. From Seney east to St. Ignace, snow on the railroad was reported "very light." After the storm, it "froze sharply." The mercury hit 10 degrees below zero in Michigamme Sunday night, while Ishpeming registered 14 below. In Negaunee, many water pipes were frozen by the early, unseasonable cold.

The early wintry blast brought smiles to area lumbermen. Enough snow fell to facilitate logging operations, while the cold froze the roads solid. The weather also brought inconvenience, misery and even tragedy on both land and sea. The fragile infrastructure of the nascent telephone company in the area saw "no end to trouble" because of the storm. The rain of Saturday froze on contact in the highlands west of Marquette. The ice accumulated on telephone wires, while the wind blew them together, forming a ground that knocked out telephone service. A company employee had to make a trip on horse-drawn sleigh to Eagle Mills, a few miles east of Negaunee. He brought back service to the area by climbing a pole at that location, and breaking the ice off the wires and then pulling them apart. In Wisconsin, a mother and her daughter lost their way in the bitter cold and were found in swamp country several days later, frozen stiff.

On Lake Superior, several vessels went aground in the stormy November weather and another came near disaster. The steamer *S. F. Hodge* left Marquette for Houghton and traveled through a blinding snowstorm the entire trip. At one point, in rounding Point Abbaye into Keweenaw Bay, the ship clerk, expecting the vessel to founder, wrote a note that he stuffed in a bottle as a last message from the *Hodge*. The boat escaped sinking, but when it reached Portage Entry the next day it was completely covered with three to four inches of ice. The ice became so thick, the windows to the pilothouse had to be broken in order to see. The poor lookout then had his outer clothes frozen to his underwear. His shipmates had to break the ice off his clothes before they could be removed.

"Soft," thawing weather prevailed through the first part of December. A reporter, writing on December 13, apparently blocked out the severe end to November when he wrote: "[The winter]…so far has been extremely open; in fact, we haven't had enough cold to freeze anything but houseplants." Less than a week later, winter closed in with a vengeance; the official thermometer in Marquette plunged to 17 below zero with readings as low as 27 below to the west. Just before Christmas, a wind-driven snowstorm buried the entire peninsula from Houghton to St. Ignace. By year's end, it reached a mercury-congealing 40 degrees below zero at Michigamme.

Early 1885 brought consistent severe winter conditions. The year opened in Calumet with "five degrees below zero and the wind blowing a gale." The cold was consistent enough for teams to safely cross Little Bay de Noc at Escanaba from New Year's Day on. January 13, Negaunee experienced its "coldest day yet," with an early morning reading of

With the cold came the snow. This is a scene from Negaunee in mid-January 1885. (Courtesy of the Negaunee Historical Society)

27 below. The next morning, Champion reported an impressive 47 degrees below zero.

Calumet, on the Keweenaw Peninsula, normally experiences significant moderation in winter temperatures because of its proximity to the relatively warm waters of Lake Superior; not so in the bitter January of 1885. Early morning readings from Calumet's official thermometer illustrate the severity and persistence of the cold:

Calumet Low Temperature	
January 12: -8	January 20: -5
January 13: -15	January 21: -17
January 14: -11	January 22: -16
January 15: -5	January 23: +5
January 16: -5	January 24: +14
January 17: -6	January 25: -5
January 18: -17	January 26: -20
January 19: -15	January 27: -30

It "stormed hard" during the warm-up of the 23rd with a full-blown blizzard accompanying the 20 below zero three days later. On January 27, the noon temperature struggled to only 16 degrees below zero.

The extreme cold meant danger and even death to travelers. Henry Wood, a resident of Seney, left town during the height of the late January cold wave to walk to an area lumber camp. His frozen body was found a half-mile from his destination two days later. A few days earlier, a Copper Country resident, Peter Pearce, left his home in the settlement of Eagle bound for Eagle Harbor. He made the first leg of the journey successfully, but on the return trip,

Bundled up and snowbound in Calumet. Normally, clouds from lake-effect snow keep it relatively mild in the Copper Country. January 1885 saw consistent, bone-chilling cold along with the snow. (Courtesy of Superior View)

**VICTORIAN JOURNALISM:
TELLING IT LIKE IT IS**

Keweenaw pioneer John Senter found the body of Peter Pearce "lying face upward and eyes open," after the man lost his way in a January 1885 blizzard. Journalists of the late 19th century gave much more information than their contemporary counterparts do. For instance, a young man's body was found in the spring of 1885 outside of Sault Ste. Marie. It was discovered to be that of Alfred Sherman who had been missing since early January. Today the story would end there, but not in 1885. "The body presented the most horrible spectacle when found," stated the article in the local paper, "the face and hands having been devoured by wild animals or vermin." It went on: "His satchel and one boot were found a short distance from the body. How Sherman came to lose his boot will remain an unexplainable mystery."

During a cold wave in 1899, a fire broke out at a residence in Marquette. The headline read: "Nellie Howard Loses Her Life in a Sunday Morning Fire on Bluff Street." The story went on to describe the difficulty firefighters had putting out the fire in the subzero cold. It then went on to recount the discovery of the dead woman: "The body was so badly burnt that it was charred. One foot was gone, and of hair and clothing, not a vestige

Pearce apparently lost his way and was found dead several days later. The tragedy was blamed on the fact that "the evening was very stormy for an old man…to travel so far." Pearce was about fifty years old at the time of his death.

As February 1885 began, the cold wave continued "to roll over the land." On the 1st, it reached 20 degrees below zero in Calumet. Then on the 11th it bottomed out at 22 below. Ishpeming reached minus 28 on February 5. February 1885, like its counterpart the year before, actually averaged colder than January, finishing at 6.7 degrees versus 7.4 degrees in January.

Excessive snow accompanied the cold. Even in southern sections like Escanaba there was "more snow than anyone desires." In the northern snow belts a huge cover accumulated by the beginning of February. Lumbermen around Ishpeming complained about the deep snow. "Roads had to be made for every stick of lumber hauled" as snow depths approached four and even five feet in the woods. Grand Marais turned in similar depths and a reporter added the following qualifier to avoid accusations of exaggeration: "This is not a romance, but the result of actual measurement."

The latter part of February into March brought a bout of "spring like weather." In Norway, the thaw was welcomed, though the large amount of snow on the ground brought concerns. "Should the present large amount of snow go off with a rush," wrote a reporter in the *Norway Current*, "The towns at the mouth of the river had better anchor themselves, or there won't be a shovleful [sic] of sawdust left to tell the tale." Roads for sleighing between Ishpeming and Negaunee became damaged by the melting during the first part of March.

Then the bottom fell out; Ishpeming reported 10 below zero on the morning of March 11 and Negaunee residents endured more frozen water pipes during severe cold on March 15. During mid-month, temperatures plunged as low as 28 below in the mining districts of Marquette County. By the latter part of the month, water was "a scarce article" in Norway. Nearly every water pump in town froze or had gone dry during the severe cold wave.

The changeable March weather slowed down one of Marquette's first settlers. 55-year-old Peter White was reported "confined to his room" because of a severe cold "contracted during the...changeable weather." The article stated, "his condition is not such...as to cause alarm... [and]...he is gaining nicely." The writer hoped to "chronicle his reappearance on the streets shortly."

March 1885 became the coldest third month ever recorded in Marquette, with an average temperature of 12.1 degrees, an incredible 11.6 degrees below the long-term average. To put this number in perspective, the cold Januarys of the 1870s and 80s averaged around 16 degrees.

The winter cold retarded the maple sap run in the spring of 1885. Normally, maple sugar farmers head into the sugar bush around March 20. At the end of March, several camps around Negaunee reported the sap run "greatly retarded" by the late cold snap. At mid-April, no maple syrup had shown up on city store shelves in Ishpeming as "cold, raw weather" continued.

Spring 1885 arrived slowly, as winter refused to give up. The first of April started with sunshine in Calumet "but wound up with an old-fashioned blizzard." Eight inches of snow fell in Michigamme that day and by the 3rd, the temperature hit zero again. In Marquette, one could look out on Lake Superior during early April and gaze on ice as far as the eye could see. Gamblers were putting money on May 15 as the arrival date of the first boat.

remained."

Today's journalists leave out the gory details. "We're more sensitive to the victims, and particularly to their families," says long-time WLUC-TV News Director Ed Kearney. "In those days, when there was nothing but print, they probably thought, 'well, the gorier it is, the more sensational it is, the more papers we sell.'" Even now, he explains, the old television newsroom adage still applies: "If it bleeds, it leads." Today's journalists, however, refrain from describing or showing how much blood there is.

In Escanaba, a snowstorm occurred on April 10 and 11. The question was asked, "Was this the last storm of the winter of '84-'85 or the first of the winter of '85-'86?" On the 12th, ice in Bay De Noc seemed "as firm as at the winter solstice." There was no sign of wasting along the shores or shallow places, and the massive ice field had neither cracked nor moved. Farther south, the *Marinette Eagle* reported the ice still solid on the Menominee the third week of April.

Up in the Iron Mountains, inhabitants endured the miserable commingling of seasons. "Poor wheeling" occurred between Ishpeming and Negaunee due to the large amount of snow that still covered the roads. Two inches of new snow covered Michigamme in late April and reports from the Sault said the ice showed no signs of weakening on the St. Marys River.

May featured more backward weather. The tug *City of Marquette* left Marquette on May 6 with crews for the lighthouses on Stannard Rock, Granite Island and Huron Island. The vessel returned during a snowstorm on the evening of the 8th with the crew of Stannard Rock light still aboard. The tug had labored through heavy ice, and succeeded in reaching the islands; she then began hammering her way out to the "the rock" some forty miles into the

THE OPENING OF NAVIGATION

The arrival of the Peerless *on May 11, 1885 was not the latest opening of navigation at Marquette. After the cold winter of 1875, the first boat did not make the harbor until May 20. The latest opening*

Another view of the famous ice blockade at Marquette in June 1873. At least one account claimed that Fourth of July picnickers cooled their drinks with chunks of ice from the lake. (Courtesy of Superior View)

occurred two years earlier in 1873; the spring of the famous "ice blockade." That year the first arrival was delayed until May 21.

Official record of spring's first arrival began at Marquette in 1864. Typically, in these early cold years, navigation did not open until the beginning of May. There was one glaring exception in 1878, a year in which the harbor remained ice-free all season (See "1877-78: The Warmest Winter" page 119). After the turn of the

center of the lake. About ten miles from Huron Island, the captain of the vessel found himself "surrounded by icebergs and an immense field of ice." He tried to break through, but was turned back by the low visibility of the snowstorm. Five inches of snow fell in the Copper Country from this late-season storm.

The steamer *Owen* finally ran out of the Escanaba harbor on May 3. It was the first marine movement at the Lake Michigan port in the spring of 1885. Gamblers who put their money on May 15 were only a few days late in Marquette. The first propeller of the season, *Peerless,* finally arrived on May 11.

In Ontonagon, the first boat arrived on May 6 and was greeted by a northeast gale and snow, which lasted until morning on the 8th. Lingering ice, blown about by the strong winds, did considerable damage to newly installed cribs at the entrance to the harbor. More snow and wind occurred the night of the 9th. Finally, the "first genuine spring day" was felt on May 12. Two days later, Ontonagon's lightkeeper declared it "a sultry summer day."

The seven-month wait for spring became unbearable for one old prospector in Ishpeming. He ventured into the woods during mid-May, looking for the mother lode; but he was turned back by mosquitoes "of the largest size made", which clouded the riverbanks despite the fact that snow still laid two feet deep in the woods!

The Arctic Attack of February 1899

"Winter's Back is Broken" read the headline of a front-page story in the Marquette *Mining Journal* on January 21, 1899. A reporter visited the U.S. Weather Bureau observer at his office in downtown Marquette. The observer "looked out the tower windows to see how fast the snow was going away." As he looked out on the mild, sunny day, he declared that if the cold did not arrive soon, it never would. A little over a week later, it arrived with a vengeance, unleashing a historic arctic outbreak from the northern Rockies to the Gulf coast.

A severe snowstorm preceded the cold wave. Snow began falling in Marquette shortly before midnight on January 25 and continued through the next day. The wind picked up and built drifts ten to twelve feet deep.

On Lake Superior, the gale whipped the unfrozen water into a chaotic frenzy: "The seas on the lake were something fearful. No ice field has formed in the bay so far this winter and the wind had every opportunity to lash it into furious waves." The waves took out a boathouse in the harbor but the launches were saved. The water came over the breakwater in such volumes that the structure could hardly be seen all day.

Streetcars were blocked and railroads were delayed all over Upper Michigan. In Ishpeming, the storm was welcomed. It put down a good blanket of snow, which had been "a very scarce article up to date." In Calumet, the storm was dubbed "a screamer…almost without equal in the history of the village." It dumped 33 inches on the town, while Marquette collected 15 inches. Even in the southern U.P. a substantial 10 inches piled up at Manistique. For Iron Mountain it was the "first real blizzard of the season."

After the snow, came the cold. On January 31, Marquette recorded its coldest temperature in years with a bone-chilling 18 degrees below zero. Quickly, Marquette Bay was covered with a "solid sheet of ice" six inches thick. Frozen water pipes became a problem all over the peninsula as the cold intensified the first week of February. Trains were delayed as frost on the tracks made for very slippery

A massive arctic high pressure system in southwestern Canada brought record cold to much of the nation in early February 1899. (NOAA Central Library Data Imaging Project)

century, warmer winters and larger, faster boats promoted earlier and earlier starts to the shipping season. In 1907, the coldest spring on record (See sidebar "The Long Winter and Backward Spring of 1995-96", page 195), the first steamer landed at Marquette on April 27.

Back in the old days, the first arrival was a cause for celebration. "The coming of the first boat was something that was the sole topic of conversation for days," remembered early settler and weather observer Judge L.P. Crary. "No man ever had more than one eye on his work after the ice began to go out, as the other eye was turned lakeward in the hopes of seeing a sail." Finally, as the first boat made port, bells rang, whistles blew and everyone made as much noise as possible.

"When the first boat arrived," explained Crary, "it was considered excusable to get 'loaded' and nearly everyone availed themselves of the privilege." He went on to recall that the small boats of the bygone years carried less weight, so there were more of them. "I have seen as many as sixty or seventy little craft in Marquette Harbor at one time. That brought lots of sailors and made things lively on occasions."

A great snowstorm followed the arctic attack of 1899 and buried much of Upper Michigan. This is a scene from Ishpeming just after the blizzard. (Courtesy of Marquette County History Museum)

conditions.

The coldest weather came during February. Iron Mountain checked in with 30 below zero on February 7. On the 8th, it bottomed out at 24 below. The peak of the cold wave arrived mid month with the 40 below zero reading on February 13 termed "a record breaker." At the same time, just down the road in Norway, many fire hydrants were frozen. Half the town was borrowing water from the hydrants of the other half.

In Chocolay Township, just south of Marquette, farmers reported the loss of a number of horses due to the protracted cold. In Negaunee, old-timers said they had never seen the Carp River so thickly covered with ice. By mid-February the river was frozen to a depth of two feet.

The Arctic Attack of 1899 brought misery and inconvenience to a vast portion of the nation. Blizzards raged with bitter cold over the Rockies. The storm was declared "one of the severest in the history of Idaho." The peak of the cold wave began in Montana on February 11; a thermometer in one town registered a brutal 61 degrees below zero. By the 12th, record cold reached the southern U.S.; Fort Worth, Texas reached 8 below, while at the same time nearly four inches of snow fell in Charleston, South Carolina. The next day, Tallahassee, Florida plunged to 2 below zero; the coldest temperature ever recorded in the sunshine state.

A memorable cold snowstorm roared up the East Coast on the 14th, burying Washington under 20 inches of snow. After the storm, the snow cover reached an incredible 34 inches on the level. As New Orleans shivered through its coldest temperature ever, a numbing 7 degrees above zero, ice floes appeared at the mouth of the Mississippi; a phenomenon observed only once before in 1784.

The cold lingered in Upper Michigan into March, culminating in a "great snowstorm" at mid month. The wintry blast reversed a warming trend that had persisted for almost a decade.

January 1912: The Coldest Month

The fall of 1911 was mild. The growing season that began on May 3 in Marquette extended to October 24 in 1911. The local newspaper boasted that the length of this growing season was "as long a period as…the average in south-central Illinois." December was more than five degrees above the long-term average. Then, a two-day snowstorm commenced on New Year's Day, followed by the unloading of arctic air that had been building over the northwestern portion of the continent.

On January 4, the temperature struggled to zero for a high in the "Queen City" by the lake, with a low of 12 degrees below zero. Then from the 5th through the 7th, the mercury failed to reach zero in Marquette, with a nadir of 22 below. Only nine times since the brutal winter of 1875 had the high temperature in Marquette stayed below zero. The three consecutive days of subzero highs bore witness to the record cold that became established over much of the country in January 1912.

The bitter weather was felt throughout the region westward to the Rockies and eastward to the Atlantic coast. A huge ice jam formed on the Fox River in Wisconsin near Appleton, causing the suspension of most manufacturing operations up and down the Fox Valley. Crews of men tried in vain to blast through the nearly two feet of ice with dynamite; but with temperatures hovering near 20 below, the broken ice froze together as fast as it was blown apart. In Yonkers, New York, the Hudson River froze over for the first time in eighteen years. New York

Menominee in the 1920s. The cold month of January 1912 brought transportation delays. Streetcars, like this one, as well as trains, froze to the tracks as far south as Virginia.
(Courtesy of Delta County Historical Society)

City's harbor was reported "nearly as icebound as it gets." Trains were reported frozen to the tracks as far south as Virginia, while to the west in Minnesota, the temperature tumbled as low as 46 degrees below zero.

Back in Upper Michigan, the early winter cold wave brought on lake effect snow in abundance, especially in the Copper Country. West to northwesterly winds typical in an arctic cold wave generated perpetual snow showers. Houghton already had three feet of snow on the ground near the end of the first week in January, a "very heavy" amount for so early in the month. A Copper Country reporter wrongly speculated that the arctic intrusion of the last few days "marked the zenith of the winter's cold." By January 11, the Houghton weather observer declared there was "no prospect of a change in the weather." He reported

Marquette's Temperatures: Comparing Apples with Oranges?

Official temperature records in Marquette began with the Signal Service, a department of the Army, in 1874. Later, the U.S. Weather Bureau was formed and it kept a station in and around the present downtown area. Then in 1979, the now National Weather Service, in an effort to provide wider coverage for a new radar installation, moved "up the hill" to Negaunee Township. The site is about eight miles from town, and more importantly, 800 feet above Lake Superior.

The present site has a significantly different climate than any of the old observing sites. Its location on a high plateau away from the lake gives the climate a definite continental character. Typically, there are wider swings in temperatures than in areas close to the lake. At lake level, where the old sites were situated, the air remains warmer in autumn and winter and cooler in spring and summer. This marine influence leads to a substantial difference in average temperatures between sites. For instance, the downtown site averages around 38 degrees for November, while up the hill in Negaunee Township, the average for the month is only around 30 degrees.

So when using data from

a temperature of 7 below "with the second edition" of the blizzard from a couple of days earlier.

Arctic high pressure that brought 50 below zero weather to Montana edged east and probably settled over the Upper Lakes January 9 through 11. The clear skies and light winds attending the high led to a free-fall in temperatures. Ishpeming reported a minimum of 24 below the morning of the 9th, while it reached 36 below zero at the newly constructed Silver Lake Dam, to the northwest. At the same time, some readings in Minnesota tumbled to 46 below. On the night of January 11, all records for low temperatures since the arctic attack of 1899 were shattered. Humboldt, in western Marquette County, plummeted to 40 degrees below zero.

The Mining Journal reported on the experience of a family who lived in the woods outside Republic. They shivered through this bitter month in a little four room, uninsulated house. Their only inside plumbing was a pitcher pump in the kitchen that had to be watched carefully, lest it freeze up. Most nights fell to 30^0 - 35^0 below zero in the Republic area that January. Their wood stove had to be stoked almost continuously, day and night. Even so, the house always remained bitter cold around the edges.

January 1912 ended with an average temperature of 1.3 degrees, the coldest month in Marquette's history. No month since then, even in the cold winters of the 1960s and 70s, came close.

Duluth, with a predominant wind off land, also experienced its coldest month with an incredible 7.2 below zero average. The bitter weather produced ice in abundance on the Great Lakes. In Marquette, the hope for a big ice crop was brighter than it had been in years. As in 1875, the ice harvest, which usually began in late February, commenced at the end of January. Off Copper Harbor, "for the first time in the memory of white men in northern Michigan" the thirteen miles of water between the mainland and Manitou Island was "frozen thick enough to bear a team" by the end of February. The ice was reported "30 inches deep...clear...[and]...blue." In mid-February, Lake Michigan was reported frozen "from shore to shore" for the first time since 1875.

The harsh winter severely strained the wildlife of Upper

Michigan. John Rough, a deputy game warden, reported four feet of snow on the level near Silver Lake Dam. He also came upon five deer carcasses. Wolves had killed the animals, easily running them down in the deep snow. The tone of the newspaper report implied that the wolves slaughtered the deer indiscriminately, as if it was a sport to them. As evidence, the story reported that only a small portion of each deer was eaten.

While in the area, Rough took the time to check in on 74-year-old Peter Moore, the caretaker of the new dam at Silver Lake Basin. The reclusive Moore lived alone at the dam site for 23 years. He ventured into the city of Ishpeming only twice a year to pick up supplies.

At the end of March 1912, Captain F. E. Nelson arrived in Sault Ste. Marie after a 60 mile trip over the frozen St. Marys River. Nelson said the ice on the channel was three feet thick and "so smooth…one could skate the entire distance." Soon after, the ice began to melt. April 1912 featured persistent southerly winds and a relatively quick breakup after one of the coldest winters of the 20th century.

these sites, it is important to consider the recording location. It is interesting to note that the coldest January, February and March occurred at the "warmer" downtown site. These low temperature marks were set during the colder cycle of the 19th and early 20th centuries, and can provide the necessary fuel to heat up the global warming debate.

The Cold, Windy Siege of 1936

Relatively mild winters were the rule in Upper Michigan from the 1920s into the early '30s, so residents were likely unprepared for the "most severe and prolonged cold wave of many winters" that blew in during late January 1936. The arctic blast was preceded by "a raging blizzard" on January 22 and 23, judged "the worst in years." The storm brought travel to a virtual halt, as street crews in Iron Mountain, Escanaba, Menominee and the Sault were called off the roads. Strong winds blew the new snow into huge drifts, making travel nearly impossible. The snow finally let up, but the wind continued, transporting bitter arctic air which had been banked up to the northwest. While the blizzard raged in the U. P., Duluth reached 30 degrees below zero along with a brutal northwesterly wind that gusted to 40 miles an hour.

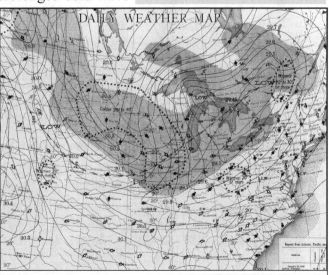

Low pressure developed in the Rockies, dipped into the Central Plains and cut up to the Great Lakes on January 22, 1936. This blizzard-producing storm was followed by one of the most prolonged, harshest cold waves of the 20th century. (NOAA Central Library Data Imaging Project)

Is Lake Superior Frozen?

The question as to whether Lake Superior was completely frozen over provided a lively debate in the local paper during late February 1912.

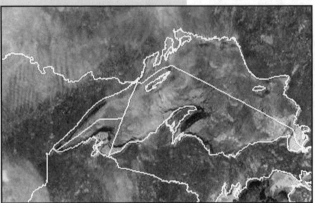

After one of the coldest winters in years, a visible satellite image in early March 2003 showed Lake Superior nearly frozen over. (University Corporation for Atmospheric Research)

Robert Blemhuber of Marquette contended that the lake was not frozen over and "by gum, it never has been." Colonel J.W. Wyckoff, of the Keweenaw, maintained it had been, and probably was now and he had proof: "Bob Blemhuber...is one of these Missouri fellows and will have to be shown I guess."

Wyckoff explained that he made a "stage trip" in February of 1872. He boarded the stage at L'Anse and among the passengers was a party of about 20 Englishmen who had walked across Lake Superior from Canada to the Keweenaw Peninsula. They were surveying the mainland in Canada adjacent to Isle Royale when their provisions ran out. It was a familiar story: They had expected a full

An incredible 55 below zero was measured at a bridge linking the U. S. and Canada at International Falls.

The cold wave of 1936 will be remembered for its harsh combination of wind and cold that persisted for nearly a month over a wide area of the Midwest and Great Lakes. In the Copper Country, poor visibility proved dangerous. A Calumet motorist wished he had stayed put when he accidentally drove his car onto railroad tracks. In the haze of the blinding snow, he saw the rear end of a switch engine approaching. He frantically tried to flag down the engine, but to no avail; the train struck the car and pushed it thirty feet, ditching it on the side of the tracks.

Mail service to Upper Michigan, shipped primarily by rail, was the worst in years; it became tied up by an unprecedented series of snowstorms and ground blizzards that blocked the tracks to the south in Wisconsin.

My father, John Bohnak, grew up on a farm in northwestern Wisconsin and vividly recalls what it was like being "holed up" for nearly a month: "We couldn't go anywhere. I remember when it started. It was about the middle of January. There was a terrific wind and it was snowing and it was real, real cold. You didn't even know where your barn was, you couldn't even see the barn. We milked cows and my dad had to take the milk to the cheese factory. He got up the first little hill on the horse-drawn sleigh and the horses just balked. They stopped and wouldn't go any farther.

"We had no mail for two weeks, and then we had to go to the cheese factory to get it when things let up a little bit. Later, when the let up came, the horses could travel right on top of the three foot snow cover, it was packed so hard by the wind."

In Upper Michigan, many villages such as Garden, in Delta County, were also experiencing isolation as incessant drifting snow and bitter cold cut off the village from the outside world. The town was facing serious food shortages when plows finally broke through the drifts in mid-February.

Menominee reached 30 below zero on February 18. During the peak of the bitter cold there, two small boys froze their hands and feet while the family home and barn were consumed by fire. Wildlife also suffered in the region. Extreme cold and deep snow brought death and starvation to hundreds of pheasants around Menominee. During the second week of February, a starving pheasant was spotted on the west side of Menominee on Ogden Avenue. The Menominee Sportsmen's Club began searching for starving flocks to feed. Farmers and residents on the outskirts of town were asked to notify the local sportsmen's club if they spotted a flock.

Marquette experienced subzero cold during 16 of the first 19 days of February 1936. Bitter northwesterly winds brought Munising its heaviest lake-effect snow in years, while numbing cold froze most of the city's fire hydrants and water pipes. On one day in early February, the lakeside community plummeted to 24 degrees below zero with a thermometer on the east side of town registering 40 below.

Day after day of brutal cold led to a quick freeze on the Great Lakes. By mid-February, ice from a foot to a foot-and-a-half thick clogged most harbors along Lake Superior. Duluth measured 31 inches in its harbor with thick ice extending out about 20 miles from shore. In Marquette, broken drift ice and ice floes extended well beyond the field of vision into the lake.

Lake Michigan became even more icebound. By the middle of February, the 80 miles of lake between Milwaukee and Muskegon was ice-covered except for a 13-mile stretch near the middle. Earlier, tragedy struck on the northern end of the lake when two fishermen found themselves drifting on an ice floe that separated from the main ice shield near Charlevoix. A surfman of the Coast Guard station there went out in a rowboat to rescue the men. He succeeded in getting them off the ice floe into the boat, but then the boat got stuck in the floe. Drifting fast, the boat disappeared from view into a low-hanging haze.

The three men became marooned in the boat miles from shore. They tried to keep warm by jumping up and down in the boat, but two of the men became exhausted. One died that night, while the other, the surfman, passed the next morning. At that point, the third man started across the ice

store of supplies by steamer, but winter came in early and the vessel was frozen in and never arrived.

The party held on as long as it could, but the situation became desperate. In February of 1872, they had no recourse but to hike out of the woods and head for "civilization." They stepped onto the ice and walked to Isle Royale, crossed it, and "then struck across the wastes of ice on Lake Superior to Keweenaw point." There were no mishaps on their roughly 70 mile journey, and they journeyed safely over the frozen lake. Wyckoff did concede that it is possible that Lake Superior was not frozen at its widest part.

*Robert Blemhuber 1861 - 1950
(Courtesy Marquette County
History Museum)*

That was the point Blemhuber made; the center of the lake would not freeze over. He offered the following as evidence: "From Sauks Head Point to Granite Island [located to the north of Marquette] is a matter of twenty miles. Ever since...a southwest wind set in, I have been able to see open water beyond the island."

"I am willing to wager $1000 against a dollar that the center of Lake Superior has never been frozen over and never will be," Blemhuber offered.

He went on to explain that for some miles beyond shore there is shoal and that section will freeze. "Toward the center," he contended, "the ice absorbs the chill from the water and the result is that the center of the lake's surface is never sufficiently chilled to cause it to freeze." Blemhuber concluded: "I defy anyone to show the contrary."

Modern satellite technology has shown the contrary, to a point. Satellite images showed Lake Superior entirely covered with ice during the winters of 1979 and 1994. However, the ice in the center, at least in 1994, was quite thin. On February 7, 1994, an image showed the lake completely ice-covered. Then, on February 22 and 23, a storm moving through the eastern lakes caused an increase in wind from the north to northeast. The strong winds broke up the thin mid-lake ice and created open water, leading to the development of lake-effect snow. Up to eight inches of snow fell in the highlands of north-central Upper Michigan—at least partially vindicating the claims of Mr. Blemhuber. ❈

toward shore; thinking that he would "rather die walking." After an all-day struggle across the jagged, shifting field of ice, the badly frozen, semi-conscious man reached the safety and warmth of a cabin along the lake. He wound up roughly fifteen miles north of where he and his partner had set out for some ice fishing two days earlier.

By the third week of February, Escanaba had recorded twenty consecutive days with temperatures below zero, tying a record set during the historic cold blast thirty-seven years earlier (*see "The Arctic Attack of 1899", page 130*). At the same time, Weather Bureau forecasters noticed pressures lowering in northwestern Canada, a sign the cold was about to break. True to the Bureau's forecast, Marquette popped above freezing for the first time in well over a month on February 23. It then stayed above freezing through the next night and all the next day.

Two days later, a blizzard, dumping "the biggest accumulation in years" roared into Upper Michigan; a foot of new snow fell in Marquette. Ishpeming residents had to wade through waist-deep snow the morning after the snow diminished. Only a moderate chill followed the storm, and a relatively mild spring unfolded. A few months later, the most intense heat wave ever experienced in the United States poked its way from the Plains into Upper Michigan (*see "Heat Waves, Hot Summers" page 238*).

The Long, Steady Cold of 1963

Like a number of other bitter winters in this survey, the 1963 cold season started out mild. November 1962 saw much-below-average snowfall; the warmest days occurred at the end of the month. In Marquette, temperatures reached 50 degrees or higher on four of the last five days of November. October weather then continued into December 1962, culminating in a record-shattering high of 59 on the 3rd.

The first inkling of what lay ahead came the day after Christmas when the high temperature struggled to only 6 above zero; the low that morning was a bitter 10 below. Mild, tranquil weather covered Upper Michigan the first week and a half of 1963. Persistent warmth whittled away a good deal of the thin snow cover. Then, in time-honored fashion, a healthy snowstorm hit Upper Michigan on January 12 followed by a bitter cold wave. Marquette recorded its coldest temperature since 1936 on January 15, with 18 degrees below zero. Locations away from the warming influence of Lake Superior dropped even lower. Iron Mountain and Escanaba both registered 22 below and Menominee plunged to 24 below zero.

On January 22, the mandatory cold weather story in the local paper began with this dramatic opening: "Severest cold wave in decades raged on today with bitter west winds ripping pedestrians like razor blades." The

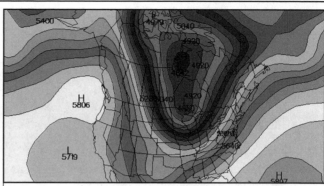

A typical upper-air map during the bitter winter of 1963. A deep trough remained anchored over the central portion of North America by huge ridge along the West Coast and by blocking high pressure in the North Atlantic. (Courtesy of Plymouth State Weather Center NCEP/NCAR Reanalysis Map Generator)

next day, Iron Mountain recorded its 11th straight day with temperatures below zero; it bottomed out there at 30 below. Outlying areas in Dickinson County had readings as low as 40 below zero. Most schools in the U.P. were closed due to the brutal cold. A thermometer at the Herman post office in Baraga County registered 43 degrees below zero. Farther east, it also plunged to 43 below at Wetmore in Alger County. At the foot of Lake Superior, Sault Ste. Marie checked in with 30 below and Marquette endured its coldest January day in recorded history on the 23rd with a high of 8 below and a low down to 21 below zero.

The cold spread southward during late January 1963. Atlanta recorded its first subzero temperature of the 20th century late in the month, and Chicago experienced its coldest month in history; registering 19 consecutive days below zero in January 1963.

An extensive front-page story from the Associated Press explained that while "air circulation may not be an ear-perking conversational tidbit" it was having "a jolting impact" on millions of people in the United States. The article went on to explain how a huge ridge of high pressure stalled off the west coast of North America kept directing mild southerly airflow into Alaska, while north to northwesterly flow directed bitter air from the "inexhaustible supply of cold" in the arctic through much of interior North America. The winter of 1963 saw exceptionally strong intrusions of cold all the way to the citrus regions of Florida and even southern California.

Like the winters of 1875 and 1885, North America shared the bitter siege with the Old World. The "Great Cold of 1963" spread "death, misery and chaos" across much of Western Europe. The Thames River froze from bank to bank at Kingston for the first time since 1895. It would be the only time in the 20th century the river froze to such an extent. At Southampton, fish reportedly froze where they swam, sticking their heads out of the ice. Seabirds then skated along the ice and picked at them. In central Italy, the Venice lagoon was reported covered with ice. In Salonika, Greece, there were reports of snow drifts up to five feet deep, while snow piled up on Italy's Adriatic Coast. The phenomenon there was declared "a rare sight." Farther north on the Oresund, the strip of water separating Denmark from Sweden, some Danes walked halfway across it, while others "rode bicycles on the sea" and got in the way of icebreakers.

Freighters caught in lake ice. Little or no movement occurred during late winter 1963 as all the Great Lakes became virtually ice covered. (Courtesy of Superior View)

As February advanced and the cold hung on, ice began to clog the Great Lakes. By February 19, Arthur J. Myers, chief meteorologist at the Sault Ste. Marie Weather Bureau, declared Lakes Superior, Huron and Michigan virtually ice-covered. It was an occurrence he deemed "most unusual." A Coast Guard icebreaker reported ice three inches thick with several inches of snow on top from Port Huron all the way to Detroit.

The Chippewa County car ferry regularly transported Drummond Island High school students across Detour passage to the mainland of eastern Upper Michigan. Finally, in mid-February the captain tied up at Detour after his steering gear broke for the third time under the pressure of ice up to 18 inches thick. Students then got written permission from their parents to drive their cars over the ice bridge of the passage to get to school. At Menominee, three feet of ice on Green Bay forced the suspension of car ferry service to Lower Michigan. By the end of February, a Trans-Canada Airlines pilot reported only scattered patches of open water on Lake Superior no more than an acre or two in size.

Richard Wright began teaching at Northern Michigan College in the fall of 1962. Flying back to his home in Indiana for spring break in early March, he received visual confirmation that Lake Superior was frozen: "The pilot of what was then North Central Airlines took the plane far out over the lake and banked both left and right to show us the surface of the lake, which was frozen as far as the eye could see."

After the coldest January and February since the early part of the century, March 1963 showed some signs that winter would eventually end. On March 15, Marquette climbed to 42 degrees, the warmest temperature since December 4, 1962. Old man winter rose up for another attack several days later, stirring up the biggest snowstorm of the winter. It affected the entire Upper Peninsula, with more than a foot of snow falling in many locations over northern portions. Strong winds created "hip high" drifts in the Marquette area while drifting snow around Calumet and Wakefield closed side roads. The storm brought the biggest March snow in 24 years.

In sharp contrast to the blistering cold of winter, spring 1963 brought some warm weather to the Upper Great Lakes. The temperature reached 72 degrees on April 3 with two more 70 degree days that month. The rapid meltdown led to a historic ice jam flood in Ontonagon (see "Floods", page 226).

As spring wore on, the warm weather continued. "What was surprising to me," remembers Wright, "around the 12th of May the weather became hot, something near 90. At just before eleven that night, the temp was 83. There was a wind shift and within 20 minutes the temp was 43." The shift in wind brought the airflow off Lake Superior, still holding the residual chill of the long, steady cold winter of 1963.

Winter of 1976-77: A Quick Start

This was the first in a series of three severe winters during the late 1970s. Unusually cold air masses made an appearance early this season. Once the cold came, it did not leave, making this one of the coldest winters of the Twentieth Century.

"It was mid-October, a Friday," remembers Don Michelin, a resident of Newberry in 1976. "It had been a real nice day. We had been out goose hunting all day and the weather changed in the afternoon; it started snowing." Michelin recalls that by half-time of the football game that evening it had snowed eight inches. Over a foot fell by the time the storm ended on Saturday. "And it never thawed," adds Michelin. "It stuck and kept snowing."

Cross country runners slogged through snow during a meet in October 1976. (Courtesy of the Marquette County History Museum)

With the snow came the cold. Marquette endured one of it coldest Octobers, with an average temperature 5.3 degrees below normal. It was also the snowiest October in 91 years, as abnormal cold got the lake-effect machine going early. Snowfall was nearly nine times the average for October with 17.5 inches. November continued the building cold. By late in the month, the weather map looked like one more typical of mid-winter than late fall. In Negaunee Township, the last three days of the month dipped below zero, with a nadir of 13 below on the 29th.

Eight record low temperatures were established in December; records which still stand as of this writing. The month started cold with records of 10 and 12 below on the 2nd and 3rd. December 1976 ended frigid with a numbing 25 degrees below zero on the 30th. The average temperature was 14.6 degrees, an impressive 8.9 degrees below the long-term average.

The cold deepened as 1977 began. Mercury-congealing cold hit south central sections of Upper Michigan. The low hit 42 below zero at Stambaugh in Iron County on January 9. It was the coldest reading in nearly 60 years; settling only a handful of degrees from the all-time low of 47 below during the historic February cold wave of 1899. A little farther north, Amasa, a perennial Iron County cold spot, registered 45 below. The same night, the temperature dropped to 30 below at Iron Mountain. In Marquette, while the influence of

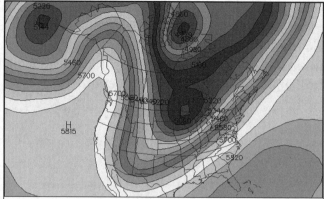

November 28, 1976—a highly amplified pattern saw a deep, cold trough over the Upper Midwest. (Courtesy of Plymouth State Weather Center NCEP/NCAR Reanalysis Map Generator)

The last three winters of the 70s were cold and snowy over Upper Michigan. This is a view from Escanaba in January 1979. (Courtesy of the Delta County Historical Society)

Lake Superior kept things a little milder, the average for the month was still more than 8 degrees below normal.

The cold of '76-'77 was far reaching. Lake Erie was already completely frozen over by the second week of January. The largest ice buildup in years formed on the rest of the Great Lakes. On Chesapeake Bay, several ships were reported trapped in thick ice. The two tugboats that tried to rescue them also became stuck. By month's end, a historic blizzard swept off frozen Lake Erie and isolated Buffalo, New York for nearly a week.

The bitter cold began to moderate during the middle of February but a couple more snowstorms visited the area in March. April and May 1977 turned into balmy spring months. Despite a relatively quick ending, the winter of 1976-77 made an impression on many U.P. residents. "That was about the longest, harshest winter that I'd seen," recalls Michelin.

The Big Freeze Up: The Bitter Cold Winter of 1993-1994

A severely cold winter descended on Upper Michigan and much of the rest of the country during the winter of 1993-1994. The protracted periods of cold and wind rivaled the great cold waves of the past. The frigid weather damaged infrastructure across the peninsula, and caused significant disruption to the lives of many residents.

The winter started early in northern sections, with plowable snow just before Halloween (the snow laid down in this event provided a continuous cover over some higher elevations from October 30th until early April of 1994). Snow and cold weather then continued well into November. Both October and November came in more than 3 degrees below average.

December 1993 began mild, and continued warm for nearly three weeks. Little snow fell and temperatures popped above freezing for a few hours most afternoons. It appeared another in a series of mild winters was underway. Then profound changes began to take place in the circulation over North America during the latter part of the third week. The broad, warm ridge of high pressure that had taken up residence over the central part of the continent was gradually replaced by a deep, cold upper-air trough. This would be the predominant pattern for the next seven weeks.

Upper Michigan's first widespread subzero readings occurred on Christmas Eve. Shoppers who turned out for after-Christmas sales on the 26th had to brave below zero readings all day; the first of many such days this bitter winter. December ended with seven of the last eight days below zero.

January 1994 evolved into one of the coldest months on record. It started with moderate, bearable cold the first week or so, punctuated by a heavy snowstorm over scattered sections on the 6th and 7th.

After a brief mild spell January 10 through 12, the harshest cold blast in years settled over the peninsula. Temperatures stayed below zero in most sections for a week. The cold reached its nadir on the 18th. Larry Wanic in Bark River observed a high temperature

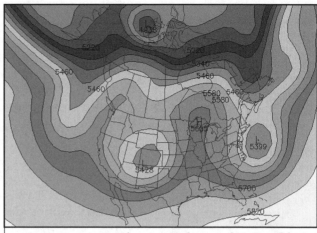

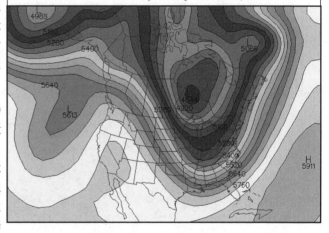

A strong upper-air ridge sat over the central portion of the U.S. on December 16, 1993. Little more than a week later, the pattern flipped—a deep, cold trough took up residence in the same spot. (Courtesy of Plymouth State Weather Center NCEP/NCAR Reanalysis Map Generator)

of 11 degrees below zero. "That's the second coldest day I ever had," says Wanic.

In north-central Upper Michigan, the National Weather Service (NWS) recorded a blistering cold high of 15 below; the coldest high temperature in 117 years. Brisk west-to-northwesterly winds accompanied the cold, dropping wind chills out of sight and compounding the misery factor. As the wind calmed down a little, some remarkable low temperatures occurred. It fell to 27 below in Bark River and 31 below in Spalding and Ironwood. In Caspian, near Iron River, the temperature fell to minus 35 for the second time during this bitter stretch. An observer in Amasa had an alcohol thermometer drop to 53 degrees below zero early on the morning of the 19th.

As the brutal cold persisted, water pipes began to freeze and crack in communities throughout the U.P. In Marinette-Menominee, lateral lines that run from the water main to private residences began to freeze up. Crews worked overtime all that bitter week into the weekend thawing pipes and restoring water service to area homes. As the weather warmed, the ground began to heave, which caused pipes to crack, compounding the problem. Farther north in Stephenson, the city council ordered all residents to leave their water running, as

MENOMINEE'S HISTORIC SNOW: JANUARY 6-7, 1994

An unusual lake-enhanced-snow event brought record breaking totals to Menominee in early January 1994. The system was not a major, wound-up storm, but a weak low that developed to the south in response to an upper-air trough drifting in from the west. A persistent northeasterly wind set in, picking up moisture off the still-unfrozen Green Bay.

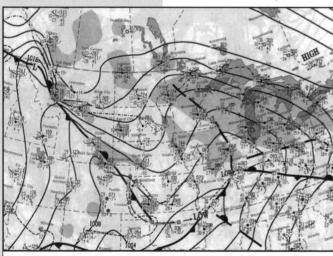

This innocuous-looking set up brought big snows to parts of the Upper Great Lakes, including an unusual lake-enhanced event in Menominee during early January 1994. (NOAA Central Library Data Imaging Project)

"It just came in spells," remembers Greg Albrecht, a resident of Menominee at the time. *"It just constantly came and when the snow squalls would come, the wind would really increase out of the east or northeast."* The fluffy snow piled up all along and just inland from the bay. Stephenson had 13 inches, while Spalding, to

bitter cold persisted into early February. The order was given as a preventative measure to avoid major problems with freezing pipes.

On the east end, the worst freezing conditions on record assaulted Sault Ste. Marie. "It's been like fighting a war day after day," said Water Department Superintendent Bud Clarke. "We had 800 some freeze-ups. There were people who had no water in the mains and we had to run plastic lines over ground from fire hydrants. It was a really tough one."

Clarke's crew put in tremendous amounts of overtime. As February wound down, his crew of nine had accrued some 1,256 overtime hours; normal overtime for an entire year averaged only 125 hours. "The guys, they'd get tired out," Clarke says. "So they had to go home, of course. They'd sleep for a few hours and come back again."

The men worked at thawing lines, sometimes working around the clock. "We were always scared at nighttime that a fire might start," explains Clarke. "That year we had one problem; we set a house on fire. The current jumped over...and jumped into the house. It...burned pretty badly by the time firemen got there." He says they never liked to thaw during the night, but had no choice if they wanted to keep up with the long list of freeze-ups.

"I had 43 years in the water department, so I've seen a lot of freeze ups," declares Clarke. "The winter of 1994 was the worst for us. We had some bad ones in the '60s and '70s, but nothing like this."

Some of the worst water problems occurred in Ishpeming. "Our large water main on Cleveland Street was one of the first or second ones to explode about the 18th of January," recalls city manager John Korhonen. "Once the frost started going below six feet...we began having some major problems. Our community is actually built on an old cedar swamp that was filled in with mine rock to pick it up out of the water table, so a lot of the lines are shallow."

"We had a difficult time even identifying leaks," he remembers. Since much of the area is built on old mine

January 1994. As the bitter cold persisted, water pipes started freezing in towns all across Upper Michigan. (Photo by E. Yelland)

rock, water from a leak did not always come to the surface; it just seeped down into the rock. At one point, engineers from Milwaukee were contracted to locate a leak. But their electronic detection devices were no match for the problem. "They would say, 'Yes, it's here,'" he says. We'd dig there, there'd be no leak. We'd dig in another place, there's no leak. I think we dug up a whole block of a street and didn't find a leak."

It turned out that the water main in that section was not responsible for the leak. In the old days, logs were hollowed out and tied together as wooden pipes which brought water into area homes. Some of these old, deteriorating wooden pipes were still in place and leaking. "So it wasn't coming from our new main, but it was coming from this old main," explains Korhonen.

He also says that the shut-off valves were at the depth of the water mains, so when they froze, the water could not be shut off. "We were really in a desperate situation," he recalls. "It was not possible for us to make the repairs. We had to make the decision to shut the whole system down. Everything in the system had to be drained out prior to… [fixing]… these leaks. That took hours and hours and hours. We had to do that twice."

Any time a municipal water system is shut down, there is

the north, was buried under 10 inches of fluffy snow. But Menominee hit the snow jackpot.

"It lasted for two-and-a-half days," says Albrecht. "I must have shoveled a half-dozen times. After living in Marquette for a year, I can definitely say what we had in Menominee was a typical lake-effect snow event." Albrecht's three-day total was 31.5 inches. The snow came over a long duration and caused little disruption; schools remained in session, though roads were described as "horrible" south of Escanaba.

The heavy snow tapered off quickly from Escanaba north and south of Marinette. Farther to the north, over the Lake Superior snow belts, Houghton had a three-day total of 32.4 inches, while around Marquette, the ideal flow for heavy snow never developed; only 2.2 inches was measured at the Weather Service office on the 6th. In the arrowhead of Minnesota, some astounding totals were turned in. The community of Finland, in the high country adjacent to Lake Superior, was buried under 44 inches of snow from the storm.

The Winter of '93-'94

Average Temperatures

January 2.8

9.1 degrees below average

February 7.7

6.3 degrees below average

42 days below zero; 9 calendar days with high temperatures below zero

Data provided by the National Weather Service

a possibility of contamination because of siphoning from higher elevations into the water system. "We then were under boil orders," says Korhonen. "That was a real inconvenience. All restaurants had to boil everything, even water for coffee."

He says the community provided lots of support through the crisis. "I thought they were going to get very angry," he laughs. "But everybody pitched in and just bit their upper lip and got through it alright. It was, by far, the most serious crisis I had to deal with as a city manager," declares Korhonen. "I had many sleepless nights over that period of time, but I think our community is better for it now."

The period of intense cold lasted from the end of December through a good share of February. Around December 21, the winter solstice, Lake Superior was ice-free; by February 9, satellite pictures showed the lake had completely frozen over for the first time since 1979.

While frozen pipes plagued a number of Upper Michigan residents well into spring, the cold left early. March started lamb-like and continued mild with the majority of days above freezing. The winter of 1993-94 will be remembered for its unrelenting intensity, though the bitter cold was confined to a roughly 50 day period.

CHAPTER 7

Upper Michigan claims the distinction as the snowiest non-mountainous location east of the Rockies. While the Lake Superior snow belts may not see the extreme snowstorms found downwind of Lake Erie and Ontario, whose width and orientation to prevailing westerly wind flow produce "mid-lake convergent" snow bands that dump huge amounts of snow over small areas, the frequency of snow in the Upper Peninsula, combined with a cold climate that holds snow through the winter, make it a snow-lover's paradise. This section will examine some of the more noteworthy snowstorms, including the unusual storms that have occurred outside the normal season. Let's look at some of the U.P.'s snowiest weather, jumping back briefly to the pioneer period.

1856-1857: The Snowiest Winter?

This harsh winter may have been the snowiest of all time if you believe the snow total that came out of the frontier community of Marquette. Dr. G. H. Blaker kept a tally of snowfall during the late 1850s and claims he measured 27 feet, 8 inches of snow (332 inches) in 1856-57! The highest total measured in the city between 1885 and 1979 was about 189 inches, an amount attained in the winter of 1890-91 and nearly achieved (188.1 inches) in 1959-60 and (188.0 inches) 1949-50. The 1856-57 figure is extraordinary when one considers the heaviest snows of modern times, measured in the highest

1856-57: The Snowiest Winter?
Marquette's Average Snowfall 1885-1979: **110"**
Record Snowfall: **189.1" 1890-91**
Dr. Blaker's 1856-57 Total: **27'8"** **332"**

elevations (where about five feet more snow falls in an average winter than at lake level), range from 337" at Herman in the higher elevations of Baraga County during the winter of 1995-96, to a whopping 390.4 in Keweenaw County during the long, snowy winter of 1978-79.

The unequaled snow total of 1856-57 may not be an exaggeration. The winter started early. Peter White's father, who lived in Green Bay, wrote a letter to his son stating that navigation on Green Bay and the Fox River ended early, on November 30, 1856. This incredible winter was "the severest ever known" on the frontier, with unprecedented cold and heavy snow. At Ridgely, near present-day New Ulm in south-central Minnesota a total of 4.38 inches of precipitation (= melted snow) fell during December 1856. Assuming a 15 to 1 snow-to-water ratio would yield nearly 66" of snow, an extraordinary monthly total for this location. January 1857 brought two feet of snow to Fort Snelling; February brought two more major storms.

We can assume this stormy pattern headed to the east and north into Upper Michigan. Here, enhancement off Lake Superior would have added tremendously to the accumulations, undoubtedly piling up huge totals in Marquette and over much of the rest of the peninsula.

The publishers of The Lake Superior Miner in Ontonagon began rationing paper in early December 1856, anticipating no more supplies until spring 1857. The small top paper is the December 6 issue, published three days before the General Taylor arrived. (Courtesy of the Marquette County History Museum)

This presumption is confirmed by news from the west end in December 1856. The *Lake Superior Miner* in Ontonagon reported "over two feet of snow on the range" (the higher elevations southeast of town) as early as December 6. On the 9th, "much to the astonishment" of the town, the propeller *General Taylor* entered Ontonagon harbor with a large mail delivery, winter provisions and a supply of paper for the *Miner.* The previous week's edition was laid out in tiny print on paper half the normal size in anticipation that paper would have to be rationed for the winter.

The *Taylor*, under the command of Captain Ryder, left Detroit on November 22 and spent over two weeks battling storms and then ice in an effort to bring winter supplies to the tiny, struggling communities on the Lake Superior frontier (*see Chapter 3, "Will Winter Supplies Arrive?"*, see page 82). It was the latest departure, up to that time, of a vessel from Detroit and the latest arrival in Ontonagon. "Her arrival brought much joy throughout the town," and Captain Ryder was given a hero's welcome along with a "valuable gold watch and chain" (still on display at the Ontonagon Historical Society Museum); a token of appreciation for making the voyage during such a "tempestuous season."

The rest of December 1856 turned out to be tempestuous *and* snowy. A four-day snowstorm before mid-month already brought the snow cover to four feet on the range. Another extended storm between the 13th and 17th buried the Village of Ontonagon under "unusual deep snow." The continuous storm made "all communication to the mines, and even house to house…very difficult." Cold accompanied the snowy weather; by the 20th, the Ontonagon River was "solidly closed" and a solid sheet of ice extended nearly a half-mile out into Lake Superior.

While Minnesota suffered through the coldest January of the frontier period, more heavy snow accompanied the bitter weather in Upper Michigan. In late January, "a severe and violent storm and blow from the north, north-west and north-east…continued for nearly nine days" in Ontonagon. The final crescendo of the tempest occurred on the 26th when "a perfect hurricane" set in. All communications with the mines to the southeast of the village were cut off for nearly a week by the blizzard.

Benjamin Ryder, captain of the General Taylor, *made the latest trip to date on Lake Superior to deliver supplies to Marquette and Ontonagon. (Courtesy of the Ontonagon Historical Society)*

The harsh, stormy weather continued well into February. About mid-month, a group of villagers gathered around a fire and asked: "How many storms have we had this winter?" The majority decided "one, with few and short interruptions." The weather had never been calm for over two days and nights in succession since Christmas. Snow depths during this time reached nearly five feet on the level in the mining district to the southeast. On February 10, the temperature fell to 35 degrees below zero in the village, the coldest reading of the long, bitter season.

Spring was incredibly backward in 1857. By early April, the five-foot cover had shrunk to about three-and-a-half feet. Then another storm struck, dumping nearly a foot of new snow on the 4th and 5th. The temperature at Norwich Mine, near Ontonagon, fell to 16 below zero the morning of the 7th. The region was besieged by another "continued storm" from April 13 through 17; the northeast gale gradually backed to the northwest, "bringing a small addition to the old snow."

A *Lake Superior Miner* article reviewed the blustery, inclement highlights of April 1857: "The first three weeks of April was singularly cold and stormy. Up to the 15th there have been but three bright days…up to the 20th we had three considerable snowstorms, of which the depth of snow, measured light, would equal two feet. And the entire range is at present (23rd) covered with very compact snow to the depth of three to four feet. The ice on the lake still extends as far as the eye can reach. It may be said we have at present more snow than

The gold watch presented to Captain Ryder by the townspeople of Ontonagon is still on display at the Ontonagon Historical Society Museum. (Photo by E. Yelland)

at anytime during the winter of 1855-6, and the season is at least a month later."

The first signs of spring held off until the tail end of the month when on April 29 the "south wind mastered his cold opponents" and blew all night. Ice was temporarily driven out of Ontonagon Harbor and the "first spring rain" fell. By the beginning of May 1857, the north wind, an almost constant inhabitant of the area for the last six months, set in again and the ice moved back to shore; only a "small opening" was observed at the entry to the harbor on the 2nd. On May 9, yet another "snowstorm with a cold and severe northeast wind" raged, locking the winter's accumulation of ice fast to the shore until mid-month.

A weather observer near Eagle Harbor on the tip of Keweenaw Point described the unseasonable May 9 storm at that location. The day started relatively mild with an early morning temperature of 46 degrees. Then the wind shifted to the north about mid-morning and dense fog flowed inland off the Lake. The temperature fell to 28 degrees and stayed steady throughout the rest of the day. The wind then veered to the northeast and picked up to near gale force by late in the day when snow began falling. Two to three inches of snow fell and ended that night. By the next morning, the temperature stood at 17 degrees and rose to only 23 by mid-day on the 10th!

The "backward" spring was felt down to the south as evidenced by "floating ice" in Green Bay on May 7. Just under a week later at the Sault on May 13, Bishop Baraga noted that "the last little pile of winter snow" beneath his window disappeared. On May 16, it "snowed again heavily."

We have little information from Marquette that winter except the unprecedented snow total from Dr. Blaker. The June 20, 1857 edition of the *Lake Superior Journal* (then published in Marquette) gives another bit of evidence confirming the length and severity of the winter: "This is rather an unpleasant as well as unusual subject for discussion at this time of year, particularly when the ice floats on the Lake before us…The Steamer *North Star* passed us on her way up after approaching within a very short distance of the town, and we have no hesitation in saying that if she had had the perseverance of other boats she *could* have come in." Ice in Marquette Harbor on the third week of June provides further evidence that the winter of 1856-57 was an extraordinary one.

December 27-28, 1904: "Worst Storm in Years"

A howling snowstorm began over the western Upper Peninsula early on the morning of December 27, 1904 "and raged with unabated fury for more than thirty hours." The snow, driven before a wind that gusted at times to 60 miles an hour, piled "in great banks that were a sight to behold." Drifts in Ironwood were estimated at 12 to 15 feet deep after the storm. The blizzard piled on top of snow that was already 20 inches on the level before the storm began, forcing people to "tunnel" from their houses to the street.

In the country, two young men from Ewen experienced a harrowing journey to Ontonagon during the height of the storm. Stanley Brown and Leon Garvin left Ewen Monday morning in a horse and cutter. They stayed the night at a friend's camp and woke to the raging snowstorm. They struck out into the blizzard anyway, heading right into the teeth of a furious north wind replete with blinding snow. They arrived at Rockland about noon, had linner, and then set out on the last 14 miles of their journey.

Travel was slow and difficult as the snow accumulated rapidly. Finally, their horse became stuck in a huge snow drift. It was getting dark and the young men decided they could go no farther. They freed the horse from the cutter and, fortunately, came upon a barn, where they found comfortable quarters for the animal along with a good supply of hay.

Brown and Garvin now focused on their own comfort. After a 17-mile ride through the ferocious storm, the pair was cold, wet and exhausted. They approached the farmhouse near the barn

A low-pressure area dropped through the Rockies into the Southern Plains and hooked northeastward, socking much of Upper Michigan with heavy snow and strong winds in late December 1904. (NOAA Central Library Data Imaging Project)

and found it unoccupied and locked. Since they did not want to break in, they resigned themselves to a night with the horse in the barn.

Following a sleepless night, Brown and Garvin crawled out of their haystack beds and both realized they were frostbitten in several places. Once out of the barn, they also fully grasped their bleak circumstances; all they could see of their cutter was one shaft protruding from the snow, while the blizzard still raged. The young men made sure their horse was well stocked with hay and then they set out on foot for Ontonagon.

Walking was extremely difficult through the mountainous drifts and biting wind and snow. It took seven hours for the lads to reach a farmhouse outside of the village. There they were fed and took time to thaw out. After making arrangements for getting their horse after the storm ended, they resumed their journey. They arrived in Ontonagon during that afternoon and found businesses paralyzed and trains stalled. Engines tried to go to the aid of mired trains and became stuck themselves. It took several days before plows succeeded in pulling out the trains. Some stranded passengers on one of the trains broke into a meat car. The express manager acted as chef, cooking the meat on a small oil stove. Mail, which moved exclusively by rail at the turn of the century, was delayed for two days.

Back in Ironwood, all streets were rendered impassable to teams except for a few blocks in the center of town. At the conclusion of the storm, the sidewalks were so deeply buried, a newspaper reporter wrote that no one expected to see any of them until April. While it is possible sidewalks remained covered the winter of 1904-05, the rest of the season featured near average snowfall and well-above-average temperatures.

Menominee's "Worst Storm": The Washington's Day Blizzard of 1922

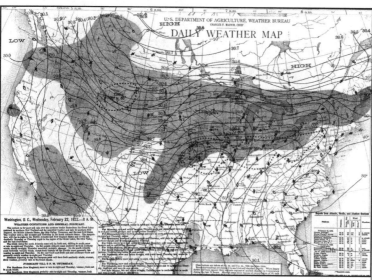

A strong disturbance drifted from the Pacific into the Inter-mountain region on February 21-22, 1922. Low pressure developed and sent a warm front eastward to the Lower Great Lakes. A huge shield of overrunning precipitation developed north of the front. The next day, an intense storm moved through the Central Great Lakes, paralyzing much of the Upper Mississippi Valley and Western Great Lakes with heavy snow and ice. (NOAA Central Library Data Imaging Project)

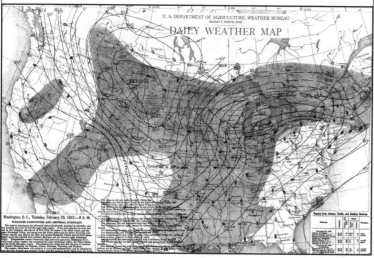

"The storm was ushered in…like the arrival of a commanding officer before his troops when cannon boom the salutes." With this military analogy, a newspaper reporter in Menominee tied in Washington's Birthday with this unprecedented blitzkrieg of snow and wind. During the peak of the storm, the "cannon boom" of thunder could be heard following lightning strikes, which were "the most vivid ever seen…before in the winter time."

The storm began late on the 21st and contained the key elements found in a crippling event: prolonged snow and raging wind. Two feet of snow fell on the Twin Cities of Marinette-Menominee, blown into drifts up to 10 feet deep by northeasterly winds as high as 50 miles per hour. In addition, sleet and freezing rain fell for a time on the 22nd, leading to a hard, frozen covering over the top of the huge mass of freshly fallen snow.

Telegraph and telephone service was disrupted and trains and streetcars became snowbound. By nightfall on Washington's Birthday, Menominee was virtually isolated from the rest of the world. While there had been greater falls of snow, this blizzard was unrivaled in its duration, coupled with the ice that even caused railroad plows to slide off the tracks into the ditch.

The storm slammed the entire Upper Peninsula. Escanaba endured its worst storm in at least a decade. Drifts piled 15 to 20 feet high throughout Delta County, bringing all traffic to a halt. Disruptions in communication and travel were reported all the way north to the Keweenaw, west to Ironwood and east to the Sault.

While Menominee residents waited out the two-day blizzard, one of its young men battled the gale and snowstorm on the frozen waters of Green Bay. Seventeen-year-old Walter Fiedorowicz left town with a friend just before the storm started to recover an ice boat left on Green Island. The pair quickly skimmed across the bay in an ice yacht, propelled by an increasing northeasterly wind. In a short time they reached the island and recovered the abandoned boat. They set off back to town with Fiedorowicz piloting the recovered boat, while his friend commandeered the ice yacht.

The Washington's Day Blizzard buried Menominee under one of its deepest snowfalls on record. Street cars became snowbound and plows like this had trouble staying on the tracks due to freezing rain that fell during the storm. (Courtesy of Menominee County Historical Society)

Before long, Fiedorowicz, in the smaller of the two boats, fell behind his friend and drifted north. His friend immediately gave chase but lost his bearings and his companion. Eventually his ice boat was wrecked and he battled his way back to shore on foot, reaching Menominee about midnight.

Blinded by the blizzard, Fiedorowicz continued sailing north at full speed until a great gust of wind hit the boat. The boom, caught by the wind, hit the lad and threw him from the craft. Lying in the snow, he watched the boat continue for a short distance before it swung into the wind and came to a stop.

Luckily, Fiedorowicz was uninjured. He assessed his situation and decided to abandon his boat for fear that he would hit a windrow or an unseen crack in the ice. He set out on foot over the blizzard-swept bay, making very slow progress in which he assumed was the direction of town.

After two hours of floundering through heavy snow, the drenched, cold and exhausted young man heard the faint blast of the Menominee Fire Department whistle. He then changed course, thinking he was headed toward Menominee. After another two-hour struggle, he became hungry and even more exhausted. By this time, his clothes were frozen stiff and covered with ice. Mustering every bit of strength, he continued against the wind, stumbling through deep drifts until he finally made it to shore.

On shore, he believed he had arrived on Peshtigo Point, about eight miles south of Marinette. Nearly frozen and almost out of hope, he chanced upon a farmhouse where he learned that he was actually more than eight miles north of Menominee; a full sixteen miles north of where he thought he had landed.

Fiedorowicz spent the night at the farmhouse and left for Menominee the next morning. He finally arrived home after a harrowing journey, with no boats.

Outside of Negaunee, the Chicago & Northwestern's Railway telegraph operator sent an S.O.S. call after he became trapped in his office. The operator worked the night shift during the peak of the snowstorm. By morning, he realized he was snowed in; drifts surrounded the telegraph office and blocked the doors. Fortunately, the operator was able to wire division headquarters in Escanaba for help. A big railroad plow eventually made its way north to Cascade and the men aboard dug out the imprisoned operator, who could have been trapped for days if he had not made the call. The snow around Cascade Junction drifted 10 to 12 feet high and in a few spots the drifts piled up to 20 feet.

Mountains of snow were left after the big storm. (Courtesy of Superior View, Marquette)

Three Ishpeming girls spent a harrowing night in the blizzard. They attended a dance in Negaunee and afterward went to the train station and waited for the midnight train, which finally arrived at 5 a.m.

When they reached Ishpeming, they started for their homes in Cleveland location, but the storm was so severe they lost their way. Confused, exhausted and frozen, they took shelter in the doorway of a factory. In the morning, a passerby noticed the girls huddled together, crying.

The man realized they were "in a bad way" and urged them to seek shelter at the depot. Neither of the three seemed able to walk, so he carried them, one by one, to the station. After about an hour spent thawing out, the girls set out on another, and this time successful, attempt to reach their homes.

The system raked a wide area. The Green Bay region southwest into the Fox Valley sustained heavy damage due to ice. Thousands of trees were toppled when ice up to an inch thick accumulated on branches near Manitowoc. In Minnesota, twelve people died, including four found frozen in snow drifts at Minneapolis. In Duluth, a northeasterly gale blew for three days, piling the heavy snow into 30-foot drifts. These mountains of snow were "the deepest ever known" at the Zenith City.

Tragedy in the Mining District: The Storm of October 1925

This storm, "unprecedented for October in this territory," began the afternoon of October 18. The headline on the 19th, in huge letters, read "Storm Isolates Marquette." While mostly rain and mixed precipitation fell in the city due to the warming influence of Lake Superior, heavy, wet snow and sleet just outside of town to the west and south brought down telephone and telegraph wires, cutting off communications. Six to eight inches fell in Ishpeming and

Negaunee, while more than a foot piled up west of Ishpeming. More than two feet of wet, windblown snow was reported in interior Alger County at Rumely.

"It stormed and stormed and stormed," remembers Margaret Mullins, who was 12 years old at the time. Her family, the Gustavsons, were residents of Diorite, a community on the Iron Range of western Marquette County. She remembers the storm so vividly after so many years because of the tragedy it brought her hometown that mid-October weekend.

"It was nice out," recalls Mullins. "Five lads went back up in the bluff behind Diorite. They went in their shirt sleeves then all of a sudden, a storm came up." The boys were about two miles north of Diorite when it began to snow and they decided to head for home. When the snow became heavy, they lost their way and wandered in the woods and swamps about three hours.

Finally they came upon familiar markings and three boys in the party decided they were on the right track. Two other youngsters in the group, Waino Maki, 14, and his young uncle, Aino Johnson, 17, disagreed. The five argued, and Maki and Johnson said they would get home first. Despite pleading from their three companions to stick together, Maki and Johnson persisted and the two parties separated. Neither of the two young relatives was familiar with the woods and this was the farthest they had ever been from home. They quickly lost their way in the blinding snowstorm, while their three companions arrived home about mid-afternoon.

A search party led by Tom Johnson, Aino's father, was quickly assembled. The severity of the storm impeded their efforts and they were unable to reach the camp and farmhouse where they thought the young men may have sought refuge. The search party remained in the snowbound woods until 11 that night without finding any trace of the missing pair.

Negaunee, March 1926: ironically, little snow fell the rest of winter of 1925-26. Calumet received only 84.5 inches the whole winter, while Ishpeming tallied a paltry 68 inches with nearly a third of that total coming in a tremendous early-March 1926 storm. (Photos courtesy Superior View, Marquette)

Meanwhile, the cold, wet and exhausted boys knew they would have to spend the night in the woods. They constructed a crude lean-to out of fallen wood to protect themselves from the snow and wind. Then they tried to rest but were unnerved by the howling of a pack of wolves.

The animals kept circling their improvised camp, and the boys, afraid of being attacked, did not fall asleep until morning.

When Aino Johnson woke about noon, he realized Maki was gone and immediately followed the younger boy's trail. He trudged through knee-deep snow for what seemed like an eternity. Then, he thought he heard voices. Buoyed by the prospect of being rescued, he followed the sound through a swamp. Johnson then most likely fell into the hallucinatory state of the winter sojourner (*see 'Hallucination', page 95*) and wandered aimlessly the rest of that day then through the night. He finally arrived at a farm five miles north of Clarksburg, "exhausted and deranged" the next morning. His hands and face were swollen and his feet frozen. "He had to get both legs cut off below the knee," remembers Mullins.

A search party was finally assembled early Tuesday. While several Diorite men familiar with the area went out Monday to search for the boys, a more organized hunt involving state police and conservation officers was delayed by communication problems; telephone service was out due to downed lines. When the Johnson boy showed up at the Clarksburg farm, searchers backtracked, following his trail through the snow until they came to where he had left Maki's trail. They then picked up where Johnson had left off, and a short time later found Maki under a tree. A state police officer said the boy put up a "game fight for his life" and had only been dead a few hours. Waino Maki appeared to have dropped down by the tree, covered his face with branches as protection from the storm, fallen asleep and died. His death and his young uncle's crippling injuries serve as reminders of the perils of venturing into Upper Michigan's woods unprepared.

The Storm of '38: Upper Michigan's Storm of the Century

In late January 1938, the country was still in the process of emerging from the Great Depression, while President Roosevelt asked Congress for a larger army, "concerned by world events." Downstate, a probate judge ruled that a welfare grant of two dollars a week for a family of two was not adequate, after he tried to live on the allowance himself.

Upper Michigan must have seemed a world away from its political neighbors across the Straits of Mackinac. The Mackinac Bridge would not be built for another two decades and the ice-choked straits hindered ferry passage to the Lower Peninsula. The Upper Peninsula may have seemed isolated, but it was not in hibernation. Despite the lingering effects of the Depression, the area was bustling with activity.

In Marquette, the major "Queen City" and center of commerce for the region, a January thaw was gradually whittling down the snowbanks left by a New Year's Eve storm. The holiday weekend snowstorm was actually a blessing; it kept the majority of people home and accidents to a minimum. The mild, tranquil weather of the last few days had allowed workers to erect a new tower for radio station WBEO on top of *The Mining Journal* building downtown. Back then, the regional newspaper owned the only radio station in the county, too. The tower project was a difficult one, and it took the better part of a week before it was raised.

Up the road in Ishpeming, the balmy weather made it a perfect time to take in a movie at the Ishpeming Theatre. The screwball, Oscar-winning comedy *The Awful Truth* starring

Cary Grant and Irene Dunne, was just ending an extended run. Down south in Escanaba, the Delft Theatre was showing the action-packed Western *Wells Fargo* starring Joel McCrea and Frances Dee.

The residents of Upper Michigan were enduring the mid-winter doldrums quite well as they began a new week on January 24, 1938. The day dawned cloudy with a stiff northeasterly wind and a Weather Bureau forecast of rain or snow with much colder weather and flurries the next day. A storm followed by a cold wave; it was all part of the time-honored sequence of events during a normal winter. But this storm was to be different. Somehow, the atmosphere delivered up just the right combination of energy, moisture and cold air in just the right spot to unleash a blizzard of historic proportions from Ironwood to Newberry and from Houghton to Menominee.

Do you remember the "Storm of the Century" along the East Coast in March 1993? This monstrous low took shape in the Gulf of Mexico, caused a storm surge worthy of a small hurricane on the west coast of Florida, and then surged northeastward. It drew arctic air into its circulation, which led to record snows from Alabama to New York and New England. The blizzard of 1938 was the U.P.'s "Storm of the Century" and those who lived through it hold it up as a yardstick against which all other storms are measured.

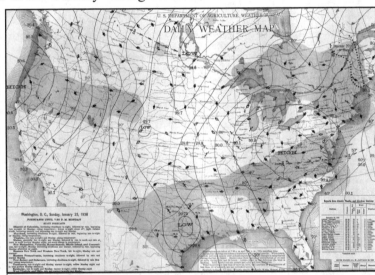

The storm of '38 developed out of two systems. The low in the Northern Plains provided the cold air, while the Texas low pumped up the moisture. The two disturbances formed into one massive storm over the Upper Midwest. (NOAA Central Library Data Imaging Project)

In the late 1930s, weather information was gathered by telegraph, and the quantity and quality of this data was very meager by today's computer-age standards. Upper-air observations were in their infancy, numerical weather prediction was just a theory and surface weather maps were produced only a couple of times a day.

What small bits of data we have indicate the probable "phasing" of weather systems

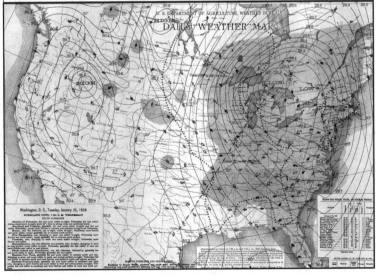

Snow Measurement

Over the last quarter of the 20th century the 1938 Ironwood total of 32 inches of snow from one storm has been equaled or exceeded several times. But it must be kept in mind that snow-measuring techniques have changed since the 1930s. The actual measuring of the snow has stayed the same—a ruler is used. But instead of measuring snow once a day as observers did back in the '30s, snow is now measured several times a day, and in some cases hourly. The more often snow is measured, the less time it has to settle; less settling could mean higher snow-depth totals in modern times.

over the central section of North America, which developed this storm into a memorable one. On January 23, a low-pressure system was developing over eastern Texas along a stationary front that ran eastward through the Deep South. At the same time, a cold front extending from low pressure near Lake Winnipeg, Canada into the Northern Plains was heading southeastward. As energy from the northern stream system "dug" toward the Texas low, it caused the low to deepen, while it drifted northeastward. The low drew up tremendous amounts of moisture from the Gulf, generating an expanding area of precipitation. By early the 24th, a strengthening storm was situated near Springfield, Illinois, with heavy, wet snow already falling over much of northern Wisconsin and the southwestern Upper Peninsula. Farther south, heavy rains triggered river flooding in northern Illinois.

During the next 24 hours the storm really wound up, as phasing of the polar stream from the north and the subtropical stream out of the south was completed over the Upper Great Lakes. The low drifted from central Illinois to east of Sault Ste. Marie, drawing arctic air into its northern and western flank. The introduction of cold air developed blizzard conditions in the cold sector of the storm, while the deepening and slow movement exposed Upper Michigan to an unusually long period of heavy snow and gale force winds. As the air cooled and the northerly winds increased, Lake Superior undoubtedly became a player, adding moisture that contributed to snowfall totals.

Snow measurement is difficult when it piles to the top of utility poles like this scene from the Copper Country. (Courtesy of Superior View, Marquette)

Accurate snow measurement is extremely difficult when the wind blows as strong and as long as it did during the '38 blizzard. The Weather Bureau reported a total of about 18 inches of snow in the city of Marquette from the storm. Judging by the stories, the pictures and the fact that snow fell for at least 30 hours, this storm total seems conservative. The 32 inches reported in Ironwood during the two-day event appears a much more realistic figure.

The snow began wet and heavy with an early morning temperature of 34 degrees in Marquette on the 24th. Gale-force winds then drove the sticky snow into mountainous drifts that became the consistency of sand. These drifts brought transportation, both vehicular and rail, to a standstill for days. In Baraga County, a north-bound Chicago train stalled in a drift

30 feet high between Nestoria and Herman.

Snow removal technology was no match for this historic blizzard. "They had big tractors at that time," Margaret Mullins of Diorite in western Marquette County remembers, "not snowplows like we have now." Today the trucks that carry the huge plows get up enough speed to plow through the snow and push it back away from the road. "The tractor moved so slowly," explains Mullins, "all it did was make a rut and great big banks." The snow piled within several feet of the tops of telephone poles where Mullins lived on Highway 41. "Nothing moved except by foot for three days," she says. "The people that came walking could reach the telephone wires with their hands." She went on to explain that the exposed tops of the poles served as a guide to help hikers stay on the road.

The huge snow tractors would bog down in the colossal drifts piled up on area roads. In some cases, shovel crews would then have to remove enough snow by hand before the tractor plow could get through. "A friend of mine, his dad was on a shovel crew," recalls Cliff (Kip) Waters of Negaunee. He explains the "tier" shoveling technique of these crews: "They had to back the truck in and the guys up here would shovel down to this guy, then to this guy, to this guy and then they'd shovel it into the truck." He explains that this snow removal method took a lot of manpower and time. "The county hired them for six-hour shifts. It took them six days to get from Negaunee to Palmer," a distance of about ten miles.

Not only was the equipment less powerful and efficient, there was less of it. Back in 1938, Marquette County had 19 snow plows and tractors responsible for keeping 742 miles of roads cleared. Sixty years later, the county had 32 plows and 7 graders responsible for taking care of 1,262 miles of highways and county roads. The equipment more than doubled, while the amount of roads increased by only 70 percent. Obviously the road

In many instances, snow-removal equipment proved nearly useless in removing the mountains of snow left by the storm. It took days of back-breaking labor by crews of men to clear some roads in the central and western U.P. (Courtesy of Delta County Historical Society)

crews of today are much better equipped with better designed and more powerful equipment; though a storm of comparable intensity today can still create major problems.

There were major problems aplenty during the Storm of 1938. They included stranded travelers and workers, marooned vehicles and a disastrous fire that threatened to take a good share of Marquette's downtown business district. Since the storm started early in the day and the weather forecast failed to adequately describe its eventual intensity, schools opened as usual that morning. As new information came in and the Weather Bureau got a handle on the scope of the event, Bureau officials called school authorities, advising them that snow and wind would continue, accompanied by a cold wave. As the wet snow quickly piled up and the wind increased, all Marquette County schools were ordered closed.

The call came too late for some of the school districts, especially in the western part of the county. Buses in the mining districts of Diorite, West Ishpeming and Eagle Mills did not leave until late afternoon when the blizzard was nearing its peak. All buses in these communities became snowbound along their routes. The Eagle Mills bus finished most of its route but was forced to turn back to Negaunee because of almost zero visibility and severe drifting. Five children still on the bus had to spend the night in Negaunee homes. The West Ishpeming bus floundered and came to a halt in deep drifts at North Lake. County plows made two emergency trips to take children off the stranded bus to their homes.

The biggest scare came from the Dorite district west of Ishpeming. The bus first pulled out of Diorite with its cargo of young passengers at 4 that afternoon. Margaret Mullins's husband drove that bus for the district at the time, and operated the gas station on Highway 41 near Greenwood. Somehow he managed to get most of the children home. "He had four students left," she remembers. "He had to travel over to South Greenwood to get them home." Fortunately, a father of two passengers on board was following behind in a 1935 Ford equipped with chains. "My husband got stuck by the railroad crossing," recalls Mullins. "So the kids got out and the father took all of them home."

Ray (Kayo) Mullins then had no choice but to face the raging blizzard and find his way home. "It was getting dark and he had a flashlight," recounts Mullins. "The road he was traveling on was where the Wawanowin Golf Club is now. There was a farm just opposite where the golf club is. It had a fence line and he followed that fence line to know where he was. You could see one of the fence posts sticking up through the snow every now and then. He made it home. At that time, we didn't have a telephone, so we didn't think about notifying anybody."

The bus was reported late, and receiving no word from Mullins, school officials assumed the worst—that the bus was stranded with children on board. They contacted the county and an all-out search was mounted as the storm peaked. Three plows and a tractor searched more than six hours for the bus and its passengers. Finally, at about 11 o'clock the empty, snowbound bus was found. "In 1938 not many people had telephones," says Mullins. "We had one ever since then, though."

High school students in Ironwood holed up in Roosevelt Elementary school. Students were also stranded at a school in the Iron County community of Alpha for several days. (Courtesy of Ironwood Carnegie Library)

In Ironwood, students had to endure many a child's nightmare—they became trapped in school as the blizzard reached a crescendo. Students from the high school were being transported home but conditions became so bad that the bus driver stopped at Roosevelt Elementary near the airport and decided he would not chance trying to plow through the deep drifts. For the next four nights the students slept on exercise mats in the gym. The school had a stove and cooking utensils and food was brought to them, but no attempt was made to take them home through the 12-foot drifts that piled up on city streets.

Six children also became snowbound in an Iron County school. Their school bus left the small community of Alpha, south of Crystal Falls, but the driver was forced to turn back when huge drifts made highways impassable. Food and beds were provided for the four girls and two boys whose ages ranged from six to 12 years old. "Life became monotonous and weary" for the students—they were held prisoner by the drifted roads until the end of the week.

The 36-hour storm is still considered "the worst of them all" by old timers in the Copper Country. While only 7 ½ inches of new snow was measured at Calumet, 50 mile-per-hour wind gusts built 20-foot drifts in business and residential districts. Here too, snow removal equipment became bogged down trying to break through the huge mounds of snow.

Two area residents died due to the storm. A Houghton County Road Commission employee was asphyxiated in his cab. He was on his way to Atlantic Mine to open a road so an area doctor could reach a patient. Outside of Lake Linden, a lumberjack was found dead. He apparently succumbed to the blizzard on his way back to lumber camp.

The fierce winds knocked out power to many Keweenaw residents. Eagle Harbor was without electricity from Monday night until Thursday evening. The lighthouse there was left with a coating of ice eight inches thick; the violent gale caused waves to crash over the structure. The cascading water smashed windows there and at the Coast Guard lookout. The keeper of the light said it was the worst storm in his 32 years of service.

The Eagle Harbor lighthouse. The keeper declared the 1938 storm the worst in over three decades of service. (Courtesy of Superior View, Marquette)

Out in rural areas, virtual mountains of snow developed. In Dickinson County, roads were shut by drifts as high as 18 feet in some places. "You may go along for 10 miles or more, in areas where the highway has been swept clean by the wind," said the county highway engineer. "Then you will suddenly come upon a huge drift that blocks all traffic." On U.S.-2 near Wakefield in Gogebic County, a drift 15 feet high and 700 feet long was reported!

Marguerite (Johnson) Waters grew up in Ironwood and remembers how deep the snow got: "I was eleven at the time and we were tickled because we were out of school four or five days. We lived on U.S.-2 at the time. It was only a two-lane road called Cloverland Drive then." She explains that there was a huge lilac, not really a bush, but a grove of lilac

Children all over the Upper Peninsula enjoyed an extended vacation from school after the massive storm. Most played on the mountains of snow left by the storm, while this youngster preferred taking his sled through a doorway tunnel constructed in a Negaunee snowbank. (Courtesy of Superior View, Marquette)

trees over a story high. "The grove of trees was completely drifted over," she remembers. "You couldn't tell there were any trees under… [the snow]. So of course, we climbed on top of it, we played around and we could almost touch the telephone wires. That was an adventure."

The children she played with made a game out of tumbling down the huge snow bank. She said they slid down into a "sort of depression that was the highway, although it was about six or eight feet" under the bottom of the mound of snow they were playing on. "One of my friends got stuck headfirst when he rolled down," she recalls. "So we had to pull him out by the feet. It was packed hard enough so that he was really stuck."

Waters explains that after a few days the bread and milk trucks could finally get through to restock the store shelves. "A couple of my little neighbors got the idea 'If we push some snow into there [the highway], they'll have trouble getting through, and then we can push them out and they'll give us something.'" She remembers that these "enterprising" kids earned bread and milk for their families that way.

Lots of folks tell stories of being trapped in their houses by the deep snow and escaping through second story windows. Most houses had doors that opened outward and when the dense, drifted snow packed up against them they became impossible to open. Kathy (Mullins) Lundin was not born until after the storm, but her husband was three years old at the time. "His father worked at the Marquette prison and he never got home for three days," she explains. "My husband was home with his mother at Cleveland location in Ishpeming for three days and their fire went out." The fire died because the chimney became plugged with snow. Her husband's uncle came to their rescue, snowshoeing up to the second story window and leading them to safety.

Many other workers, including scores of miners, became snowbound at their work places and were stuck there for several days. Two Works Progress Administration watchmen became marooned atop Mount Zion just outside Ironwood during the height of the storm. Several attempts were made to bring the men food but in each case the would-be rescuers were turned back by gale-force winds and heavy snow. Finally, Joseph Maurin and a friend strapped a three-day supply of food on their backs and headed into the teeth of the blizzard to aid the stranded men. Maurin was on skis and his friend on snowshoes. They labored through the mountains of snow and eventually reached the base of the summit. There Maurin took off his skis and used them in his hands as supports to crawl through the 10-foot drifts. The wind was so strong and the snow so heavy, the two could only see a few feet in front of them throughout the slow, tortuous climb to the top. The two-mile trip took an hour and a half to complete. "Once we started to turn back," said Maurin. "But when we thought of them being up there for probably a week without food, we decided to continue."

Others were unable to get to work. "That was the first time my dad ever missed a shift at the LS&I" (The Lake Superior and Ishpeming Railroad), recalls Kip Waters, who grew up in Negaunee. "He started at the railroad in 1910. He went to work the next day on a pair of skis." Waters laughs when he tells the story; his father was not very proficient on skis. "I wish I could have seen him go up Snow Street hill, because the depot was on top of the hill."

In Escanaba, the weatherman became snowbound. A young assistant weather observer was just promoted to the Milwaukee Weather Bureau Office. He was delayed in his departure because the train was not running. While only seven inches of snow was reported from this southern Upper Michigan town, the drifts left by the storm rivaled those found in the snow belts farther north.

A young lad resorted to snowshoes in order to deliver the paper to his customers in Escanaba following the storm. (From Delta County Historical Society's Pearl Larsen Collection, Vol. 1)

Up north in Marquette, the storm created and exacerbated another unique set of problems. On Monday, the north wind kept building in strength as the day came to a close. At about five that evening, a gale force gust toppled the upper half of WBEO's new radio tower in downtown Marquette. It was the same tower the workmen had finally erected with so much difficulty the week before. The new antenna severed the station's old antenna as it fell, knocking the station off the air. The crumbled mass of metal also put a small hole in the roof of the Mining Journal building.

Fred Rydholm, Marquette native, local historian and storyteller, was 14 years old at the time of the blizzard. He says the storm was "the worst in my recollection." Even as the storm built toward a crescendo, many residents still tried to maintain their schedules. A concert featuring a 60 member male choir from Finland was held at the local high school auditorium despite the snow and wind. "I had gone to the concert that night," recalls Rydholm, "and it wasn't until the concert was over and we left that we realized we had a big storm on our hands." The choir members were stranded in town and spent the next three days holed up at the Northland Hotel. Rydholm remembers the choir giving free concerts at the hotel during their stay.

Later that night a fire broke out in downtown Marquette.

The Opera House Fire: suspicious origin?

The 1938 Marquette Opera House blaze apparently originated nearby in the Masonic Temple and was thought by many to have started suspiciously. The treasurer of the Masonic Temple, who was also the treasurer of the Episcopal Church in town, had been accused, along with the bishop of the Episcopal Church, of misappropriating church funds.

"Some folks thought that the fire was started by the treasurer, while he was trying to destroy church documents stored in the temple safe," says Rydholm. The man was never questioned about the incident—he collapsed and died of a heart attack on a city street a short time later. The bishop was eventually charged with embezzlement and sent to prison. ❄

The blaze was first reported by newspaper boys on their way to deliver the morning paper. By that time, the Masonic Temple and the old Opera House built by city pioneer Peter White were engulfed in flames. Firemen worked well into Tuesday desperately trying to save the rest of the downtown district. They fought against gale-force, bitter winds, blinding snow and a lack of water pressure, but they managed to save all but four buildings. Even so, the fire was the worst since the conflagration that consumed much of Marquette in 1868. It caused damage estimated at $400,000, a huge sum in 1938.

On the lighter side, the severe snowstorm did not prevent some people from engaging in their favorite vices. Marilyn (Anderson) Baker grew up in Ironwood and remembers watching the storm out the front window of her home. "You could hardly see across the street," she remembers. "My mother…called to my dad to tell him there was someone walking up the street and he kept falling down." Baker went on to explain that her father thought his wife was seeing things. She persisted and insisted that he come and look for himself. "Sure enough it was Jalmer from across the street," says Baker. "He was drunk as a skunk. He was a young bachelor who lived with his aged mother." Apparently Jalmer's favorite watering hole stayed open long enough for him to get a snoot-full. "He would take a couple of steps and down he would go," she chuckles. "Finally, he didn't get up and my dad bundled up and managed to drag him home. The door opened and his mother let loose with a tirade in Swedish."

At the height of the storm, a devastating fire roared through the downtown business district of Marquette. (Courtesy of Superior View, Marquette)

Drifts halted a double-header snow plow train near Ford River south of Escanaba following the storm. (Courtesy of Delta County Historical Society)

Rydholm tells of a man who lost his car on a back road in Baraga County. His car became stuck and he abandoned it. When he went back to fetch it, he could find no sign of it; the whole area was covered in snow higher than his car. He later came back with an iron pole and did "soundings"— sticking the pole into the snow until he located his vehicle.

A farmer in North Bessemer slapped on a pair of snowshoes and set out on foot to deliver milk to a few preferred customers. He hauled the milk on a toboggan that he pulled along with a rope. The man decided to take a shortcut across an open field; the roads were totally clogged with snow, so it did not matter where he walked. As he was crossing the field, he stumbled against a fairly substantial object and he looked to see what he tripped on. As he cleared away the snow, he stepped back and gasped realizing it was the chimney of a house! Tall tale or fact, this story symbolizes the magnitude of a storm that defines severe winter weather in Upper Michigan; a storm that lives on as one of *the* major weather events of the region.

The March 1939 Blizzard: Flashback to '38

A "severe storm…reminiscent of the destructive blizzard of January 1938" struck Upper Michigan on March 14 and 15, 1939. A foot or more of snow came down over central

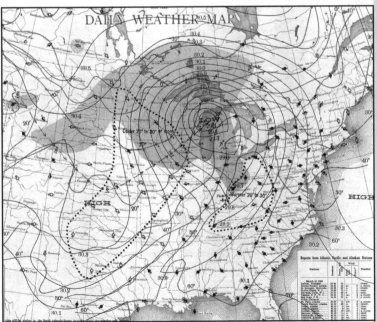

An intense winter storm took a familiar path in mid-March 1939. It buried a large area of the U.P. in over a foot of snow.
(NOAA Central Library Data Imaging Project)

ESCANABA: UPPER MICHIGAN'S "BANANA BELT"

If the brisk, invigorating climate of Upper Michigan suits you, but you are not a fan of the huge snowfalls found over many areas, Escanaba is the place to be. Located on Lake Michigan's Little Bay De Noc, the city is far enough removed from the snow belts to the north. Northerly winds off Lake Superior push lake effect snow far inland, but the majority of snow falls over the ridges to Escanaba's north. By the time the snow bands reach the city, there is little left in them but a few flurries or very light snow.

While many locations in the northern U.P. push or exceed 100 inches of snow annually, Escanaba averages a mere 56.7 inches. Occasionally, Lake Michigan will produce lake effect, but most of the time the wind blows from a northwesterly direction, diverting Lake Michigan's lake effect to the Lower Peninsula. Even in these relatively rare Lake Michigan events, this city on the bay usually escapes the heaviest snow. For instance, on December 20, 2004, a vigorous "clipper" low-pressure system moved into a very cold air mass over Upper Michigan. The strong southerly flow ahead of the system produced tremendous snows off Lake Michigan. Manistique, roughly 40 miles to the east, was buried under nearly two feet of wind-

blown snow. Escanaba, too far to the west to receive the lake influence, wound up with only a few inches.

The heaviest seasonal snowfall on record in Escanaba is 90.8 inches set in 1908-09. Its least snowy winter was 1899-1900, when a scant 14.8 inches fell. All areas too far from the influence of Lake Superior receive less than the snow belt areas, but Escanaba, with its moderate climate on the shore of Lake Michigan, is the capital of Upper Michigan's "Banana Belt."

sections, with Republic reporting 20 inches. Marquette was buried under 19 inches, while Munising tallied 20. After the storm, Munising in the east-central snow belt of the U.P., measured a massive 52-inch snow cover.

Even in Escanaba, the "banana belt" of Upper Michigan, 13 inches of new snow fell, whipped by tremendous winds. A correspondent reported what it was like there at the peak of the storm: "The snow's fallin' like fury. There's a 42-mile gale. Ya can't see across Ludington Street. Everything's tied up." The 42-mile-an-hour wind gust set a record wind speed for March at that location.

In Marquette, approximately 60 people were again stranded by the storm at the Northland Hotel. One of them was Ted Kingsford of Iron Mountain, attending a car dealer meeting at the hotel. Kingsford was determined to get his station wagon shoveled out so he could drive back home. He and eight car dealer buddies, all attired in 10-gallon hats, worked feverishly to get his car excavated from the drifts in front of the hotel. Kingsford's pals eventually abandoned him, convinced it was a lost cause. They retired to the hotel lobby to watch their determined friend continue working. One of them told a reporter, "We would no sooner shovel out the front end after clearing the rear than the rear end of the car would be snowed under again." Kingsford finally gave up, after a two-and-a-half-hour, all-out effort enabled him to move his car about 100 feet.

While Escanaba may be the center of Upper Michigan's "Banana Belt," it is not immune from snowstorms like this heavy, wet one that brought down trees and interrupted power and telephone service in late November 1945. (Courtesy of the Delta County Historical Society)

Another fire occurred in Marquette during the height of the storm, this time at the Knights of Columbus building on Washington Street. The blaze caused $100,000 dollars in damage.

After the 1938 storm, little additional snow fell the rest of the winter and the weather was mild. On March 22, 1938 only a trace of snow remained in some shady areas around Marquette. Some people were even out golfing. The 1939 snowstorm was the "crown of winter" storm that sometimes hits the U.P., bringing the snow cover to maximum winter depths near the first day of astronomical spring. After one of these storms, the snow lingers; the slow march toward true spring warmth is delayed, sometimes for a month or more, until the last of the crusty, old drifts melt.

Stranded on the Ice: March 16, 1941

A storm, "the worst blizzard of the winter," caught up with 20 people fishing on the ice off Skanee, in northern Baraga County on March 16, 1941, causing a near catastrophe. The storm developed out of a trough of low pressure extending from El Paso, Texas to near Duluth. As the system intensified to the west, "the severest blizzard of the modern era" struck North Dakota and Minnesota the night of the 15th. Seventy-one people perished in the two states when caught in the ferocious gale, plummeting temperatures and blinding snow. Winds reached 85 miles an hour in Grand Forks and 75 miles per hour in Duluth. The low then passed over the west end of Upper Michigan. It was when the cold front extending south of the low pushed through Skanee that trouble began for those out on the ice of Lake Superior.

A gentle snow fell early that morning, then about 8:00 a.m.,

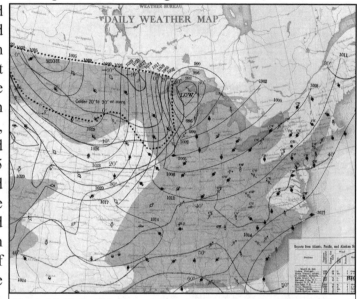

March 16, 1941. This intense winter storm over western Upper Michigan was followed by a rush of cold air and a blizzard. Twenty ice anglers near Skanee were left stranded on a piece of ice that began floating toward the open water of Lake Superior. (NOAA Central Library Data Imaging Project)

the front plowed through with a blast of cold air from the west. "A terrible wind came," remembered John Koski, one of the fishermen, "like a tornado. We were near Point Abbey and we could see the branches bending and falling off the trees." The strong westerly winds eventually started breaking up the ice Koski and his fellow anglers were on. "It wasn't long before there was 10 feet between our piece of ice and the ice connected to the shore," he recounted.

Myrna Koski Ward was nine years old at the time. She remembers that her father was supposed to pick her up at her aunt's in Skanee that afternoon. He did not show up and her cousin, an older boy, came instead. "He whispered to my aunt, and I knew something was amiss," recalls Koski Ward.

The party drifted for several hours as the west wind continued howling. Finally, the wind veered more northerly and the ice flow began drifting back toward shore. Koski and four companions were the first to reach shore, escaping from their ice floe and working through a maze of rough, partially frozen ice about three miles east of the Little Huron River. The five men walked several miles through deep snow in near zero visibility. Eventually, the other men in the party became exhausted and built a fire. Koski was familiar with the area and kept hiking for a friend's logging camp.

Another group wound up stranded on the Huron Islands. The five men jumped off their icy prison as high seas tossed the ice floe they were on against the rocks. They had to jump from one small cake of ice to another, eventually making it to the rocky shore of Macintyre Island. They found shelter in a fish shanty and subsisted on a pound of beans left by some other fishermen.

Two other men in the group were not able to get off the ice floe in time before it whirled away from the island. They were left drifting toward the open water of Lake Superior, moving in an easterly direction. Finally, the wind swung around and they were carried toward the beach along the shore of extreme northern Baraga County. The floe they were on began breaking up and they, too, were forced to jump from cake to cake to keep from going under. After several harrowing hours on the ice, they made it to shore; the two had floated approximately 28 miles from where they had been fishing.

The men walked for several miles along the shore where they came upon a group of six men and a woman who had escaped their ice floe around the Huron River. They built a fire and a windbreak out of ice, deciding to spend the night there rather than risk getting lost in the woods.

Back in the woods, John Koski pressed on. "Finally, through the dark, I could see a little light shining out of that cabin," he remembered years later. He had arrived at his friend's camp. Inside camp, Edmund LeClaire was trying to settle down to sleep when he heard strange noises that differed from the howling of the storm. He began to wonder what was going on outside the cabin.

"Then all of a sudden," he recounted, "the door flew open." There stood a big man, "so covered with snow and ice, you could not recognize him." As the man talked, the others in camp immediately identified him as Koski. He explained what happened and that he had left the others back in the woods.

This snow and ice "volcanoe" was formed on the Lake Superior shore near Marquette by the strong winds of the March 16, 1941 storm. (Courtesy of the Marquette History Museum)

A rescue party was formed. A sleigh was hooked to a tractor and LeClaire along with a camp companion and the frozen, wet Koski took off into the storm. The tractor had no headlights so they took a lantern and followed Koski's tracks as best they could through the two feet of new snow. After traveling some distance down the trail, they began to distinguish some sort of light ahead. As they got closer, they recognized it as the fire of Koski's companions. "There were some happy faces when they saw us," LeClaire remembered. The four men warming themselves around the fire jumped on the sleigh and were taken back to shelter and a hot meal.

The next morning, LeClaire took off in a pick up truck for town. The storm had quit but the road to town was still blocked. On his way back to camp, he stopped at another logging camp and found three other ice floe survivors. These men "were in pretty tough shape" and told him there were still other people in the woods near the Little Huron.

LeClaire went back to camp, hooked up the tractor and sleigh, and headed toward the river mouth. Some companions left before him on snowshoes. When he got to a swamp just before the river mouth, his companions were already helping six, wet, frozen people across it.

LeClaire tells the story of one survivor who wanted to throw himself off the sleigh; he was in such pain from frozen hands and feet. When they arrived at camp a local doctor was there to provide treatment, including some good, stiff drinks. As the survivors told their tales, they realized that five more people had been stranded on one of the Huron Islands. LeClaire again sprang into action and made his way to Portage Entry. There he alerted the Coast Guard, who launched a boat and pulled the five off Macintyre Island; they had been stranded there for nearly 30 hours.

All survivors suffered from exposure, many of them had frostbitten hands, feet and faces. "I remember my father being in bed with frostbite a couple of days and getting a letter from his congressman," remembers Myrna Koski Ward. The congressman's letter congratulated him for his courageous walk through the blizzard to get help for his companions.

The ice floe incident was an event no one in the area ever forgot. The local paper summed up why all the townsfolk were so grateful: "No one can realize what a near catastrophe it was unless he could have seen the huge seas pound the rocky shoreline and the ice floes rapidly being ground to bits under the feet of their human freight."

Blizzard of '47:

Wisconsin's Worst Scrapes the U.P.

"Wisconsin's worst snowstorm", of January 30-31, 1947, edged into southern Upper Michigan, bringing Menominee and surrounding areas to a standstill. The intense storm, borne over the Southern Plains, lifted far enough northward to affect far southern Upper Michigan.

Winds were the most outstanding feature of this storm. Because of the geography of the region, a northeast wind tends to "funnel down" Green Bay and pick up speed into the east-facing twin cities of

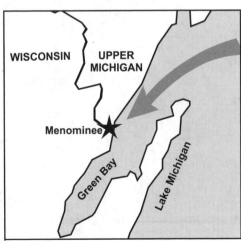

Northeast winds are channeled down Green Bay into Menominee. This funneling effect causes high winds speeds like the 74 mile-per-hour gust measured during the January 1947 storm.

Menominee-Marinette. In this storm the peak wind reached an incredible 74 miles an hour. The drifting and heavy snow isolated Menominee and much of the county.

Gales over 50 miles an hour at the Straits of Mackinac forced cancellation of state ferry service; it was too dangerous to be near the boat or the docks. Easterly winds blowing up the straits reportedly broke windows on the ferry, while light standards on the dock at St. Ignace were blown down.

Farther northwest, Marquette collected only three inches, while the strong northeast wind blowing up into the higher elevations enhanced snowfall; Ishpeming received 12 inches and many secondary roads in Marquette County were closed due to heavy drifting. At the same time, Houghton, even more removed from the path of the storm, got little more than a dusting.

The epicenter of this snowstorm was the central Great Lakes. Milwaukee was crippled by 18 inches of wet snow whipped by gale-force winds. Hundreds of people became stranded throughout the city, taking refuge in hotels, businesses and even street cars. In the Lower Peninsula, the worst conditions existed north of a line from Bay City to Muskegon. There, 15-foot drifts made travel impossible. Train service from Wisconsin and Lower Michigan to the Upper Peninsula was hampered for days.

March 5-6, 1959: "Wild March Blizzard"

"The worst storm since the storm of March…1939" buried all of Upper Michigan with a foot or more of wind-whipped snow in early March 1959. It was a wide-ranging system, dropping 17 inches of snow on Ottumwa in south-central Iowa, and a foot or more from northern Missouri into Wisconsin. This March classic developed from the Rockies into the Texas Panhandle on March 4, moved to southwestern Missouri near Springfield on the 5th, then took a sharp left turn to southern Lake Michigan, as the upper low supporting it closed off and intensified over the Mid-Mississippi Valley. On the morning of March 6, a deep low with a pressure of 29.20 inches of mercury (988mb) was situated over the southwest corner of Lower Michigan.

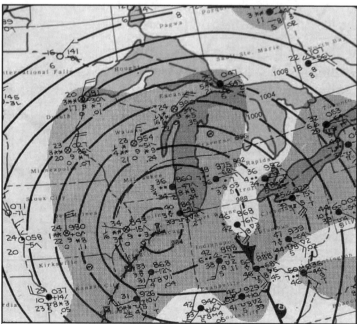

March 6, 1959 at 1:00 a.m. This March classic formed in the Lower Mississippi Valley and headed north-northeastward putting the entire U.P. in a heavy snow shield and resulting blizzard. Note the heavy snow, 25-knot-sustained northeast wind and one-sixteenth-mile visibility report at Escanaba. (NOAA Central Library Data Imaging Project)

The storm was unforgettable for Pard Bess of Iron River, who lived in Ishpeming at the time. "My daughter, Sarah, was born then. We lived on Michigan and I worked for Selin's [Furniture] Store. We were having a sale," he remembers, "buy a living room set you'd get a bedroom set free." Bess says not a single living room set was sold because of the storm—there were no customers. He closed the store as the snow picked up and immediately headed home. When he got into the driveway of the apartment where he and his wife lived, his cousin, who lived downstairs, hollered out the door, "Don't put the car away, because Jeanie is going into labor."

A big snow year got bigger late in the winter of 1958-59. This policeman in Munising poses near street signs buried in deep snow during January 1959. (Courtesy of Superior View, Marquette)

Bess drove the ten blocks or so to the hospital in the worsening storm. Sarah was delivered successfully and when Bess knew everything was OK with Jeanie and their newborn daughter, he decided to head back home. "It took me two-and-a-half hours to get the car home…ten blocks," he remembers. "I got stuck a few times, so I kept shoveling and shoveling."

Near Sault Ste. Marie, Jim Bennett's wife went into labor at the peak of the storm. Bennett immediately called for the fire department ambulance at Sault Ste. Marie, six miles to the north. The ambulance, with a snowplow escort, set out for the Bennett residence. It became

bogged down anyway, and the plow driver, not able to see the ambulance's predicament in the swirling snow, drove on. Meanwhile, Bennett called his aunt for help. She waded a mile through waist-deep snow to his house and with phone instructions from the family doctor, delivered the baby. A short time later, the ambulance arrived and transported mom and her new baby boy to War Memorial Hospital in the Sault.

At least two lives were lost on U.P. highways due to the March 1959 blizzard. A snowplow driver found the bodies of an elderly couple, a brother and sister, inside a car on a snowbound road near Carney in northern Menominee County. They apparently became stuck in a drift, and made

A school official checks on the nearly four dozen children that were stranded at an elementary school in Munising because of the storm. (Courtesy of Marquette County History Museum)

the mistake of keeping their car running with their windows closed to stay warm. They died of carbon monoxide poisoning.

During the height of the storm, severe drifting closed most of Delta County's 840 miles of roads. It took a while to clear them all, and eventually a county plow driver discovered a stranded vehicle on a back road, nine miles or so north of Rapid River. Much to the surprise of the plow driver, there was a couple with the car waiting to be rescued. They had been stranded almost three days!

The couple, from Round Lake in rural northern Delta County, had left their camp for a grocery-shopping trip to Rapid River. On the way back that evening, their vehicle became snowbound. They thought about abandoning the car and seeking help, but wisely decided to stay put as the blizzard was reaching its crescendo, piling hip-deep drifts across the open fields and roads. Fortunately, they were heavily dressed and had a 10-day supply of food from their shopping trip. The couple knew enough to run the car at short intervals, and after the storm abated they got out of the car every once in a while to exercise. The road was impassable until the county plow came through three days after the storm began.

Farther north in Munising, the blizzard was so ferocious a "lifeline" was set up to help guide workers into the paper mill. "The snow was so deep," remembers Dan McCollum who worked at the mill, "that they parked cars along H-58 at the old plywood plant and then followed a rope into the paper mill. The next day the cars were gone…buried in the snow." When the road was finally cleared, a long bamboo pole was used to find the buried cars. A "Snowgo" then cleared around each vehicle and a tow truck pulled them out of the snow bank. In town, 45 students at Washington Elementary were forced to sleep in their classrooms after their bus "became hopelessly stuck."

The Dedication and Persistence award could have been presented to the driver of a diary truck that left Marquette bound for delivery in Munising. He left on the roughly 40 mile journey at 5 in the morning Friday, finally arriving in Munising at 2:30 that afternoon! He had to maneuver around many stalled vehicles—fifty alone became stranded on U.S.-41 south of Marquette in Harvey. A newspaper reporter, walking back from a visit to the State Police Post in that area, noticed rather strange footing at one point as he waded through the deep snow. He dug down a little and realized he was on top of a car buried in a huge drift.

After the storm, more moderate weather prevailed the rest of the month. The last half of March 1959 saw a majority of days with temperatures above average. The warm weather ate away at snowbanks left by the severe blizzard. At the same time, Marquette County prepared for the arrival of the cast and crew of Otto Preminger's *Anatomy of a Murder*. Filming began on location in the county just as the last remnants of the great blizzard melted away. The movie was based on the book by local author John (Robert Traver) Voelker.

November 27-28, 1966: Ferocious Gale and Snowstorm

This storm hit at the peak of Thanksgiving weekend return-trip travel. The week leading up to the storm had been mild and the thawing weather and rain put a damper on the second week of deer hunting season. During Thanksgiving weekend, an upper-air trough began to form and deepen over the central United States. At the surface, low pressure in south-central

Canada, which had been pumping mild, southerly winds into the Upper Great Lakes, began to fill, while new low pressure formed in northern Missouri ahead of the deepening trough in the Plains. The Missouri low became the main system and strengthened rapidly, drawing in cold air from the north. Rain quickly changed to freezing precipitation and then snow from northwest to southeast across Upper Michigan. As the storm intensified and lifted northeastward, gale force winds began to buffet the region.

Richard Wright, an instructor at Northern Michigan University in Marquette at the time, was visiting family in the Menominee County community of Daggett that Sunday. "It was raining and blowing," he recalls, "and we

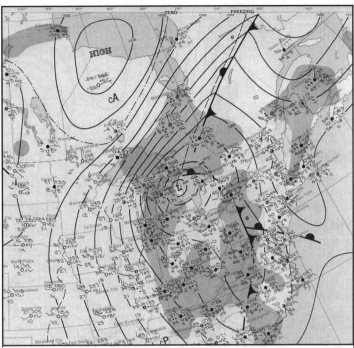

Low pressure deepened tremendously as it moved from the Central Plains into the Great Lakes on Sunday, November 27, 1966. Note the close spacing of the pressure lines or isobars on the back-side of the low. The tight pressure gradient led to very strong winds. (NOAA Central Library Data Imaging Project)

were concerned about the weather farther north. We left right after lunch and things were fine until we got to the snow belt around Trenary. It started to deteriorate fast and by the time we got around Skandia, traffic was down to one lane." He and his wife made it to their home in Harvey. Later that evening they lost power, and with it, their source of heat.

They were not alone. Thousands of homes throughout an eight-county region of central and eastern Upper Michigan lost heat and cooking facilities as wind gusts to 60 miles-an-hour caused massive power failures. Curtis, in Mackinac County, went without power from 4 p.m. Sunday until well into Monday. The Chippewa County community of Rudyard was blacked out too, as five miles of ice-laden utility poles around the town were brought down by the wind. Farther west, Munising also experienced a blackout that caused the city's hospital to use emergency backup power. Vicious winds snapped trees and flung them onto power lines around Marquette. The wind was so strong it blew spray from Lake Superior across U.S.-41 near the prison. It was the first time residents had witnessed that spectacle in many years. Half the city was without power at the height of the storm. Baraga and Delta counties also suffered extensive outages.

Only a few inches of snow fell in the Copper Country during the storm, while on the east end four to five inches accumulated at the Sault with no real problems. The central and much of the rest of eastern Upper Michigan bore the brunt of the storm. Over a foot of snow accumulated in Marquette. The full gale accompanying the blizzard piled up drifts eight to nine feet deep between Marquette and Negaunee with even deeper drifts around Skandia.

Huge drifts took days to clear after the late November snowstorm in 1966. (Courtesy of the Marquette County History Museum)

Larry Wanic grew up near La Branche in northern Menominee County and enjoyed an extra day of Thanksgiving holiday vacation because of the storm. "I remember the fields," he recalls. "There was hardly any snow. It didn't snow more than six or seven inches in this area, but the fields were like you see in North Dakota. They were bare and then you'd have places where the drifts would be five feet."

The blinding, blowing snow brought traffic to a complete standstill during one of the busiest travel days of the year. Hundreds of vehicles became stranded along main thoroughfares throughout the region, from the straits westward to Baraga County. In the Green Garden-Skandia area alone, about 200 vehicles became mired in drifts on U.S.-41 south of Marquette. Most of the stranded travelers camped out on the floor of the Idletime Bar near Yalmer Road and stayed there through much of the next morning. Stalled vehicles still lined the highway on Tuesday morning the 29th, a day after the storm ended.

Joe Freeman of Engadine, a small town in western Mackinac County just north of U.S.-2 on M-117, remembers a Greyhound bus stranded in the main intersection of the town at the height of the storm. "Its windshield was busted," he says. "It was the wind that must have blew an evergreen branch or something…through the window." The bus was full of students heading back to Northern Michigan University and Michigan Technological University from downstate. The students were herded over to the Town Hall where they were forced to spend the night. "The manager of our store opened up and made sandwiches for the kids," recalls Freeman.

The store manager made lots of sandwiches that evening. After a 75-mile stretch of U.S.-2 from the straits to Blaney Park became impassable, 500 students and motorists took shelter in the Engadine Town Hall. Freeman says the students had no galoshes or boots, so some of them put on the town's firemen's boots housed at the hall. "The powers-to-be didn't like that too well," remembers Freeman with a chuckle.

Farther north in the woods of northern Luce County, tragedy struck as the blizzard peaked. The proprietors of Pike Lake Resort had just closed the

Memorial to Faye Leighton and Doc Purnam who lost their way in the blizzard and perished less than a half mile from the shelter they were seeking. (Photo by E. Yelland)

place down for the winter, as the last of the deer hunters headed south. Faye Leighton had operated the resort since 1941. A widow for over 20 years, she married a longtime family friend, Leslie "Doc" Purman in 1964.

As darkness fell that Sunday evening, the couple left isolated Pike Lake and drove toward Newberry on one of the backwoods roads. They became stuck along the way and apparently decided to walk to the Pine Stump Junction Bar for help. The pair struggled through the biting wind and blinding snow for nearly four miles. Exhausted, they probably decided to rest for a while. Their frozen bodies were found cuddled up in a snowdrift beneath a cedar tree on December 1, three days after the storm ended. Ironically, they were less than a half-mile from their destination. The ferocious gale and snowstorm rendered a short hike an insurmountable obstacle that evening in late November 1966.

Dec. 21-23, 1968 Snowstorm: "Worst Since '38"

A raging, howling snowstorm choked Upper Michigan with up to three feet of snow just

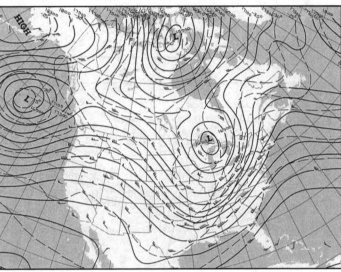

before Christmas in 1968. The brunt of the storm hit the west, specifically the Gogebic Range, where it was declared the worst storm since the famous late January blizzard 30 years earlier.

The system was the second and most intense low that developed out of an upper-air trough which formed over the western U.S. almost a week earlier. The first system dropped a general half-foot of snow over a good share of the U.P. on December 19. By that time, the next system had slid southeastward out of the Gulf of Alaska and was dropping

December 23, 1968. The weather charts showed a mature, intense storm over the Upper Great Lakes. All the Upper Peninsula got heavy snow from the system, with the west end receiving the greatest accumulations. (NOAA Central Library Data Imaging Project)

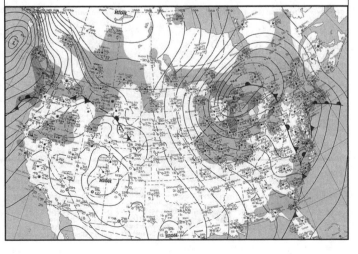

through the inter-mountain region. This disturbance cranked up low pressure in the southern Rockies where it already began tapping Gulf of Mexico moisture. The developing storm then headed northeast.

This system differed from the 1938 blizzard in that it developed and moved farther north and west. While the '38 storm tracked from east Texas to central Illinois then east of the Sault dumping heavy snow on much of the U.P., the 1968 system tracked from northern New Mexico to near Kansas City across central Wisconsin then very close to Sault Ste. Marie. The 1968 track put the heaviest snow axis farther west into far western Upper Michigan and northeastern Minnesota.

The 1938 storm moved into an initially warm environment, leading to flooding rains in parts of the southern Great Lakes, while this 1968 system moved into a cold environment leading to widespread snow. My home town of Milwaukee received a quick four inches late the night of the 21st before the usual turn to rain occurred as the storm center moved west of the city, drawing in warmer air.

Over Upper Michigan, Sault Ste. Marie and Marquette both received a foot of snow, while in Minnesota, Duluth also accumulated a foot. On the Keweenaw Peninsula, roads were blocked around Houghton-Hancock as 21 inches buried the twin cities. The snow "jackpot" was won by the Gogebic Range—a total of 35 inches buried Ironwood over three days. Two feet fell during the passage of the storm itself, while close to another foot accumulated due to lake-effect in the wake of the storm.

Howling north then northwesterly winds up to 45 miles an hour built huge drifts that brought traffic to a virtual standstill. Highway 2 from the Michigan line to Ashland, Wisconsin was closed for a time when blowing and drifting snow stalled a half-dozen cars around Birch Hill, midway between Ironwood-Hurley and Ashland. Work crews were frustrated as drifting closed area roads as quickly as plows opened them.

Despite the hazardous roads, Ironwood retailers refused to close their stores and were rewarded for their resolve; Christmas shoppers flocked to area stores in surprising numbers from all parts of Gogebic County. Business was as good, if not better, than on some days before the storm. Shoppers seemed unfazed by the storm and boldly waded through snow-choked and, in some cases, impassable sidewalks in search of last-minute Christmas presents.

The Blizzard of '78

The second severe winter of the late 1970s (*see "Winter of 1976-77" page 141 and "The Long, Snowy Winter of 1978-79" page 179*) produced one outstanding event. In late January 1978, a mighty storm developed over the eastern Great Lakes and substantially disrupted the lives of Michigan residents.

The storm grew out of the phasing of the subtropical and polar jet streams. Low pressure formed in the southwestern United States into Mexico early in the fourth week of January. It pushed slowly eastward, creating heavy rain through much of the southeastern United States. At the same time, blocking high pressure in far northern Canada combined with ridging along the west coast of North America began forcing the polar vortex southward through central Canada.

The systems began to coalesce on the evening of January 25. The surface map at that time revealed a low pressure area over northern Georgia. Its circulation already covered half the country, from the far eastern Plains to the east coast. The polar vortex dropped into the Upper Mississippi Valley. Ahead of it, a south-southwesterly flow aloft pumped warmth and moisture from the Gulf Coast states to New York and New England. The vortex itself brought down bitter cold air that began driving southeastward through the Plains into the Mississippi Valley.

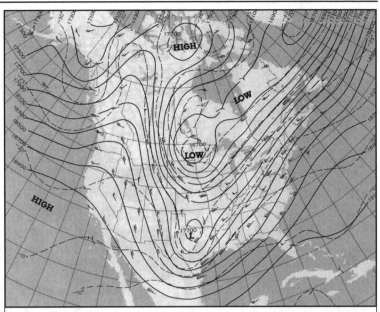

A monumental clash of air masses ensued. During that night, the phasing of jet streams was completed; the low "bombed out," falling from a pressure of 29.06 inches (984mb) to an astounding 28.32 inches (959mb) as it headed north. Rarely has a storm over land undergone such explosive deepening or achieved such a low pressure. By the next morning, a powerful circulation was situated over Lake Erie near Cleveland.

High-latitude blocking forced the polar vortex southward into the Northern Plains on January 25, 1978. At the surface, an arctic cold front was sagging through the Plains, while low pressure developed over the central Gulf States. (NOAA Central Library Data Imaging Project)

A low pressure area of that depth creates tremendous winds. This became the unforgettable feature of this storm over Upper Michigan. "I had wind gusts to 70 miles an hour," remembers Larry Wanic, who lived in Escanaba at the time. "I recorded nine and a half inches of snow, but that's only a guesstimate; I thought there was more than

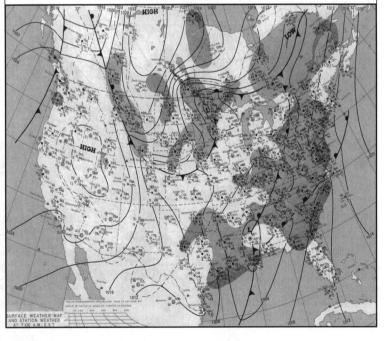

that. It was nearly impossible to measure because of the wind."

In the northern Menominee County community of Spalding, Lyn Veeser measured only 3.2 inches of new snow. "Yeah, winds, strong gusty winds," he notes. "I recorded frequent whiteouts, too."

Farther north, the influence of Lake Superior added to snowfall totals. Seventeen inches was reported in the hills near Marquette. Incessant wind gusts to near 50 miles per hour

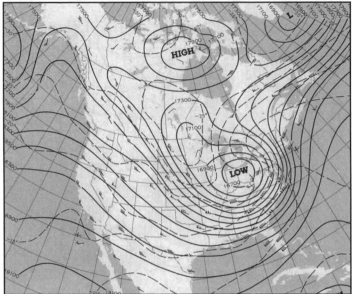

The morning of January 26, 1978. Phasing of the polar and subtropical jet streams was complete. The merger brought about a historic storm that lashed the entire Great Lakes region with high winds and heavy snow. (NOOA Central Library Data Imaging Project)

made travel impossible. U.S.-41, M-28 and M-35, were shut down the entire day.

"That was really something," remembers Wanic. The northerly gale blew the falling snow, along with the large existing snow cover, into huge drifts. "The snowdrifts were packed so densely after the storm, you could walk right on top of them without breaking through."

The strong southerly flow east of the circulation produced record warmth, heavy rain and snowmelt, which resulted in flooding over many East Coast states. The brunt of the blizzard was unleashed on the Lower Peninsula, nearer the low center. Almost two feet of snow, along with bitter cold and ferocious winds paralyzed much of the region. The locus of the storm's fury centered itself around Lansing. Drifts, as high as 27 feet,

were reported. During the height of the storm, as many as 400,000 homes were without power.

Seasonable cold followed the blizzard. The same blocking pattern that set the stage for the storm's explosive development suppressed the storm track far south of Upper Michigan the rest of the winter. No more significant storms occurred and the winter

The northerly gales of the storm completely encased Marquette's Lower Harbor Breakwater light in ice. (Photo by Tom Buchkoe)

slowly and peacefully gave way to spring during late March and April. The Blizzard of '78 was the one event that made this winter a memorable one.

The Long, Snowy Winter of 1978-79

This was the final and most severe of the wintry triumvirate of the late 1970s. Late fall in 1978 was especially pleasant. The unusually warm, dry weather extended into November; three of the first eight days of the month had temperatures above 60 degrees in Keweenaw County. The road commission in Delaware keeps temperature and precipitation records with an emphasis on snowfall in this snowiest spot in Upper Michigan.

The snow around this woman's house was about as deep as she was tall after the '78 blizzard. (Photo by Tom Buchkoe)

Their records show a change in this warm regime starting on the 13th. The high temperature that day hovered in the low 40s with heavy rain accompanied by over four inches of wet, sloppy snow. This snow did not stick—it disappeared the next day under a quarter inch of freezing rain.

Real winter commenced on November 19 when more than a foot of snow fell. The snow contained over an inch of water; laying a good, sturdy base for the massive blanket that was to follow. Observers in Delaware measured new snow on 10 of the last 12 days of the month. During this span, 44.7 inches came accumulated, putting down a snow cover of 21 inches by November 30, 1978. This late November surge in snowfall was a mere warm-up for what was to follow.

December began with over a foot of snow in Delaware. By the 11th, Houghton County had cracked the 100 inch mark for the season—the earliest date that milestone has been reached. Measurable snow fell on all but eight days that month in Keweenaw County.

The weather pattern during December 1978 was dominated by a general upper-air low pressure trough over the central North American continent. This trough held sufficiently cold air over the Upper Great Lakes (the high temperature never exceeded 32 degrees in Delaware the entire month), while at the same

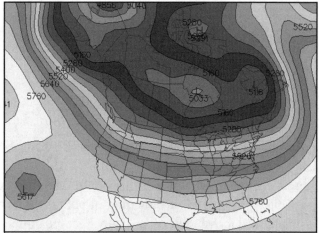

A typical upper-air map during December 1978. A westerly flow brought snow-bearing disturbance after disturbance to the Keweenaw. Each was followed by a healthy dose of lake-effect. (Courtesy of Plymouth State Weather Center NCEP/NCAR Reanalysis Map Generator)

time, an endless series of disturbances passed through the trough. These disturbances would produce "system" snow ahead of them, and then lake-effect in the cold northwesterly flow behind them.

As the white stuff piled up, people began running out of room to put it. Paul Lehto, long-time Calumet Township Supervisor, says a winter like the one in '78-'79 was not one for beginners: "If you're an amateur with a plow, you run out of room in one heck of a hurry." During this long, snowy winter, everyone, including seasoned snow-plow veterans, eventually had no place to put the snow.

"There was an awful lot of snow," remembers Owen "Obie" O'Brien. He operated a grader for the Keweenaw County Road Commission that winter. "Day after day after day after day, this'll get to you. In one stretch we worked 38 days in a row."

O'Brien describes a typical day during the ceaseless snow in December and January that winter: "The foreman gets up in the morning to see how much snow has fallen. He'd call at four and you'd leave the shop at five o'clock. You'd work your eight hours, you'd be done around 1 or 1:30 maybe a little longer. You'd come home, you'd be home for a couple of hours, maybe until 4 o'clock or so, they'd call us out and we'd go out again until 10 o'clock at night." He considered himself lucky: "I was on the grader; I was all alone," he laughs. "When you work in a big cab with two guys, that cab starts to get pretty small after sitting in there with the same guy for 14 or 15 hours a day; you just kind of get on each other's nerves."

Calumet at an earlier time with snow piled to the rooftops.
(Courtesy of Superior View, Marquette)

In Ontonagon, road crews plowed 60 out of 61 days between November 17 and January 16. One plow driver did not have a night off during that entire stretch.

Jim Heikkila spent 39 years with the Keweenaw County Road Commission and was the Engineer-Manager during the winter of 1978-79. "I hated to go talk to the guys between January and the end of February into March," he remembers, half-joking. "They were plowing so often and so long, and of course, once they got done plowing snow, they had to go home and move their own. They became quite ornery; their tempers flared and they were not easy to get along with. I just didn't go visit them."

After more than 14 inches of new snow on January 24, the snow cover reached an extraordinary 60 inches at Delaware. This huge mass of snow began putting a strain on area buildings. National Guard officials closed the Calumet Armory to the public after cracks were discovered in the roof beams of the 70-year-old building. Snow had piled waist deep on the roof.

In Lake Linden, "a disaster and a miracle" occurred at the same time on January 17 when the Torch Lake Ice Arena collapsed. Two-and-a-half feet of snow had been shoveled off the roof as recently as a week before, but that did not matter. The building could not take any more weight. Miraculously, no hockey or ice skating was going on when the structure came down. Three men inside the arena raced for the door at the first sound of rumbling. They were actually blown out of the building by the force of the collapse.

In Greenland southeast of Ontonagon, a large portion of the township hall crumbled beneath the weight of the snow. The building was more than 100 years old and had not been used in recent years. Many other sheds and garages collapsed throughout Keweenaw, Houghton and Ontonagon counties. "That's our urban renewal in the Copper Country," Lehto says with a chuckle. "Somebody neglects an old garage or something like that.

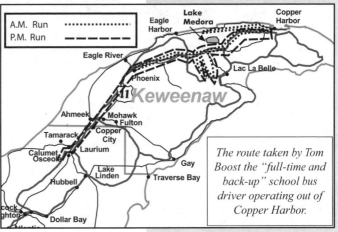

The route taken by Tom Boost the "full-time and back-up" school bus driver operating out of Copper Harbor.

A building ready for "urban renewal" in the Keweenaw. (Photo by E. Yelland)

You can be sure that if it's going to go, it'll go during a winter like that."

While snowy days decreased in February (snow fell

A LONG, SNOWY DRIVE

Driving a school bus day after day through the snowiest spot in Michigan can be quite a challenge. "Going through there with the wind blowing in the morning—it's dark; it's about 6:30," says Tom Boost, a full-time and back-up school bus driver for Keweenaw County's school system. "Of course, you have to more or less remember where the road is. You have to know where the curves are because with some of the whiteouts through there, you just can't see at all." Boost is referring to a three-quarter mile stretch of U.S.-41 along Lake Medora. The road narrows with little in the way of a shoulder, while the tree-free area of the lake provides an opening for snow to blow through.

"The plows get through there early enough that they get the majority of the drifts now," Boost says. "Years ago, I would plow drifts going through there; the snow packed up in the engine, got around

The "scenic route" through the heavy forest canopy on a portion of Boost's route can be driven without much problem because the trees catch a good deal of snow, keeping some of it off the road. (Photo by E. Yelland)

on half the days of the month), Keweenaw County still collected a healthy 57 inches. Cold weather the balance of the month led to little melting. Finally on the 28th, the temperature rose to 52 degrees, the warmest reading by far since the snow blitz began three-and-a-half months earlier.

Judy Johnson of Skandia, lived alone in a cabin in Pequaming on Keweenaw Bay during this harsh winter. "The piles of shoveled snow on the path to my front door were well over my head," she remembers. "You could only see white looking out the windows." In late February, she left for a business trip to Chicago. While away, the 52-degree temperature occurred,

your circuit time belt and your belt quits pulling and the lights go all dim. Then I'd drive a hundred yards down the road, and it would catch again; the lights would come back on."

Boost starts his day early. He's up by 5:00 or so. By 5: 15 he gets a call if school is called off. Despite the almost-constant snowfall, school is usually in session. Boost has a good working relationship with the snowplow drivers, and that helps. "I got with the road foreman this past fall and told him what my schedule was," he explains. The plow comes through before Boost leaves on his route.

Boost's daily itinerary takes him through "the scenic route" to Delaware. "This stretch is not bad," Boost says, "because the trees absorb most of the snow." Once he gets past Delaware, he takes the steep road down to Lac La Belle. "I make four trips to Lac La Belle

A Calumet building before and after winter sets in. Cross-country skiers have been known to ski up one side of the building and down the other during exceptional winters like '78-'79. (Courtesy of Paul Lehto; inset photo by E. Yelland)

unleashing a major meltdown. Three-foot ice dams on the edge of her cabin roof virtually disappeared in the thaw.

"The melt water ran right down the walls, flooded the floor and put out the flame on my little furnace," she recalls. Unaware of what was going on up north, Johnson made her way back from Chicago, driving into a "terrific" ice storm in Wisconsin. She explains that her car defroster could not keep up with the ice. "I'd hunch over the wheel peeking out a little circle of clear windshield," she recounts. "I did this for many miles, till I was exhausted."

The next day she arrived back at her Pequaming cabin on a crisp, cold sunny morning. She tried opening the door inward, but it would not budge—the water that flowed off the ice dams flooded the floor of her cabin and then froze solid because the furnace went out. "I shoveled to a window, which luckily could be opened without breaking," she explains. "After borrowing ice fishing equipment, I chipped and chopped my things out of the ice, packed up my car and moved, temporarily, to my grandparent's home in Skandia (a town about 10 mile southeast of Marquette)."

To the northwest on the Keweenaw, relatively mild weather continued the first couple of days in March. If winter-weary denizens of the region thought they saw light at the end of the tunnel with this taste of spring, they were mistaken. The tunnel collapsed under the weight of the heaviest snowstorm of the season on March 4-5. A low pressure system developed in west Texas, tapped Gulf of Mexico moisture, drifted east and then shot northeastward. The majority of the snow that fell during this long winter was the fluffy, lake-effect variety with little wind. "It was basically like gum drops," remembers Heikkila, "It just

every day; going up and down that hill can be a challenge."

After a thorough inspection of the bus, Boost shovels the entry way to the school and then takes off to collect his first student at about 6:12. There are not too many students to pick up in this remote area of the Keweenaw. "We had three days when my regular twenty one-passenger bus was down in December," he recalls. "Calumet let me borrow one of their seventy-passenger buses. So I had a seventy-passenger bus for six students. I would look in the rearview mirror and it looked like a bowling alley behind me."

It takes about two hours for Boost to complete his route in the morning. In the afternoon, he drives all the way to Calumet and then brings up to a half-dozen students back to Keweenaw County. The schedule gives him a fair amount of flexibility. "I get back here about quarter after eight or eight thirty," says Boost. "If it snowed overnight, then I can start moving snow, or come in and have breakfast and then go out and move snow." Sometimes, after fighting off the hypnotic effect of watching billions of snowflakes fly past his headlights for two hours, he does neither. "Then," he says, "I get back here and pop a couple of ibuprofen and lay on the couch until the headache's gone."

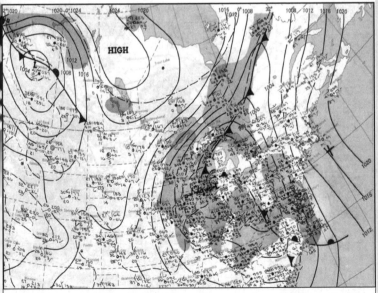

Saturday, March 24, 1979: Low pressure crept northeastward from the Mid-Mississippi Valley into the Central Great Lakes, impeded in its eastward progress by a blocky pattern to the east. This slow movement resulted in a prolonged snow and wind event over a good portion of Upper Michigan. (NOAA Central Library Data Imaging Project)

piled and piled and piled." This early March storm was the wet and heavy variety, driven by strong east to northeasterly winds. By the time the storm wound down, over two feet had come down, once more raising the snow cover to 60 inches.

Little snow fell over the next two and a half weeks. The cover shrunk to 38 inches by the 23rd as several warm days and a rising sun angle conspired to begin the big meltdown. A serious setback occurred, however, on March 24—a whopping 20.4 inches dumped on Delaware. Ironically, the greatest impact from this blizzard was felt to the southeast, away from the center of heaviest winter snow.

The storm of March 23-25, 1979 was one of the largest, most intense post-equinox snowstorms on record in the central Upper Peninsula. The same storm that affected the Keweenaw brought Marquette, Dickinson and Alger counties to a standstill. The blizzard grew out of a slow-moving upper-air disturbance that emerged from the Desert Southwest on the first day of spring. Low pressure connected with the trough, gradually developed to the northeast, impeded in its eastward progress by blocking over the western Atlantic.

Mild air ahead of the low caused rain to develop the night of the 23rd. Then colder air started pouring in on stiffening northeast to north winds, changing the rain to snow the next afternoon. The storm then cut loose, dumping heavy snow through the 25th. As the snow piled up, travel became nearly impossible. Numerous vehicles were abandoned, hampering snow-removal efforts. Eventually, authorities in Marquette, Alger and Dickinson counties were forced to close roads. The Marquette County Airport shut down for two days as winds gusted to 45 miles per hour. Gusts to 55 mile per hour were reported at Sawyer Air Force Base.

In Baraga County, John Johnson of the tiny community of Aura, near L'Anse, almost made it home as the storm intensified. Wet snow was quickly piling up, and he had trouble entering his unplowed driveway. He drove down a hill near his home and turned around, but could not make it up the icy road. Johnson turned around again and headed for Pequaming where he planned to stay with relatives.

Johnson missed a turn and became snowbound on a desolate stretch of Point Abbaye Road, some 14 miles from his home. There he stayed for almost a day and a half, keeping a minimal amount of heat in his car by running the engine intermittently. Finally, he was found by two snowmobilers. Outside of being stiff, sore and tired, Johnson pulled through the ordeal without serious injury.

In Skandia, Judy Johnson (no relation to John) was still living with her grandparents after her northern Baraga County cabin flooded, then froze a few weeks earlier. She was about to leave on another trip, this time to Virginia, when the snowstorm hit. The day of her departure was the day the storm finally ended. "I brought my suitcases to the porch to load into my car," she remembers, "but could not see my car. Ohhh, there's a bit of the roof and front window there peeking out the drifts." She recalls that it took a couple of hours of shoveling to free the car and get on her way. A couple of days later, she was driving through the Blue Ridge Mountains, enjoying spring flowers and greening trees. "What a dramatic difference in weather from the U.P. to Virginia," she exclaims.

Back up north, the storm reached a crescendo and brought blizzard conditions that isolated and stranded a number of residents. The volunteer rescue unit in Marquette County made about 70 runs to assist 240 persons during the storm. The most dramatic rescue involved 39 high school youths trapped at a vacated house on Lakeshore Boulevard. The kids, ranging in age from 16 to 18, had gathered for a party at the house. When they tried to leave, they found their cars buried in five- to 15-foot drifts. The house had no phone, so one of the students waded through the drifts to a neighbor's house to contact police.

Rescuers arrived and took much of the next day to evacuate the students. They were led out five at a time and had to walk more than two miles through drifts up to 15 feet deep. Visibility was so poor that the kids were tied together so none would be lost in the driving snow. After 30 students were evacuated in this manner, a DNR vehicle used for grooming snowmobile trails arrived and took out the remaining nine.

Outside of some frostbite, no serious injuries were reported. None of the youths were taken to the hospital; they just wanted to go home.

The memorial to a record-breaking winter. The "snow thermometer" along U.S.-41 in Keweenaw County shows how high 390.4 inches or 32 1/2 feet of unsettled snow looks. (Photo by E. Yelland)

"The thing I remember about this storm," recalls Barrett Ludlow of Newberry who lived in Marquette in 1979, "was that the winds intensified at night. You would think each night, OK, the storm is going to end, and it would pick up again at night. The storm went on for three days with a north wind. We haven't had one like that in a long time."

The city of Marquette tallied 18 inches of snow from the storm, while the new NWS site in Negaunee Township, 10 miles west of town, measured 27 inches of wind-whipped snow from the event.

April 1979 came to the Keweenaw with winter's hangover still affecting the area. Delaware carried a snow cover of three and a half feet the first few days of the month. Temperatures refused to warm, remaining in the 30s to near 40 during the day and dropping as low as the single numbers at night. A little rain fell on April 2, but with temperatures in the 30s, the snow cover went down only a couple of inches. Then a strong, unseasonably cold trough dug into the Great Lakes, spawning a storm that essentially bypassed the snowbound Keweenaw, but thrust winter's worst on eastern sections of the peninsula.

A blinding snowstorm, "easily the worst...of the season," socked Sault Ste. Marie and much of the eastern U.P on April 5. It started in central sections around Marquette just after noon and reached the Sault by evening. The snow came down furiously, falling at the rate of three inches an hour for a time.

The snow let up for a while and it appeared the storm was over. Then the wind set in along

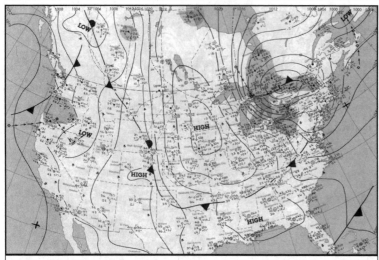

This powerful spring storm developed over the Upper Great Lakes on April 5-6, 1979. It reached its greatest intensity over the far eastern U.P. where Sault Ste. Marie was paralyzed by heavy snow and wind gusts to 60 miles-per hour. (NOAA Central Library Data Imaging Project)

with increasing snowfall; gusts to 60 miles per hour rocked the area through the night, creating whiteouts and massive power outages. Trees were blown down on houses, cars and garages. Plows were called off the roads and the Chippewa County Sheriff's Department quit patrolling.

A state of emergency was declared in Chippewa County and Sault Ste. Marie. The power outage caused the water pumping station in the city to go down, cutting off water to much of the city until noon the next day. For the first time in nearly 35 years, mail service in and out of the Sault was cancelled. The howling blizzard kept some county road commission plow drivers from getting to work, while other plows became stuck. It took until Saturday morning for most roads to be cleared and the state of emergency to be lifted.

At Bay Mills, a 30-foot wall of ice came onshore during the storm. The long winter made for massive ice buildup on Lake Superior. Area residents claim the Coast Guard ice breaker loosened the ice, and then when the storm blew in from the north, the ice headed to shore.

"The wall of ice thundered from Whitefish Bay, steamrolled up the shoreline and crashed down," read the local newspaper. The account went on to describe how a fisherman's shed housing his boat and several snowmobiles was crushed like "so much balsawood." The structure was pushed back some 25 feet from shore by the ice. Other commercial fishing operations were damaged and a summer cottage came within a couple of feet of being smashed by the mountain of ice.

Record cold followed the blizzard. Marquette's temperature fell to 8 degrees the day after the storm. It was considered the worst blow to hit the Sault since the famous "Fitzgerald Storm" four years earlier.

While this vicious system missed the Keweenaw, the winter of '79 had one more snowstorm up its sleeve. Four days later, on the April 9th, 7.8 inches fell at Delaware, bringing its season total to an astounding 390.4 inches. By mid-month, mild weather set in for good and the snow began to leave. Fortunately, April 1979 was a dry month and the massive mantle of white disappeared slowly but steadily with little flooding. On the 30th, a mere 3 inches of the record snowpack remained. The last of it disappeared after the first few days of May.

The Post-Thanksgiving's Day Storm of 1985

This massive, far-reaching storm grew out of an unsettled pattern that developed early in November 1985. A series of troughs dug into the western United States, while cold air began massing in Canada after mid-month. On Friday the 29th, a strong low dove from the Gulf of Alaska into northern California. The system meandered southeastward, eventually redeveloping in south Texas on the following evening.

An inverted trough poked north-northeastward from the low into the Mid-Mississippi Valley, developing a wide area of precipitation between the cold air west of the trough and the mild, moist air to the east. Meanwhile, a disturbance containing arctic air dropped from western Canada into the northwestern United States. By the morning of December 1, a deepening low-pressure area was situated near St. Louis. As the low gradually pulled northeastward, it grew into a massive winter storm over the southern Great Lakes that evening.

Like the '66 blizzard, this storm occurred during the return trip home for many travelers on Thanksgiving weekend. Snow broke out on Saturday night to the southwest and spread northeastward. "When I woke up," remembers Greg Albrecht who grew up in Menominee,

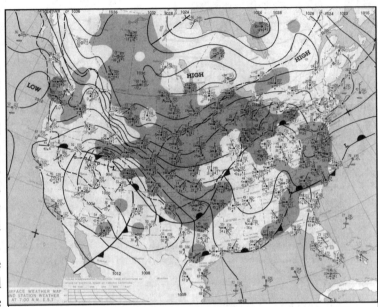

Low pressure was developing in the Rockies on November 30, 1985. Extensive arctic high pressure covered Canada into the northern United States, setting the table for a major, wide-spread snowstorm. The next morning, December 1st, the system was near St. Louis, ready to deepen and move northeastward. (NOAA Central Library Data Imaging Project)

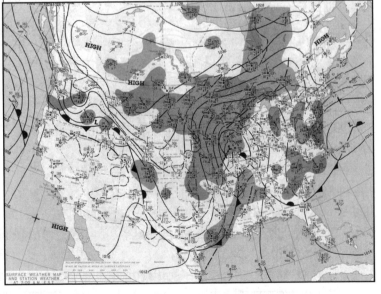

"there was probably four inches of new snow on the ground. I remember the wind really howling out of the east and northeast."

The combination of wind and snow quickly made roads nearly impassable over a vast

An example of Lake Superior's handiwork along the Lake Superior shore during the December 1, 1985 storm. (Photo by Tom Buchkoe)

area of Minnesota, Wisconsin, northern Lower Michigan and the U.P. Home or college-bound travelers, many from large cities of the southern Great Lakes, drove into a nightmare of snow-covered roads and near-zero visibility.

One of those travelers was Beth Hoy of Greenville, northeast of Grand Rapids. "It was my first year attending Michigan Tech," remembers Hoy. "My parents loaded me into this car to carpool back up with three other Tech students. It was an old, beat-up car, like Tech students often have. There wasn't a working heater in it and the defroster didn't work." Beth recalls her parents being a little nervous sending her back up to the U.P.

"The weather was horrible. We made it across the Mackinac Bridge just before they closed it." Hoy and her fellow travelers drove straight into the storm as evening set in. "The snow and ice scraper broke so we were using credit cards and licenses to scrape off the inside of the windows so we could see." Scraping did not help that much, though. "The visibility outside was ridiculous," recalls Hoy with a chuckle. "It was probably illegal to be driving that way."

They moved on—slowly, finally reaching Marquette. A trip that would take about seven hours under normal conditions took 17 ½ hours. They had to stop in Marquette—authorities closed portions of U.S.-41 between Marquette and Houghton. The section of highway between L'Anse and Baraga was the worst. High winds drove water off Keweenaw Bay onto the roadway, where it froze. In addition, rocks and other debris were swept off the bay onto the highway.

A number of students bound for Tech were stranded in Marquette. Some were housed on gymnasium floors, but Hoy and her companions were lucky: "We knew somebody who was going to Northern; we stayed in that person's apartment."

A number of students did not make it that far. Many became stranded at Munising after severe blowing and drifting shut down M-28, the road winding along Lake Superior to Marquette. Area motels became jammed with students and other travelers who took refuge from the howling blizzard.

The next morning, snow was still falling, but the worst of the storm was over. Hoy and her companions got into their beat-up car and made their way northwest. She remembers driving through the section of highway adjacent to Keweenaw Bay: "There were almost like these frozen waves in time hanging next to the road. And there was obviously a lot of ice that had been broken and pushed off to the side to clear the highway." Hoy and her companions finally made it to Tech late that Monday afternoon after spending more than 21 hours on the road.

Steve Asplund, long-time news anchor at TV6 in Marquette, was spending the weekend with relatives in suburban Milwaukee. He got up that Sunday morning, saw that it was raining, and started watching the football pre-game show. He and his

A pedestrian scurries across Ludington Avenue in Escanaba during the height of the snowstorm. (Courtesy of Delta County Historical Society)

wife, Ann, who was eight-months pregnant, along with a friend, were planning on leaving for home in the late afternoon.

During the pre-game, the network went live to Lambeau Field in Green Bay. The Packers were playing the Tampa Bay Buccaneers with a noon starting time. Asplund watched as the street sweepers cleared the field of several inches of snow. Soon the game started, and they watched about 10 minutes of it.

"It was just like a white sheet in front of the TV, it was snowing so hard," remembers Asplund. A call to the TV station in Negaunee gave him an idea of the breadth of the storm; it had already started snowing heavily there and a large accumulation was expected. Immediately, they decided to pack up and leave.

"We got into our vehicle, a Chevy panel van, and headed north," says Asplund. I-43 was in decent shape until about Sheboygan; then the road became snow covered. Soon the freeway was down to a single lane. They were listening to the radio and heard that the tower bridge, the main freeway bypassing the city of Green Bay, was closed due to the blinding snow and wind. "We ducked through town in Green Bay on 141," recalls Asplund. It took nearly four hours to get to Green Bay; a trip that would normally take about an hour and 45 minutes.

They stopped in town for gas. "We talked to some people there who asked, 'Where are you going,'" he remembers, "We said we were going to the U.P. and they said, 'You're crazy to continue on.'" They decided to press on, anyway. He recalls that many streets in Green Bay were blocked and the city was virtually shut down. The Packer game had ended and the fans made their way home or took refuge from the storm in area motels.

The game was a rout. The Packers solidified their reputation as a bad-weather team by pounding the hapless Buccaneers 44-0. To add insult to injury, Tampa was stranded for the night in snowbound Green Bay.

Asplund headed north out of town and found the highway to be in decent shape. "The roads were kind of wind-swept," he says. North of Menominee the snow started picking up and the wind was ferocious. Conditions steadily deteriorated as they drove north until there were just "two ruts in the middle of 41." By the time they reached Trenary in Alger County,

A house along the shore in Marquette undermined by huge waves during the storm of December 1st, 1985. (Photo by Tom Buchkoe)

Asplund remembers creeping along at 25 miles per hour, "just plowing through snow."

Finally, they reached Marquette. A five-and-a-half- hour-under-normal-conditions trip took 11 hours. They dropped their friend off in town. Their friend urged them to stay, but they had a mere 10 miles left to Negaunee. "Little did we know," recounts Aplund, "that this would be the worst part of the trip." They headed west and drove into a whiteout. "You couldn't see anything," he says. "Ann was looking out the right side window; I was looking out the left side just so we wouldn't go off the road." Asplund drove blind at 20 miles per hour.

Their tandem side-viewing technique worked— they kept the van on the road and eventually made it to Negaunee. The main street they lived on was plowed clean; however, the driveway in front of their house was clogged with four feet of snow. Asplund backed up, got up a head of steam and drove his van straight into the snowbank. "I then crawled out the window," he recalls, "because I couldn't open the door." He waded through the snow, grabbed a shovel and made a pathway back to the van so his wife could get to the house.

The next morning Asplund called the TV station and found that the crew that did the Sunday night news was still there. No one could get out of the parking lot. This same crew did the Monday morning news. It was the last time a storm would keep employees at WLUC-TV overnight.

Asplund recalls that his evening news co-anchor left the Milwaukee area on Sunday later than he did. "She got as far as Grafton [about 20 miles north of Milwaukee]. She ended up spending a day and a half at an armory there because they shut down I-43."

Across the Upper Peninsula, snowfall totals were impressive. Over 30 inches came down in the hills west of Marquette. Ironwood reported 19.5 inches with five-foot drifts. Even away from Lake Superior's influence, deep snow fell—Menominee collected 15 inches. To the northwest, Norway checked in with around 20 inches and to the east Bark River, tallied 14.5 inches with a wind gust to 42 miles an hour.

That wind raised havoc along the shore of Lake Superior. Photographer Tom Buchkoe lives along the lake just north of Marquette. "Usually when storms are blowing like that one was, you look at them through a window," he says. "That one I wanted to go out and look at because that was the first and only time that I had waves hitting the crest of the beach. They were big waves."

On another beach, waves undermined the foundation of a beachfront home. At Shot Point and Bayou Roads east of Marquette, trees were uprooted, boulders were washed up on shore and basements were flooded. The Coast Guard station in Marquette had waves wash away a fuel shed. Doors on a boathouse were pushed in and the building was strewn with rocks and ice. Other shoreline homes received severe property damage. "It was unbelievable," the county sheriff later recalled. "The waves cracked four-inch slabs of concrete…it looked like an explosion."

The post-Thanksgiving Storm of '85 brought out the best in area residents. John Turausky, longtime Parks and Recreation Director for the city of Marquette, was a relative newcomer to the area. He moved up with his family from Chicago a few years before and was impressed at how people pulled together and helped each other out. "I saw people out plowing out other people's driveways," he recalls.

He himself had a "Chicago snowblower," a small "carpet sweeper" with an 18-inch cut. It was no match for the mountain of snow, so he began shoveling his driveway. One of his neighbors saw him shoveling and asked if he wanted to borrow a snowblower. "The guy came from a block and a half away to bring me his machine," remembers Turausky. "It was one of those animals, a 42-inch cut or whatever. He asked, 'Can I help you?' That's how people do things around here."

Students all over Upper Michigan had their Thanksgiving vacation extended a day as all schools, as well as colleges and universities were shut down on Monday, December 2. "We spent the whole day playing outside," says meteorologist Steve Brown who grew up in Norway and was 12 years old at the time. "It was still snowing on Monday. That was the largest snow accumulation that I remember from a single storm."

Big Early Snow on the Gogebic Range: Nov. 1-3, 1989

Just the right combination of wind direction, cold air and moisture teamed up to blast the Ironwood area with a big early season snow in November 1989. Seven inches of snow already accumulated on Halloween as northerly winds drove snow bands off Lake Superior into the higher terrain around Ironwood and Hurley. The big dump came on November 1-2 when 20 inches of snow fell in a 24-hours period. Then, to add frosting to the cake, the sky opened up and an additional seven inches fell in the following 3 ½ hours.

"Every day I was going out to shovel," remembers Mary Baginski. "Every day the banks were higher and higher." Baginski will not forget this early season snow. She had just moved back to her hometown from Minneapolis. As she continually cleared snow from her walk, her neighbors stopped by and instead of welcoming her back would ask, "Don't you wish you were back in Minneapolis? They don't get as much snow as we get." To all her neighbor's inquiries Baginski responded with a simple "No". "I had lived there for about 10 years and it was just getting too big and too crowded and I just didn't like it anymore. So I decided to pack up and move back here to Ironwood." She admits she is not a big outdoor person but does not mind the snow. "Snow you can shovel; you can move it out of the way," she says.

Baginski and the rest of her neighbors in Ironwood moved plenty of the white stuff the first few days of November 1989. Forty-six inches fell in four days, leading to one of the earliest openings of the snowmobile and ski seasons in Big Snow Country's history.

December 1995: The Sault's Big Snow

Rarely, perhaps once in a lifetime, a weather event occurs in a region or community that is so extraordinary that it becomes etched in the collective memory of its residents. An experience

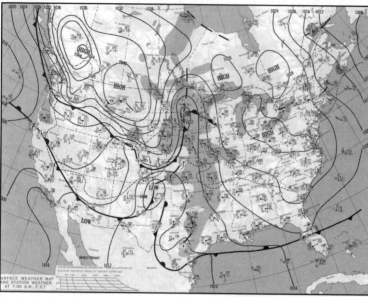

like this then becomes part of the history of that community. Sault Ste. Marie's Big Snow of December 1995 was such an event.

On Friday, December 8, low pressure was forming over South Dakota. It would bring substantial snow across Upper Michigan that night. The next day, its position over eastern Lake Superior set up an ideal flow for heavy lake-effect snow in Sault Ste. Marie. (NOAA Central Library Data Imaging Project)

The winter showed early signs of being a big one when the west end of Upper Michigan caught an unseasonably early snow in September (*see sidebar "September Snows", see page 59*). By November, cold and snow became the rule over the U.P.; a nine-inch snow fell on the Sault as early as November 2. By Thanksgiving, the entire peninsula had at least some snow cover. This cover would remain well into spring 1996.

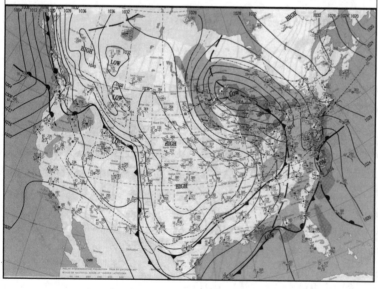

In the week preceding the big weekend snow, a cold front marched across the Upper Midwest, ushering in a healthy cold shot, which developed lake-effect snow. Through the first week of December, over 20 inches of snow accumulated at Sault Ste. Marie. At the same time, a strong disturbance formed in the Gulf of Alaska and began dropping slowly southeastward. As the disturbance dug toward the lower 48, low pressure took shape along the foothills of the Rocky Mountains. By the morning of December 8, the healthy low had moved to northeastern South Dakota. Snow had already begun falling on the west end of Lake Superior at Duluth.

"It was a triple whammy," explains John Wallis, former head of the NWS in Sault Ste. Marie. First, there was "system" snow associated with the low-pressure area. Second, there was "enhancement" of the system snow due to a southeasterly wind off of Lake Huron. "Very seldom do we get a fetch off of Lake Huron that will produce enhanced snowfall," says Wallis. Finally, as the low slowly lifted toward Wawa, Canada on the northeast end of Lake Superior, a west-northwesterly wind produced enhancement and lake-effect off Lake Superior.

"I woke up Saturday morning, my day off," remembers Tom Ewing, longtime manager of WSOO Radio. "I didn't think anything of it, because we get a

Fireman attempts to clear snow and ice off the roof of the fire hall in the Sault.
(Courtesy of The Evening News, Sault Ste. Marie)

lot of snow here all the time." He recalls noticing it snowing when he went to bed the night before. It seemed like a light snow to him. "I then went into the [attached] garage to make a morning run for some bread and milk," he explains. "I hit the garage door opener over my visor in my truck and nothing happened, apparently. I heard a little noise but the door didn't seem to go up. I thought, 'something's wrong with my garage door opener.'"

As it turned out, the opener was working fine; the door was moving up, but it had to go up five feet before any light came into the garage because the snow was that deep outside the door. "On that horrible realization," Ewing says, "I decided to drive right out of the garage and bull my way through." He explains that rarely, if ever, had he seen snow so deep that he could not plow or drive through it. "I had a four-wheel-drive truck with a plow attached to it and five feet of snow behind me just three feet from my bumper. I put it in four wheel drive and low range and went about three feet into the snow and stopped like I hit a brick wall. Fortunately, I was able to get back in the garage."

Ewing then moved outdoors into the storm to survey the situation. He thought maybe a huge drift had packed up against the garage. "I saw that it was that deep everywhere, virtually as far as you could see!" Immediately his "alarms" went off. "In broadcasting," he explains, "when something big happens, whatever it is, you've got to tell people about it."

Across the road from the Ewings, Sault Ste. Marie Fire Chief Ken Eagle had a sense of the gravity of the situation much earlier. "We had an emergency call early, one or two, on Saturday morning," remembers Eagle. "I was thinking to myself that it's extremely dark in the house. I have night lights outside but there was no light in the house." Eagle looked out the windows and realized why he could not see anything. "All the window pockets were completely filled with snow," he explains.

He left his house, got in the four wheel drive he used when on city business and began making his way down his 1000-foot driveway. "It was snowing heavily," he remembers, "and at the same time, snow was coming over the top of the truck." He made his way to the call and was met by other emergency vehicles. "The snow was going right over our vehicles," he explains. "It was unreal; it was like your truck was a snowplow."

There's no place to walk but in the middle of the road as the storm finally begins to wind down. (Courtesy of Marcia Morse-Mullins)

Lots of shoveling to do. A view down Portage Street in Sault Ste. Marie. (Courtesy Marcia Morse-Mullins)

On his way back home after the call, he noticed someone flagging him down. He stopped to see what was going on. "It was a young kid," Eagle says. "He was on a snowmobile and became disoriented; he didn't know if he was on the railroad grade, where he should have been, or the railroad tracks." It turns out he was stuck on the tracks. "One of his skis got lodged into part of the track" recounts Eagle. "We ended up trenching down through the snow and freed his machine up before the train came through."

Eagle arrived home about 5:00 that morning; he had been gone about three or four hours. "My tracks were completely filled in," he recalls with amazement. "I couldn't even get back in." Fortunately, he had a full-size tractor with a snowblower attached. "I cleared the snow every couple of hours around the clock," he explains. "I had to, so I could respond to emergencies."

When Eagle arrived at the fire hall later that day, he realized there was a full-blown emergency. "We couldn't leave the hall," he says. "The fire truck would get as far as the ramp and then it was dead—it was stuck. There was nothing we could do; we were at a standstill. Our city plows could not handle the volume of snow."

Eagle gave an assessment of the situation to city officials later that day. "I told them point blank," he remembers, "We need to get help in here because you have no fire protection and you have no ambulance service." Quickly, a call was put in to the governor's office, then to the emergency management division. A state of emergency was declared and the National Guard was sent in to help the city dig out.

Jim Hutcheson of Ishpeming was one of the National Guard troops who got the call to come to the Sault. "It was really something," he remembers. "As I went down M-28 and turned on I-75 there was only maybe a foot or two of snow on the level. I turned off of I-75 at Three Mile Road Exit; it still didn't look like much. But the closer I got to town, the deeper it got. It was something like I had never seen before."

Hutcheson, along with his 107th Engineer battalion and 1437th Engineer–Bridge Company of the Sault, worked 24-hour shifts for a solid week to open the roads. "We brought in equipment from as far as Calumet and Baraga, Ironwood, Iron River and Gladstone," remembers Hutcheson. "There was also a very large snowblower that had been used to clear runways at K.I. Sawyer. It was moved to Camp Grayling after the base closed. That was also brought up to move snow." The blower was used to open up the large thoroughfares. In the heart of the city, where the streets were narrow, bucket loaders and dump trucks removed the snow.

"It was just wild," remembers Eagle. "We had all kinds of things happening." Once the roads were opened, his staff spent lots of time digging out gas meters. Eagle explains that gas meters need to breathe. When the big snow buried many of them around the city, a dangerous situation developed. "We had one apartment complex catch on fire," he recalls. "There were torches blowing out of gas furnaces, water heaters and so on. Once we understood the problem we put out the word to dig out your meter."

In his spare time, Eagle also helped keep WSOO Radio on the air. "He was nice enough to come by, pick me up and take me to the radio station," acknowledges Tom Ewing. "Things like that happened all over town; people helping each other, carpooling and so on."

A fistful of records was shattered by the December 8-11 storm. The most impressive was the largest storm snowfall in the history of Sault Ste. Marie: 61.7 inches. In addition, the highest 24-hour snowfall was set on the 9th and 10th with 27.8 inches. The deepest snow depth of all time was equaled at 50 inches. December 1995 became the snowiest month in the history of the Sault with a whopping 98.8 inches; 82.5 of which came down through the first twelve days of the month. This incredibly snowy month contributed to the all-time season total of 222 inches, eclipsing the old record of just under 179 inches set in the long winter of '76-'77 (see "Cold Waves, Cold Winters", page 141).

The Long Winter and Backward Spring of 1995-96

A long, harsh winter affected the rest of Upper Michigan in 1995-96. Major storms occurred in every month from December through April, leading to record or near record season snowfall totals. Along with the snow came cold weather; late January and early February brought the lowest minimum temperatures in years. But the main feature of this winter (and spring) was snow.

Parts of the western U.P. shared in the Big Snow that buried Sault Ste. Marie. Ontonagon collected 40 inches during the long weekend event; other areas favored by west to northwest winds also wound up with impressive early-season snows. The winter did not show its true character until the third week of January 1996. Arctic air, massing in Canada, began to collapse southward into a deepening trough over the intermountain region. By early morning on January 18, a 1035-mb high pressure perched over northern Alberta was squeezing on

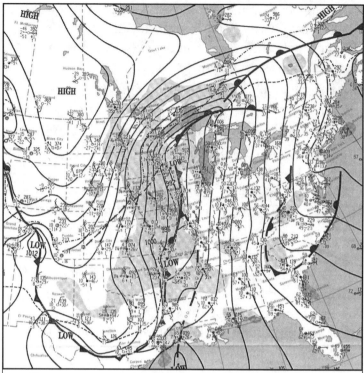

This strung-out storm brought a variety of nasty weather to Upper Michigan on January 17-18, 1996 including rain, freezing rain, sleet and heavy snow. Up to two feet of snow piled up in some western sections. (NOAA Central Library Data Imaging Project)

a 982-mb low developing near Denver. The difference in pressure between the high and the low led to high winds, numbing cold and snow through the Northern Rockies and High Plains.

The Colorado low then made a move northeastward. It brought with it a surge of warmth and moisture that turned snow into freezing rain and then plain rain around Marquette. The temperature spiked at 44 degrees at the NWS in Negaunee early on January 19, a record for the date. The low then moved eastward and began to fill, as another one developed farther south. Rain changed to sleet in central Upper Michigan as very cold air poured in behind the departing low.

Western sections remained in snow through the entire event. A reporter writing in the *Ironwood Daily Globe* claimed the storm "was a doozy, even for the Gogebic Range" after 18 inches of snow fell overnight. The wind whipped the snow into five-foot drifts and brought Big Snow Country to a standstill. The double dose of low pressure produced more than two feet of snow in many areas of the west from January 17 through 19.

Less than a week later, a wave moved off the Pacific into the Rockies, setting the stage for a storm that has become one of my personal favorites. Low pressure developed over the intermountain region and slid southeastward to a position over the Texas Panhandle on the evening of January 25. The low shot to near Springfield, Missouri the next day as the upper-air trough supporting it began to deepen. By late afternoon, a shield of heavy snow spread from the Central Plains to the Mid-Mississippi Valley. Des Moines, Iowa reported heavy snow, accompanied by thunder with temperatures only in the teens. When I saw that observation, I knew a large section of the Upper Peninsula was in for a dandy; I was not disappointed.

The low moved on a perfect track for heavy snow over a large portion of Upper Michigan. It traveled northeastward from its position over Missouri to northwestern Illinois by evening. That is when snow entered southern sections of the peninsula. It then spread rapidly northeastward.

Another snow fanatic was watching the situation closely. Steve Brown, who grew up in

Norway, Michigan, was studying meteorology at Central Michigan University. Most people will travel to avoid a storm if possible; Brown decided to drive into it. "I knew where I was in Mount Pleasant, there wasn't going to be any snow because the low was going to track right over us," he remembers. "So I decided to drive home for the weekend. My brother and another friend came with me. As we drove west we ran into snow around Manistique. By the time we reached Escanaba it was snowing hard—heavy, heavy snow."

Brown says it seemed to take forever to drive the last 40 miles home through snow-filled roads and quarter-mile visibility. A foot of new snow was added to the deep covering already on the ground. "My parents had trouble getting in and out of the garage because there was so much snow, there was nowhere else to push the snow," remembers Brown. "That was, by far, the most snow I'd ever seen on the ground in Norway."

Farther north, the influence of Lake Superior added significantly to snowfall totals. As the storm center shot from Illinois to near the Sault by the next morning, strong northeast to northerly winds brought added moisture off the lake. The NWS near Negaunee measured just under

1907: THE MOST "BACKWARD" SPRING

The headline in the mid-May paper read "An Almost Unprecedented Backward

A scene in the Copper Country on May 3, 1907 during the most backward spring. (Courtesy of Superior View, Marquette)

Spring." The story that followed gave details on how cold weather had affected farming and business across a large part of the nation during the spring of 1907. In Upper Michigan, this historically cold spring began with a snowstorm on April 7. Up to a foot of wet snow fell in many parts of the Keweenaw and in the hills west of Marquette. Trains were completely blocked around Houghton for the first time that winter.

Another storm "resumed hostilities" over the entire area on the 11th and still another dumped more snow about mid month. At that point, an old Copper Country resident declared, "I have been here since 1851, and I have never seen anything like this."

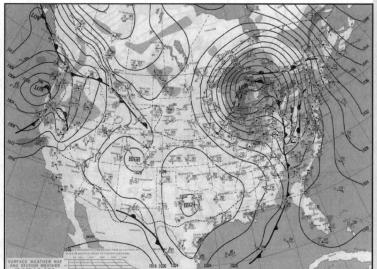

January 27, 1996: This quick-hitting low buried most of Upper Michigan southwestward into Wisconsin and Iowa. A bitter, extended cold siege ended the month and extended into February. (NOAA Central Library Data Imaging Project)

While strong April sunshine depreciated the snow cover significantly the third week of the month, cold weather remained the rule. The high temperature in Marquette on the 25th struggled to only 28 degrees. Through the end of the month, highs in the 30s were common.

The cold weather slowed navigation. The first boat reached the dock at Marquette on April 27, the latest arrival in years. At the end of the month, some 200 vessels were reported stuck in ice at Whitefish Bay. One captain, who plowed his vessel through the bay, stated the ice "is not of the crumbly variety either, but good thick ice and it is being piled up at an astonishing rate by the wind." On Big Portage in the Copper Country, ice was still more than a foot thick at the beginning of May, the thickest on record so late in the season.

Fishermen had a rough opener on May 1; the ground was too frozen to dig worms, "a necessity in trout fishing early in the season." Farmers became discouraged early the second week of May. Snow one to three feet deep still drifted on some fields around Ishpeming. On May 17, farmers were "doing nothing" owing to the wetness of the fields. A farmer east of Negaunee claimed his timbered land was still covered with one to two feet of snow.

High temperatures in Marquette failed to get out of the 30s from May 12-15.

The cold of late January and early February brought beautiful ice formations on Lake Superior. A cold spring would keep ice along the shore into early June. (Photo by Tom Buchkoe)

two feet of snow; all of it falling in the span of about 15 hours. Skandia, in the hills southeast of Marquette, tallied 28 inches. Wind gusts to 40 miles per hour built huge drifts.

The quick-hitting storm brought near paralysis to the U.P., though disruption and inconvenience was mitigated by the fact the storm extended into the weekend and most people exercised the option of staying home. Some residents of Ishpeming had a long wait for their Saturday morning paper. My sons, Ian and Alek, had a paper route at the time. The papers were dropped off at the house in the predawn hours; they would then deliver them to their customers, usually before 8:00. This Saturday brought a disruption to their usual routine. They first had to search for the bundle of papers beneath the fresh mantle of snow. "We finally found them," remembers Alek. "They were way on the bottom of a drift. Luckily they had a plastic bag around them."

Delivering the papers was a great adventure. "It took us three hours," explains Ian, normally it would take an hour." "No one had cleared their sidewalks, yet," recalls his younger brother. "Ian and I would swim through the snow, kind of just dive in and swim to the door. The drifts were as tall as I was."

The massive cleanup was just finished when another significant snowfall greeted Monday-morning commuters. This moderate storm ushered in severe cold which closed out the month of January and extended into February.

Many residents over interior sections of the U.P. reported temperatures in the 30-to-40 below zero range on a couple of nights in early February. Amasa, a perennial cold spot in northwestern Iron County, registered unofficial lows of 50 degrees below zero on February 3 and 51 below on the 4th.

City Park in Escanaba following a sprinkling of snow on May 27, 1907. The most remarkable feature of the photo are the trees in the foreground, totally devoid of leaf growth—a result of the very cold spring. (Courtesy of Delta County Historical Society)

February 1996 evolved into a moderate month with a couple of significant warm-ups sandwiched between two healthy snowstorms. March was an uneventful month over the U.P. until another major storm lifted in from the southwest, dropping a foot or more of snow on many western and central locations.

April usually brings spring to Upper Michigan. An inexorable meltdown occurs as longer days and a higher and higher sun angle warm the earth. April 1996 was different; weather conditions in the Northern Hemisphere conspired to produce what early New England settlers called a "backward" spring.

The main weather player this month was high latitude blocking over the North Atlantic. This high pressure area aloft drove the storm track south of its usual position and held enough cold air over Canada into the Upper Midwest to produce a succession of late-season snows over Upper Michigan. The first eight days of the month saw highs only

After a brief warm spell where readings popped into the 50s, more cold, wet and even snowy weather greeted residents after the 20th. Snow fell across much of Upper Michigan on May 27. It melted rapidly, wrote a reporter in the Copper Country, because "the language used when the beautiful started to fall was sufficiently warm to melt more than snow." The reporter went on to state that while there had been snowstorms this late in the Copper Country, the persistence of the "cold wave...is a record breaker in itself."

April 1907 came in with an average temperature of 29.8 degrees, almost 8 degrees below the long-term average. May registered an astounding 39.8 degree average, more than 9 degrees below the standard for the month. Both April and May 1907 were, by far, the coldest of their respective months on record.

Upper Michigan Seasonal Snowfall Records Set in 1995-96			
	1995-96	*Record*	*Avg. Snow*
Alberta	*217.8*	*194.8 1971-72*	*151.1*
Bergland	*284.2*	*244.1 1976-77*	*171.1*
Chatham	*315.5*	*227.0 1983-84*	*146.1*
Herman	*337.0*	*308.4 1875-76*	*N/A*
Iron River	*114.5*	*113.7 1959-60*	*77.5*
Ironwood	*283.1*	*255.0 1970-71*	*171.8*
NWS	*251.4*	*243.2 1981-82*	*165.3*
S. S. Marie	*222.0*	*178.6 1976-77*	*127.1*

Figures from the National Weather Service in Marquette, MI

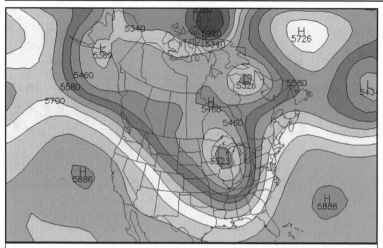

Not very spring like: The upper air chart the morning of April 30, 1996 showed a strong, blocking high over the North Atlantic and an equally strong low over the Upper Great Lakes. A late-season storm buried parts of northern Wisconsin and the U.P. to cap-off the long winter of 1995-96. (Courtesy of Plymouth State Weather Center NCEP/NCAR Reanalysis Map Generator)

reaching the 20s and 30s with lows in the single numbers and teens. Measurable snow fell on five of these days.

To illustrate the back-wardness of the month, the heaviest snows did not begin until well into the second week. Low pressure emerged onto the Plains on April 11. The low pushed slowly northeastward toward Upper Michigan, while high pressure north of Lake Superior funneled cold air in on north to northeasterly winds.

The next day, rain changed to freezing rain, sleet and then snow. Temperatures south of the low reached into the 80-degree range as far north as Milwaukee, providing a source of unstable, relatively moist air. Thunderstorms with rain and sleet broke out over southern sections of the U.P. that afternoon. By the 13th, just over a foot of wet, heavy snow had fallen on Negaunee Township. This system was quickly followed by another southwestern low that dropped up to a half-foot of fresh snow the 15th.

Warming set in during the third week of April and by all appearances, the long winter was finally through. High temperatures reached into the 60-degree range over many areas on April 18 and 19. Light rain fell as the temperature rose, and flooding soon became a problem on many rivers and streams.

Against the backdrop of this mild interlude, the pattern driving the circulation over North America had not fundamentally changed. A strong disturbance shot eastward out of the Pacific storm factory during the fourth week of the month. Forced southeastward by a persistent block over the Atlantic, it brought more snow to sections of Upper Michigan on April 26 along with record low temperatures in the teens.

The culmination and climax of this anomalous month grew out of a low-pressure area that formed over west Texas the evening of the 27th. The system slowly shuffled east-northeastward as the upper-air trough supporting it began to amplify over the Plains. On the 29th, low pressure sat over eastern Illinois. Clouds thickened over the Upper Great Lakes and rain broke out in southern Wisconsin. As the precipitation lifted northward, it turned to snow over northern sections of the state into Upper Michigan. Heavy, wet snow fell all night and through most of the next day as the Illinois low drifted into the eastern Lower Peninsula.

The weather map featured the classic signature of a backward spring; a strong upper ridge of high pressure sat over Greenland while an equally strong low, causing Upper Michigan's snowstorm, was anchored over the Western Great Lakes. Just over 14 inches of snow ell; bringing the season total to a record-setting 251 inches at the NWS. Similar amounts fell over a good share of the rest of central Upper Michigan into northern Wisconsin.

May 1996 began with an unusually thick snowpack over a good portion of the Peninsula. To add insult to injury, a weak disturbance brought another couple of inches of snow to the Iron Mountain area on May 4. Fortunately, dry, mild weather gradually eroded the enormous mass of snow, keeping further flooding to a minimum.

Ken Michels (right) and his brother, Tom enjoying a mid-May snowmobile ride. (Courtesy of Ken Michels)

Snow covering the ground continually for nearly six months can be a source of depression for some—others make the best of it. "We went for a snowmobile ride on May 11," says Ken Michels of Ishpeming. "There wasn't much snow and we could only go about a mile in the woods before we ran out of snow. But we did it—we were out snowmobiling." While he is proud of his late-season feat, he is not eager to do it again. "The season can end in March," he adds. "I never want to snowmobile that late again."

May 1996 brought a quirky juxtaposition of seasons. On the 18th, temperatures soared into the 80s. The last few piles of snow were eaten away by the warm wind and hot sun and the ice finally left Negaunee's Teal Lake. That evening, a friend of mine had a party. Most of us remained outdoors enjoying the warm, almost muggy night. Some of us remarked at how quickly the weather had turned. Most of us spent time swatting at the first crop of mosquitoes. The pesky creatures arose from the melt water of the last snow piles as if to assure us that, indeed, the long, snowy winter of 1995-96 was over.

1996-97: The Snow Hammer Falls on Upper Michigan Again

Record snowfall blasted sections of the U.P. the next winter. Big lake-effect snows descended on Lake Superior snow belts favored by northwesterly winds the first weekend in November, but a period of warmth and rain washed away most of the snow later in the month. The first general storm of the season held off until the middle of December when a Colorado low brought a half-foot or more of snow to western sections.

The real snow blitz began just before Christmas. In a two-week period, from December 23 to January 4, 1997, three major storms hit north central Upper Michigan. Each one dropped over a foot of fresh snow. From late December to late January, nearly 122 inches of snow fell in the hills west of Marquette.

Like their predecessors in the Keweenaw nearly two decades earlier, a new generation of snowplow drivers had to endure long hours and many consecutive days clearing snow. "It was

The Lake Superior shoreline became encased in ice after a series of storms beginning in late December 1996. (Photo by Jerry Bielicki)

getting sickening going to work all the time," remembers Ken Michels, a plow driver for the Marquette County Road Commission. "You work 12 hours, then you come home and you have two hours of snow removal to do at home. Then it goes on and on and on."

Fortunately for Michels and other road commission workers in the area, the snow let up in February. However, a thick snow cover was established over the entire peninsula and seasonable cold promoted little melting. February 1997 was a quiet winter month; no major storms occurred and temperatures settled close to the long-term average. Even one brief, sharp warming trend pushed temperatures into the 40s and 50s around the 20th.

While some U.P. inhabitants take flight to warmer southern climates during the dead of winter, Jeff Howell, a resident of Colorado Springs, Colorado at the time, was preparing a move to Upper Michigan. "I grew up in the Portland, Oregon area," he explains. "I loved snow; and while we had a big snow winter there in the late 60s, most years it snowed very little. It was frustrating living in an area that got rain all winter, while not far to the west heavy snow would be falling in the mountains." Howell lived in various parts of the country while he served in the military and even spent some time overseas. He had lived in Colorado a number of years and it was time for a change.

"I looked for areas of the country where there was lots of snow," he says. "I chose the Upper Peninsula because of the amount of snow that fell, the small communities and because it just looked like a great place to live. Ever since the *Edmund Fitzgerald* went down and the Gordon Lightfoot song, I was always intrigued by Lake Superior, too."

Howell arrived in the Marquette area in early March. The heavy snow cover impeded his move into a house he had rented. "The moving truck couldn't get to the house because of the snow piles on each side of the road," he recalls. "It was stuck for over eight hours. I then spent five days in a hotel."

His move was completed before the largest snowfall of the winter arrived. This particular event would become the literal "icing on the cake" for snow fans like Howell—a phenomenon colonial New Englanders called the "Crown of Winter Storm."

This system gradually developed the second week of March out of a large ocean storm centered off the West Coast. On March 12, nascent low pressure was situated over western

Kansas. The next day, a vast amount of warm, moist air began lifting over the dome of cold air entrenched over parts of Minnesota, Iowa and Wisconsin. As the system sent its energy slowly northeastward, snow broke out in these areas. It took quite a while, though, before the snow lifted into Upper Michigan.

"The radar image I saw on television showed the snow staying in the same spot over Wisconsin all day," remembers Howell. "I even heard a local store owner say there was only supposed to be one to three inches of snow out of the storm. Back at that time, I had no Internet access, so I didn't know what was going on. I had expected a big storm, so I was disappointed."

Howell and other snow lovers throughout the U.P. had nothing to worry about. The Kansas low initially slid into to southern Missouri, keeping snow to the south. Then as the

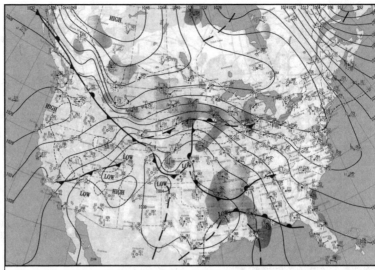

Low pressure formed over the Central and Southern Plains on March 13, 1997. It took a while to reach Upper Michigan but when it did, it dumped record snows on north-central sections. (NOAA Central Library Data Imaging Project)

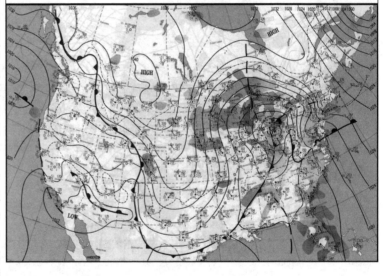

upper trough started amplifying in the Plains, the southwesterly flow ahead of it drew the storm northeastward. Snow began falling lightly across the U.P. on the evening of March 13 and then began to pick up. By morning, the deepening low had drifted northeastward, producing a heavy snowstorm over much of the Upper Peninsula.

The local paper called it a "St. Paddy's winter blowout." A foot of snow fell in Escanaba and also around the Iron Mountain area. Farther north, the influence of Lake Superior added considerably to storm totals. The system's movement created the perfect environment for lake enhancement. Very heavy snow fell all day around Marquette as the low continued intensifying to the southeast and the upper trough deepened overhead.

The heavy snow came in bursts. "There were times when I couldn't see the house across the street, because it was snowing and blowing so hard," recalls Howell. "I spent a large

Five people were injured when a roof collapsed on an Ishpeming building following the record snows of the winter of 1996-97.
(Courtesy of Paul Arsenault)

portion of the day shooting video to show to the folks back home."

He and others throughout the area spent a good deal of time clearing snow, too. About 18 inches fell in the city of Marquette, while road commission crews in Big Bay encountered over two feet of fresh snow along with drifting. Plow drivers were hindered by other vehicles bogged down in the deep snow. This was especially true in the higher elevations west of Marquette, which received the greatest snow amounts.

A combination of moist north-northeasterly flow and added lift provided by elevation produced exceptionally heavy snow in the north central U.P. highlands. A 24-hour snowfall record of 26.2 inches was set at the Weather Service on the 14th. The 63 inch snow cover measured that evening became the deepest snow cover ever reported at the station. This storm, combined with minor snowfalls that followed, established a record seasonal snowfall (272.2 inches) for the second year in a row.

The rest of March 1997 turned peaceful; no more major storms occurred and temperatures slowly warmed under the influence of the increasing sun angle. The thick snow cover melted only slowly; 50 inches or more remained on the ground through the end of the month. April began with an exceptional warm-up. Temperatures rose into the 60s on two days early in the month and the snow melted quickly. While the majority of the winter's snowpack left the first half of the month, the cold season was not entirely through. May 1997 brought more "backward spring" weather to a large portion of Upper Michigan (*see "May 1997: The Snowy Week", page 215*).

The Winter of 2001-02: A Slow Start, an Extraordinary Finish

This winter began extraordinarily mild. November 2001 averaged an astounding 9.8 degrees above the long-term average. Very little snow fell. Just after Thanksgiving, a storm developed off the Rockies and pushed toward the southern Great Lakes. It encountered a massive, cold, high pressure system in Canada and began to weaken; however, it still had enough strength to produce a substantial snowstorm over a large portion of western and central Upper Michigan.

This was an "elevation storm." Snow fell at temperatures around the freezing mark and the added warmth of Lake Superior kept the precipitation a mixture of rain and snow near the lakeshore. Almost no snow accumulated at the shore in Marquette. The farther inland away from lake-level, the more snow fell. Roughly ten miles to the west, the 36 hour storm dumped over 33 inches near Negaunee. The snow was incredibly wet and heavy. At the height of the storm on November 27, the NWS tallied just over 19" of snow, containing over two inches of water—an approximate 9 to 1 snow to water ratio.

Residents worked their "yooper scoopers" overtime in February and March of 2002. (Photo by E. Yelland)

The sloppy load of snow brought down some trees and caused power outages over the higher terrain of north central Upper Michigan. It was supplemented by an additional few inches of very wet snow the last day of the month. Normally, the snow that falls at this time in November stays on the ground the rest of the winter. This was not the case in 2001. Mild, fall-like weather set in as the new month began and it stayed through the winter solstice.

December 2001 averaged almost 8 degrees above average. A 20 inch snow cover in the hills west of Marquette at the beginning of the month dwindled to patches and piles of crusty, dirty snow by the 15th. Virtually no snow fell the first three weeks of the month. Those areas that missed the late November storm had bare ground until just before Christmas.

A pattern change brought moderate cold and some snow, especially near Lake Superior from the holiday into the first few days of 2002. But true winter continued to elude the U.P. as mild air again washed over the mid latitudes of North America. January wound up nearly 9 degrees above average.

Snowfall remained light; areas away from Lake Superior's influence continued with bare ground or a mere dusting through the end of the month. The lack of snow cover around Escanaba forced organizers of the U.P. 200, Upper Michigan's premier sled dog race, to change the race route, avoiding southern areas in favor of the snow belts farther north. As of

The 2002 U.P. 200 Sled dog race course was permanently moved due to lack of snow early in the winter of 2001-2002. (Drawing by E. Yelland)

Does the bicycle have chains? A student pedals to class during one of the many snowstorms of this late-blooming, record-breaking winter. (Drawing by E. Yelland)

this writing, the new course from Marquette to Grand Marais and back has become the permanent race trail.

While February 2002 remained much warmer than average, the snow situation changed dramatically. The skies opened up over a good share of the peninsula, dropping a season's worth of snow over the next seven weeks. The first day of February brought the area's first significant snowstorm. A trough over the southwestern U.S. the last couple of days of January redeveloped into the Plains. Low pressure, spawned in south Texas, deepened and headed northeastward through the Mid-Mississippi Valley to the Central Great Lakes. Anywhere from 6 to 10 inches fell over the south, while some northern areas, helped by lake enhancement, received over a foot.

The "snow machine" kept operating at full tilt the rest of the month. A series of minor, moderate and major snows laid down a thick covering. "What stands out about this winter is that the shortest month produced the record snow total for any month," remember snow aficionado Jeff Howell of Negaunee. "That's huge. And then it just kept coming."

February 2002 became the snowiest month on record at the NWS in Negaunee Township. An incredible 91.9 inches fell during the month, and as Howell alluded, the snow blitz continued well into the next month. March 2002 featured three major storms the first 15 days. Several more moderate falls laid down an impressive covering by the latter part of the month. "I couldn't see a car driving past my house after the last big snowstorm," says Howell. "That was the largest snow cover I'd seen since moving up here."

The massive, waterlogged mantle remained in place into the first part of April, as chilly weather prevailed. Another sudden and dramatic change in the pattern at mid month set the stage for one of the worst snowmelt floods in Upper Michigan's history (*see "The Snowmelt Flood of 2002", page 229).*

Chapter 8

Spring arrives slowly in Upper Michigan. Most of its land lies north of the 45th parallel of latitude and the proximity to large bodies of water that retain winter's chill usually make for a slow march to the warm season. Occasionally, the atmosphere conjures up just the right combination of cold air, moisture and energy to produce a memorable late spring snowstorm. Here is a survey of some of the more outstanding ones:

1870s-1880s

These cold years produced some late snows. On May 5, 1871, 8 inches of snow fell in Negaunee, providing two good days of sleighing. After one of the coldest winters on record, there were still ten-foot snow banks on Iron Street in that mining community as late as April 20, 1875. Gladstone, on the northwest shore of Little Bay de Noc, had only been a village for two years when it was hit with a freak, 24-hour snowstorm on May 13-14, 1888. Farther north around Marquette, the storm lasted four days.

June 2-3, 1945: The Latest Big Snow

"They changed the song...to 'It's January in June' as startled Ishpeming residents, thinking they had seen the worst in a record cold May, watched a cold June rain turn into a swirling snowstorm." The opening sentence in the local paper described the latest, heaviest snowfall in Upper Michigan history.

The date was June 2, 1945. It was a Saturday and Kip Waters of

A snowman in Negaunee proudly displays his birth date. Up to six inches of snow accumulated from late Saturday, June 2 into Sunday. (Courtesy of the Negaunee Historical Society)

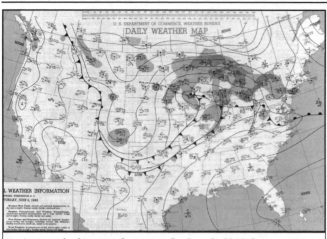

A wintry looking weather map. On June 2, 1945, low pressure was drifting over the Upper Mississippi Valley toward the Great Lakes, while chilly high pressure dominated to the north and west. Rain changed to snow over most of western and central Upper Michigan. (NOAA Central Library Data Imaging Project)

Negaunee had gotten back home from camp at Goose Lake. He left on foot Friday afternoon with a friend. "It was a beautiful day, 70 degrees," he recalls. "We got half way out there and it rained, from out of nowhere." They decided to keep going and arrived at the cabin thoroughly drenched. After building a fire in the stove the two boys dried out and took to the lake for some fishing. They got soaked again, dried out by the fire and stayed in for the night. On Saturday morning, they fished a little, then Waters said, "we better get out of here," after he became convinced the weather would not improve. Later that afternoon, "about four o'clock, five o'clock," he remembers, "I was walking across Main Street in Negaunee at Iron Street and it started snowing."

It snowed into Sunday and it stuck. Veteran highway employees declared that never before had equipment been brought out of the county garages in June to clear snow off the roads. Waters says he went to Sunday school the next morning but first had to shovel the sidewalk and in front of the garage before his father could pull out the family car. He remembers hearing of a number of cars getting stuck just east of Negaunee near the Carp River Bridge on old Highway 41 (now Heritage Drive). The cars got down the hill into the river valley and could not plow through the greasy, wet snow back up the hills on either side of the bridge.

In Ishpeming "some of the finest snow pictures of the year" were missed because "no films were available." Shrubbery and trees were coated with a thick mantle of white and some residents were concerned about their flowering fruit trees and the gardens they had just planted.

Luckily there was a camera and film available in Ironwood to catch a father and daughter in the latest big snow on record, June 1945. (Courtesy of Ironwood Carnegie Library)

In Diorite, Margaret Mullins remembers the extraordinary snowstorm because she had visitors. "My husband's sister and her friend came up from Chicago," she says. The couple arrived that evening in about six inches of heavy, wet snow. "They couldn't get over that," recalls Mullins, "especially the fellow. He was from Chicago, and, of course, nothing like that ever happens down there." And at least in the last one hundred and some-odd years, it only happened once in Upper Michigan—in June 1945.

Memorial Day Snow of 1947

Just two years after the June 1945 snow, another aberrant, late storm occurred, this time over the Memorial Day holiday. Spar Sager was employed by the U.S. Forest Service and was looking forward to the holiday off. "Rather than come straight home," he remembers, "I decided to stop on the way and pitch my little shelter tent and catch some fish in the morning." Sager drove off the road in the Carp Plains area in Schoolcraft County found a good spot, pitched his tent and settled in for the night.

The next morning he awoke to the feeling of the cold, wet canvas roof of the tent against his body. He removed the tent from his face, extended his elbows and maneuvered his way to the door to see what had happened. Sager was startled as he gazed out on a snow-covered landscape—about six inches of the wettest, sloppiest snow had come down while he slept.

"That cancelled the fishing trip," he recalls. The snow weighed down the tag alders across the stream, rendering fly-fishing impossible. Worse yet, he was stuck. His car could not be driven over the rough, hummocky ground covered with six inches of slush. "It would just slide and slide, so I had to sit there and do nothing until late afternoon before I could get out." Sager explains that while there was still some snow left even after the warmth of a late May day, it melted enough so he could drive out. The tires cut right through the remaining slush to the

An example of U.P. tenacity—even a late-season snow will not hold back a hardy, outdoor enthusiast.
(Courtesy of Marquette County History Museum)

brush underneath, which provided enough traction to keep the car moving forward.

Farther east, nearly a foot of snow was said to have come down between Eckerman and Paradise. Officially, Sault Ste. Marie reported three inches of snow out of the storm while Marquette received less than an inch. The storm came out of the Plains where a section of Nebraska had a foot of snow and parts of Iowa had a remarkable four inches. In North Dakota, the town of Eckman reported a low temperature of 15 degrees and in Detroit, residents shivered through the coldest Memorial Day since the frigid spring of 1884.

Extraordinarily Cold, Snowy Start to May 1954

A wet, cold and snowy period plagued Upper Michigan the first week of May 1954, rivaling any other nasty start to the fifth month on record. May Day brought spring warmth after a period of showers affected central sections. The temperature in Marquette soared to 66 degrees under brisk southwesterly flow. A careful inspection of upper-air charts that morning would have tipped the weather-savvy observer that this pleasant spring pattern would not last.

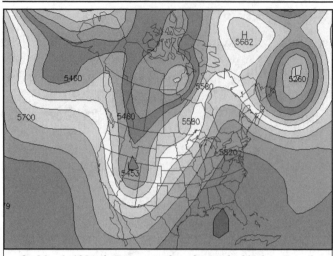

On May 1, 1954, the upper-air chart featured a block in Canada and the North Atlantic and a developing storm out west. The atmosphere was getting ready to unload a late bout of winter on Upper Michigan. (Courtesy of Plymouth State Weather Center NCEP/NCAR Reanalysis Map Generator)

A sharp, deep trough of low pressure was situated over the intermountain west, while a tremendous, blocking ridge of high pressure held sway over the northwest Atlantic. This strong ridge was a signal that stormy weather, developing with the trough in the west, would not be able to progress through the continent in a normal manner. Over the next couple of days, the western system crept eastward, while residual cold in Canada oozed southward into the north central states, including Upper Michigan. Cold rain and snow developed ahead of the western low and then lingered as the system wound up and parked itself overhead.

Road conditions were declared the "worst in years" around Ironwood as 17 inches of wet snow fell inside of 48 hours from May 2-4. Many plows became "hung up" in the mire when they attempted to clear snow from unpaved roads where the frost had left the ground. In one instance, a plow became stuck in soft ground on North Douglas Boulevard; a city truck, sent to pull the plow out, also became mired in the mud.

Stannard Rock—the loneliest lighthouse in the United States was manned until the early 60s. (Courtesy of Superior View, Marquette)

The Keweenaw waited for its main snowstorm until the 7th. A wet, heavy snow of eight to ten inches came down with a temperature hovering right around freezing. This snow along with other smaller falls the first week of the month, contributed to over 11 inches at Houghton in May 1954. This figure remains the greatest May snow total in the Copper Country.

Out on Lake Superior, the lighthouse keepers settled into life at the most isolated beacon in all the United States. Stannard Rock light kept its reputation for being encased in ice from December to May. Assistant Keeper Elmer Sormunen of Chassell reported in May that the tower of the lighthouse was covered with ice on the northwest side. He and three other keepers had to chop their way through ice to get up to the first landing.

The lighthouse on a shoal in Lake Superior, roughly forty miles due north of Marquette and due east of Gay on the Keweenaw Peninsula, was still manned through the navigation season during the 1950s. The keepers would be deposited at their post on the "rock" around the beginning of May; they would then stay there for the next six months. Through years of experience, the personnel knew what confronted them when they arrived in early May. In 1954, as soon as they landed, they built fires and began to thaw out the mattresses they would sleep on, which were rigidly frozen.

This year the furnace failed to function and a man had to be shipped in from the Sault to fix it. The men were without heat in the beacon building for three days and this fact may have contributed to Sormunen coming down with a severe cold. He was taken back to his home in Chassell, where he convalesced for a few days.

Back on land, Marquette received 7.8 inches of snow on the 7th. It was the heaviest snowfall ever recorded up to that time on a single day in May. In the four days preceding the storm, a little snow fell each day, contributing to a total of 8.7 inches for the month. The temperature from May 2-13 averaged a chilly 35.8 degrees, the longest cold spell for any May on record. During the same period in 1907, the coldest spring on record (*see sidebar in "The Long Winter and Backward Spring of 1995-96", page 197*), the temperature averaged nearly a degree warmer.

May 6-7, 1960: Heavy Snow Follows Record Rains

One of the wettest periods on record in Upper Michigan (*see "Floods", page 224*) culminated in a snowstorm over many sections in early May 1960. Old timers in Negaunee and Ishpeming were unable to remember worse weather the first week of May. May Day was preceded by a sloppy four to eight inches of snow over central sections on April 30. After a brief dry spell, new low pressure formed in the Plains on May 3, while a frontal boundary set up from the low into the Upper Great Lakes, paralleling the developing southwest flow aloft. Waves of low pressure rippled along the stalled boundary, drawing abundant moisture northward, producing more unwanted rain over the waterlogged U.P. May 4-5.

Finally, the main storm lifted northeastward out of the Texas Panhandle, drawing in cold air from an extensive pool of chill trapped over central Canada by persistent high-latitude blocking to the north. The low lifted slowly northeastward to

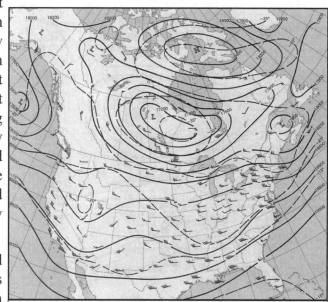

High-latitude blocking was a constant feature during the late winter and spring of 1960. On May 3, higher-than-normal pressure over northern Canada trapped cold air farther south, which led to a major late-season snowstorm over the U.P. several days later. (NOAA Central Library Data Imaging Project)

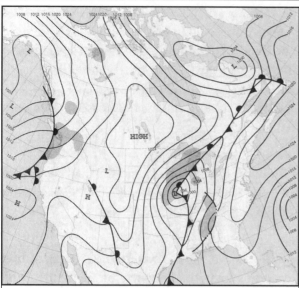

Low pressure crept from northeastern Missouri Friday afternoon, May 6 to northern Lake Michigan 24 hours later. It brought nearly two feet of snow to parts of Upper Michigan. (NOAA Central Library Data Imaging Project)

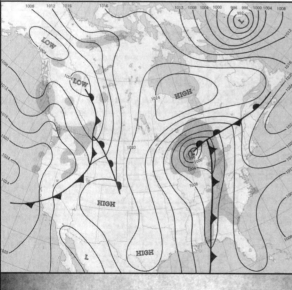

May 7, 1960—the scene looked more like mid-winter than early May at the Marquette County Airport. (Courtesy of Marquette County History Museum)

Wisconsin then the Lower Peninsula while deepening, providing a perfect set-up for heavy snow over Upper Michigan.

Helen Lepola remembers this weekend storm well. "Our daughter was born prior to the storm," explains Lepola, "so I did get to L'Anse hospital but my husband could not get to see me during that weekend." L'Anse high school had its prom that weekend and she remembers lying in the hospital bed, looking out the window "watching the girls trample in the snow with their lovely gowns."

Roads around her hometown of Watton were a mess. Lepola explains that M-28 running through the village was under construction at the time and she was later told that the detours around the town were littered with vehicles stuck in the mud and snow. Later, the cars and trucks required tractors to pull them out. Stranded travelers had to spend the night in people's homes and even saunas. Lepola's mother walked a "young Air Force man" to the neighbors through the dark during the storm. "Needless to say that man…was very appreciative," says Lepola. He sent her mother a Christmas card and note of thanks, which she still keeps after almost 50 years.

Snow amounts from this storm were worthy of a mid-winter snowfall. Marquette only tallied 8.8 inches because a good share of the precipitation mixed with rain. The higher elevations west of town had mostly snow. Ishpeming reported 14 inches with three-to-four-foot drifts. The high temperature there on Saturday only made 32 degrees and on Sunday 33. The Marquette County Airport in Negaunee Township was buried under nearly two feet of wet, heavy snow. "Extremely dangerous" driving was reported down south in Dickinson County and up north the May chill allowed Houghton to retain a 3 inch snow cover on May 9, two days after the unseasonable storm.

The Freak Snowstorm of May 9-10, 1990

On the surface, this appears to be a repeat of the storm thirty years and three days earlier; but it occurred against a weather backdrop vastly different from the 1960 storm. In contrast to wet, cold weather in 1960, record-breaking early season heat began around April 20, 1990 and continued right up to the day before the storm.

Steve Brown, a high school student living in Norway at the time, remembers that day: "It felt really warm. I was up in Marquette. There were thunderstorms, it was like summer." The official high on May 8 was 76 degrees—a record for the date. Bark River in western Delta County topped out at 82. It was the

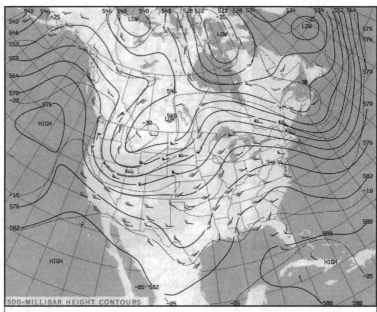

An unusually deep, cold trough of low pressure dropped into the western U.S. on May 8, 1990, while Upper Michigan enjoyed one more day of warm spring weather ahead of it. (NOAA Central Library Data Imaging Project)

last day in a series of six record highs within 16 days that included a sultry 89 degrees on April 25. The thundershowers that developed that afternoon formed along a cold front that sank into the area from the northwest. The temperature fell sharply after the frontal passage and the bout of warm spring weather that induced a remarkably early green-up, came to an abrupt end.

Out west, an upper-air trough in the Rockies supported low-pressure development in the Western High Plains, and the weather map suddenly took on a wintry look. I remember looking at the maps and charts and computer forecast models and thinking to myself, "If this was a month earlier, we'd get hammered with heavy snow." The low in the Plains was forecast to come toward the Great Lakes and deepen while drawing in colder air from the north. The time of the year and the fact that it had been so warm the last two weeks provided a forecast quandary: How much snow would actually fall and with the warm ground, how much would stick? It seemed wise to mention how wintry the system looked and warn folks that there would likely be a change from rain to snow, at least at the tail end of the event.

The next day saw a thickening overcast as the morning wore on. The air remained chilly, with the temperature rising little from an early-morning start in the 30s to 40s over Upper Michigan. About mid-day a few ice pellets and a flake of snow came down in Marquette. Sprinkles of rain followed and then the precipitation quit.

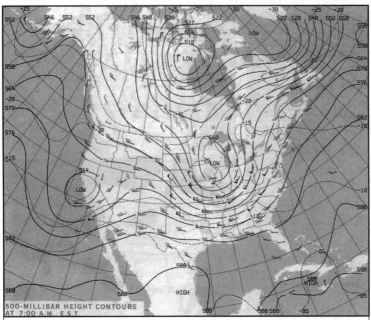

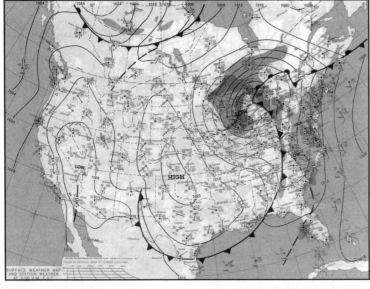

On May 10, the trough had moved east and deepened further over the Western Great Lakes, supporting a late-season snowstorm from Wisconsin into Upper Michigan. (NOAA Central Library Data Imaging Project)

As part of my television duties, I spoke to a class at Gilbert Elementary School in Gwinn during the early afternoon. At the time, I showed slides as part of my presentation, so the shades in the classroom were drawn and the lights were out. I was telling the students how interesting this developing storm looked; how "if it was a month earlier, we would get a big snow," and so on. At that point, the teacher interrupted me. She pulled up the shade and said, "Look." Outside, a thick fall of heavy, wet snowflakes had begun.

It never did change back to rain over a good portion of the north central highlands of Upper Michigan. At lake-level, it was a different story; a mixture of rain and snow changed to a driving rain that continued all night in Marquette. Down in Norway, Steve Brown was in history class when the leading edge of the storm's precipitation shield reached there. "I remember looking out the window," Brown recalls, "and it looked like it was starting to mix with some flakes of wet snow. I thought, 'that can't be.' But, it started to mix with snow, and then changed back to rain." It rained there all night, too. Brown, a cooperative observer for the NWS, measured two inches of rain and it was still raining the next morning.

In the highlands of the north central U.P., it snowed all night and was still snowing heavily the morning of the 10th, with an increasing northerly wind. The snow took a while to accumulate because of the warm ground. The snow cover never amounted to more than a foot or so, yet there was over three inches water-equivalent and an estimated total of just over 22 inches in Negaunee Township. In Marquette, the precipitation changed to snow in the early morning and began to accumulate slowly. Total accumulation near lake-level amounted to around 8 inches.

In Norway, the changeover occurred during the morning commute. "At ten in the morning it was probably a quarter mile visibility, just heavy, heavy snow," remembers Brown. "No one could pay attention in school because it was May and just a whiteout, huge flakes…it just came down like crazy." Schools in Norway were dismissed at noon. "We hadn't been let out that whole

The wet snow clung to everything it fell on. (Photo by Tom Buchkoe)

winter and it was May and we got let out because it was so bad," says Brown. Along with the two inches of rain, he measured 10 inches of snow from the storm.

To the east, in Bark River, NWS cooperative observer Larry Wanic checked in with 6.5 inches of snow and a storm total of over 2.33 inches water equivalent. In Menominee, the combination of heavy snow and strong winds caused damage to cable and power lines. "We've got so many outages I can't begin to list them," said a power company spokesman during the height of the storm. "We've got outages from Daggett to Pensaukee [Wisconsin] and all the way west to Suring." The freakish storm dumped significant snow as far south as the western suburbs of Milwaukee.

Up north in Negaunee, Marguerite Waters looked out her window and noticed that all her daffodils, which had been standing "so brave and proud," were flattened by the storm—all except one. She threw open the window and leaned out with her camera to get a picture of the last courageous blossom standing. "As I took the picture, it went Phht!" she remembers while laughing and gesturing with her hand, demonstrating how the flower keeled over from the weight of the snow.

The aftermath of the 1990 storm turned out significantly different from the storm 30 years earlier. This storm did not linger like the 1960 system, but moved steadily northeastward out of the area. In 1960, the day after the storm high temperatures struggled into the low 30s with a thick overcast. In 1990, the sun shone brightly all the next day with highs topping out in the 50s. The snow disappeared quickly, and while there was a lot of standing water and a brief rise in stream levels, dry, warm weather preceding the storm allowed the ground to easily soak up the last vestiges of the May 1990 snowstorm without major flooding problems.

May 1997: The Snowy Week

A motorist pulled up along side me as I was jogging down a Negaunee street sometime in mid-May 1997, rolled down his window and hollered, "This has been the worst May that I can remember and I've lived here all my seventy years." I could not disagree with him;

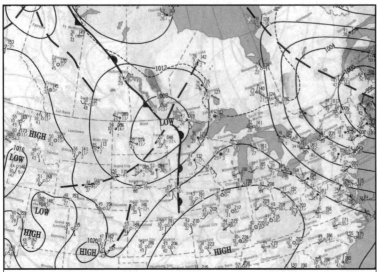

On Friday morning, May 16, 1997, a "clipper" was located over northwestern Minnesota. It would bring another snowfall to a good share of Upper Michigan to cap off an unusually-snowy May week (NOAA Central Library Data Imaging Project)

if one were an aficionado of mild spring weather, May 1997 was a trying time indeed. After the snowiest winter recorded at the time, a warm spell in early April quickly whittled down the huge banks left by a record March snowstorm. Then the typical slow struggle to spring settled in; a generally disagreeable weather pattern dominated the rest of the month into early May, punctuated by a nice early spring day here and there. Then from May 9-16 it snowed six out of eight days in most sections of the western and central Upper Peninsula.

The big snow of this period hit the far west on the 12th. Ironwood collected a foot of snow, while Ontonagon measured 13.6 inches. Porcupine Mountains Wilderness State Park, straddling Gogebic and Ontonagon counties, accumulated even more: 16 inches at the park office and workers who visited Summit Peak (1,950 feet) at the conclusion of the storm measured an astounding 36 inches! While the snow was wet and heavy at the office, typical of a late season fall, the summit snowfall was said to be as fluffy and dry as if it had fallen in January.

The last snow in the series began quickly during the afternoon of the 16th. A strong, clipper-like low-pressure system raced in from the northwest. At 4:00 eastern daylight time, moderate snow was reported at both the Houghton County and Marquette County airports. A quick 3.2 inches fell at the NWS in Negaunee Township, causing slippery roads, which resulted in a number of accidents. The snow disappeared just as quickly the next morning.

Warmer weather finally visited Upper Michigan the last half of May 1997. More moderate weather the last two weeks raised the average temperature at month's end to 44.8 degrees, still a remarkable 5.4 degrees below the long-term average. The NWS recorded its first official 70 degree day on May 23, 1997, one of the latest on record. The latest 70-degree high in Marquette occurred on June 2, 1907 after the coldest May on record (*See sidebar, "1907: The Most 'Backward' Spring", page 197*).

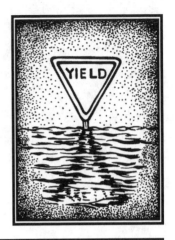

CHAPTER 9

FLOODS

Most floods in Upper Michigan occur as the result of snow melt. Even this type of flooding is relatively rare; usually, the winter's snow cover melts slowly, as dry, cool weather dominates during most springs. Occasionally, a surge of heat, exacerbated by heavy rain, will send rivers and streams over their banks. While even less frequent, a heavy summer rain on saturated ground can cause flash flooding. The following is a survey of some of the more infamous spring floods and flash floods.

September 1881: The Wettest Month

The wettest month in the recorded history of Marquette culminated in "The Deluge" of September 29, 1881. "The flood-gates of heaven were opened" and almost 5.5 inches fell, the greatest one-day rainfall ever recorded. A number of sidewalks in the city were undermined by the torrent, while many cellars flooded.

In Ishpeming, flash flooding occurred. Partridge Creek lost no time in flowing out of its banks "and over everything else for blocks on either side of its course." Water kept rising all night, and by daylight, a large part of town was flooded. Alleys and backyards were covered with up to four feet of water, and in many cases people had to build bridges from their houses to the sidewalks. All area mines were flooded to some extent, with the Winthrop mine suffering the worst inundation. A creek running past it became blocked with floating debris, diverting its course into the mine. The deluge washed the soft ground from the foot-wall to the bottom of the open pit, filling the mine with 30 feet of water.

The local paper declared it the "severest rainstorm…within the memory of the oldest inhabitants." The downpour added to an already soggy month. September 1881 concluded with a total of 12.73 inches of rain in Marquette—the wettest month on record.

July 19-22, 1909: Downpour on the Gogebic Range

The historic snowmelt flood of 2002 in Wakefield, Michigan. (Courtesy of the Wakefield Chamber of Commerce)

Flooding rain poured down on the Gogebic Range July 19-22, 1909. The first installment of the deluge "fell in sheets" and then attained "cloudburst proportions". The second torrent descended on the water-soaked region two days later, dumping more than three inches of rain in less than four hours. Nearly 10 inches of rain swamped much of western Upper Michigan and northwest Wisconsin during this four day period.

Basements and cellars in all sections of Ironwood were flooded during the first part of the storm, then again during the second installment. Storm sewers backed up in the downtown district; the water rose so quickly that goods stored in basements of businesses could not be moved to higher ground fast enough, causing heavy losses. The Montreal River rose over a foot higher than ever observed, but bridges across the river managed to hold out against the flood. A break occurred in the city water main after the second storm. It took a few days to locate and repair the leak and bring running water back to the entire city.

Heavy rain was widespread. Hancock sustained much damage during the rain on the 19th. Many residents' cellars were inundated. A large portion of Front Street was washed away. A barber shop in the western part of the "Hill City" was flooded up to its chairs. Then another storm brought the "season's heaviest downpour" two days later. In Duluth, the hillside on which the city is built "became practically one great waterfall." Three children drowned during the torrential cloudburst of the second storm. About 20 homes were washed away along creeks in the city's suburbs.

In Wisconsin, the Indian village of Odanah suffered the worst flooding of any town in the Lake Superior country. The town is situated at the confluence of several rivers and only a few feet above the level of the lake. On Wednesday, the water rose four feet in just over an hour after two dams broke. Fortunately, early warning was given to the village, preventing loss of life, but many buildings were washed away in the ensuing flood.

A Torrent at the Sault: September 3-4, 1916

Flooding rain, "the worst of its kind ever seen," descended on Sault Ste. Marie in early September 1916. As a prelude to the deluge, the Copper Country was "visited by a violent electrical storm" the evening of September 3. The storm was judged "about as widespread in scope as any storm in recent years." In Negaunee, a lightning bolt struck a residence that night, slightly injuring four people. Two occupants were thrown to the ground by the force of the strike, while two others were injured by falling plaster.

The complex of storms pushed east, arriving in the Sault later that night. Few cellars escaped flooding in the Easterday district. On Prospect Street, in the hill section, flooding occurred for the first time ever. The city health officer offered advice to those with flooded basements: "Open all windows and sprinkle liberal amounts of lime or some other disinfectant in the cellar. The atmosphere will be foul for some time to come, and will be detrimental to the health of the residents in the house unless precautions are taken."

There was no time for precautions or preparations during the height of the storm in Soo Township. Lightning struck a farmhouse completely destroying the chimney and tearing up portions of the roof, ceiling and floor. A fire broke out in the structure while its occupants, a couple and their young son, slept. Miraculously, the three escaped injury, though their beds were covered with debris. The tremendous downpour helped extinguish the flames, but likely damaged the house's interior and furnishings.

A barn at Parkerville was also struck and burst into flames. The building, along with a horse, 70 tons of hay and some farm implements, was destroyed. The rest of the livestock was led out of the barn and saved by the farmer with help from his neighbors.

Rain from the storm totaled 5.64 inches in 24 hours with a total of 5.83 inches in 31 hours. This Sault Ste. Marie rainfall record stood until August 3, 1974 when 5.92 inches fell. The 1974 torrent featured rainfall rates as high as an inch in 10 minutes but did little damage other than some flooded basements.

Manistique's "Worst Catastrophe in History": The Flood of 1920

The Manistique River ran higher than average in the spring of 1920. Its swift current grabbed some logs, leftovers of the big logging drives that ended some years before, and drove them up against a dam just above the city that bears its name. A small break developed in the dam early on the morning of March 28, pouring a torrent of water into the city.

Sections north of Deer Street and west of Delta Gardens in Manistique were initially hit by the flood, which, at first, was mild enough "to prevent any alarm among the residents." But the water kept rising. Residents on Weston Avenue eventually evacuated their homes. By 4:30 that afternoon, water gushed over Deer Street onto property to the south. Even then, the flood did not cut off traffic between the east and west sides of town.

The water still kept rising; Manistique's mayor drove the last auto from the west side to the east. After that, traffic over the city bridge was suspended. On April 1, five days after the flood began, water was still sweeping through the west side. The break in the bank was originally a few feet deep and approximately 30 feet wide but soon, five to 15 feet of water surged through an opening nearly 100 feet wide.

The river rushed through a residential district where seventy families were rendered homeless. Disaster overwhelmed the industrial district nearby. Among the sufferers was Waddell Lumber Company sustaining damage to a number of buildings. The first floor of the paper mill was flooded with up to two feet of water. The raging river tore out windows and waterlogged valuable machinery. Utility poles near the mill collapsed early the second morning of the flood, cutting off electric and water service to the city for 12 hours. The Goodwillie Brothers box factory was wrecked. It was swept by a torrent hundreds of feet wide traveling at 10 to 15 miles per hour. The raging flood washed out foundations and sent 125,000 feet of lumber into the bay. This business never rebuilt and eventually left town.

The industrial section of Manistique was devastated by the flood of 1920. (Photos courtesy of Superior View, Marquette)

On the lighter side, a horse owned by a family on Weston Avenue seemed more like a mule when it refused to "give up the ship." It remained on a small, dry piece of ground near the house. "No amount of urging or persuasion would make him forsake his island home," read the newspaper account. The next day, while the water still rose, hay and oats were shipped in to the horse by boat. A last-ditch effort was made to coax the animal to safety. Finally, after much time and effort, the horse took to the water and was led out of harm's way.

Nearby on Deer Street, the fishing was great. A gentleman was crossing the street at a point where there was a foot or more of water. While he waded across the street, he stepped on a large northern pike. The fish squirmed and fought, but the man grabbed it firmly with two hands. He carried it a short way to his house and prepared the fish for dinner.

After nearly a week, the river began receding. A coffer dam was built at the site of the break, and the river was finally coaxed into its normal channel. The Flood of 1920 was one of Manistique's worst natural disasters. It made a mess of a good portion of town and its impact was remembered for a generation or more.

August 21-22, 1942: Ontonagon County's Killer Flood

The largest recorded flood due to rain occurred on the Ontonagon River system August 21 and 22, 1942. The oldest residents of Ontonagon could not remember a more violent rainstorm. Roads were washed out, bridges flooded over and three people were drowned during the raging torrent.

The three people killed were swept to their deaths while they slept. A flash flood estimated at 10 to 12 feet deep tore down the valley occupied by a branch of the Ontonagon River. The victims, George Dent, 79, Tommy Mason, 31 and Joseph Paul Garsanki, 53, had no chance to escape as their creek-side cabin was stripped off its foundation and sent downstream. The 39-by-36 foot structure struck a bridge. The roof of the house came to rest on the bridge, while the rest of the building, including furniture, was smashed to bits.

A portion of Highway 45 north of Bruce Crossing was washed away. In Ontonagon, the large cement bridge over the river was in danger of being wrecked, as floating debris completely blocked river channels. The tremendous amount of water forced through the west channel undermined the west pier, so that the western third of the bridge began to sink. When that portion of the bridge was down almost two feet, cars were kept off.

This flood was unusual in that it occurred solely due to rain. Most Ontonagon River floods are caused by snowmelt and resulting ice jams. Serious 20th century ice jam flooding occurred in 1912, 1923 and 1963 (*See page 226*).

Flood aftermath—a washout on a section of U.S.-45 near Bruce Crossing. (Courtesy of the Ontonagon Historical Society)

June 23-25, 1946: Severe Flooding on the West End

A series of severe thunderstorms accompanied by torrential rains devastated the Gogebic Range and adjacent parts of northwest Wisconsin in late June 1946. The onslaught of storms began late June 23, accompanied by strong winds, hail and severe flooding. By early June 25, numerous roads and bridges in the area were washed out, homes flooded and communities isolated.

Bessemer suffered extensive damage during the first wave of thunderstorms. A portion of the grandstand at the high school athletic field was torn off by high winds, hurled high above the tree tops and deposited on a home close by. Portions of the home's roof caved in, leaving a mass of lumber partially covering the residence; parts of the roof were also strewn about the yard. Huge trees were split and snapped off near the roots. Lightning damaged chimneys and started fires.

The worst damage and disruption came from flooding. Six inches of rain poured down in Ironwood over 48 hours, most of it occurring in less than 8 hours overnight. Wakefield residents could not recall a harder rain in such a short period of time. Nearly 3.5 inches of rain fell in less than an hour and a half.

The torrential rains quickly

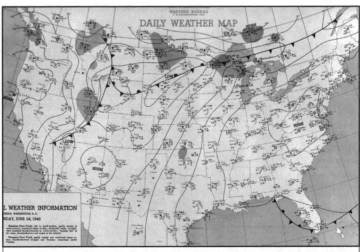

A stalled frontal boundary draped over the Upper Great Lakes became a focus for waves of heavy thunderstorms that pounded the west end of the U.P. in late June 1946. (NOAA Central Library Data Imaging Project)

raised rivers and streams in the area over their banks. In Ironwood, the west end of Cedar Street in the "flats" district was inundated by the Montreal River. A woman had to be rescued from her home at the edge of the river and several other houses on the street could only be reached by boat. The Black River became obstructed with numerous large trees and logs felled by the storm. Its swift current carried three boats moored at the harbor out into Lake Superior. Sport and commercial fishermen suspended operations until the water subsided for fear the strong current would prevent them from returning to harbor.

Bridges and culverts were washed out all over the Gogebic Range into adjacent areas of Wisconsin. A bridge on M-28 at Kenton washed out, forcing traffic to take the long detour to U.S.-2. The North Bessemer farming community was isolated when the last round of heavy rain pushed the waters of the Black River and Powder Mill Creek over the bridges on roads leading into the settlement.

In the town of Bessemer, raging flood waters carried away a garage on the north side. A man went to the aid of a neighbor during flash flooding when water from a nearby creek overflowed the banks and began entering the neighbor's house. The man was swept off his feet by the current and had to swim across the lot.

In Wisconsin, residents of Odanah were evacuated to the surrounding hills as back waters of the White River lapped two to three feet high on all buildings in town. Ashland was virtually isolated as both roads and rails were inundated by flood waters. With rail service at a complete standstill, mail delivery reverted to methods employed during the pioneer era. First-class mail was trucked from Ironwood to the Black River harbor, loaded on a fishing boat and dispatched to Ashland, Wisconsin. Then outgoing mail was loaded on the boat for the return trip. It took a week for rail and mail service to get back to normal. The flooding rains were confined to a relatively small area of Wisconsin and Upper Michigan. Farther east, Marquette actually in contrast, registered below-average rainfall during June 1946.

July 28, 1949: Record Rainstorm Hits Marquette County

Torrential rains battered Marquette and vicinity the evening of June 28, 1949. It had been a wet and stormy period throughout the Great Lakes. In Milwaukee, three people were killed the day before when a high-tension wire fell on their car during a severe thunderstorm. Two inches of rain fell in Green Bay in less than an hour, causing flooded basements. In Detroit, a man was struck and killed by lightning as he walked down the street. A power outage caused by the storm forced a doctor to complete an operation with a flashlight.

A strong, hot, high-pressure ridge brought record heat to much of the eastern United States in the days leading up to the deluge. On the backside of the eastern ridge, a stream of rich moisture surged from the Deep South into the Great Lakes, providing fuel for severe weather. In addition, a slow-moving low-pressure system and cold front approached from the west. Heavy thunderstorms developed ahead of the cold front and reached their peak intensity over Marquette County. In just over two hours, nearly 5.5 inches of rain fell on the city of Marquette, leading to considerable damage.

Flash flooding caused washouts on streets and sidewalks and damage to buildings near downtown. A huge washout at the intersection of Lake and Spring Streets brought about chain reaction of damage to infrastructure and buildings in the area. The flooding caused a fuel tank owned by Michigan Gas and Electric Company to tumble into a gully, leading to the loss of 12,000 gallons of fuel oil. At the same time, a pipe broke, allowing the escape of some 50,000 cubic feet of gas. The washout caused a water main to break, cutting off fresh water to a large section of the city. Repair of the water main was delayed for several days until workmen shored up the wall of a building in the area undermined by the high water. The building, a garage housing a service station, was one of at least two in the area that sustained heavy damage. The other, a stone building containing a rug shop, saw 40 feet of its north wall give way when the ground around it was washed away.

To the west, train service was disrupted as three miles of track washed out near Goose Lake. Kip Waters remembers driving on the back road between Ishpeming and Negaunee: "We just got through the bottom of the hill at Suicide Ski Jump, and then it was under water." He laughs when he remembers the kids diving off the bridge and swimming under the viaduct on Silver Street in Negaunee.

For one Ishpeming couple, the flooding was no laughing matter. They spent a good share of the night marooned on high ground after their vehicle stalled in floodwaters on M-35 between Palmer and Gwinn. At about 11:00 p.m., Frank Hennessey spotted water on the highway in front of him as he and his wife were returning home from dinner at a friend's camp near Gwinn. Suddenly, he heard a roar and rumble as the wall of water rushed at his car.

"I started to turn the car around on the highway with the thought of going the other way," he said, "but the water

A man and woman pose in the basement of an Ishpeming business flooded by a torrential downpour in Marquette County in July 1949. (Courtesy of The Marquette County History Museum)

Workers repairing a Marquette street devastated by floodwaters from the record-breaking rainstorm. (Courtesy of Superior View, Marquette)

came too fast and killed the motor."

He noticed a rising cliff off to the side of the vehicle. He and his wife managed to extricate themselves from the car and waded in waist-deep water to the dry ground. There they yelled for help. Finally, at about 1:30 in the morning they heard what sounded like another woman yelling for help. They called back, but got no reply.

"We resigned ourselves to waiting on the cliff until daylight because it was pitch dark," Hennessey said. "In daylight we knew we could safely start out. But about 4 a.m. we heard a man whistle, so we whistled and called in answer. The man told us to stay where we were."

A short time later, the man, rowing a boat up the flooded highway, rescued them. "I have seen pictures of such things," said Hennessey, "but I never realized it could be so terrifying. It was something I wouldn't wish on anyone."

In Ishpeming, where damage to homes and stores mounted to many thousands of dollars, there was a bit of comic relief: The basement of the A & P grocery store got a super cleaning when flood waters hit a big supply of soap, creating mountains of suds.

The thunderstorms took down a number of telephone poles around Iron Mountain, knocking out service until the next morning. Otherwise, the system was confined mainly to north central Upper Michigan. Only a half inch of rain fell in Sault Ste. Marie, while a mere trace was reported in Escanaba.

April 22-24, 1960: A "Desperate Situation"

Heavy rains poured down on a large section of Upper Michigan in late April 1960, leading to serious flooding in many areas. Roads were washed out, bridges swept away and a number of residents were forced to flee their homes. The rainstorm, which began early on April 23, was the opening salvo in one of the wettest onslaughts in the history of the central Upper Peninsula.

The deluge was spawned by a rather innocuous looking frontal system that set up from the Plains to the Upper Great Lakes. Waves of low pressure moving along the front just south of Upper Michigan generated the rain. "It was a tremendous rainstorm," remembers Ed Holmgren of Ishpeming. "It really came down in sheets." Around Ironwood, more than five inches of rain poured down over three days, while Gurney, a town across the border in Wisconsin, was inundated with over eight

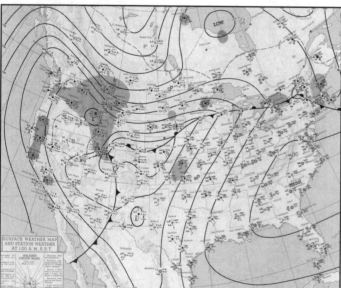

A frontal boundary draped just south of Upper Michigan triggered heavy rains and began one of the wettest periods on record. (NOAA Central Library Data Imaging Project)

inches, seven of which came down in just a 24-hour period.

The excessive rain brought the Montreal River bordering Ironwood and Hurley, Wisconsin into high flood. Two Ironwood police officers noticed the flood danger increasing in the wee hours of the morning while on patrol. They notified headquarters and immediately started arousing occupants of homes along the river. At least 15 families were evacuated from their homes, while scores of others were temporarily stranded as rivers and streams throughout the Gogebic Range went on a rampage.

Floodwaters made a muddy lake around these homes on Silver Street in Ironwood. (Courtesy of Ironwood Carnegie Library)

Silver Street at the bridge linking Ironwood and Hurley was flooded over a block wide. Many homes along Hemlock Street became flooded, as the street became a catch basin for the surging water. Spectators flocked to the flooded area. Children frolicked in the water, while their parents stared at the devastation.

Three rural North Bessemer residents had a scare early Sunday morning, when the car they were in was swept 150 feet into a field by overflow from the Black River. Passersby helped the three to safety with no injuries. Residents in that vicinity were stranded for a time by high water from the raging river.

In Marenisco, about 25 families were forced to leave their homes when the Big Presque Isle River overflowed its banks. The main street running through town still looked like a lake April 25. Road graders were employed to pull cars through the flooded area.

Farther east in the central U.P., record smashing rainfall resulted in a "desperate situation" on Marquette County roads. A combination of a high water table from excessive rain the preceding fall, heavy winter snow and a rapid spring break-up already created "the worst roads in memory." The weekend rains were the "nail in the coffin" that pushed the roads and road workers over the edge.

"There is just nothing we can do," said County road superintendent Dick Shroeger. "Even the repairs we were able to make have been washed out by the weekend rains."

Skandia was especially hard hit. Most roads in the area were already closed before the rain due to a combination of frost and water; after the rains, the "roads would not hold traffic at all." In Ely and Humboldt Townships, school buses were asked not to operate because of poor road conditions. The Milwaukee Road train was unable to leave Champion because of flooding off Lake Michigamme from Van Riper State Park west to near the town of Michigamme.

"Our road conditions here are every bit as bad as in major flood areas of the country," declared Shroeger. "But it just isn't as obvious because the county is not under water."

Residents near streams and rivers may not have agreed with Shroeger. Their residences were threatened by rising water, and in some cases, families were forced to evacuate their homes. In Gwinn, the east branch of the Escanaba River was 10 to 12 feet above normal after the rain. Numerous garbage cans and trash barrels were swept away by the flood. The river was "the highest in the memory" of the oldest residents.

Partridge Creek went on a rampage, flooding a large section of Ishpeming in late April 1960. (Courtesy of The Marquette County History Museum)

Near Republic, parts of M-95 were under water. Leif Erickson Park along the highway, normally well above the river, was inundated and water from the park ran across the highway. Farther northeast, most secondary roads in the Ishpeming area were closed, while an estimated third of the basements in the city were flooded.

Ed Holmgren remembers the problems his cousin Edgar had in Ishpeming. He explains that Partridge Creek runs through the Ridge Street area of the city. The heavy rains grew the creek into a raging torrent which flowed into area basements. "I remember Edgar telling my dad there were times when he had to dive off his basement steps and go under water to get certain things out of his basement," he recalls. "His furnace and everything was under water."

The rainstorm of April 22-24, 1960 was the beginning of an 18 day siege in which almost 11 inches of precipitation was recorded in Marquette. The period culminated in a tremendous rain and snow storm in the first week of May (*see Chapter 8, "Late Season Snows", page 211*).

March 31-April 1, 1963: Ontonagon's Worst Flood

A combination of unseasonably warm weather and thick, solid ice left from one of the coldest winters of the 20th century (*see " Cold Waves, Cold Winters", page 136*) resulted in record flooding of the Ontonagon River in early April 1963. On March 31, the temperature rose to 72 degrees, a welcome change after the area endured severe, consistent cold from early January into the first half of March. Trouble began quickly that day as heavy runoff from rapidly melting snow met with a solid ice pack on Lake Superior. In addition, river ice began to break apart. The first heavy ice flow came down the Ontonagon April 1 and jammed up against the railroad bridge. Heavy flooding swept over the entire island between the river and slough and then spread throughout the center of the village, spreading icy water from two to three feet deep.

Damage to property and businesses was extensive. Boat houses were demolished along with the watercraft in them. The boats were then swept into Lake Superior or wrecked by the ice, piled high on adjoining land. In area businesses, the water rose so fast there was no time to move or shift stock. Buildings on the south side of River Street were soaked with up to four feet of water. As the water receded, a thick coat of red silt mixed in places with oily substances was deposited over everything the flood touched. Truckloads of flooded food and other merchandise ended up in the village dump—a precaution taken to prevent the possible spread of waterborne disease.

The village slowly got back to normal as the water receded and found its way into Lake Superior; this despite a two-mile ice jam which still held on the lake. Conservative estimates of damage was placed at over a half million dollars.

Ontonagon streets became navigable after an ice jam that developed during a spring warm up following the cold winter of 1963. (Courtesy of Superior View, Marquette)

The "100 Year Flood": April 1985

Early spring 1985 was a snowy one in Upper Michigan. March was "book ended" by two major storms. The first, in the early part of the month, was a mighty cyclonic whirl that buried vast sections of the Rockies and Plains. It brought over 20 inches of snow to the NWS site in Negaunee Township. The second storm dumped just as much; it began on the last day of March and extended into April Fools Day.

Wintry weather then held on through the first week of the fourth month. Another half-foot of wet snow fell on the 6th, leaving a thick, waterlogged covering that would inevitably melt at some point over the next few weeks. The pattern began a gradual change; a deep, cold trough that dominated the early part of the month slowly lifted out and weakened, while the flow over Upper Michigan brought milder air in off the Plains. More typical spring

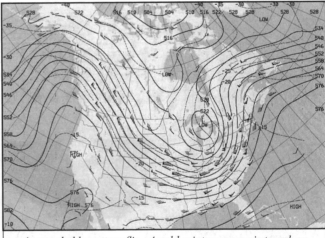

A remarkable pattern flip. A cold, wintry upper-air trough on April 6, 1985 was replaced by a warm ridge less than two weeks later. (NOAA Central Library Data Imaging Project)

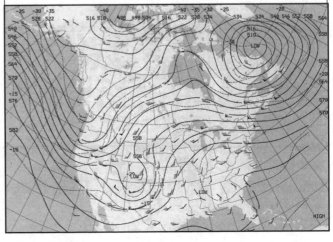

The trees in the background mark the normal bank of the Michigamme River. (Photo by Gerry Gardner)

weather followed the second week, promoting some slow melting of the dense snow pack.

The natural evolution of the spring pattern brought drastic changes during the third week. A mild, moist, southwesterly flow developed, which led to thunderstorms. Heavy rain poured into the remaining snow cover over the Upper Peninsula. Over three inches fell on April 19. The rain was immediately followed by record warmth.

"We had a lot of warm weather, so the snow melted really fast," remembers Gerry Gardner of South Republic. She lives in a home set back along the Michigamme River. "The river kept coming up," recounts Gardner. "It was gradually coming up to our house and it finally made it in."

Floodwaters made it in to hundreds of residences along rivers and streams in central Upper Michigan. Marquette County bore the worst of the snowmelt flood; at its peak, officials estimated as many as 500 homes were affected. This figure did not include summer camps. Numerous roads were closed by flooding and at least one bridge was washed out on a county road. In Alger County, four secondary roads were washed out.

But the flooding of homes caused the greatest hardship. "It was a trauma for me," explains Gardner. "It went on for three days." Her family, neighbors and friends manned four wet vacs to keep the water down. They even began moving belongings out of the house. "The girls took all my pictures off the walls because we didn't know what was going to happen with the house," she says. "One man was kind of cute; he took my microwave off the stand and he said, 'I just bought one of these and I don't want you to lose this one.'" Gardner and her family had to leave their home and turn off the power, but they were lucky; water only came up to their first basement step.

Farther down the road, Margie Isaacson was not as fortunate. "It was really bad," she remembers. "My house is one hundred years old; it's built close to the river. The pressure from the water started cracking the basement floor. We had five feet of water down there. We also lost three cords of real nice hardwood, which took a ride down the river." After the 1985 flood, the city put storm sewers in to handle run-off. She adds that while there is still the occasional flood; none have been as bad since.

Along the Escanaba River, a historic deluge occurred. "I've been here for sixty years," says Jim Ghiardi of Gwinn. "That's the highest I've ever seen the river. In the 35 years we've been in our home, that's the only time I've ever had water that came up high enough so it came in our basement."

Like Gerry Gardner in Republic, Ghiardi was fortunate. "Here on Spruce Street in Gwinn, on my end, we're probably the highest," he explains. "Farther down the street to the north, where it's lower, it was a lot worse. One person down there was pumping water out of their basement and noticed the foundation was beginning to cave in. They were afraid they were going to lose their home, so they had to hurry up and pump water back into the basement to equalize the pressure on both sides of the wall. They had just remodeled the area, too. They had something like five or six feet of water and lost everything in the basement."

Ghiardi, whose home sits about 100 to 150 yards from the normal riverbank had two pumps going at full tilt during the time the river was rising to its record crest. "I also had

to make a hole in the floor to put a third pump in," he adds. "So I was able to keep the water level in the basement at about three or four inches. I think we were in the basement for three or four days."

He was principal at Gwinn Middle School at the time, which is located a short distance from his home. "The yard at the school was completely flooded. It was right up to the school

Some buildings in central Upper Michigan became surrounded by water during the snow-melt flood of April 1985. (Photo by Ralph Gardner)

building. Some water flowed into the furnace room and into a few lower-lying rooms." The flood cancelled school the next Monday and Tuesday, April 22 and 23.

The river surrounded houses in some sections of Ghiardi's neighborhood. "There was a home just across the alley from us," he recalls. "A young lady came out of the house that Saturday morning to take a test at the school. She had to wear a garbage bag, because the water was up to her waist as she came out of her house."

Some officials termed the Flood of '85 a 100 year flood: a flood of historic proportions that is likely to occur on average just once every hundred years. The elements needed for a deluge like this were all in alignment; a thick, waterlogged snow cover, followed by heavy rain, followed by record heat. Ironically, these same conditions lined up in a similar fashion over a good share of Upper Michigan just 17 years later.

The Snowmelt Flood of 2002

The worst combination of meteorological conditions again combined to bring record flooding to parts of western Upper Michigan in April 2002. After a slow start, the winter of 2001-02 ended with frequent heavy snowfalls from early February through mid-March (*see "Snowstorms, Snowy Winters", page 204*). By early April, a three- to four-foot snowpack remained over much of central and western Upper Michigan, containing nine to 10 inches of water. The first week or so of April remained cool and the snow melted slowly. Then, on April 11, 1.5 inches of rain fell on the Montreal River watershed. The river rushed with snow melt, but aside from some flooded basements in Ironwood and some plugged ditches that caused road flooding around Bessemer, there were no major problems.

Rain continued into the morning of April 12. More than two inches poured down on the thick snowpack and swollen rivers of western Upper Michigan inside 48 hours. The rain, combined with four inches of snow melt raised concern as basements continued to flood in Ironwood and water continued to collect in low spots. Over the next few days, a warm-up continued to melt snow.

Then disaster struck. An unseasonably warm air mass flooded Upper Michigan on brisk, southerly winds. On April 16, low temperatures never fell below 60 degrees, while daytime highs soared above 80. A massive meltdown occurred. "On Sunday we had three feet of snow", remembers Marko Movrich of Wakefield. "Tuesday the snow was just gone, there was nothing." After the instant melt-down, record flooding ensued.

"We were isolated," says Joe Carlson of Ironwood. "The floods of 2002 were horrible." The Montreal River, which serves as a state border and geographic divider between Ironwood and Hurley, Wisconsin, flooded 250 to 300 feet from the riverbank into the City of Ironwood. The river rose across U.S.-2, making it impossible to cross west into Hurley. To the east, the highway was flooded at Wakefield. "We couldn't get out of this area," remembers Carlson, "We were an isolated island for about a week…it was pretty bad."

Sunday Lake Street in Wakefield became part of the lake in April 2002.
(Photo by Marko Movrich)

Movrich's hometown of Wakefield was inundated. "The night before, my wife and I took a walk," he remembers. "There was just a little bit of water." In some spots near Sunday Lake water was beginning to creep up toward nearby homes. The next morning, Movrich got a call from his wife who headed up the lunch program at Wakefield's school. She said, "You're not going to believe this. School is going to be evacuated and 28 is flooded." Movrich headed down to where they had walked the night before. "It was unbelievable," he recalls, "you just look at it and say, 'What's going on here?'" At the junction of U.S.-2 and M-28 the water was rising steadily and the roads were becoming impassable.

Homes began to flood as Sunday Lake continued its relentless rise, becoming a catch basin for the tremendous runoff. One resident reported his washer and dryer floating in his basement. A resident of Smith Street, one of the hardest hit areas, assessed her home after the floodwaters subsided: "I think our house is just shot. The foundation is cracked…everything in the house is permeated with fuel oil. When the water was so high, it took our oil barrel. We had 130 gallons of oil. Now we have a basement full of sewage, mud and oil. Where we go from there, I just don't know."

Some houses were lost as well as some businesses, but an all-out disaster was averted by wise engineering decisions. A culvert system was opened up on Verona Road just outside of town. In addition, an arsenal of five pumps was put into operation on one end of Sunday Lake, moving 12,000 gallons of water a minute out of the flood plain. A suggestion was made to cut a channel through M-28 to relieve the flow, but that plan was abandoned; if the flow of water got out of control, public utilities downstream may have been undermined and then the entire town would have been evacuated.

Volunteer efforts proved crucial in saving Wakefield from complete inundation. A combination of National Guardsmen, city workers, high school students from the surrounding area and inmates from local prisons worked around the clock on sandbag lines, salvaging as many homes and businesses as possible. Among the most heroic efforts involved city workers and volunteer firefighters. A crew worked in icy, rising water to keep the city substation—the town's main power supply—from flooding. The men worked overnight, carefully piling sand around folded plastic sheeting; the sand creating a berm that held back the flood and kept Wakefield's lights on.

A Red Cross director sent from downstate to assist in disaster relief declared he had never seen an area pull together like the residents of the Gogebic Range did: "I've seen cooperation, but nothing like this. The outpouring in these communities is mind-boggling." A flood victim from Ironwood personified this spirit of pulling together during the height of the flooding; "Skippy" Lombardo worked to save his house, then when the danger passed, he went to Wakefield and manned the sandbag lines there.

Brotherton Street near Pierce in Wakefield on April 16, 2002.
(Photo by Marko Movrich)

The weather took an ironic twist just after the floodwaters receded. The next weekend, snow fell over much of southern Upper Michigan as cold air settled in again. The last weekend of the month saw a major snowstorm affect much of northern Wisconsin and Upper Michigan. The unprecedented heat of mid-April 2002 was nothing more than an anomalous spike in an overall chilly spring.

When asked about the Flood of 2002, Marko Movrich leafs through a stack of pictures he took back then and puts the event into perspective: "Lots of talk about it still. You look at these pictures I have and you shake your head and say, 'Is this really so, did this really happen here?'"

The Dead River Flood of May 2003

A heavy rainstorm on Mother's Day 2003 contributed to a devastating flood on the Dead River system in Marquette County several days later. In the process, Silver Lake, near the headwaters of the river, returned to its original size. The 1400 acre storage basin shrunk to about 400 acres and the lost water rushed downstream into Lake Superior.

Prior to the Mother's Day deluge, it had been stormy for nearly a week over portions of the central United States. Repeated surges of energy, peeling off a trough anchored over the west, initiated rounds of deadly thunderstorms from the Southern and Central Plains to the Mid-Mississippi Valley. Upper Michigan stayed to the north and east of the stormy weather. As the weekend approached, the western trough began to progress eastward. Low pressure formed over the Southern Plains in response to this progression and shot northeastward toward Upper Michigan.

Thunderstorms with heavy rain formed quickly over the U.P. on Saturday evening, May 10. By morning, steady, heavy rain continued to fall over northern and western sections, as the strong low moved across northeast Wisconsin and then slowly crawled eastward. Three- to more than five-inch rain totals were common over the watersheds of most rivers in the northwest third of the peninsula. A number of these rivers were pushed over their banks from late Sunday into early the next week.

Water began to slowly recede as the next week wore on, and flood warnings and advisories, issued on Mother's Day, were gradually lifted. On May 14, John Mullins drove out to his camp on the Dead River north of Ishpeming. "Everything was normal when I went out there in the morning," he recalls. "I headed home about 3 or so. The river was running over the road; about a foot of water was coming over the road, oh, I'd say twenty yards or so before the bridge. I put it in four wheel drive and went through."

Mullins made his way back to his business in Diorite and called the road commission. "I told them, 'Something's wrong at Silver Lake.'" He was told they would send someone there right away to check things out. The road commission worker, dispatched to the scene, found water flowing out of Silver Lake at a rapid rate, while the river downstream quickly rose.

Informed of the situation, authorities from law enforcement, Emergency Management and the National Weather Service (NWS) determined that a crisis was in the making. It appeared that an earthen dike had given way on Silver Lake; a large portion of the formerly impounded lake was

An aerial view of the Hoist Dam holding back the waters of Silver Lake.
(Courtesy of the City of Marquette)

now heading toward the city of Marquette, about 20 miles downstream.

About four in the morning, Jeff Marshall, a resident of Marquette near the Dead River, was awakened by a knock on his door. "Honestly," he remembers, "they were just announcing on TV that they were doing emergency drills for the 9/11 thing, practicing for disaster management and so on. I looked out the window and saw police cars parked and I thought, 'You've got to be kidding me. Why would they run one of these drills in Marquette at this time of day—at this time of the morning?'" He went to the door and was greeted by a police officer who told him that Silver Lake was draining and that the water was heading toward Marquette.

The first thing Marshall did was walk down to look at the river. "It was really low at that point because they opened up the Tourist Park dam," explains Marshall, referring to a dam in north Marquette. He and the rest of his neighbors were awake for the day; they had just been told that the picturesque river that flowed by them would continue to rise and might flood their homes. At that point, they were asked to voluntarily leave the area. "We got ready," Marshall says. "We kind of moved pictures upstairs and about 9 o'clock, we walked down and saw that the river was really starting to rise."

Back up the hill in Diorite, John Mullins was talking with a friend. "He asked me, 'Aren't you afraid for your cabin?' I said, 'It will never get to my cabin.' We're a couple of hundred feet from the river. I'm also on a bit of a hill, so I didn't think it would get that high."

Emergency personnel watched closely as the river continued rising and the remains of what was the Silver Lake Storage Basin charged into it. The Hoist Dam, at the foot of the Dead River Basin,

The floodwaters of the Dead River made it to John Mullins's camp some 200 feet back from the river up a hill. Mullins points to the high-water mark. (Photo by Chris Mullins)

now held back an enormous amount of water; if it failed, all of the Dead River flood plain, which included the north side of Marquette, would be inundated. Nearly 1,800 residents were ordered to leave their homes and all streets north of Wright Street were closed.

Several feet of water gushed over the dam along with whole trees, boats and other debris. The crush of water and jammed debris proved too much for the bridge that Mullins took to his camp—the steel and concrete structure let go and cascaded downstream. Several other bridges were washed out along with numerous roads. The Hoist Dam held and the danger passed, however, the river flooded out about 100 seasonal and permanent residences, including Mullins'.

"I got up to the cabin," he recalls. "I had four and a half feet of water in it. I have some outbuildings that flooded. My front porch floated; it's made out of cedar and was just sitting on the ground. That floated down in the swamp."

The rampaging Dead River drastically changed the landscape. Art Maki watches while his granddaughters fish from the riverbank in 2001. The same view after the 2003 flood. (Courtesy of Art Maki)

Mullins was one of the many residents who had to deal with the aftermath of the flood. "My refrigerator, I just bought a brand new refrigerator," he exclaims, "it was laying on its back on top of a five gallon pail full of water. The stove, everything went under—all my appliances were wet. I had to take them all home and cleaned everything out. I pressure washed them. I tore the carpeting out—ohh! It was a total mess."

Downstream in Marquette, Art Maki, who lives on the river near the Marshalls, also had a mess when he arrived back at his place later that day. "We had pretty close to two and a half feet of water in the basement," he says. "Everything in the basement was ruined up to that point. The furnace had to be redone. The wash machine went to heck. I lost quite a bit of land in the center of my property, pretty close to twenty feet."

Maki also lost about a dozen trees, which were lying in a tangled heap when he returned. "Huge trees," Maki declares. "I had one pine tree go way down the river—the whole works, stump and all. It was an awful thing to come back here and look at."

The landscape changed significantly in the aftermath of the flood. Silver Lake shrunk to less than a third of its pre-flood size. The Tourist Park basin in Marquette completely drained. The river changed course in some spots. Two years later, John Mullins took a walking tour of the area where the dam broke. "There's a beautiful stream going down through there now," he says. "It looks good in spots; when it was happening, it sure didn't look too good."

Downstream, Jeff Marshall does not like what he sees. "There's white pines that came out of Mr. Maki's yard … 70 feet tall that are lying in the river," he says. "There are stumps—it's just terrible. My son and I used to fish in the river every night. Now you can't. There's no water there. It's sand and trees knocked down everywhere."

As of this writing, a number of lawsuits have been filed in connection with the earthen dike failure at Silver Lake. Nature conspired with technology to bring a disaster to north central Upper Michigan in May 2003. The changes wrought by the flood will be discernible for generations.

CHAPTER 10

HEAT WAVES, HOT WEATHER

Upper Michigan is famous for its comfortable summer weather. The first summer I spent in the U.P. was the hot summer of 1988 (*see "The Hot, Dry Summer of 1988", page 241*). I quickly learned from a neighbor a term that I have used ever since to describe one of the most cherished aspects of our climate. The morning after a remarkable early season hot spell his neighbor greeted me with, "Now this is U.P. summer weather." The day was sunny with a few puffy fair weather clouds; there was a light breeze, and the air was pleasantly cool and dry. This combination of atmospheric ingredients is the rule during a typical summer and helps make the region a summer destination for tourists and winter snowbirds who want to escape the heat and humidity farther south.

Hot weather does occasionally visit Upper Michigan. On average, the National Weather Service (NWS) records three days a summer with 90 degrees or above. When the air gets hot and the humidity rises, it is a big deal because sultry weather is an exception to the rule.

While most businesses have central air conditioning, many

A gathering of Upper Michigan ladies model the latest swimwear fashion of the day in about 1910. (Courtesy of Jane John)

residents forgo that luxury or get by with a battery of fans or a window air conditioner. "We don't have any air conditioners," says Chicago transplant John Turausky of Marquette who lived through sweltering summer days and muggy nights at the southern end of Lake Michigan until 1982. "The few days that it gets hot around here are no big problem for us."

The following is a survey of some memorable heat waves and hot days.

1852: "Troubled by a 'Drought'"

One of the earliest allusions to an Upper Michigan heat wave was reported in *The Lake Superior Mining Journal* September 1, 1852: "Since the summer of 1846 there has not been in this northern region as dry and warm a season as at present." The correspondent complained about the lack of rain over the past two months and that "the ground is parched with heat and thirst."

A local merchant's advertisement for cool fashions of the day during the first decade of the 20th Century. (Courtesy of Marquette County History Museum)

A month earlier, correspondent "J.L.C." declared "we have indubitable summer weather—equatorial weather." Back in the pioneer days, a stretch of summery weather was probably appreciated; however, the inevitable companion of the heat was troublesome to a population at the complete mercy of the elements. "We are very much troubled by a drough [sic]," wrote J.L.C., "and only need a heavy shower to ensure a profitable return from the few crops which have been put in the ground."

While a drought may have persisted in the mining country of western Upper Michigan in 1852, over southeastern sections a heavy thundershower occurred on at least one occasion. Mackinac Island had already been a tourist destination for over a decade. Juliette Starr Dana, of New York City, kept a journal while traveling through the Great Lakes that summer. She wrote that a "most terrific thunder storm accompanied by hail" struck the island during the afternoon of July 29.

"It was really fearful to hear and see," she penned. The hailstones, "some as large as walnuts," broke nearly all the windows on one side of the Mission House Hotel on the island. During the storm, she and a companion looked out on the lake and watched as the wind, generated by the storm, built high waves that were "covered with foam." The day after the storm, in typical U.P. fashion, she reported that "the air was like a fine November morning in New York, with a fresh breeze that curled the waves nicely."

July 15, 1901: The Hottest Day

"Marquette had better take down her shingle as the Queen summer resort of the north," said the U.S Weather Bureau observer. He made the remark after a sweltering high of 108 degrees on July 15, 1901. The all-time hottest temperature on record came at the peak of a three-day heat wave that affected the entire region.

"Copperdom" first felt the excessive heat on July 13 when the temperature in Houghton popped above 90 degrees. The next day it had already reached 95 at 11:00 a.m. and by 2:00 the official thermometer read 103 degrees. Residents then suffered with no let-up the rest of the day as the "sun beat down relentlessly on those who passed in the streets." The usual lake breeze was lacking—there was little if any breeze at all.

No casualties were reported due to the torrid temperatures, though a horse "dropped dead at Hancock" in the morning. The next day was a different story. Andrew Swenson, chef of the Douglass House in Houghton, fell ill at noon. A physician was called, "but medical skill was of no avail." The 38-year-old was pronounced dead later that afternoon. Several others succumbed to

From a painting by A.B. Wentzell, 1903, man in shirtsleeves and straw hat; a rare occurrence to see among the fairer sex. (Courtesy of the Judy Johnson collection)

the heat, including a waitress at the same restaurant, a couple of "coal heavers" and an elderly Calumet man whose poor condition the next day engendered "fears for his recovery."

Despite the heat, work went on as usual that day. Even at area foundries and smelters, men continued their labors over molten copper and iron with few delays. The workers did take more frequent breaks Barrels of ice water were brought into them and they drank the water "in large quantities."

In Marquette, work was partially suspended at the Powder Mill and at a veneer factory, but otherwise the daily routine continued. In fact, few people realized that it was the hottest day ever, because there was at least a "slight prevailing breeze." Many residents in town boarded the open-air street cars in an attempt to catch a stronger wind. Business was brisk to Presque Isle well into the evening as it stayed "uncomfortably warm for some time after the supper hour."

New fashion ground was broken during this turn-of-the-century hot spell. Prior to 1901, "men felt it was their manly duties to swelter in scorching weather for dignity's sake." They would keep their coats on no matter how hot it got. During this heat wave, men in Marquette were "emboldened to cast their coats aside." They walked the streets and did their business in shirtsleeves, hiding their suspenders or casting them aside completely, using a belt to hold up their pants. Some of the more daring males even donned the more "feminine" garment called the "shirt waist." Local historians say this hot weather garment was likely a loose-fitting cotton shirt sans the usual starched collar and cuffs.

Even area horses blazed a new fashion trail in July 1901. Houghton horses were seen wearing straw hats, part of the latest fad from the big cities to the south. The stylish hat was specially tooled for the equine population. There were slits on each side for the ears, and the hat came to a peak. Just like its counterpart for humans, the straw hat came with a colored band and was "altogether…not unbecoming."

The record blast of heat came to a merciful end just after midmonth. July 1901 ended in Marquette only a modest 3 degrees above average, indicating a more normal U.P. summer weather pattern the majority of the month.

The Greatest Heat Wave: July 1936

Scorching heat, borne off the bone-dry Plains, poured over Upper Michigan just after the Independence Day weekend in 1936. The temperature soared to 98 in Ironwood on the 7th and moderated slightly under the influence of a fresh breeze the next day. The heat wave gradually reached a crescendo over the next several days; it reached 103 degrees on the 12th and an all-time record of 104 the next day.

Midge Waters grew up in the Ironwood area and remembers how hot it was: "We dragged our mattresses off the beds upstairs and put them in the glassed-in porch downstairs so we could sleep; there was a little bit more fresh air there." Her birthday was moved to an unusual location because of the heat. "The party was held in the basement very near our wood burning furnace," she recalls. "There was not much space, but it was cool down there."

The stifling heat was blamed for 13 deaths on the Gogebic Range. Most victims were elderly and died of heat stroke. Gust Lindquist, 83 years old and a pioneer of the Norrie location near Ironwood, lost his wife on July 12 due to complications brought on by the hot weather. The following day, Lindquist himself succumbed to heat stroke. When admitted to the hospital his body temperature topped out at 108 degrees. The hardy pioneer pulled through; the next day his condition improved. At the same time, cooler air began filtering into the region.

While Escanaba wilted under 104-degree heat on July 8, the lightkeeper in that town "enjoyed the fresh breezes from the lake" that "made living comfortable" at his shoreline location. The next day the temperature uptown soared to 102 at 10 a.m., while at the same time at the lighthouse, the mercury leveled off at a more comfortable 88 degrees.

Escanaba endured the searing heat with most of its natural ice supply lost. On July 7, fire leveled the Swanson Ice House, melting the precious contents of the building in a matter of two hours.

It got so hot a thermometer broke in Menominee. Actually, the thermometer was overexposed. City employees at the water works placed a thermometer directly in the sun; minutes later, the temperature rose to 120 degrees and broke the glass containing the mercury. Menominee reached 99 degrees in the shade on July 7 and 102 on the 8th.

Record breaking heat was experienced in the "Queen City" by the lake. Marquette reached 103 degrees on July 7, and 101 on both the 8th and 9th. It was the first time since 1901 that the weather bureau recorded three days in a month with a temperature above 100 degrees,

DROUGHT LOSS OVER BILLION

The heat wave and resulting drought had a devastating impact on farmers across the country. (Courtesy of Ironwood Carnegie Library)

and the first time ever this milestone was reached over consecutive days. Even out on the area's "largest natural air conditioner" there was no escape from the hot air mass. Sailors on an ore carrier 10 miles offshore on Lake Superior said the temperature there climbed over 100 degrees.

Lake Superior did provide relief for one young couple. "My dad had a little sailboat," says Jane John. Her father, Kenyon Boyer, along with his soon-to-be bride, Dorothy, would take the boat out into the lake. "They would just slide off the boat and float around to cool off. They told me it was just beastly," she recalls. The weather finally cooled off in time for their wedding on July 17 that year.

The climax of this historic heat wave came on July 13. Just like Ironwood, Marquette suffered with a 104 degree high accompanied by excessive humidity. The temperature stayed above 100 for nearly four hours late that afternoon and early evening. In Munising, the thermometer peaked above 100 degrees from noon to 7pm. In Republic, it topped out at a sizzling 107.

Records for extreme heat were set in 16 states from the Plains to the East Coast during the second week of July 1936; this after many spots set or approached records for duration of cold the winter before. Mio, in northeast Lower Michigan, set the all-time state high temperature record of 112 degrees during the heat wave. In North Dakota, the temperature in one town rose to 120 degrees; this Death Valley-like temperature has never been equaled since. Texas, Arkansas and Oklahoma also reached the 120-degree mark; the only instances in recorded history of 120 degrees or more outside the Desert Southwest. The Heat Wave of July 1936 still stands as the most intense in United States history.

May 28, 1969: Record-Shattering Heat

A brief, but intense heat wave brought the earliest 100-degree reading to Marquette in late May 1969. An upper-level ridge shot northeastward from the Southern Plains as low pressure formed in the Northern Plains. Strong, dry southwest winds ahead of the low brought a blast of heat into Upper Michigan. Temperatures had already soared into the 80s by 7:30 a.m. in Marquette. It reached 96 by noon and crept up from there, topping 100 by mid-afternoon.

"There was no way anyone could get used to it," remembers Jane John. "We were living in a third-floor apartment and I was expecting my first baby on June 13. It was just like an oven." John's cousin was attending high school, and exams were taking place. "He came home and sat in a cold bathtub for an hour," she chuckles. "Then he went back to school for more exams."

Some folks tried to cool off in Lake Superior, but found it more than an exhilarating experience. "It was too cold to swim in it," remembers John. "You could walk on the edge of it and get your feet cold and then hope that would cool off the rest of your body."

The quick, intense heat wave beat up area roads. The heat caused deterioration of expansion joints; pressure built up and concrete literally "exploded." Sections of U.S.-41 from Chocolay Township to Ishpeming needed emergency repairs. The worst eruptions occurred on concrete stretches that were 25 years or older.

While Marquette sweltered at the century mark, Calumet registered 95 degrees. A cooling breeze off Lake Michigan kept Escanaba a comfortable 81 degrees. It was still a sweltering 81 in Marquette at midnight. By early the next morning, a cool front slid through from the west, ending the extreme heat in time for the Memorial Day weekend.

Hot Tuesday of April 22, 1980

This day was noted for its extreme heat and the remarkable turnaround which followed. The temperature soared quickly to the hottest reading for so early in the season and then fell just as fast.

April 1980 exhibited spastic variations in temperature typical of spring in Upper Michigan. A near average beginning to the month led to unseasonable cold the second week. The NWS recorded a high of only 29 degrees on April 13, culminating in a nadir of 7 degrees for a low on the 16th.

Often, the lowest temperatures in a cold pattern will be followed by a rather quick and decided warm-up. This occurred after the cold morning of the 16th. The last high-pressure system in the series settled overhead and drifted east as the cold trough which spawned it lifted northeastward away from the lakes.

The warming trend that followed was impressive. It brought positive temperature departure from normal even greater than the negative departures earlier in the month. Temperatures soared into the 60s and 70s the next five days as a warm ridge replaced the cold trough. The ridge reached its greatest amplitude over the Upper Great Lakes on Monday evening, April 21.

The next morning, the stage was set for the hot blast. With the upper ridge in place, surface low pressure in the Plains sent a hot, very dry, southwest wind into Upper Michigan. Upstream, serious grass and forest fires broke out in parts of central Wisconsin in the bone-dry, torrid air mass. Quickly, the thermometer reached mid-summer heat-wave proportions. The official high topped out at 92 degrees, but the conditions that promoted the heat soon worked in concert to bring its demise.

The Plains low moved eastward and its trailing cold front passed through in the evening, bringing a gush of cooling northwest winds behind it. A number of factors then led to a rapid, complete reversal of the pattern. A cold trough pounded down the hot ridge and dove into the Upper Great Lakes the next day.

On the 23rd, the Weather Service recorded a low of 21 degrees, a record, which, as of this writing, still stands. To add insult to injury to residents who hoped warm weather was here to stay, it began snowing that afternoon. By late morning, April 24, a total of 6.4 inches had come down. Warm ground heated by 90-plus-degree air the day before led to lots of melting—never more than a couple of inches remained on the ground when official measurements were made.

Hot Tuesday, April 22, 1980, went down as the

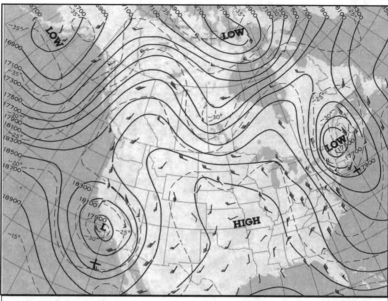

A sharp, spring turn-around is graphically illustrated in these upper-air maps for April 22 & 23, 1980. (NOAA Central Library Data Imaging Project)

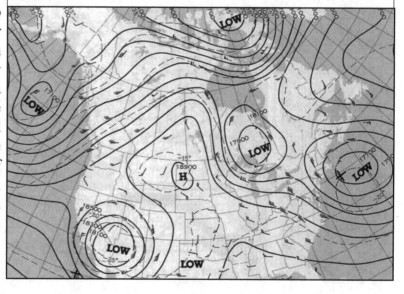

warmest temperature ever recorded in April. The turnaround that followed is one of the more profound in the record and an extreme example of the drastic changes that the U.P. experiences during the transitional seasons.

The Hot, Dry Summer of 1988

Heat and drought go hand and hand. Upper Michigan heats up the most during dry summers. If the ground is wet, a large portion of the sun's energy is used to evaporate the water in the ground and there is less energy available to heat the air. Dry ground allows the air to heat more effectively. This point was graphically illustrated during the summer of 1988.

After a gradual spring melt-down warm, dry weather began showing up in the spring.

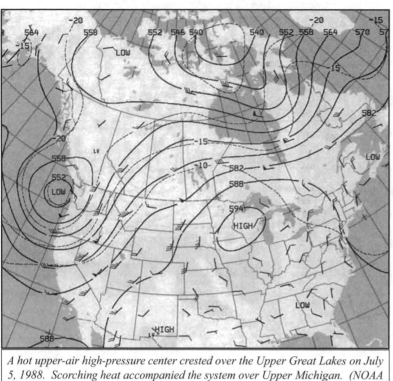

A hot upper-air high-pressure center crested over the Upper Great Lakes on July 5, 1988. Scorching heat accompanied the system over Upper Michigan. (NOAA Central Library Data Imaging Project)

May came in at 4.5 degrees above average at the NWS Negaunee township location, while precipitation came in at only a third of the long-term average.

June was hot and exceedingly dry. Nine record highs were set during the month, with a stretch of five days of 90 degrees or above. The dryness of the air kept the humidity in check; however, the lack of rain (less than 20 percent of the average) put a stress on crops throughout the Midwest.

A small, anomalous complex of thunderstorms fired over south-central Upper Michigan the night of June 21, 1988. Larry Wanic of Bark River reported 2.77 inches of rain in a short period of time. Wanic remembers the little island of green that developed in a sea of drought because of those storms: "Later that summer if you flew over with an airplane you could see where those storms developed, kind of like a triangle toward the lake of green; heaviest right through about here. Nobody else had rain; it was real dry."

July 1988 was a scorcher. The temperature reached 90 degrees or above on 11 July days at Spalding in Menominee County. After a pleasantly cool interlude at the close of June into the first couple of days of July, a heat wave commenced on Independence Day that measured up to hot spells normally felt much farther south. The five-day mean temperature from July 4-8 reached a sweltering 80.2 degrees. This stretch included a maximum of 98 on July 7 and 8. The hot, dry weather aided in spreading a wildfire near Rapid River that injured a firefighter and backed up holiday traffic on U.S.-2 (*see "Fire Weather", page 287*). Later in the month, the official high temperature reached 99 degrees, tying the all-time record high at the NWS in Negaunee Township.

While rainfall still averaged below the long-term normal at most locations, humidity became a factor as the seasonal circulation shift brought up air from the Gulf of Mexico. The stifling heat and humidity reached a peak in Spalding on August 2 when the high hit 102 degrees. That night, severe thunderstorms and flooding rains hit parts of the U.P., signaling a gradual shift in the overall weather pattern. By mid-month, a remarkable severe weather outbreak (see *"Severe Weather", page 257*) brought one of hottest summers in Upper Michigan's history to an end.

Other Hot Summers

July 1921 remains the hottest month in the record. Its average temperature of 72.4 degrees far exceeds the 69.4 average registered during the month of the greatest heat wave, in July 1936.

August 1947 comes in as the hottest eighth month on record. The heat made an impression on John Wallis, long-time chief of the Weather Bureau at the Sault. "I could tell you as a boy in Rudyard looking out my grandmother's window at the thermometer," he recalls. "It said 100 degrees. Now that's really hot. Both days it reached 100, August 5-6, 1947."

A couple of Negaunee girls enjoy a picnic on a warm, summer day.
(Courtesy of the Negaunee Historical Society)

The searing heat reached also reached the Copper Country. Houghton wilted under a high temperature of 103 degrees on August 5, 1947. It also topped 100 in Marquette. The high reached 102 on the 5th, while the low only fell to a stifling 82 degrees—the highest minimum temperature ever recorded in August. The average temperature measured in Marquette during August 1947 was a record-breaking 70.9 degrees.

"The warmest summer was 1955," remembers Wallis. "It was the centennial summer; the locks were opened in 1855." That summer saw consistent, hot, muggy weather over a good share of the country.

The summer heat in '55 was known for its persistent nature and lack of really hot temperatures. At the same time, the extremely high mean temperatures during July and August 1955 suggest high nighttime low temperatures. There also was a lack of drought accompanying the heat throughout the country.

Marquette's records bear out these trends. While there were some hot days, there was no excessive heat; just consistent warmth through July and August. July came in more than 5 degrees above the long-term average, at 71.1 degrees, while August registered 69.6, a solid 4.3 above normal. During the two months, the high temperature reached into the 90s in Marquette on eight days. August 17-21 was the warmest period, with a sweltering mean temperature of 78.4 degrees. A cool spell closed out the month, but summer made a comeback later in September. It reached an even 90 on both September 16 and 17, 1955. Rainfall during the period was close to average.

In Iron Mountain, July 1955 was the hottest in 53 years of record keeping. The average high temperature exceeded 85 degrees with the hottest maximum reaching 102. By late

August, contrary to trends elsewhere, Dickinson County farmers were suffering from moderate drought. During a 50 day period beginning July 1, the area received just over half the average rainfall. Damage to crops was reported heavy due to the dry weather and heat.

It was not until 40 years later that Upper Michigan experienced its warmest June. A heat wave began on Friday, June 16, 1995 and continued for over a week. That Sunday, a number of communities from the U.P. into Ontario reported temperatures near or above the century mark as a huge, hot, high-pressure ridge aloft formed from Texas into southern Ontario. The heat pumped by the ridge into the Upper Great Lakes lingered; records were set eight days in a row from June 16-23. While the summer of 1995 remained warm, the second half of June was, by far, the hottest part of the season.

1992: The Year without a Summer

Just as the famous warm winter of 1877-78 won a spot in the section on cold winters (see "Cold Waves, Cold Winters", page119) to illustrate the opposite extreme, the cold summer of 1992 deserves a special place in the hot summer section. The summer of '92 stands out for consistent chill through all three meteorological summer months (June, July and August). It also holds the distinction of producing the coldest July on record.

The summer of '92 started with promise for warm weather enthusiasts. The temperature popped well into the 80s at the NWS from June 11-13. The warmest reading in that stretch was an 88-degree high on the 12th. It would be the warmest day of the entire summer.

While this mini heat wave was in progress, close inspection of the upper-air charts gave an indication of what lay ahead. A ridge of high pressure aloft sat over western Canada— a breeding ground for cool air masses just downwind from it. This ridge would become a semi-permanent feature during the summer of 1992.

The pattern established in Canada began sending cool air masses southeastward into Upper Michigan after mid month. By the

Summer is finally here! Beach goers cool their beverages with ice from Lake Superior on June 1 after the backward spring of 1996. (Courtesy of the Ed Kearney Collection)

19th, the official high only struggled to 45, while the low slipped to 37. A trace of snow was reported over parts of the northern U.P. early the morning of June 20. Alpena, in the Lower Peninsula, had snow for 45 minutes around noon the same day. The temperature crashed to 32 degrees on the 22nd; the latest official freeze and the coldest temperature for so late in the season.

The pattern that produced the chill refused to let go through the end of the month. As July began, cool air remained entrenched over central Canada into the north central United

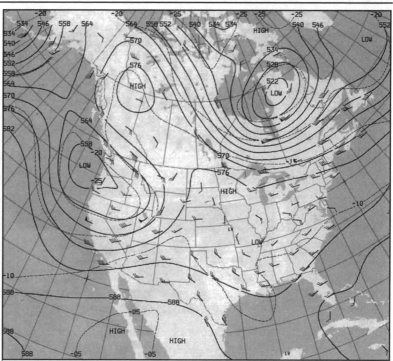

June 13, 1992. This upper-air high-pressure system remained over the Northwest Territories of Canada much of the summer. It generated cool air masses that plunged southeastward into Upper Michigan. (NOAA Central Library Data Imaging Project)

States, while a low-pressure trough drifted in off the Pacific. This trough spawned a storm that brought a heavy, pre-July 4th rainstorm to much of Upper Michigan.

It came down in buckets on July 2. Republic, in the central U.P., collected over 5.5 inches, while Bruce Crossing on the west end was inundated with 6.5 inches of rain. The system then lingered through the holiday, producing a cloudy, damp Fourth over most sections.

July, the warmest summer month on average, did not live up to its billing in 1992. There were some brief warm spells over parts of the peninsula, including one which led to a destructive tornado in Gladstone on the 19th (*see "Severe Weather", page 262*). However, chilly weather predominated. Officially, the temperature managed to reach the 80-degree mark only once, on July 25. On the other hand, readings in the 30s occurred on two nights. In the wake of the severe weather on the 19th, a thermometer in Rapid River registered an astounding low of 24 degrees the morning of July 21.

July's average temperature wound up at 58.4 degrees, a remarkable 6.2 degrees below the long-term average. The only other July that came close to this level of cold was in 1891; that month averaged 59.7 degrees.

The extended cool spells that marked the summer of 1992 continued into the eighth month. Between the 12th and 15th, official lows fell into the 30s each night at the NWS. This included a low of 34 on August 12, the coldest for so early in the season. That

Mt. Pinatubo eruption on June 12, 1991. The debris from the volcano was pushed over 65,000 feet into the atmosphere and was one of the causes of Upper Michigan's coolest summer on record the next year. (USGS photo)

same night, an observer just outside the Houghton County community of Chassell noted a low of 29 degrees. August ended warmer than July, but not much. Its average came in at 59.2 degrees, 3.4 below average.

This cold summer resulted from the persistent generation of cool air masses in Canada, exacerbated by the eruption of Mt. Pinatubo in the Philippines a year earlier. Massive quantities of volcanic dust and gas pushed into the stratosphere and acted as a veil, filtering sunlight throughout the summer of 1992. Temperatures worldwide averaged a half degree Celsius cooler; the greatest climate disruption from a volcano in the 20th century.

CHAPTER 11

While far removed from Tornado Alley, Upper Michigan still receives its fair share of summer thunderstorms. Occasionally, these storms produce damaging winds, dangerous lightning, large hail and even tornadoes. This section reviews a few of the more memorable events.

June 19, 1878: Lightning Invades an Ishpeming Home

It was a late spring afternoon. The weather was not all that warm because Mrs. Siluts of Ishpeming had a fire going in the stove at her home situated in the Strawberry Hill area on Main Street. Suddenly, a heavy thunderstorm blew in, accompanied by intense cloud-to-ground lightning. A bolt struck the Siluts' chimney, completely demolishing it, then traveled into the house. It toppled the stove containing the fire, and then knocked the poor woman, standing near the stove, to the floor. Her shoes and stockings were ripped from her feet, while her clothes were "rent and torn." Siluts received serious injuries; her face and limbs were blackened and lacerated.

A neighbor rushed to the scene immediately after the strike and entered the house, which was "filled with blinding smoke." He quickly put out the scattered fires caused by the toppled stove, preventing a conflagration. He then rushed

Possibly due to the lack of trees because of clear-cutting, lightning often struck buildings including homes around the turn of the century, with devastating consequences.
(Detail of a mural by E. Yelland)

to Mrs. Siluts' aid; at first he thought she was dead, but she soon regained consciousness. Another woman in the house was knocked to the ground by the bolt but was only stunned, while several other occupants "were almost out of their wits." Other than the chimney, the house sustained only minor damage. As for Mrs. Siluts, she recovered, but probably carried scars from the thunderstorm the rest of her life.

Stormy Weather in Ontonagon: August 1878

Ontonagon's lighthouse keeper noted some stormy weather on his watch in mid August 1878. On August 14, lightning struck the schooner *Donston* and "knocked ten feet of the Main Mast." The next day, three water spouts were observed about two miles from the light out over Lake Superior.

September 6, 1899: Killer Storm hits Rockland

"Severe electrical storms" hit Rockland in Ontonagon County with "great frequency" late in the summer of 1899. The one that struck the small community on September 6 was among "the most severe…ever." The rain fell in torrents, washing out a section of railroad bed between the village and Ontonagon. The washout delayed train service from Ontonagon until afternoon the next day. The thunderstorm also produced an "electrical display that was sublimely grand" and also deadly. A bolt entered a home and killed a woman as she left her upstairs bedroom and attempted to seek shelter on the lower floor.

The morning of September 7, 1899. The U.P. experienced frequent severe thunderstorms all summer and the violent weather continued into the early fall. Low pressure moved from Nebraska on the 6th to a position north of Lake Superior. It dragged a thunderstorm-producing cold front through western sections during the early morning hours. An intense storm produced a lightning strike that killed a woman in Ontonagon. (NOAA Central Library Data Imaging Project)

Mr. and Mrs. Hull of Rockland were awakened by the storm about 11:00 p.m. Mrs. Hull "overcome by fear and excitement," got up and left their upstairs bedroom. "Mr. Hull admonished her to remain in the bedroom," but she did not listen. Moments later, there was a flash, then a sudden crash of thunder. Mr. Hull reported smelling "sulphurous fumes" and immediately jumped out of bed to check on his wife. He entered the hallway and found his wife on the floor "her apparel burning and smoking."

She was dead. The bolt struck the chimney, passed

through it and then through the poor woman. The newspaper account, in typical fashion of the day (*see "Victorian Journalism: Telling it like it is" , page 128*), gave a graphic account of how it happened: "The bolt…struck her squarely on the head, as her hair, head and shoulders showed, thence passed through the body and went out at the left foot, which had a shoe and stocking on and which must have been placed upon the floor. The other foot must have been raised, the lady evidently being in the act of putting on…her shoe when struck."

The Hull house sustained heavy damage. The chimney was demolished, while the ceiling partitions around it were "but little better." The bolt also knocked out a panel of a downstairs door, while ruining a screen door and breaking out a window. It ricocheted around the house, blasting several large holes on its east side. Finally, it shot through the basement, "shattering the joist and splintering the foundation posts."

Hundreds of people turned out the next day to view the remains of Mrs. Hull and express their sympathy to her husband. They also noted "the havoc wrought" by the storm—a storm that found a "place exclusively its own in the pages of Rockland history."

Freak Lightning Strike in Ontonagon: September 6, 1902

Lightning struck the home of H. A. Savage on Ontonagon's south side the evening of September 6, 1902. The strike "badly frightened" the Savage family and did considerable damage to the residence.

The bolt struck the building on the roof near the top of the gable, tearing a small hole. From that hole, it followed down a rafter and poured into the house's interior. It tore off plaster and singed wallpaper on the second floor hallway. Afterward, it "played a veritable game of hide and seek in nearly every room of the house." A window on the second floor was smashed, while a chair piled with clothes was thrown into another room. Several rolls of wallpaper, stored in an empty room, were cut to threads, resembling "the work of rats."

The most frightening episode came during the bolt's course on the first floor. There, it entered the front room where the family's children were sleeping. The lightning singed, scorched and loosened the lath and plaster "but strange as it may seem, the children were not even stunned."

Even more miraculously, the house was not set on fire. However, the structure was filled with smoke that smelled like burning dynamite for several hours after the strike.

Mr. Savage said later that the sound given off as the bolt hit was "almost deafening." As corroboration to Savage's assertion, a neighbor, who was walking home on the other side of the street when the report came, was "partly dazed" by the thunderous crash.

April 25, 1906: "Bad Electrical Storm" in Houghton

A spring thunderstorm struck Houghton on the evening of April 25, 1906 causing destruction and "severely frightening…nervous people." The storm lasted about an hour and during this time several homes were struck. One house lost a corner of its roof.

A man walking near the county bridge was struck by lightning. The umbrella he was carrying acted as a conductor, directing the bolt right at him. The shock knocked him to the ground and destroyed his umbrella, but he was not seriously injured. The same bolt then struck an arc lamp on the bridge and destroyed it.

Another house received considerable damage as a lightning bolt struck it, ripping a hole in its roof, and then tearing plaster off its walls. The local telephone company "suffered considerably." Its big switchboard was thrown out of commission for nearly an hour, while several "hello girls" suffered light shocks.

For all the ruckus this event created, the official Weather Bureau observer said "there was nothing remarkable about the storm." He never observed winds over 20 miles an hour or more than a "very light" rain.

Escanaba Storm, July 9, 1906: A "Miraculous" Escape

A violent thunderstorm struck Escanaba July 9th. A lightning bolt struck the lighthouse and produced tremendous damage. But three members of the keeper's family, home at the time, were uninjured. Their escape from harm was truly miraculous when one considers what the bolt did to the structure and its contents.

Lightning flashes over schooners moored in Marquette Harbor about the turn of the century. (Courtesy of Superior View, Marquette)

Every window on the first and second floors was broken, and interior doors were cracked off their hinges. A pantry full of dishes was thrown from the shelves and broken. All the silverware was touched by the current and turned a deep brown. An organ, stored on the second floor, was demolished. Nails, heated by electricity from the bolt, were ejected from the walls and burned holes in the carpets. Tools in a chest were "converted into powerful magnets and the temper removed," rendering them useless.

Outside, brick walls were cracked in many places. Inside, the bolt bored twenty holes into interior walls ranging in size from small punctures to gaping hollows a foot in diameter.

None of the occupants even felt a shock from the lightning strike, but all were badly frightened. Despite the damage, operation of the lighthouse was uninterrupted.

June 18, 1908: Big Hail Storm

"The worst wind and hail storm in the history of Ironwood" broke over the city shortly after 6:00 p.m. June 18, 1908. Hailstones measuring as large as four inches in circumference rained down during the height of the storm, accompanied by a torrential downpour. Driven by high winds, the hail smashed windows in every section of the city.

Florist R. Lutey suffered the most damage of any Ironwood area business as the majority of he windows in his greenhouse were shattered. Forty windows were broken at Central School with all other school buildings sustaining significant window damage. Stained glass in area churches "were pierced as if there had been a fusillade of bullets." In all cases, damage was he worst on west and north sides of buildings facing the storm's prevailing wind.

With windows broken, flooding rain freely entered homes, soaking floors and damaging carpets, rugs and hangings. Shade trees were broken and uprooted. The next day everyone n town was busy cleaning up. Window glass soon became a precious commodity; no glass dealer in town was prepared for the demand caused by this fierce hailstorm.

July 29, 1909: Tornado on the Gogebic Range

An incredibly stormy two-week period in Ironwood (*See "Floods", page 218*) culminated in a vicious early morning windstorm, probably a tornado on July 29, 1909. Buildings were unroofed, windows smashed and trees uprooted throughout the city and surrounding area. The early morning storm did thousands of dollars in damage, but no deaths or serious injuries were reported.

The heaviest losses were incurred by the Newport Mining Company. The storm descended on Newport Hill, where most of the Mine's infrastructure was located. At least three buildings were unroofed, including the new "change" house, the new power house and the "dry" house. The power plant also had its 14 inch brick walls blown in by the force of the storm. The plant sustained severe damage to the machinery as the west wall of the structure caved in. An instant later, 60 feet of the south wall imploded, bringing down the steel-trussed roof. The mine was forced to suspend underground mining operations for several days. Two hundred feet of the dry house roof blew away. Roof timbers twelve feet long were hurled several hundred feet from the site. One timber was flung through the window of the doctor's office. There was so much debris piled against the little structure, it looked like "it had been struck by a cyclone."

Several workers in the buildings narrowly escaped serious injury. Two men were in the north side of the power plant when the south wall caved in; both fled the building without a scratch. In the engine house, one of the workmen said he jumped out the window as the funnel descended on the building and when he "came to earth again" he was sprawled out among the wreckage, some 250 feet from the engine house. Another man ran out the front door and claims he was picked up and carried to the company barn about 100 yards away!

Big "Hailers" of the 1930s

The Escanaba lighthouse keeper reported a "heavy electric storm" the afternoon of July 23, 1936. Hailstones the size of hen's eggs accompanied the storm; they were declared "the largest ever seen" around Escanaba. The severe thunderstorm occurred late in a month that featured the most intense heat wave ever felt in Upper Michigan and much of the central United States (*see "Heat Waves, Hot Days", page 238*).

A "Giant Hailstone Downpour" hit the Gogebic Range early the morning of June 16, 1939. Stones the size of marbles to larger than baseballs covered the ground; they did not completely melt until noon in some places. In Hurley, a mammoth stone eight inches in

A stormy period in Escanaba: The weather map on the morning of July 23, 1936 showed low pressure dropping into the Great Lakes from the Northern Plains. Escanaba had already had a thunderstorm in the previous twelve hours and would have at least one more producing the largest hailstones ever observed in the area. (NOAA Central Library Data Imaging Project)

circumference was found shortly after the storm ended.

Just like in a hailstorm 31 years earlier, the greatest losses occurred at area greenhouses. At one greenhouse just north of Ironwood an estimated 800 panes were shattered. Accurate estimates of damage could not be made immediately because it was too dangerous to enter the glass buildings; jagged pieces of hanging glass kept falling from the roof, shaken loose by high winds following the storm.

Ironwood, Bessemer and Wakefield all reported extensive damage to businesses and homes. In Bessemer Township, 103 windows were broken at the Puritan School, while many homes in town had windows smashed. Automobiles throughout the range were badly dented and fabric covered convertible tops were perforated by the huge stones.

Gardens and farm crops throughout the area sustained extensive damage, limited to some extent by late planting due to a wet spring. A number of workers at a Civilian Conservation Corps camp in the area were caught in the storm and pelted by hailstones. One young man required medical attention after being struck on the hand by one of the ice chunks.

Farther east, wind caused the most damage. At least a dozen barns and outbuildings were demolished as the severe squall line rolled through Trout Creek about an hour after hitting the Gogebic Range. The storm tore through the Ontonagon County community with "cyclonic intensity," bringing down telephone and electric power lines and uprooting 37 large trees on Main Street. The trees, most about two feet in diameter, tore out large sections of sidewalks and displaced sewer pipe. Just to the north in Bruce Crossing, a bad streak of luck continued on the Walter Schroeder homestead, blowing down the barn and hay shed located just south of town. The home on the farm had been destroyed by fire only two weeks before.

The storms marched across the entire peninsula. In Newberry, a mother and her two children were treated for shock after lightning struck their home, blasting a two-foot hole in the roof and wrecking the electrical equipment inside.

The remarkable storm and seiche were part of a record-breaking month. Marquette recorded 8.64 inches of rain in June 1939, the wettest sixth month in its history.

The "Root Beer" Tornado:
Spalding, July 20, 1972

Lyn Veeser had just come home from work and was busy peeling poplar logs when he looked west-southwestward to a threatening sky. An avid weather watcher, this Upper Michigan native could not believe his eyes—a tornado appeared to be heading right at him. "It looked like a pencil in the air," remembers Veeser. "All of a sudden thirty seconds later, it did it again. It had a little flip to it." He assumed his wife, "an Indiana girl," would recognize a tornado so he called her out of the house to witness the spectacle. As he waited for her, the pencil-like object flipped a third time and he noticed debris flying into the air.

At that point, he did not need confirmation that what he saw was a tornado. Veeser recalls yelling to his wife, "Grab the baby, we're running over to Julia's." They lived in a mobile home at the time and he knew it was the worst place to be during a tornado. The couple had about a 300 hundred yard sprint to Julia's home where they passed a big Chinese Elm on the west side of her house. "We ran by that and got to the east side of the house," says Veeser. "The door was locked, she wasn't home. I hung onto the door. It sounded just like a railroad train coming." The small funnel passed within a relatively short distance of the couple and their baby. No one was injured or even felt a thing as the twister passed by.

About 30 feet away, some homemade wooden lawn chairs "went up in the air…just like a helicopter brought them up." The chairs rose about twelve feet off the ground, hit a tree and blew apart. The large Chinese Elm just west of the house was uprooted. "I never heard it go down," says Veeser. "That's how loud the roar was. All the telephone poles were

The effect of the historic seiche near the mouth of the Dead River in Marquette. On the left (top) is high "tide." On the right (bottom) is the view when the water receded. (Courtesy of the Marquette History Museum)

MARQUETTE'S HISTORIC SEICHE

A tremendous "tidal wave," or seiche, occurred on the Lake Superior basin in conjunction with the severe weather of June 16, 1939. A seiche is the rhythmic oscillation of a body of water. Seiches on the Great Lakes occur, often in conjunction with severe weather, when prolonged strong winds push water toward one side of the lake causing water levels to rise on the downwind side of the lake and to drop on the windward side. When the wind stops, the water sloshes back and forth. The process can be likened to water sloshing back and forth in a pan after the pan is disturbed.

This seiche pushed and pulled the water of Lake Superior in and out of Marquette Bay at half-hour intervals beginning shortly after the storm passed through at 10:30 a.m. The freakish surge, "unprecedented in the memory of marine men," rose and fell five feet over several hours. At the same time, the Weather Bureau observed a tremendously "jumpy" barometer, with a change of 0.30 inches in just 15 minutes.

Docks, fish houses and small boats sustained extensive damage. Andrew Anderson, a Great Lakes fisherman of 38 years, said that he had never seen the lake rise so high before. It covered his landings, flooded his fish cleaning and packing house and rushed up behind the house to the road. Houses and docks were moved up and down by the lake waters.

A man points to the high water mark during the seiche. On the right (bottom) is the same structure a relatively short time later when the periodic sloshing of Lake Superior brought the water back in. (Courtesy of the Marquette History Museum)

"Everything had just been fixed up for the season," Anderson said while interviewed during the seiche. "Now look at it." He pointed to the landing, from which planks had been torn, and which sagged precariously in one spot. As he spoke, the water began to surge in again.

Farther up the shoreline to the west, the highway between L'Anse and Baraga was closed; surging water brought debris from the lake over the roadway. On the north shore of Lake Superior, Canadian officials reported a rise of eight feet in 20 minutes in the waters of Heron Bay. It took until the next morning before the lake there reached normal levels.

❄

slanted; they had a six-inch gap on the northwest side of them." The Veeser's had some screening blown off their mobile home, but it sustained no serious damage.

No rain fell with the storm, but at one point the air was filled with water. As Veeser watched the tornado toboggan down the hill away from him, it hit a sewer pond at the bottom of the hill. The brackish water in the pond was sucked into the tornado's vortex, creating a huge, whirling geyser. "It looked just like root beer," remembers Veeser. "It had foam and everything."

July 7, 1980: Escanaba's $2 Million Storm

A severe thunderstorm lashed the south side of Escanaba in the early morning hours of July 7, 1980. The storm, packing winds gusts near 100 miles-an-hour, injured eight people and caused heavy damage at the Delta County Airport. Numerous homes and vehicles were damaged by falling trees and limbs. Thousands were left without power and Escanaba's city manager declared a state of emergency for much of the rest of the day.

Winds from the storm "took a plane and put it over the top of the cyclone fence and it landed upside down in the road," remembers longtime weather observer Spar Sager. In all, 25 planes and two buildings, including the main terminal, were damaged at the airport. A mobile home park close by had six trailers flipped over by the wind. One mobile home was completely demolished, its debris scattered over a wide area. A man inside the structure suffered internal injuries, while his wife and daughter received cuts and bruises as they were hurled to the ground when the trailer flipped over.

Torrential rain and small hail accompanied the storm. Two to four inches of rain came down in a short time and caused flash flooding. Some main streets became lakes for a short period of time at the storm's conclusion. Sager's home sustained hail damage. "They weren't big hailstones," he recalls. "But the wind was, I don't know, probably 90 or 100 miles-an-hour. It put dents in the cedar shingles. The dents are still there."

Planes flipped by winds estimated at 100 miles an hour during the July 8, 1980 storm. (Courtesy of the Delta County Historical Society)

Damage at the airport and trailer park alone was placed at $600,000. Total damage in the brief but violent storm amounted to $2 million.

The Faithorn-Nadeau Tornado of July 4, 1986

A tornado, as powerful as any Great Plains twister, tore across a portion of northeastern Wisconsin into northern Menominee County the early evening of July 4, 1986. The funnel touched down near Faithorn, east of Niagara, Wisconsin, on the Menominee County line, and stayed on the ground for 17 miles to just north of Nadeau. It destroyed a number of homes and barns, and injured several people.

Steve Brown of Norway will never forget that evening: "Big hail started falling…golf-ball size. I knew something was going on at that moment. Probably five miles south of my parent's house there was a tornado that was producing F-3 damage. It went right through our main power line five miles south. Our power was out for 12 hours. Later, I remember driving back there with my parents to look at the damage. There was a house that was completely destroyed; nothing left except the foundation."

Scale	Wind	F-Scale Typical Damage Description
F0	< 73 mph	**Light damage**. Some damage to chimneys; branches broken off trees; shallow-rooted trees pushed over; sign boards damaged.
F1	73-112	**Moderate damage**. Peels surface off roofs; mobile homes pushed off foundations or overturned; moving autos blown off roads.
F2	113-157	**Considerable damage**. Roofs torn off frame houses; mobile homes demolished; boxcars overturned; large trees snapped or uprooted; light-object missiles generated; cars lifted off ground.
F3	158-206	**Severe damage**. Roofs and some walls torn off well-constructed houses; trains overturned; most trees in forest uprooted; heavy cars lifted off the ground and thrown.
F4	207-260	**Devastating damage**. Well-constructed houses leveled; structures with weak foundations blown away some distance; cars thrown and large missiles generated.
F5	261-318	**Incredible damage**. Strong frame houses leveled off foundations and swept away; automobile-sized missiles y through the air in excess of 100 yards; trees debarked; incredible phenomena will occur.

About twenty miles east in Spalding, Lyn Veeser was hosting a party for about 30 people when the sky grew black. "I told them, 'There's something that really looks bad,'" he remembers. "I put everyone in the house. The rain was…hitting the north wall coming in the south way." Large hailstones also accompanied the rain.

Around 20 miles down U.S. 41 at Stephenson, Alvin and Claudia Lauren saw the storm from a southern vantage point. "That night, the strangest thing was the yellow sky," remembers Alvin. "It was yellow and pink…weird, you know," adds Claudia. The Laurens were visiting Claudia's brother, waiting for Fourth of July fireworks, when her father called and said part of his barn blew down and the cows were out. He had a farm about a mile west of their home—a new house they had built a mile north of Nadeau and had just moved into about a month earlier.

The Laurens left to help Claudia's father put the cows back in. As they drove over the last

The Lauren home had two walls and its roof blown away.
(Photo by Lyn Veeser)

hill before the turnoff to their home, they witnessed a scene of devastation; a home along the highway was demolished with a fire truck and other emergency vehicles at the scene. Alvin recalls what happened next: "I said, 'If it hit him, it hit us.' We got this far and the house was gone. Saved the floor but the roof and the walls, everything was gone."

Claudia's other brother along with his wife, Geraldine, and their children lived next door in the Laurens' old house. Geraldine was doing the dishes when the storm struck. She called to her children: "Come and look at these clouds." She then observed three small tornados rotating around a central axis heading straight for them. She decided to seek shelter at Uncle Alvin's because it had a walk-out basement they could easily access and the house was newer, so she figured it would hold better. As the family rushed next door, the tornado, now one large funnel nearly a quarter-mile wide, took down a big tree in the field in front of them. The family huddled together under a big table in the basement as the twister passed overhead.

"They said they didn't think much of it," remembers Lauren. "It sounded noisy like a train going through, real noisy." When they felt the danger had passed, each family member slowly emerged from the basement walk-out. It almost seemed as if the storm had spared the new structure; until they turned around. "They looked back and the house over their heads was gone," recounts Lauren.

While the Laurens lost the walls and roof of their new house, they fared better than some of their neighbors. A new house just over a hill downwind from their house disappeared nearly altogether. "The only thing left was the fireplace and chimney," says Lauren. "The one across the road, the garage and the trailer both got taken away." A brother and sister lived in the trailer and as the twister approached they decided to take shelter under a vehicle in the garage. As they ran toward the garage, the sister decided to go back to the trailer to get her dog just as the storm struck. A short time later, the brother emerged from the rubble of the garage and realized his sister was gone. She was swept away by the tornado. "About an hour later she came walking out of the woods; didn't even know where she was," explains Lauren.

This home was completely destroyed by the tornado. (Photo by Lyn Veeser)

Claudia recounts what motorists driving north on U.S.-41 witnessed: "They saw it come through. It…literally picked the whole house right up in the air and then they said it twisted and just blew. That house completely disintegrated. If anyone…had been in that basement they wouldn't have been saved. The only thing you could see in that basement was where the hot water tank was…everything else was gone."

The twister just missed the village of Nadeau, so an even larger disaster was avoided. While the storm created havoc and devastation along its 17 mile path, there was not enough monetary damage to qualify for state or federal funds. The Laurens were grateful, regardless, for all the help they received. "The whole community helped us rebuild," says Alvin. They quickly raised a new building on top of the wood floor and basement spared by one of the most violent tornadoes to ever hit Upper Michigan.

August 16, 1988: A Violent Climax to a Hot, Dry Summer

The storm that pummeled Marquette the morning of August 16, 1988 will long be remembered as one of the most violent and damaging ever. Hundreds of trees were blown down, a fisherman was drowned, buildings were damaged and thousands of residents lost power, some for several days.

This storm was unusual in a couple of ways. First, the complex of thunderstorms developed over the relatively cold waters of Lake Superior before tearing through Marquette eastward into parts of Alger County. And second, most summer thunderstorms reach their peak of frequency and intensity during the late afternoon and evening; this squall developed during mid morning.

The summer of 1988 was a hot one over all of the Midwest. Records were set for duration and extremes of heat from the Canadian border to the Mid-Mississippi Valley. Temperatures soared above 100 degrees on a number of days in cities like Chicago and Milwaukee. Even Marquette recorded 13 days with temperatures of 90 degrees or above; the long-term average is only three days.

The balance of this scorching summer featured drought conditions. "It was real dry," says Larry Wanic of Bark River. On the evening of June 21 Wanic recorded a heavy thunderstorm at his location. It was an isolated event. "I had 2.77 inches," he remembers. "Later that summer if you flew over in an airplane you could see where those storms developed." The pattern of rainfall left by those thunderstorms was very distinctive. Wanic describes it as "kind of a triangle of green toward the lake." All around that triangle was a sea of brown, parched grass. In the summer of 1988, Michigan wildfires were considered the worst in years (*see "Fire Weather", page 287*). June and much of July were especially dry.

It took until July 30 before a large line of severe thunderstorms brought brief heavy rain to some spots. The heat built back a few days later. On August 2, the high temperature reached 101 degrees in the northern Menominee County community of Spalding. That evening, a complex of heavy thunderstorms rolled through north central Upper Michigan. Marquette recorded over three inches of rain during the deluge. The rainfall in this one event exceeded the total precipitation for the months of June and July combined. This occurrence foreshadowed things to come; the pattern was changing, setting the stage for the August 16 assault.

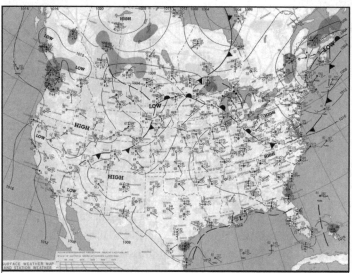

A warm front developed just south of Upper Michigan early on August 16, 1988. Severe thunderstorms developed in its vicinity throughout the day. (NOAA Central Library Data Imaging Project)

A frontal boundary set up over the northern Great Lakes early August 16. This front separated searing 100-degree heat to the south from relatively cool, dry air to its north. An unseasonably strong jet stream was associated with the boundary, ready to add energy to any storms that "popped." Extremely moist, hot and unstable air from the south glided over the cooler drier air and rapidly developed areas of thunderstorms. At about 4:00 a.m., an intense, rapidly moving storm dropped one-inch hailstones on downtown Marquette. This system moved east and later drenched areas around Munising with over two inches of rain.

Dan Hornbogen lives on Lake Superior just north of Marquette. That morning, about 8: 15, he stepped out onto his porch and saw a huge, black cloud mass to the northwest. "The unnerving part about it," he recalls, "was that it started at the horizon and seemed to have an altitude of many miles in height." He thought that he had better head out on his morning run immediately, so he took off down the path that would take him around Presque Isle and back—a total of about 5 miles.

Just after 8:30 a.m. National Weather Service (NWS) radar detected some showers over Lake Superior just southeast of the Keweenaw Peninsula. They moved rapidly southeastward in the strong, energetic flow aloft. At first these developing thunderstorms looked rather benign. "The storms blew up in about ten minutes' time," recalls Marv Taulbee, a long-time head of the cooperative observer network at the Marquette NWS. "Our radar showed level twos, basically 'garden variety' storms as they approached Marquette over the lake. When they passed our ground clutter, they were level fives," (the strongest returns on the radar).

Hornbogen moved down the trail and soon found himself at the Presque Isle marina. "I looked back," he recounts, "and that cloud or mass of weather had moved about halfway to me from where I saw it originally. So my better judgment told me to go home rather than run around the island." This decision may have saved him from injury and could possibly have saved his life.

It began to rain and a violent wind came up as he retraced his steps back home. He made it to the wooded trail less than a half mile from his house. "Branches and tree limbs were coming down around me," he remembers. "Lots of the branches were near misses." Hornbogen got through this segment of woods without injury and emerged onto the beach. About 100 feet away was Lake Superior but he could not see it through the maelstrom of rain and

Trees taken down by the storm in the vicinity of Dan Hornbogen's residence.
(Photo by Tom Buchkoe)

wind-whipped spray off the frenetic lake surface. "My impression was that it was raining up," he recalls. "Later I found out that for water to rain up, it takes a wind of around 90 miles an hour."

For fishermen on the lake, the violent wind turned a pleasant morning of fishing into an instant nightmare. Seas went from calm to eight feet with blinding rain in a matter of moments. Even the most cautious boaters were caught off guard by the sudden squall. One of them, an avid Lake Superior fisherman, managed to get off a distress signal to the Coast Guard just as the storm peaked. But he drowned when his boat went down near White Rocks, about two to three miles offshore.

Others got caught in the blow but managed to survive. One fisherman told a newspaper reporter he made a run for the Upper Harbor and was about 100 yards from safety when a violent gust spun his craft around. The wind ripped the canvas canopy clear off his boat. Then in a wall of rain, he was swept toward McCarty's Cove. He eventually made it to safety, as did a couple of fishermen I talked to years after the storm. They had the same

This sign on Hwy 28 was demolished by the straight-line winds of the storm.
(Photo by Tom Buchkoe)

experience; the wind ripped off their boat canopy, while they found themselves caught in a blizzard of blinding rain and pounding, chaotic waves. They sought refuge in the Upper Harbor, but were swept to the Lower Harbor, almost two miles to the southeast.

Back on the beach, Hornbogen thought it would be easiest for him to run on the hard sand close to the water's edge; he quickly found that was not the best plan. "I got to the water line," he chuckles, "and the wind just knocked me right over. I crouched, no, crawled, in the sand back up into the woods. I stayed in the woods and worked my way through the tag elders to get home."

He finally came to the end of his driveway. "I watched as trees were blowing down about 75 feet north of me in back of the camp," he remembers. "I worked my way up the drive and crouched behind my station wagon for protection." As he hunkered down on the leeside of his car, more trees came down; one large oak right onto the drive, and a birch at the top of the drive.

He decided to make a break for the house. "There were no trees between myself and camp," he explains, "only an open gauntlet 30 to 40 feet wide with a hurricane-force wind blowing off the lake." Struggling against the roaring wind and driving rain, he reached the back of the house. He opened the door and could not believe his eyes. "A window, the corner one, had blown out and rain was going right down the stairwell," he explains. The upstairs door had blown open. My wife has a jewelry tree, which stands about four feet high. It had been sucked out the door leading to the rear small porch off the bedroom. I was able to reach out and pull it in from the porch and shut the door." Later, he retrieved jewelry that had been strewn over the parking area and driveway. His house was a mess. "I realized I couldn't do anything with that window," he says. "There was as much wind going through the house as there was outdoors."

The squall line tore through Big Bay about 8:55 a.m. and raced down the lakeshore, reaching Marquette just after nine. Large trees were snapped or blown over along its path. Power poles fell and trees came down on wires, causing instant, widespread power outages. Windows were blown in on some buildings and a church steeple, just north of downtown, was tilted off its base by the strong winds. At least one business on Marquette's north side lost part of its roof.

Some people reported seeing a funnel cloud at Tourist Park on the city's north side. While a small "gustnado" may have dropped out of the storm's leading edge, Taulbee of the NWS says the damage was produced by straight-line winds: "Our damage surveys indicated it wasn't a tornado but extremely strong downburst winds because most of the big trees were uprooted with no twisting. They were all blown over in the same direction."

The highest recorded wind gust in the city came in at 65 miles an hour from an anemometer on the north side. Judging by the extent of damage and the size of the trees that came down, some of the peak gusts were much higher. An anemometer on Middle Island Point, just north of town, recorded a 95-mile-per-hour gust just before the power went out.

Hornbogen walked around Presque Isle that afternoon. He counted 246 large trees down on the road he had decided not to run on earlier that day. It is estimated that about a thousand trees came down on the 323-acre park.

John Turausky was city parks and recreation director at the time of the storm. He was in charge of the massive cleanup on the island. "We didn't want to go in there and tear the place up getting the downed trees," he says. "It was decided that...we would take only the trees that were 'widow makers', if you will, across the paths or roads. Also, we were going to do this as sensitively as possible."

A steeple of the historic 1st Methodist church in Marquette tipped by the violent northwesterly winds. (Drawing by E. Yelland)

He explains that meant no bulldozers—they brought in a logger who used horses. The fallen timber was skidded out the old-fashioned way. "It took quite a while," remembers Turausky. "But the money that we paid was offset by the trees that we took out of there. If you go out to the island now and know where to look, you can still see the trees that we left alone, that had blown down."

Four distinct bands of thunderstorms plowed through the area on August 16, 1988. Later that day, a tornado watch was issued for a large portion of Upper Michigan. A tornado was spotted near Republic around 6:00 p.m., but no damage was reported. In the late evening, I stepped outside the TV station during a break between severe weather broadcasts. I remember watching the chaotic sky with some of the other station employees. In just a few minutes, the flag across the road was moved around by the wind in every direction of the compass as the clouds boiled and rolled above us. It was an awesome sight, and a fitting end to a weather day that many will never forget.

In retrospect, this stormy August day marked the end to a long, hot summer. Two days later, a low of 39 degrees was recorded by the Weather Service. In less than two months, the first measurable snow arrived, leading to one of the coldest Octobers on record.

July 19, 1992: A Tornado Rips into Gladstone

"It was a real hot day," remembers Helen Micheau. This hot July Sunday, June 19, was

A rare photograph of an Upper Michigan tornado. (Photo by Helen Micheau)

noteworthy in its own right during this "Year without a Summer" (*see "Heat Waves, Hot Summers", page 244*). What caught Micheau's attention that muggy evening from her vantage point at Flat Rock, a small settlement about 10 miles northwest of Gladstone, were the clouds. "I had never seen any clouds like that before," she remembers. "I got my camera after I saw this black cloud coming toward the house. As we were watching it, we saw all the other clouds kind of start circling and they all formed into that cloud." Micheau and her family were watching a rare event in Upper Michigan—the formation of a wall cloud, the rotating system that breeds a tornado.

She kept snapping pictures as the black cloud moved southeastward. "When the lightning started, it was going straight out of that black cloud," recounts Micheau. "It was going straight up; it would go straight across the sky instead of coming down." The rotating wall cloud began moving away from them. "As it started to move," she says, "You could see something coming out the bottom of it. It would just come out a little ways and then go back up; come out a little way and then go back up. Then all of a sudden, it came all the way down to the ground." She took one last picture as a well-developed tornado began ripping across the fields and woods, heading southeastward toward Gladstone.

Micheau ran into the house and called local law enforcement to tell them that a tornado was heading right at Gladstone. Probably accustomed to fielding outlandish, crank calls, the officer answering the phone greeted her report with skepticism. "Just by listening to him, I knew he didn't believe me," she remembers. "So he said, 'We'll check into it,' and hung up." Micheau then called her parents. "They lived right below the bluff in Gladstone," she explains. "They were in their 70s at the time and it did get real close to their house. They were in the basement and heard the tornado pass by."

The twister plowed through the bluff area, the geological formation that was supposed to protect the town from storms like this. Widespread destruction occurred along its half-mile-wide path. Several businesses sustained major damage, including one housing several large tanks. The tornado picked up an empty 20,000 gallon tank and threw it 200 yards, slamming t into another tank. A valve broke on the second tank, spilling 250,000 gallons of tar.

Half the residents in the town of 4,800 were without power after the storm. Telephone service was knocked out. A number of houses were damaged; one had its kitchen windows shattered with glass later found imbedded in the walls. The occupants of the structure had made it into the basement just as the storm struck. A number of garages were damaged or destroyed. One garage was lifted off its foundation and dropped onto a car parked in front of it. The boat inside the garage was untouched.

Only minor injuries were reported. One girl was hit by a board that flew through a window of the house she was in. A boy fell while running to the basement of his home.

Farther downstream, Terry Soderman of Gladstone was on the shore of the bay trying to protect his boat while the storm passed. "I felt alone," he remembers with a chuckle. "I was the only one on the shoreline. Here I am sitting out there holding a boat down. I'm holding the boat, while there's other boats just flipping." Soderman explains that the storm became a large waterspout as it passed across Little Bay De Noc. "The whole shoreline was peppered with debris; boat cushions, chairs, roofing, you name it."

Soderman has a camp 10 miles to the east. The F-1 tornado even left its calling card there. "We had plywood and Styrofoam from the building supply store in Gladstone out there in the woods," he recalls. "It was unbelievable."

After this muggy, stormy interlude, the summer of '92 resumed its fall-like characteristics. Two mornings later on July 21, frost was reported at Sand River east of Marquette and also north of Iron Mountain. At the same time, a thermometer just outside of Rapid River, several miles up the road from Gladstone, registered 24 degrees. The Gladstone Tornado of July 1992 was a unique event, punctuating an extraordinary summer season.

August 23, 1998: Near Miss in Menominee

A late summer thunderstorm formed over Menominee on August 23, 1998 and dropped a large tornado that just missed the city. Showers and thunderstorms had broken out in sections of Upper Michigan earlier in the day. Strong low pressure for the season over the Northern Plains formed a warm front just south of the U.P., providing a boundary for storm development. These thunderstorms brought heavy rain and damaging winds.

Tragedy struck earlier in the day at a National Forest Campground in Gogebic County when strong downburst winds blew a large pine tree down on a small camper. A person inside the camper was killed.

The warm front then lifted north as the low moved eastward along the U.S.-Canadian border, placing much of Upper Michigan in the warm sector of the system. "Temperatures were in the mid-90s in Menominee," remembers Greg Albrecht, who was back home visiting his family. "Very hot, very humid; a real strong southwest wind."

The cold front extending from the low moved east, plowing into the hot, humid air mass in place over northern Wisconsin and southern Upper Michigan. "Clouds began to increase," recalls Albrecht. "You could see lower clouds just screaming off to the north. At the same time, higher clouds were screaming off to the east."

A large thunderstorm began forming just upstream from Menominee. This type of thunderstorm is called a "supercell." Supercells are common on the Plains; the strongest ones produce large tornados and extremely large hailstones. These storms grow as distinct cells apart from other showers and storms. Supercells develop their own circulations and can extend far into the atmosphere. This particular storm could be clearly seen well over 100 miles to the north as it shot into the atmosphere some 60,000 feet.

"The sky grew increasingly dark," remembers Albrecht. He took a walk to check out the storm and before long his partner saw something and took off running. "He got scared," explains Albrecht. "He claimed he saw a funnel cloud. That couldn't have been more than a mile or so to the west northwest of my parents' house. What I then saw was definitely a wall cloud. The clouds were rotating."

At the same time, several miles north of Albrecht's position, in the Birch Creek area, residents reported a severe thunderstorm with hail up to 1.5 inches in diameter. Albrecht got back to his parents' house, as winds picked up dramatically. "It was a classic," Albrecht explains recounting the sequence of events. "First there were strong winds, then calm and then hail followed by a wind shift. That's when I got scared. Right at that time a tornado warning was issued."

A funnel was then spotted over Green Bay just east of the city. It traveled eastward and came onshore as a large tornado in Door County, Wisconsin, near the village of Egg Harbor across the bay from Menominee. The half-mile-wide twister leveled or damaged at least 25 homes and businesses in the area. An observer there described the destruction in the aftermath of the storm as "like someone came through with big claws and just raked over the entire area."

A stand of pine blown down by the tornado. Note the trees in the top part of the picture are blown down in different directions—indicating a tornado touchdown. (Courtesy of The Daily News, Iron Mountain/Kingsford, Michigan)

The near-miss made a lasting impression on Albrecht: "In my thirty one years …that was the only funnel cloud that was ever really noticeable in Menominee. It was a very intense storm."

2002: An Active Severe Season Culminates in a Fall Tornado

Severe thunderstorms with destructive downbursts and flooding rains were frequent across Upper Michigan during the summer of 2002. For instance, on July 21, a severe thunderstorm complex raked the Marquette County area from Republic to Sands to Skandia.

ntense microbursts
downed numerous trees
and created massive power
outages. Then on August
., three areas of severe
thunderstorms tore across
Upper Michigan from
morning until evening. Tree
damage was widespread
along with power outages
and flooding rains. Republic
was drenched with over 5
inches of rain.

The prevailing circulation
that summer brought
abundant heat and humidity
northward into the Upper
Great Lakes, while an
active jet stream provided
the necessary energy to set

The path and intensity of the tornado as it moved through Iron Mountain and vicinity. (Courtesy of The Daily News, Iron Mountain/Kingsford, MI)

off thunderstorms. Summer's heat lingered past Labor Day as temperatures soared into the
90s the second weekend of September. Then above-average temperatures remained through
the end of the month. This unseasonable warmth helped trigger an extraordinarily late
season tornado in Iron Mountain the evening of the 30th.

A cold front plowed into the region the last evening of September and thunderstorms
exploded across southern Upper Michigan and northern Wisconsin. One large supercell
thunderstorm developed just downwind of the greater Iron Mountain area and dropped a
tornado near the Menominee River. The entire system then proceeded eastward, affecting
Kingsford, Iron Mountain, Quinnesec, Breitung Township and Norway.

"My biggest argument was with the news media," says Bruce Martin of Quinnesec. "They
said there was only two. I think there were up to four funnel clouds that came through."
Martin explains that one of them went behind his house, while another one came down
highway 41 just the other side of his home. "That one took out the Wells Fargo sign from
the bank across the highway. It was in my backyard." Martin believes two other small
tornadoes came down across a lumberyard up the road, while another one came straight up
Lincoln Street in Quinnesec and took out a large number of pine trees.

NWS investigators officially designated the storm an F-1 tornado. The multiple bands of
damage resulted from the twister and bursts of straight-line winds. Widespread destruction
occurred along the system's eight-mile path. The roofs of several businesses and homes
were torn off and numerous garages and sheds were destroyed. Downed trees and toppled
and snapped power poles caused the most problems; up to 15,000 residents were without
power. About 10,000 homes remained in the dark into the next day.

Structural damage in the wake of the twister.
(Courtesy The Daily News, Iron Mountain/Kingsford, MI)

"There were trees all over the roads in the Quinnesec area," remembers Martin. "When I drove into my driveway, I noticed one tree down across my boat. It took me over a year to get that boat back from repair." But Martin still considers himself lucky. "There was a guy on top of the hill behind me," he says. "He had a pine tree come through his roof right into his bedroom. Had the storm occurred later that night, those people would have been killed in their bed."

Martin noticed strange windstorm antics. "When I got up to my house, I noticed there was dirt all over the porch," he explains. "My wife had a bunch of hanging flowers in the pot. The wind sucked the dirt out of the pot, but left the flowers in it. My grandson had one of those matchbox zambonis sitting next to the flower pot on the porch; it wasn't disturbed at all. Also, I have a double-house bird feeder in the middle of my yard. It took one roof and left the other untouched."

The unseasonably late tornado left a trail of destruction that was still visible several years later. The weather pattern then gradually shifted and evolved into a cold one. October 2002 ended as the coldest tenth month in history with record low temperatures the second half of the month along with heavy, early-season snows.

Chapter 12

Upper Michigan, located in the heart of the mid-latitude westerlies, usually enjoys an abundance of precipitation rather evenly distributed throughout the year. This climatic feature, along with moderate temperatures, keeps the fire threat low. Occasionally, dry weather, along with the explosive mixture of high winds, leads to wildfires. This is especially true during spring before green-up; however, some of the most disastrous fires have occurred following a hot, dry summer. This section features some of those fires and their consequences.

The Great Peshtigo Fire Jumps the Border into Upper Michigan

"Trees, trees everywhere, nothing else but trees as far as you can travel." Father Peter Pernin, parish priest at the Oconto Catholic church in 1871, wrote about northeastern Wisconsin in the 1870s: "a country covered with dense forests." Logging of the forests was proceeding at full throttle; the maple, oak, beech, ash and elm were felled indiscriminately; the slash left in piles to dry where majestic virgin timber once stood.

The litter of the logging industry combined with careless camping practices always posed a danger of

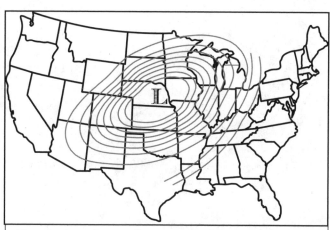

The stage is set for a conflagration. Northeastern Wisconsin and south-central Upper Michigan were in the warm sector of strong low-pressure system developing on the High Plains the evening of October 8, 1871. Strong, dry southwesterly winds whipped spot fires into one huge blaze.

fire; even more so in the fall of 1871. Drought conditions had prevailed over the last several months. Fires burned through scattered sections of Wisconsin and Michigan days before the Peshtigo holocaust. Damage from the fires was declared "incalculable," while the smoky atmosphere produced by the blazes rendered "everything obscure." Visibility got so bad from a combination of smoke and fog that navigation at Detroit was suspended—an event "unparalleled within the memory of the oldest navigators."

Against this backdrop of sporadic fire and smoky haze a "feeling of uneasiness and premonition" hung over the region. Animals behaved strangely. Dogs howled. Cats ran together in packs, while birds flocked in towns and deer ran into populated areas for safety.

On Sunday, October 8, nature provided the ingredients for disaster. A deep storm developed over Colorado with a strong trough extending from the low northeastward toward western Lake Superior. The east-northeast alignment of the trough promoted a strong southwest flow of warm, dry air in the warm sector of the system toward northern Wisconsin—the perfect setup to fan the scattered flames of the existing spot fires into one giant conflagration.

That evening, Josephine Ingalls Sawyer of Menominee accompanied her brother as he took home an employee of the family business named Mr. Merrill. They traveled in a horse-drawn carriage in a foreboding atmosphere. "There was already a roaring in the air," remembered Sawyer, "and the sky was lighted up over towards Peshtigo." They dropped off Mr. Merrill short of his home because he insisted on walking the rest of the way. On their way back, "the roaring became loud and the wind came in fierce hot gusts." Smoldering logs on the side of the road burst into flames, while trees before them "took fire." "Our horses needed no urging home," she recounted. The Ingalls were fortunate; they made it back safely to Menominee, which, for the most part, escaped the inferno.

When Mr. Merrill arrived at his settlement outside of Marinette, all the buildings were on fire. All the cattle and horses were turned loose and each person grabbed a bucket and headed for the river. He said the heat was so intense that

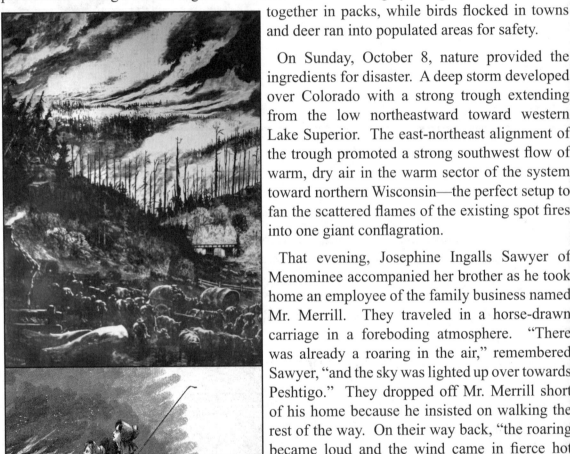

Artists' portrayals of the Great Fire. Top image from the periodical "Every Saturday", December 1871. (Courtesy of the Marquette County History Museum)

when a person rose out of the water their clothes would immediately catch on fire. If a person had a wooden bucket and flipped it upside down over their head, the bottom of the bucket would start burning.

In Peshtigo, a fiery "hurricane" burst upon the hapless community. Father Pernin wrote later that eyewitnesses reported seeing "a large black object, resembling a balloon, which…revolved in the air with great rapidity" (see "Firestorm" sidebar). He went on to explain that the object rose above the tops of the trees and made a beeline for a house "which it seemed to single out for destruction." The black balloon barely touched the house and "burst with a loud report, like that of a bombshell." Immediately "with the rapidity of thought," fire enveloped the house giving no chance for its occupants to escape.

The intense blaze created its own "tornado-like" circulation. The fierce winds reportedly blew shingles a mile out into the bay where they set fire to the sails of ships. Burning lumber was transported over miles of forest then over the Menominee River where fires sprang up on the Michigan side of the river.

The fire beast of Peshtigo, while avoiding most of Marinette-Menominee, moved northeastward parallel to Green Bay and descended upon the farming community of Birch Creek north of Menominee. Similar to Peshtigo, the rapid advance of the blaze gave residents no time to escape. One family, a husband and wife with seven children, made a mad dash for the creek. The smallest children in the family, two girls, began to stumble and fall. The father suddenly grabbed them and "threw them both into the water and mud under roots of an overturned tree, telling them to crouch down and stay there, until he came for them." They were the only ones in the family of nine to survive.

FIRESTORM

A scientific theory was advanced that sought to explain the reason for the fire's intensity. This theory stated that marsh gas from peat bogs that had been burning in the area for weeks produced "carbureted hydrogen" that then produced "great masses of combustible gas resembling balls of fire which would explode on contact with oxygen." This theory has now been discredited.

It is now accepted that wildfires intensify and produce their own violent wind circulation. Superheated air, rising in a chimney-like column, breaks through the "capping" of the pall of smoke caused by the fire. When the flames break through the cap of smoke into the colder air above, tremendous updrafts occur as the hot air suddenly rises, creating the "fire tornado," the whirling black balloon that Father Pernin wrote about, and other spectacular phenomenon seen in the Peshtigo Fire and other intense blazes.

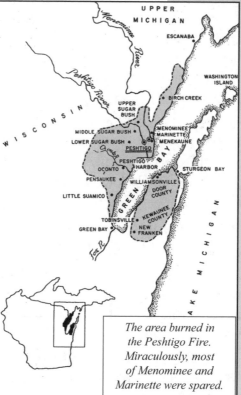

The area burned in the Peshtigo Fire. Miraculously, most of Menominee and Marinette were spared.

Another Birch Creek family miraculously escaped death or serious injury. Frederick Sieman saw the wall of flame approaching from the southwest. He gathered his wife and four children and beat a hasty retreat to a vacant field adjacent to the house. The crops had been harvested off this small plot of land and it had been burned over so it afforded a tiny if tenuous oasis in the sea of flame. Sieman and his wife huddled the children together and put wet blankets over them as the flames passed by. Later, they recounted how they heard the crashing of their buildings and the "maddened cries of their dying cattle and horses." Their next door neighbors "not 40 rods away" burned to death.

An estimated 25 people died in the fire at Birch Creek—a quarter of its population. The count did not include some newcomers to the community. A number of immigrants were in the area working on the railroad that was being built to Escanaba, and more had come to homestead in the region. Bodies that could not be identified were buried in a common grave. Legend has it that someone later planted lilac bushes over the graves. The huge, aged clump of lilacs can still be seen just off U.S. 41 in the village.

This stand of lilacs is said to mark the common grave of the victims killed in the fire at Birch Creek. (Courtesy of the Menominee County Historical Society)

In the aftermath of the fire, survivors reported scenes of utter desolation. Sawyer told of a trip she took with some friends north of Menominee several days after the fire. They got as far as Birch Creek and she described how "strange it was to see these great forests lying row after row, as though cut with a scythe, their tops pointing toward the north."

The Great Fire of October 1871 was Michigan's first recorded catastrophic fire. It occurred the same night as the Great Chicago Fire, which killed 250 persons. Besides the victims at Birch Creek, at least 175 others died in separate blazes that raged across the Lower Peninsula from October 8-18. In all, some 1,200 perished across the Upper Great Lakes in October 1871, including about 1,000 in the Peshtigo area alone. It remains the most deadly forest fire to ever occur on the North American Continent.

1896: The Year of Devastating Fires in Upper Michigan

1896 had a warm, dry spring and summer. The spring was especially warm and dry. April came in at over 5 degrees above average, while May was virtually a summer month with positive departures in excess of 7 degrees. At the same time, both months had rainfall deficits. This potent pair of meteorological conditions set the stage for a devastating fire during the second weekend in May.

L'Anse was a busy village on the southeast shore of Keweenaw Bay. May 9, 1896 was a warm day as low pressure in the Northern Plains sent a dry, brisk southwesterly wind into the Upper Peninsula. At about 3:00 that afternoon fire broke out in the L'Anse Lumber Company sawmill. The southwest wind "blowing half a gale" spread the flames rapidly and in 10 minutes, the blaze was completely out of control. In short order, the structure was devoured and the flames spread to the lumber dock where they began consuming 3 million board feet of dry lumber awaiting shipment.

Low pressure in the Northern Plains sent a warm, dry southwesterly wind that fanned a lumber mill fire in L'Anse on May 9, 1896. (NOAA Central Library Data Imaging Project)

By this time, showers of burning brands were scattered all over that side of the village and the townspeople realized their homes were doomed. Some tried to salvage their belongings, but the flames spread so rapidly that most lost everything. Twenty businesses burned. At least that many residences were consumed by the fire. Hundreds of people were rendered homeless.

On the afternoon of August 27, fire broke out in a row of wooden buildings in the business district of Sault Ste. Marie. The initial cause of the blaze did not appear weather related, however, a fresh northwest wind helped spread the flames. By 6:00 p.m., 20 buildings lay in ruins. This fire occurred just two days after one of Upper Michigan's most damaging conflagrations.

August 25, 1896: The Day Ontonagon Burned

Tinder-dry conditions in late summer 1896 led to forest fires in scattered areas of the western Upper Peninsula. Fires burned in the forests around Ironwood and Hurley, Wisconsin. As August wore on, even the swamps around Ontonagon dried out and began to burn.

Ontonagon, a boom town of the early copper mining era, found new life as a lumber center in the late 1800s. With an abundant supply of pine trees nearby, the Diamond Match Company established its headquarters in the town. Logs

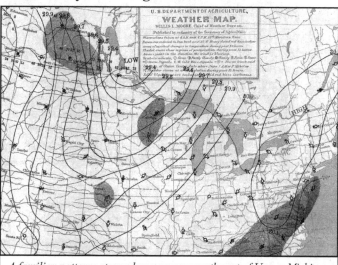

A familiar pattern: strong low pressure northwest of Upper Michigan produced a dry, "living gale" at Ontonagon on August 25, 1896. Shifting winds caused by a frontal passage late in the afternoon led to disaster. (NOAA Central Library Data Imaging Project)

were driven down the Ontonagon River and then processed into matchsticks, shingles and boxes at the company's huge sawmills near the river's mouth.

In the summer of 1896, Diamond's two mills were operating at full capacity. Wood was everywhere; stacks of lumber were said to be piled as high as three-story buildings. Sawdust, the waste of the log milling process, grew into huge mounds. Ontonagon was an enormous pile of kindling waiting to go up.

Del Woodbury was 17 years old at the time of the Great Fire. He was employed loading logs at one of the mills. Woodbury said August 25, began just like any other: "When we went to work the morning of the fire it was about 70 to 75 degrees, I would say, and we had been bothered by smoke for, oh, a number of days. The sun was just a red ball up there and since we had no covered roads then—just dirt roads—why, when a ripple of wind came which was strong enough, everything was dust and dirt."

That day the wind was much more than a mere ripple; the keeper of the Ontonagon light wrote that at around 1:00 in the afternoon it was "hot and blowing a living gale." The swamp southeast of the light caught fire and soon the gale-force winds fanned the flames toward the mill. A number of workers were called off their stations to beat back the encroaching blaze, but to no avail. The towering piles of lumber caught fire and the devastation began.

The first of the company buildings burst into flames and a chain reaction occurred—in a short time a dozen buildings were consumed. The workers-turned-firemen saw the futility in their efforts and immediately began urging women and children close to the mill to move uptown away from the conflagration. Suddenly the fire jumped the river and the mountains of sawdust ignited; now the town was doomed.

Ruins of the Diamond Match Store and Box Factory. (Courtesy of the Ontonagon Historical Society)

The Bigelow House, the grandest of the town's local hotels, was the village's first structure to go. When this four-story frame building went up like a roll of birch bark on a campfire, the townspeople realized their lives were at stake. Every person at the lower end of town either headed southeastward in the direction of Rockland or Greenland or sought refuge on the beach or in boats on Lake Superior.

The wind never eased but continued increasing, reaching gusts estimated at 75 miles an hour. Huge sticks of lumber, not yet consumed, became airborne fire-breathing missiles that struck buildings, exploding them into flames. Just after 4:00 the wind shifted from southwest to northwest with the passage of a front. Some noticed a brief burst of cool air while the light keeper recorded "a few drops of mocking rain." Now any hope of saving the rest of the town was dashed as the flames spread up the Greenland and Rockland roads.

Huge banks of smoke hid the sun from view; Ontonagon became a living hell as the darkened sky filled with fire-brands. The townspeople began a race for their lives. A scene of panic and chaos ensued; horses were lashed into a mad gallop and men, women and children ran wildly. Terror stricken, many of the escapees saw houses catch on fire in front of them, but could do nothing to help as they knew they had no alternative but to stay ahead of the advancing wall of flames. People standing a half-mile from the fire could not face it—the very air seemed charged with flame. The intense heat roasted apples on the trees. The population kept pushing out to the southeast away from the blaze, some moving as far as five miles out of town before feeling safe.

The Ontonagon County Jail—one of the dozens of structures laid to waste in the fire. (Courtesy of the Ontonagon Historical Society)

Ontonagon was laid to waste in matter of a few hours. During the height of the holocaust, the town was ablaze in 100 places at once and nothing could save it. Three hundred and forty-four buildings burnt to the ground. Among them were four churches, a bank, three hotels, a dozen stores, thirteen saloons, two newspapers, the entire Diamond Match Company plant along with 40 million feet of lumber, as well as the barge *City of Straits* and two iron bridges. The village's court house and jail were reduced to ashes along with nearly 300 residences.

Only one person died in the fire. The victim was Mrs. Pirk, "an aged German lady." She apparently refused to leave her home, and her daughter sustained severe face burns trying to drag her to safety. A number of animals perished in the firestorm. The bodies of charred cows, pigs, poultry, dogs and cats were strewn about the burn area, which encompassed a full square mile.

In one afternoon, some 2,000 people became homeless. The St. Paul railroad gave free passes to any fire victim to any town the train served. Immediately, 400 residents took advantage of the offer and left the area. A number of victims spent the first night in the open air with their only possessions—the set of clothes they escaped in. Hundreds of others found temporary shelter in farmhouses or any structure still standing.

The state militia soon arrived and put up 150 tents at the fair grounds. The refugee camp became known as White City and housed up to several hundred people well into the fall. Aid in the form of food, blankets and clothing poured in from every corner of the peninsula as well as from cities as far away as Milwaukee and Green Bay. The residents that stayed were provided with lumber. Most built tarpaper shacks to house their families over the following winter.

Diamond Match Company did not stay. In February 1897, the company announced it

Banker C. Meilleur set up a make-shift structure to conduct business only 48 hours after the fire. (Courtesy of Superior View, Marquette)

would not rebuild. The company said it would, however, take the remaining pine which escaped the fire and still floated in the Ontonagon River. Bitter town officials devised an "ad valorem" tax which they levied on the logs passing through the river in their city. Diamond Match contested the tax and after nine years of judicial wrangling, the company was ordered to pay the tax on some 40 million board feet of lumber. It was the only "aid" the village received from the corporation that once dominated the town.

The village of Ontonagon gradually rose out of the ashes of that terrible August day. In the years that followed, all residents, even newcomers, acquired a common malady—an intense fear of fire. The sound of the fire alarm would set off a ritual—everyone ran outdoors to see in which direction the crowd was running. Once it was realized there was no immediate danger in the vicinity, town folk would follow the rest of the crowd "to the scene of the action." The "fire demon" held a fear and fascination over this copper and lumber boom town well into the 20th century.

May 17-18, 1906 Fires: "Fearful Destruction"

A series of fires broke out in the dry swamps, fields and forests of Upper Michigan in the

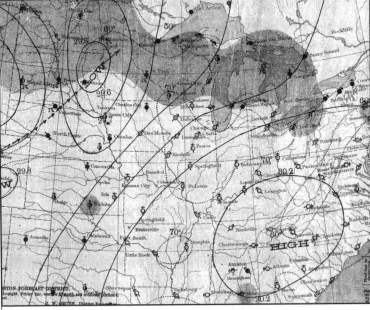

Low pressure to the west of Upper Michigan set up a strong southwesterly flow that brought a blast of hot, dry air into the Upper Great Lakes on May 17, 1906. Wildfires scorched thousands of acres across the U.P. (NOAA Central Library Data Imaging Project)

spring of 1906 and burned down portions of towns and farming settlements. The fires scorched an area roughly from Newberry in the east to Bessemer in the west and from the Lake Superior shore to the southern border of the peninsula.

April set the stage for the mid-May conflagration. The average temperature for the month came in more than five degrees above the long-term average, while precipitation was sparse. Then on May 17, an intense blast of heat flooded the U.P. on brisk, dry winds. The high reached a sizzling 91 degrees in Marquette that day. The heat, very low humidity and dry vegetation created a volatile mix; fires broke out and were fanned by winds that blew from 30 to 40 miles an hour at times.

The blazes swept over the land; farmers and homesteaders south of Marquette narrowly escaped with their lives. The Chocolay Valley, which contained some of the finest farms in Marquette County, was virtually swept clean, as if "visited by a tornado." At least 50 farmers lost their homes and their outbuildings along with cattle and other livestock. At the height of the wildfire, the woods in the vicinity "were like a roaring furnace." The highways became filled with livestock and even wild animals, all seeking to escape the flames. Flocks of birds "flew about as though dazed."

One hundred families in the area south and southeast of Marquette were rendered homeless, but miraculously, no one was killed. A Green Garden farmer lost all his personal effects in an ironic twist. As the blaze reached his clearing, he had his furniture removed from the house, which he thought would be impossible to save. The furniture was taken to a nearby pasture and then the farmer and some friends returned to battle the flames encroaching on the house. They succeeded in fighting off the fire and saving the house, but when they went after the furniture, they found it a pile of smoldering ruins.

In the city of Marquette, fires broke out as high winds carried sparks from the inferno south and west of town. The dormitory of the Normal School (now Northern Michigan University) was threatened when a spark ignited a window casing on the fourth floor and began spreading into the building. Firemen put out the flames with water and chemicals and only a small amount of damage occurred.

North of the city on the way to Big Bay, the town of Birch was saved by fighting fire with fire. A force of men set fire to slashings about three quarters of a mile from the main sawmill. The wide area burned around the town kept the fire at bay and saved the lumbering community. Farther west, the Houghton County towns of Kenton and Sidnaw were threatened but saved as the wind changed direction and directed the flames away from the towns.

Near Negaunee, a couple lost their house and narrowly escaped with their lives. Their home was located southeast of

While the city of Marquette escaped the worst of the wildfires, 38 years earlier, the then frontier town was laid to waste by flames. The June 1868 fire was not specifically weather-related. However, westerly winds fanned the flames and helped make the destruction complete. A million-and-a-half dollars worth of damage was assessed and afterward, city fathers passed a law banning wooden buildings in the business district. (Courtesy of the Marquette County History Museum)

Negaunee in the vicinity of the Iron Kilns settlement. At about noon the 18th they observed a pall of smoke to the west. A strong wind had been blowing from the west all morning. The husband and wife took every precaution to protect their buildings, and thinking the fire was a long way off, stepped inside their house to rest a bit. No sooner had they sat down when it became almost as dark as night. They heard a roar "like the approach of a tornado" and immediately ran out of the house. Outside they watched as a "sheet of flames passing with race horse speed" spread over their homestead. The wall of fire set everything combustible ablaze. As each building caught fire there was a loud explosion and for a few moments "the heat was something awful." Each had their clothing scorched and the wife's hair was badly singed, but neither was seriously hurt.

In the southern U.P., the May 1906 fire was a "catastrophe." Near Quinnesec, just east of Iron Mountain, a blaze swept out of control in a field where men were pulling stumps and burning debris. The dry wind spread the fire quickly; it moved into timber and eventually joined the inferno spreading east toward Escanaba. The fires raged 64 miles along the Escanaba and Lake Superior Railroad and then for 30 miles beyond Channing in northern Dickinson County.

Stories of heroic battles against the flames were numerous. In Northland, a southern Marquette County town of 600, the flames were beat back three times. Each time the fire was stopped within 10 yards of homes on the outside rim of the town.

Quinnesec suffered the most over southern sections. Sixteen families lost their homes, and a majority of the business district was destroyed. The victims were "provided for abundantly by the generous people from Iron Mountain and vicinity."

These deer could not escape an Upper Michigan forest fire. (Courtesy of the Marquette County History Museum)

To the north near Foster, Felch and Sagola, numerous farmers in outlying areas lost their homes and farms due to the wildfire. Sagola was saved by a last-minute shift in the wind from south to north. A number of settlers in the area had close calls, but through all-out effort and luck, they were able to save their homes.

The Iron Mountain paper criticized the "wonderful liars" reporting for the Chicago and Milwaukee papers. These "damphool" correspondents "armed...with railway maps and with cruel thoughtlessness proceeded to wipe out of existence some dozens or more towns." These reports actually showed up in the Marquette paper, but were refuted by the "diligent and careful inquiry" of the Iron Mountain paper's correspondents.

The heat wave that spawned the fires was quickly thwarted by a cold air mass from the north. On

May 19, snow flurries developed in Marquette. By the next morning, "a white pall of frost enveloped the entire region." Finally, on Monday, rain extinguished the last of the wildfires. These fires stand out as among the most widespread and destructive to ever burn across the Upper Peninsula.

May 1908: Copper Country Wildfires

Two years later in 1908, it was the Copper Country's turn to battle forest fires. "Sultry weather" the second weekend of May, along with dry vegetation, set the stage for fires from Houghton to Baraga. The first fire was discovered at the Portage Entry near Jacobsville. This fire "covered a great area" and destroyed a large amount of property. Dense smoke from the fire hung over the lake miles from shore. Boats had to "lay to" for hours before attempting the entry, because of thick haze and smoke. Over a two-day period, the wildfire consumed all of range 8 near Jacobsville (this is a large area—a range is defined as a column of townships, each six miles square).

The second fire burned especially fiercely on Sunday, May 10 from just south of Houghton through the Pilgrim River area, then southward for several miles. A number of Copper Country men, out on Sunday fishing excursions, had narrow escapes. One group had to abandon the regular trails near the river and fight their way through the underbrush as the flames approached. The men avoided smoke inhalation by covering their faces with wet handkerchiefs.

Near Baraga, two more fishermen were threatened by a third blaze that sultry Sunday. They noticed smoke, but evidently the fishing was

Fire races through a stand of aspen and pine. (Courtesy of the Marquette County History Museum)

so good they ignored the danger until the fire was only a few hundred yards from them. Finally convinced of their perilous position, they hastily hitched up their team. Soon, realizing the road they intended to take was cut off by flames, they unhitched their horses, leaving the wagon to the fire. After four miles of struggle over logs and thicket, they came to an open road, which facilitated their escape.

Twenty straight hours of rain early the next week eventually contained and extinguished the fires.

1918: Big Fire Year in the Upper Lakes

Much-below-normal rainfall and hot weather got fires going in Marquette County 10 years, to the weekend, later. Deputy game wardens reported blazes in the cut-over "wastelands" on May 5, 1918. The fires approached farms and camps in the area but were contained.

Smoke was the culprit in a two-car collision on the Marquette-Negaunee road that

A locomotive churns through a formerly wooded area laid to waste by fire. Occasionally fires were set by sparks generated from the friction of a train moving over railroad tracks. (Courtesy of Superior View, Marquette)

afternoon. A fire near Eagle Mills poured dense smoke over the road, reducing visibility to zero. The two cars, going in opposite directions, collided. "Two or three of the occupants" of the vehicles were thrown from the cars, but apparently received no serious injuries. The Negaunee-bound vehicle, a Jeffery, had its wheel knocked off, while the Marquette-bound car had its finish scorched by the intense heat of the fire.

Moisture deficits, continuing through late spring and summer of 1918, contributed to a historic wildfire at the head of Lake Superior in October. The Cloquet Fire in northeastern Minnesota gutted the city of 12,000 and laid to waste 37 other communities.

1933: "Worst Forest Fire Siege in Years"

The Dust Bowl was reaching its withering climax on the Great Plains in the early 1930s. Hot, dry weather poked northeastward into Upper Michigan in the summer of 1933. June ended 6 degrees above average, while July had 11 days with "extreme" heat. At the same time, rainfall during the seventh month was only around half the long-term average. All summer months had temperatures exceeding average, while moisture deficits plagued the region from late spring through the entire summer. No rain fell from July 23 to August 10. It was during this period that fires began popping up in scattered sections of Upper Michigan. Over the weekend of August 5-6, brisk, dry winds began fanning the flames.

The fires spread through slashings and cutover land throughout a good share of the U.P. By August 7, fires were reported from Keweenaw to Gogebic counties and from Iron to Delta counties up to Marquette County. About 2,000 men were pressed into service to fight the wildfires.

The blaze around Diorite in Marquette County was 6 miles long and 4 miles wide at its peak. Firefighters from Negaunee, Ishpeming, Gwinn and Michigamme kept the fire from the town by pumping water out of nearby Boston Lake; pouring it on brush and trees surrounding the town. After an all night vigil, the threat to the community was averted. Fires were also reported near Hogsback Mountain northwest of Marquette. At one point strong winds pushed the fire completely over the mountain.

In Baraga County, the most serious fire occurred near Arnheim, involving 700 acres. Four farm houses were saved, but not before the families occupying them fled with their belongings. The Delta and Menominee Fire District reported 65 fires during this period, the largest number of any area in the U.P.

On August 8, the *Iron Mountain News* gave a bleak assessment of the situation: "several thousand, weary, grimy firefighters prayed for rain as they vainly sought to halt the flames' advance through tinder-dry forests, brush and slashings." In the southern U.P., vast tracts of timber were destroyed, while farm buildings and at least one sawmill and logging camp were reduced to ashes. Hundreds of persons, both permanent residents and summer vacationers, fled as the fires spread. Many head of livestock were reported killed.

Just across the border in Wisconsin, fire swept toward Nelma, a village in Forest County. Most of the 100 residents fled before the advancing flames; however, nine men remained, refusing to obey the order to evacuate. They hauled a pump to the Brule River and sprayed water on houses and businesses in the village.

The flames kept advancing. A farmhouse just south of town was consumed. A hay barn on another farm was the next dwelling to go, then a sawmill and lumberyard on the town's edge.

The wildfire then roared into town, whipped by a 35-mile-per-hour wind. The *News* described what happened: "Over lawns and across balsam thickets it raced, licking at the wooden buildings as it progressed. Sheds, rubbish, shrubbery and everything combustible went up in flames—all except the houses and stores.

"Gasping in the heat, choked by smoke, the little group worked furiously at the pump until the flames…passed on to the other side of the village."

This fire then jumped the Brule into Upper Michigan's Iron County. The fire spread into the Hagerman Lake district. Flames lapped at the lakeshore opposite the shore housing a resort and a group of summer dwellings. Two farms on M-73 on the way to Iron River were threatened, but firefighters kept a vigil until the danger passed. The highway was closed for several hours because of dense smoke hanging over the road.

Heavy smoke clouds descended on Iron Mountain at the height of the fires on August 7. By the next day, only a haze remained over the city. Towermen watching from their perches across the district saw only occasional puffs of smoke, not the heavy, billowing clouds of the day before.

A relic of the past. This tower near Raco in eastern Upper Michigan once served as a lookout for spotting fires. (Photo by E. Yelland)

Fires also broke out on the east end of the U.P. at the height of the dry spell. On Sugar Island, east of the Sault, rich hardwood timberland belonging to the University of Michigan

A Futile Wildcat Strike

While the fire danger remained extreme at mid-August 1933, three Delta County fire wardens quit in protest over a wage cut. The state conservation department ordered wardens' pay reduced from $3 a day to $2.50. The wardens contended that their pay remained static, while volunteers who fought forest fires under them were paid 25 cents an hour. In a 16- or 18-hour work day, common during fires, these "impressed" firefighters would make over 50 percent more than the wardens. Times were tough during the Great Depression, and disgruntled wardens' protests fell on deaf ears. The three men were immediately replaced.

❋

was threatened, as well as the summer home of former Governor Chase Osborn. A troop of 44 Boy Scouts and 70 men fought the blaze, saving the Osborn home and minimizing damage to the forest preserve.

The fires quieted down as the month wore on, yet the situation remained dire. August 1933 was the driest summer month over most of the peninsula. Marquette received only 0.80 inches of rain the entire month, a scant 30 percent of normal.

At the end of the month, several fires broke out on the west end in Gogebic and Ontonagon counties, as well as on the east end in Mackinac County. The largest occurred near Lake Pomeroy in Marenisco Township. It consumed about 4,000 acres of cut-over land in three days. By September 1, the stubborn fire had burned several lumber camps and then jumped U.S. 2 near the intersection of M-64. Men from the communities of Bessemer and Wakefield joined the 140 Civilian Conservation Corps workers already battling the blaze.

Other fires broke out in Ontonagon County. The worst were on the White Pine Road and in the Victoria Mine territory. All fires were well under control September 5, but a high wind developed and rekindled the flames. Citizens were asked to report any fire no matter how small, and to "render all assistance possible in checking them." The call was put out when heavy smoke rendered towermen virtually helpless. One towerman near Ewen reported that smoke was so thick, he could not see the bottom of his tower. The smoke billowed eastward on the teeth of a brisk west wind. Towermen in Marquette County were "virtually crippled" by the thick smoke from the west-end fires; visibility was reduced to a half mile at times.

As the first week of September came to a close, it became evident

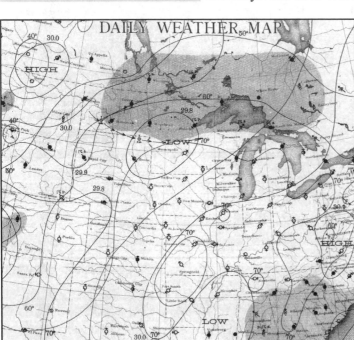

Low pressure over Minnesota early on September 8, 1933 moved across Upper Michigan bringing a soaking rain that finally ended a long, devastating fire season. (NOAA Central Library Data Imaging Project)

that the White Pine fire was set. A conservation department spokesman said the blaze had "all the earmarks" of an incendiary blaze. The main bit of evidence pointing to arson was the fact that it started on a hill. In the spokesman's view, the fire was deliberately set there so it would gain headway before being discovered.

The stubborn fires continued to flare up after a long season of drought. Up to 1,500 men continued battling the blazes. Finally, the weary firefighters received relief in the form of a heavy, steady rain on September 8.

An estimated 30,000 acres burned in Ontonagon and Gogebic Counties during the late summer of 1933. It would be the worst summer fire conditions until persistent drought set the stage for another famous fire 43 years later.

Seney 1976: Modern Michigan's Largest Wildfire

A summer drought led to a wildfire over a vast section of federal, state and private lands in east-central Upper Michigan during the late summer and fall of 1976. Dry conditions began appearing soon after the spring melt that year. April ended with only 70 percent of the long-term average precipitation. The dry weather was interrupted by a heavy, soaking rain during mid-May; it would be the last substantial precipitation for the next four months.

Summer is the time of greatest evaporation; a combination of intense sunshine and warm air dries soil and vegetation rapidly.

The summer of 1976 was dry. Vegetation, including peat and muck as deep as six feet down, became fuel for the long-lasting Seney Fire. (Courtesy of the Michigan Department of Natural Resources)

Therefore, a summer dry spell can quickly turn into a crop-wilting, fire-breeding drought. June, July and August 1976 brought only 38 percent of the long-term average precipitation. As the summer progressed, the drought worsened. Only a half inch of rain fell in Marquette the entire month of August. The compounding rainfall deficit led to tinder dry conditions across the Upper Great Lakes.

"By the end of July in 1976, we had a dangerous fire situation on our hands," remembers Greg Lusk, Michigan Department of Natural Resources (DNR) fire management officer from 1972 to 1997. "Conditions were really bad. According to information I was able to gather, the weather situation was about the same as it was during the late 1800s when the Peshtigo and Hinckley fires just burned millions of acres."

All it took was a spark to get things going. That spark was provided by a lightning strike

The "Sleeping Giant" continued to spread. In this aerial view, the smoky fire is fanned by a steady wind. (Courtesy of the Michigan Department of Natural Resources)

from a rainless thunderstorm over the Sene Wildlife Refuge in late July. On August 1, DNR airplane spotted the fire; at that time, i was a mere quarter acre in size. Normally water in the Seney swamp is "as common a black flies in June." The fire, which starte in marsh grass, would have been quickly pu out or might never have started in the firs place. But in late summer 1976, the drough had dropped the water table at the refuge . foot below average. Old vegetation, peat an muck dried out, providing an almost limitles supply of fuel for the nascent fire. It grev slowly, but continuously over the next te days.

"The Department of Natural Resources expressed their concern a number of times and i a number of ways," says Lusk. Federal Refuge personnel had no fire management plan t follow back in 1976. "Today there are very stringent regulations and rules on how to use fir naturally," Lusk explains. "They tried to get to it, but basically, it was impossible to get t it on foot." At the same time, the refuge did a test prescribed burn in another section of th refuge. "That one-acre test fire gave them no end of trouble," recalls Lusk. "It should hav been a signal as to how much trouble there would be in putting out this fire that was growin in the heart of the refuge."

The test fire eventually grew to 200 acres in size. Refuge personnel could not contain thi fire and finally called in federal forces from the Boise Inter-Agency Fire Center. By Augus 12, the combined fires had grown into one 2,000-acre blaze. It advanced to within a hal mile of state land; at that point, DNR personnel and equipment were dispatched to try t control it.

Despite all the federal and state resources that were thrown at the fire, it continued to slowl grow. Then on August 23, whipped by strong northwest winds, the fire made its largest run It burned approximately nine miles to the southeast onto state land. "This whole thing wa kind of like a 'sleeping giant,'" says Lusk. "It would lay down and smolder for just days and days and days. Then with a strong wind, it would take off."

The fire grew tenfold to about 20,000 acres by August 24. While it burned in a virtuall uninhabited area, it still made an impression on Upper Michigan residents. "There were times when you just couldn't go across the Seney Stretch because of the smoke," remembers Barrett Ludlow of the stretch of M-28 running through the refuge. His family had a cabir on South Manistique Lake well east of the fire in 1976. "The towns along the stretch were just booming," Ludlow says. He also remembers how low the lake was. "South Manistique Lake, by the end of the summer, was probably three feet down. There was nothing but sand probably ten feet past our dock." Ludlow knew there was a drought that summer, but he also thought the firefighting planes scooping water out of the lake had something to do with he low lake level. "My dad said I was crazy," he explains. "That it was just a drop in the bucket. But I think if you take out thousands of gallons every day for weeks, it will have an effect."

The fire continued moldering, and by late August, the National Guard came to help feed and transport the firefighters—a crew of men, and some women, which would soon grow to 1,000 strong. "We had crews from as far away as Texas, North

Helicopters were used to fight the fire and transport personnel quickly. (Photo by Tom Buchkoe)

Carolina, Florida," Lusk recalls. "We had help from 29 states." He explains that manpower was supplied by the feds while the DNR supplied equipment. "Kind of like infantry and armor, if you will", he reflects. "It was a pretty good match."

The fire "livened up again" on August 28. On the last day of the month, about 40,000 acres were involved. Lusk explains that a perilous aspect to the fire kept crews on alert. "There were areas in between control lines and within the fire that had not burned," he says. "That's a pretty dangerous situation for fire control folks when you have unburned fuels that can light up and take off against your control line. You can get trapped, especially in this type of situation, where the fire is laying down for days and days and days."

Despite the potential danger, there were no major injuries. Only scrapes, bumps and cuts were treated by medical personnel from Marquette, along with a few broken bones. The most serious medical condition was not caused by the fire. "I recall having to dispatch a helicopter to get a person," says Lusk. "He had an appendicitis attack. The helicopter transported him to the hospital in Munising."

In early September, the fire continued smoldering with an occasional flare-up. "On September 3, we had a massive burn-out in the northwest corner of the fire," remembers Lusk. "That increased the fire to 64,000 acres." It was officially declared contained on September 7. At that point, the fire was the largest in Michigan since 1908. Most of the loss was in the refuge; 10,000 acres of state and private property burned.

"There was a kind of demobilization," Lusk recalls. "Some staff were let go and mop up was progressing." A few days later, however, fanned by high southerly winds, the "sleeping giant" came back to life. "It was smoldering and raced over previously burned ground," he explains. Dry weather continued into September, so more peat became available to burn. "It would burn down several feet, as deep as maybe six feet down to the muck that had become so dry."

Base camp was in the process of being dismantled when the fire made a big run during a dry, windy period around September 12, 1976. (Courtesy of the Michigan Department of Natural Resources)

Airborne brands blew across M-28, the Seney Stretch, and started two blazes in the Grand Sable State Forest. One was quickly put out; the other burned out of control. "There was, of course, a retrenching," Lusk says. "The fire…quickly ran…and engulfed more than 5,000 acres that night." He took a quick relative humidity reading and found that it was in the 30 percent range at midnight. In other words, there were daytime burning conditions in the middle of the night.

To compound the problems, two other fires were burning in the Upper Peninsula while the stubborn Seney fire smoldered and flared. One was south of Ives Lake in the Huron Mountains, the other was near Hogsback Mountain, a few miles northwest of Marquette. The Hogsback fire, though small, required a continuous effort from hundreds of people. These firefighters had to work with hand tools, scratching and digging over the rugged terrain. "You couldn't get up there with a piece of equipment," explains Lusk.

Finally, fall came along with an early taste of winter (*see "Cold Waves, Cold Winters", page 141*), and the fire was permanently contained. The recalcitrant fire continued smoldering even with snow on the surface. "It did take…into January, at least, to ensure that it was out," remembers Lusk. "There were people still checking it late into the fall and early into the winter. But it was the winter snows that eventually put it out."

The final numbers on the Seney Fire were staggering. Around 74,000 acres burned involving 112 square miles and 88 miles of control line. It cost roughly $8 million to put the fire out. Lusk sums up the level of frustration felt by those charged with extinguishing it: "I used to have a full head of hair before that fire. I don't have anything left now."

May 6, 1986: Wildfires Race across the U.P.

In early May 1986, a series of fires, fanned by strong southwesterly winds, burned more than 8,000 acres, most of them in Marquette County. "Early in the day, there was evidence that we were going to have a very windy, very dry day," remembers former DNR U.P forest fire supervisor Greg Lusk. "It was related to me that there was a low level jet stream touch down in the area."

An inspection of weather charts confirms Lusk's assessment. At 8:00 a.m. local time, a strong low was lifting toward Canada from the Northern Plains. Strong southwesterly winds, about a mile above the ground, were funneled into Upper Michigan ahead of the low

enter. The very
ry air allowed
hese strong winds
o mix to the
round.

"Winds were
lowing in excess
of fifty, sixty miles
n hour," recalls
Lusk. "A number
of power lines
were blown down
nd started wild
and fires. There
were in excess of
00 fires; probably

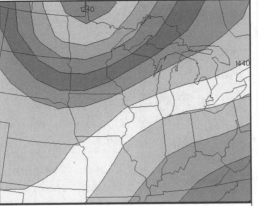

This chart is a depiction of winds at the 850 millibar level (about one mile above the ground) on the morning of May 6, 1986. Strong southwest flow over Upper Michigan is the low-level jet Lusk referred to. (Courtesy of Plymouth State Weather Center NCEP/NCAR Reanalysis Map Generator)

more...all over the U.P., but mainly in Marquette County."

One of the largest fires started near Sporley Lake in the outhern part of the county. "It was a very fast moving ack pine fire," says Lusk. "It crowned, torched and ran for everal miles."

At its peak, the Sporley Lake Fire measured 2 .5 miles wide by 5.5 miles long. DNR personnel, along with firefighters from Forsyth and Chocolay townships, worked together o evacuate people at the head of the fire, while working rantically to save structures in its path. The fire began moving toward K.I. Sawyer Air Force Base, prompting the evacuation of some 8,000 base residents from their homes.

Air Base homes were not the only things threatened that lay. "The fire itself was going right towards the sensitive weapons storage area," says Lusk. "This caused a great deal of concern among the staff at the base. They threw every resource they had available to them to keep the fire getting here. It was successfully kept from the base."

Eventually, the fire was brought under control, but it was not easy. "There is nobody in the world that can stop a crowning ack pine fire," declares Lusk. "You try to hurt it if you can. In this case, it was directed, with the help of Mother Nature, to less flammable hardwoods. The hardwoods caused the fire to come down and we were able to get a line around it."

Camps, outbuildings, boats and snowmobiles were torched

JACK PINE FIRES: THE WILDEST OF WILDFIRES IN MICHIGAN

The hottest, most dangerous wildfire in Michigan occurs in jack pine forests. The jack pine burns so hot because of the organic compounds in the tree. Once a fire starts, a waxy substance on the needles vaporizes. "A gas is given off that virtually explodes above the trees," explains Lusk. "A crowning jack pine fire [a fire moving through the crowns of trees] literally gives off the energy of nuclear weapons. We're talking flame lengths that are sixty, eighty, perhaps a hundred feet high."

Jack pine fires have ravaged Michigan, particularly the northern Lower Peninsula, many times in the past. "You can put a forest-type map on the map of Michigan," Lusk says. "It's pretty evident it has the footprints of a wind-driven fire. Lower Michigan has burned from coast to coast, probably many times within the last fifteen thousand years." The pattern of jack pine forests over the peninsula indicates fires driven by westerly or southwesterly flow. Lusk adds that the jack pine has serotinous cones—cones that pop in the intense heat of a wildfire. The tree is equipped to cast its seeds and regenerate quickly after a fire.

The last wildfire to kill a firefighter in Michigan was a crowning jack pine fire. It

A firefighter tries to keep a blaze from jumping over the road. (Courtesy of the Michigan Department of Natural Resources)

occurred near Mio in 1982. *"It started as a prescribed burn," relates Lusk. "The fire progressed very, very fast. It probably burned six to eight miles in three to four hours."* Lusk explains that the man was on the left or so-called *"cooler" flank of the fire. The intense blaze came back around, trapped and overtook him.*

by the wildfire. In one instance, the state had just sold a 90-acre tract of jack pine to a logger the day before the fire. The blaze tore through the stand valued at $71,000. "By today's standards, there were losses probably in excess of $500,000 in this very large, very dangerous fire," says Lusk.

Other damaging but smaller fires were scattered across the central Upper Peninsula. A 180-acre fire near Peavy Pond in Dickinson County damaged a cottage. At least one permanent home on County Road 581 was severely damaged in the Black River area south of Ishpeming. Four other structures were destroyed in the 500-acre fire. Another small blaze took out two buildings in Humboldt Township in western Marquette County. A stubborn fire consumed around 2,000 acres of mainly dry marsh near Rice Lake in southern Marquette County.

These were the last major fires in Upper Michigan in May 1986. It was a miracle that more did not occur as the month wore on because conditions remained tinder dry. Officially, the National Weather Service (NWS) recorded only two scant rainfalls for a monthly total of 0.06 inches—the driest May on record.

1987: Another Tinder-Dry Spring

Fires broke out again over sections of Upper Michigan in the spring of 1987; the largest resulting from arson. A lack of winter snow and a very warm, dry April led to a fire danger more critical than the year before. By early May, DNR figures showed nearly 250 wildfires, an almost three-fold increase over the same time the year before.

Fires broke out in Schoolcraft County north of Manistique on May 8 during an especially dry period. Gilbert Joy, at that time head of the Michigan Inter-Agency Wildfire Investigation Team, says a report from one of the firefighters at the scene left little doubt the fires were set. "The Forest Service had a hand crew standing by," he recalls. "They saw some smoke. They ran down there to this one fire and one of the guys looks to his right and 'boom,' another fire takes off." At least six different sites within a relatively short distance started on fire. The blazes grew into one large conflagration called the Eight Mile Road Fire.

The fire scorched more than 4,000 acres before being brought under control on May 11. Other smaller blazes brought the total acreage burned to about 5,000. Two hundred firefighters, some from as far away as Maine and Arizona, were brought in to help battle the fires, which cost $250,000 to bring under control.

These fires grew out of a familiar pattern of fires that had been going on for three years. "We had been having fire in '85, '86 and '87 in that general area—Schoolcraft County, Luce County, Mackinac County area," says Joy. "We found devices on a number of these fires." He and his team worked doggedly to find the arsonists; it took several years before arrests were made. "It takes time to establish a pattern," he explains. "You're not going to find them overnight."

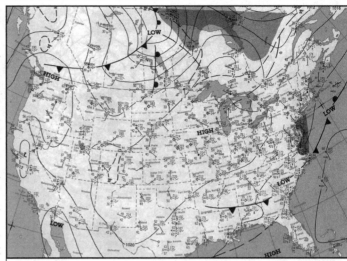

The weather map early on May 8, 1987. While the air was extremely dry, a high pressure center overhead made for light winds and kept the intentionally-set fires north of Manistique from growing even larger. (NOAA Central Library Data Imaging Project)

Finally, the perpetrators were caught. "They slipped up," says Joy. "They got over-confident. Two guys—they were arrested and they were charged and the fires sort of disappeared after that."

The fire danger did not disappear during the late '80s. The next year brought a different set of circumstances and conditions that led to more destructive wildfires in parts of Upper Michigan.

The "Stockyard" Fire of July 1988

Persistent hot, dry weather led to a wildfire near Rapid River in early July 1988. The fire, which began July 1 in grass around the site of an old stockyard east of Rapid River, consumed more than 1,000 acres and seriously injured a firefighter. Once started, the blaze spread quickly across the tinder-dry landscape and became a crowning jack pine fire, which jumped U.S. 2. The highway was then closed at the start of the busy Independence Day weekend, forcing holiday travelers to take alternate routes.

It was no holiday for firefighters or for potential victims downwind from the fire. Sixty families were evacuated from homes on the Stonington Peninsula on the evening of July 1 as the fire quickly spread toward Shelly Lake. Crews from the DNR, Forest Service and local volunteer units worked in concert to keep the blaze contained. Their efforts were successful, and the homes were saved. However, a DNR firefighter sustained serious burns.

"I was running a tractor plow on a flank of the fire," says Jeff Noble. "I was off my tractor plow to check the condition of my line and as I looked to the north, up the tractor plow line, I saw fire breaking over the line. As it got closer, it was moving like a cork screw—a vortex, breaking over the line and rolling—moving forward, towards me." The rolling vortex of fire passed over the top of him and he quickly realized his perilous position. "I got back on the tractor plow," recounts Noble, "and tried the best I could to get it out of there. I ended up abandoning the tractor and basically running for my life."

A wind gust generated by a fire-fighting plane led to a "rolling vortex" of fire that burned a DNR firefighter in July 1988 near Rapid River. (Courtesy of the Michigan Department of Natural Resources)

Noble was pulled to safety by a forest service firefighter, while the fire still rushed at them. He was transported to Milwaukee, where he spent five weeks in the burn unit of St. Mary's Hospital. He sustained second- and third-degree burns over 20 percent of his body. "I had grafting operations and stuff like that," he explains.

Noble "got back on the horse" and, as of this writing, is still with the fire fighting unit of the DNR. "I woke up the next day in the hospital," he remembers. "I said, 'If that's the worst they can throw at me, I can handle that.' I've always loved firefighting. It's something where at the end of the day, you pretty much know whether or not you've accomplished your goals for that day. And there's the whole thing about working for future generations. The work we do there on a day-to-day basis carries on into the future."

The fire that took Noble out was officially declared under control Monday afternoon, the Fourth of July—three days after it started. Officials declared that it would not be totally out until there was a three-day rain. "That was a crazy year," Noble recalls. "We were running fires around Escanaba in March; normally, we don't really start until April. The most frustrating fire is one of those that occur in drought years like 1988; especially when we get organic fuel fires…where the fire burns down beneath the surface. It's such a pain getting in there to those and eradicating every last bit of fire."

Heat and drought prolonged the high fire danger through July 1988. A quick reversal occurred the next month as record rains fell over many sections of Upper Michigan (*See "Heat Waves, Hot Summers", page 241 and "Severe Weather", page 257*).

Tower Lake Fire: May 2-5, 1999

The largest fire since the Sporley Lake Fire in 1986 began on May 2, 1999 in western Marquette County. The fire was first spotted by DNR aircraft about 4:30 in the afternoon near Tower Lake in Humboldt Township. A campfire near the lake was suspected as the initial starting point. Authorities noted that the area, popular with hikers and backpackers, was strewn with beer cans, suggesting a party had taken place earlier at the site. Once the fire started, it spread quickly and predictably.

"I looked at fire codes in our records over 30 years," explains Robert Ziel, DNR fire management specialist. "That nine-day period from April 27 through May 5 was the driest nine days in our records." Ziel says one of the striking features of this period was the humidity recovery at night. Nighttime is a time when cooling normally causes the humidity near the ground to rise. During early May 1999, this normal cycle was almost nonexistent. "The night of May 1 into May 2 the humidity recovery only got up to 46 percent," he says. "It was up at 46 for a couple of hours and it dropped immediately to 37 during the night. So you had daytime burning conditions even at night. It was pretty predictable on May 2 that a fire, if it started, would have been impossible to contain."

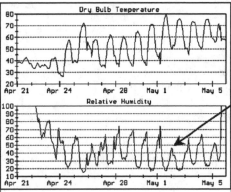

This graph shows relative humidity (vertical) over time (horizontal). The night of May 1, 1999 (arrow) showed very low relative humidity (less than 50%) at night—a time when cooling typically raises relative humidity to 70% or higher. (Courtesy of the Michigan Department of Natural Resources)

The fire spread from its position about two miles south of the intersection of U.S. 41 and M-95. Soon, it jumped the state highway and headed east, forcing the closing of the road. At least three vehicles, a mobile home and numerous outbuildings and sheds were destroyed as the flames advanced.

"The fire was a real challenge," recalls Ziel. "In that area, you have swale and ridge. You have rock, granite rock, and bluffs sticking out of marshy areas. There are also rivers running through there. It was very difficult to get any sort of a concerted effort together in controlling the fire." For instance, he explains that a tractor would be working in an area and come up to a river or stream, which would force it to back out, go around and then tie back in. While the tractor was maneuvering around the obstacle, the fire was still spreading.

At the peak of the Tower Lake Fire, 400 people were evacuated, including residents of the town of Champion a few miles to the northwest. One of the residents forced to leave his home was Dan Holsworth of Humboldt Township. It was the second time in his family's 16 years in their house that they were forced out by a forest fire. The first time was in early May 1986 (*see "May 6, 1986: Wildfires Race Across the U.P.", page 282*). Each time the Holsworth house escaped damage. "The fire probably got to within a half mile or so of us and the wind switched and turned her in a different direction," explains Holsworth. "During the first one in '86, about the same thing happened, too. The good Lord was watching over our house."

While this fire burned the area around the Holsworth residence in the central U.P., another fire started on the eastern end of the Peninsula. The eastern fire

The tinder-dry conditions caused rapid spread of the fire. It reached Highway M-95 within an hour. (Courtesy of the Michigan Department of Natural Resources)

An aerial view from the first reconnaissance flight over the Tower Lake fire at about 4 o'clock on Sunday May 2. (Courtesy of the Michigan Department of Natural Resources)

was a prescribed burn that rekindled after nine days during a period of strong winds. "We called it the 'Troll Fire,'" says Charlie Vallier, DNR fire officer in charge at Naubinway. "Because there were so many of our people from the east end at the Tower Lake Fire, we had DNR people from downstate covering our stations."

The Troll Fire, centered near Brevort, consumed 775 acres. The Tower Lake Fire burned more than 5,000 acres of predominately jack pine forest, while the Troll Fire burned in a different setting. "There is very, very little jack pine in our area," explains Vallier. "This fire here was in a red pine plantation, hardwoods and swamp. That shows how dry it was because the hardwood burned along with the red pine."

Efforts to contain both fires finally worked on May 5, four days after the Tower Lake Fire began. The primary agent in the fires' suppression was Mother Nature. A light rain began late on the 5th; over the next two days, a soaking rain put out the last embers of the fires.

CHAPTER 13

"November Gales" may be a more appropriate title for this section. From the tragic, pointless lake voyage of four Marquette pioneers in late November 1849 (*see "Pioneering on Iron Bay". page 80*) to the gale that took down the ore carrier *Edmund Fitzgerald* in 1975, November is *the* month for storms on the Upper Great Lakes.

It is no coincidence that the most infamous gales occur on or around Veteran's Day. About the second week of November, the atmosphere over the mid-latitudes of the North American continent is a "loaded gun"; rapidly increasing, intensifying cold air refrigerates over the snow cover at high latitudes. At the same time, warm weather often lingers in the far southern United States adjacent to the subtropical waters that still hold a good share of summer heat. All that is needed for a clash of air masses to begin is a strong wave of low pressure emerging off the lee of the Rockies. Arctic air moves southward, while warm, moist air is brought northward in the southerly flow ahead of the low. A mighty whirlwind can develop that may cover hundreds of miles. Air masses of vastly differing densities and heat content play about the storm, breeding the strong winds that spin around the system as well as move it along.

But these gales are not limited to November. Around Labor Day, the northern latitudes begin to cool more rapidly as the nights lengthen. Enough temperature contrast develops to begin the annual upturn in winds. Early gales can develop, like the one that marooned Henry Rowe Schoolcraft on a Lake Huron island in early September 1825 (*see "Marooned by an Early Autumn Storm", page 38*). This section will sample some of the more infamous autumn gales.

November 1869: The Wreck of the W.W. Arnold

This unusually early winter storm struck November 4, 1869 and made a mess of Marquette Harbor. The northerly gale caused ships at anchor in the harbor to crash against one another. After the storm subsided, the bay was strewn with wreckage.

About 4:00 on the afternoon of the 4th, the schooner *W.W. Arnold* pulled out of Marquette Harbor loaded with iron ore. It was commanded by Captain Beardsley and had a crew of nine on board along with two passengers. A few hours later, a storm set in with blinding snow and a ferocious northwest gale. "It was a most fearful night," read a newspaper account of the storm. "And the storm raged with utmost fury for twenty four hours." Mr. Ashman, the keeper of the light at Whitefish Point, stated that the storm at his end of the lake was "the most terrific of all others in his recollection." North of Marquette, tin sheathing was blown off the lighthouse on Granite Island.

In 1869, communication was still slow across the Upper Peninsula. Poor weather made it even slower. Sixteen days after the storm, Marquette's newspaper carried a story with the headline "Painful Rumor Probable Loss of the Schooner W.W. Arnold with All on Board." The story stated that that none of the boats passing from Sault Ste. Marie to Marquette spotted any sign of the *Arnold* and that the Sault Canal had not reported her passage through the locks.

The schooner Arnold, *like this ship pictured, was overcome by an early November gale in 1869.*

Faint hopes were still entertained that she might have somehow made it to Batchawana Bay on the east side of the lake and was disabled; but as time passed, that faint hope dissolved. In early December, a mail carrier passing through eastern Upper Michigan along the lakeshore spotted the hull of a vessel on the shore near the Two Hearted River, 35 miles east of Munising. He was prevented from getting any closer by a pack of wolves, but he got word of his find to Grand Island. Later, a search party left from there and discovered the vessel along with dead crew members encased in ice.

November into early December 1869 was exceptionally cold and stormy. An observer from Minneapolis declared that November was the "coldest...since 1857 and the cloudiest of which I have recorded." On the Great Lakes, a writer for marine interests stated, "the continued northerly storms were the most severe ever known. The loss of life and property is fearful to contemplate." In mid-November, "one of the severest snow storms...ever seen on Lake Superior" buried Marquette and vicinity under more than a foot of snow accompanied by driving winds. The early arrival of winter in 1869 prevented the retrieval of the victims of the *Arnold*. The 10 bodies were left until the next spring when a group of men from Sault Ste. Marie came and buried them on a bank above the lake.

November 11, 1883: "A Living Gale" Takes Down the Manistee

Ontonagon lighthouse keeper James Corgan put out the light for the season on December 3, 1883. He wrote in his journal he was "not sorry" to close the shipping season after a fall "fraught with disaster to shipping and life."

The first gale of the season set in at Ontonagon with rain, snow and strong winds on October 30. The blow continued through Halloween. Corgan, who took over duties at the light only a few days earlier, got "christened" during the storm; he received a thorough soaking from spray churned up

An autumn gale churns Lake Superior. (Photo by Clark Roberts)

by the northwest gale as he struggled out to relight the pier light. The storm finally abated toward evening on November 1.

The next week or so saw pleasant, even "splendid weather for this time of year." On the 10th, a "very fresh" west-northwest wind set in. The scow dredging in the harbor had to stop work because of "too much sea."

On November 11, it "blew a living gale all day." Heavy snow fell and ice formed across Corgan's walk to the beacon, while his door froze shut. Bitter cold caused ice to form and grow on the Ontonagon River "very fast." The storm finally eased late on the 12th. But the cold continued. Corgan called it "genuine Christmas weather" from November 13 through 16. A freeze hit "very hard" and the lighthouse beacon became entirely enveloped in ice, and the plate glass window on the lighthouse accrued a half inch of ice from spray off the angry lake. On the 16th, an early morning temperature of 5 degrees above zero was observed along with snow and wind.

Finally, a "splendid day" was noted on November 17. The *Joseph L. Hurd* came into port. However, the steamer *Manistee* was overdue with a load of supplies. The next few days, Corgan's entries were peppered with anxiety about the vessel's fate. The tug *Maytham*, in from Houghton, began a search and was joined by various other steamers looking for some sign of the *Manistee*.

While pleasant weather continued into the third week of November 1883, a gloom hung over the seafaring community as each day passed and the fate of the *Manistee* became more certain. On November 21, the *Maytham* picked up a pail and part of the cabin of the *Manistee*. The wreckage confirmed the loss of another vessel to a November gale, this one claiming the lives of 38 passengers and crew.

October 23-24, 1887: A "Terrible Storm" Leads to a Heroic Rescue

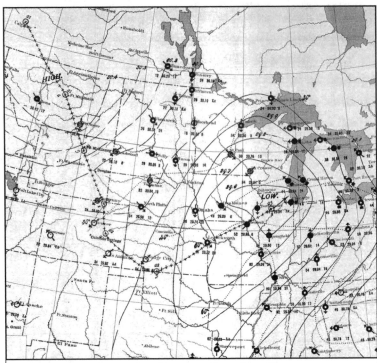

Sunday, October 23, 1887: This unusually early, cold storm system over Illinois was producing snow upstream in parts of Minnesota and Wisconsin early in the day. It later whipped Lake Superior into a frenzy and put several vessels in jeopardy. (NOAA Central Library Data Imaging Project)

A violent gale and snowstorm ravaged the southern shore of Lake Superior in late October 1887. Low pressure dropped from the Northern Rockies into the Southern Plains and then hooked northeastward into the Great Lakes. Its path just south of Upper Michigan led to a heavy, early-season snow over most of the region. Unseasonably cold weather set in with the storm. The light keeper at Ontonagon noted on October 24 that it was "freezing harder" than he had ever seen so early in the season. Later that day, a blizzard developed and continued until late the next day.

In Marquette, a "forty mile gale from the east" swung to the northeast then north, indicating the passage of low pressure to the south and east. "A terrific sea" built early in the day and by Sunday afternoon October 23, hundreds of Marquette residents braved the storm to watch the waves break over the rocks at Lighthouse Point. Snow fell so thickly along with the wind at the height of the storm that even vessels anchored in Marquette Harbor could not be seen. Rumors of disaster on the lake began flying and by late Sunday evening the first reports of shipwrecks began filtering in.

Two ships that eventually met their demise were the schooners *George Sherman* and *Alva Bradley*. Both were on the east end of the lake near Whitefish Point Saturday night when the wind began picking up. By Sunday morning it began to snow but there were no particular problems. The *Sherman* fell in with the *Bradley* and made good time along Lake Superior's south shore. Later in the day, the two vessels separated and eventually the snow came down so heavily that the captain of the *Sherman*, Nelson Gifford, could not "see a boat length ahead" of him.

Suddenly, about 12 miles from Marquette, Gifford realized he was too close to shore. He recognized the rocky beach of Shot Point ahead of him and tried desperately to maneuver his ship out of the way, but it was too late. The *Sherman* was driven up hard against the submerged rocks of the point.

Immediately the yawl, or lifeboat, was launched. While Gifford and his crew were evacuating the schooner, the main mast fell. It grazed the yawl but missed the captain and his six crewmembers. While the crew avoided getting crushed by the falling beam, the trip to the mainland was not without peril; as the boat struck the shore, Gifford was dashed against the rocks and knocked unconscious. He was dragged by his crew to safety and he recovered.

The party of seven including one woman, the ship's cook, stumbled off into the woods. The men in the party constructed a crude litter to carry the cook and wandered about in the thick snowstorm for hours until they were exhausted and almost frozen. Finally, just before dark they came upon a railroad track. After some time walking the track, an ore train came along and they hitched a ride into Marquette.

The *Bradley's* crew was not as fortunate. The schooner also hung up on the rocks, but farther offshore. The ship struck the rocks with so much force its lifeboat came loose and was lost. The 10 men became trapped as their ship split in two.

Word of the possible wreck of the *Bradley* got to Marquette from the crew of the *Sherman* and immediately a group of men from town got together and took the eastbound express. They got off near Shot Point and searched the woods, thinking that the *Bradley* crew may have been wandering in the woods, too. No trace of anyone was found and they returned to town.

The next morning the snow had subsided but a northwest storm still blew. The spars of the *Bradley* could be plainly seen from Marquette Harbor. A tug with a yawl in tow was immediately dispatched into the running sea to attempt a rescue. One of the crew shot off a gun and received confirmation that the *Bradley* was occupied when the shot was answered by the tolling of the schooner's bell. The tug's captain dared get no closer than a half mile of the *Bradley* for fear he might run up on the rocks. Crewmembers on the tug reported 20-foot waves breaking over the wounded schooner and they were compelled to return to the harbor without a rescue attempt.

Back in town it was recognized that desperate measures were called for—the Portage Canal Lifesaving Service in Houghton was contacted by telegraph. At the same time, the superintendent of the South Shore Railroad made arrangements to transport the life-saving crew and their equipment to Marquette on the night express.

By this time, the crew of the *Bradley* had spent 24 hours on the broken ship with no food, water or heat. To provide encouragement to the stranded crew as night fell, several bonfires were kept along the shore by a group of four men from Marquette. At 10:00 p.m. the express arrived with the nine-member U. S. Lifesaving crew commanded by Captain Albert Ocha along with their lifeboat.

Ocha was "an old hand at the business" (he had made another rescue in Marquette in a November storm a year earlier), "though young in years." He was "quiet, cool and daring" and there was "no braver or more skillful" a captain in the service. He was immediately briefed on the situation and in no time he and his men were in position in their lifeboat. To expedite the journey to the stricken vessel, the life-saving crew was towed by a tugboat. "It was bitter cold, a gale was blowing from the northwest and a heavy sea was running."

The schooner Plymouth *went aground in Middle Bay during the October 1887 storm.*
It spent the winter on shore but was pulled off in spring.
(Courtesy of Marquette County History Museum)

When the tug got close enough for a rescue attempt, the line connecting the boats was severed and the lifeboat "was immediately swallowed up in the blackness of the night."

Ocha maneuvered the boat through the large breakers and carefully saddled up alongside the *Bradley*. As quickly as possible the *Bradley* crew was loaded at the bottom of the lifeboat and Captain Ocha set out to find the tug. Waves splashed over the side of the lifeboat and the 19 men aboard became drenched and then ice-covered. The ten-man *Bradley* crew lying in the bottom of the boat suffered the most. The lifesaving crew rowed mile after mile in a fruitless search for the tug. Captain Ocha ordered them to row the full eight miles against the wind back to Marquette but the *Bradley* crew could no longer endure the cold, icy water at the boat's bottom. The lifesavers turned around and rowed back to the *Bradley*.

Everyone on the lifeboat boarded the crippled schooner and waited a while in the relative warmth of the ship's cabin. Then they all got back on board the lifeboat. Back on shore, the four Marquette men keeping watch devised a "land tug" and successfully towed the lifeboat to the beach. The *Bradley* and lifesaving crews warmed themselves by the fire until daybreak. In the early morning light the tug was spotted, and the lifesaving crew launched their boat to meet it. The ten-man *Bradley* crew wanted no part of the freezing, wet accommodations of the lifeboat and waited for a train to take them to town.

The Portage lifesaving crew endured a tow back to Marquette. When they arrived at the harbor they were all frozen to their seats and had to be pulled from their ice covered boat. The "Terrible Storm" of October 1887 resulted in three shipwrecks (a barge broke up on the rocky cliffs of Presque Isle) but no loss of life. This gale had a positive effect in that it moved Congress into releasing money for a lifesaving station in Marquette. The station opened in 1891.

September 19-22, 1895: "Fury of the Elements"

Not one concentric storm but persistent southwest gales pounded on the Upper Great Lakes around the autumnal equinox in 1895. A number of boats were damaged and at least two went to the bottom, one with all onboard. The stormy weather caused considerable damage on land, too.

A lifesaving crew about to make another rescue.
(Courtesy of Alger County Historical Society)

Problems started on September 19 when the steam barge *Montana* tried entering the Portage Canal on the Keweenaw. The barge had great difficulty in making the canal due to the "terrible winds and high seas rolling outside" the shelter of the canal. She successfully passed the entrance piers but immediately ran against the bank, lost her rudder and shoe and damaged her hull. The ship immediately filled with water and sank to a depth of about 16 feet. The position of the barge blocked entrance and exit to the entry for a couple of days.

In Calumet, winds blew down a wall of one new home onto another. Considerable damage was done to both structures but no one was injured. Heavy rain flooded streets in Hancock. Across the canal in Houghton, a portion of the sidewalk and railing of the bridge connecting the two cities was blown off. A number of yachts broke from their moorings at the Onigaming club and drifted to the Isle Royale sands.

Out on Lake Superior, the schooner *A. W. Comstock* in tow of the steamer *Viking* foundered off Stannard Rock. After the *Viking* released her, the *Comstock* was tossed about in the southwest gale for six hours. Finally, the crew left her in lifeboats. Another steamer, the *J. J. McWilliams*, sighted the schooner and tried to reach her but she went down in about 400 hundred feet of water before the *McWilliams* could beach the doomed ship.

The steamer did manage to pluck the crew of the *Comstock* off their lifeboats. The *Comstock* captain suffered a broken leg and had "some ribs stove in," but the rest of the crew was uninjured.

In Marquette, the steamer *Charles J. Kershaw* fell victim to the strong southwester on September 21. She went aground on a rock reef east of Marquette. Captain Henry Cleary of the lifesaving station in Marquette commandeered a spectacular rescue of the 13 man crew. He skillfully maneuvered his surfboat up to the *Kershaw* and pulled off the first nine crewmembers. On the second attempt, his surfboat was damaged and several lifesaving crew members were disabled. Undaunted, Cleary went back to Marquette, fetched his big lifeboat and with a crew partly made up of volunteers, rescued the final four crewmembers off the wrecked steamer. This lifesaving mission was called the "greatest Lake Superior rescue of the 1890s."

Finally, there would be no rescue for the *E. R. Williams*. The schooner, loaded with iron ore at Escanaba, was down bound for Toledo when it sank in Green Bay during the gale. She carried a crew of seven to their deaths.

"Freshwater Fury": The Three-Day Blow of November 8-10, 1913

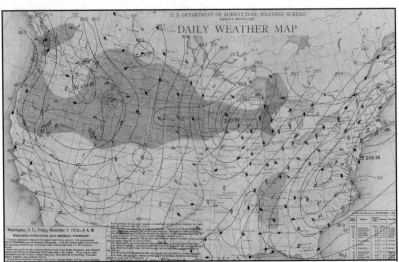

Low pressure moved on a normal course from the Northern Rockies on November 6, 1913 to a position over the Upper Mississippi Valley 24 hours later. The rogue storm then surprised even the most experienced vessel men with its behavior afterward. (NOAA Central Library Data Imaging Project)

The most deadly of the Great Lakes gales was a freak storm; a double-pronged whirling monster that blasted the region amidst the otherwise warm, dry fall and early winter of 1913. The system was born over the north Pacific and dropped southeast out of the Gulf of Alaska to a position just off the foothills of the Canadian Rockies on November 6. The low continued southeastward to near the Twin Cities 24 hours later.

In anticipation of a wind shift as the storm pulled northeast, the U.S. Weather Bureau issued a storm warning on Lake Superior for "brisk to high southwest winds…shifting northwest" the next day. This is the usual pattern for "clipper" lows originating off the Canadian Rockies; they drop into the Upper Great Lakes then turn northeastward with a rush of northwest winds behind them as they move off into eastern Canada.

Everyone, forecaster and vessel man alike, were surprised by this rogue storm. "My own forecast for November 7," stated an experienced lake captain after the gale, "was that the wind would shift from south to southwest, blowing hard from that quarter for perhaps twelve hours, then shift to northwest and blow itself out in from 24 to 36 hours."

There was never any shift in the wind once the gale set in on Lake Superior. As the primary storm crept through the Upper Lakes, wind energy continued cascading southeastward down the Rockies toward the Gulf Coast spawning the development of a "secondary" wave of low pressure in northern Georgia. This had the effect of holding a northerly wind on Lake Superior, while the Georgia wave quickly became the primary storm center by early on the 9th.

The Great Lakes low settled slowly eastward on the 8th. This movement kept Upper Michigan in the storm's cold northwest quadrant, bringing the first substantial snow along with strong northerly winds to most areas. At Escanaba, the lighthouse keeper wrote: "Wind NNW. During morning hours it increased to a severe snow storm, which raged all day."

Significant snow also fell in Menominee accompanied by winds up to 70 miles an hour. It was the earliest bout of winter that old-timers had seen in many years. Green Bay "presented a beautiful marine spectacle over the entire weekend of the 8th and 9th as the strong winds whipped the waters into a 'lashing frenzy.'"

The ferocious windstorm also brought a marine tragedy to the twin cities of Marinette-Menominee on Lake Michigan's Green Bay. The tugboat *Martin*, towing the barge *Plymouth*, left Menominee on Thursday afternoon bound for the Door Peninsula. On the evening of the 6th, the two vessels laid in the lee, or northeast side, of St. Martin Island as protection from a freshening southwest gale. All the next day the strong southwest wind continued blowing, keeping the ships at anchor. A wind shift to the northwest occurred late that night and forced the *Martin* and *Plymouth* off their anchorage.

The northwester increased in intensity, making the going difficult and dangerous. The *Martin* tried to proceed with the *Plymouth* in tow but made little or no headway against the violent gale and began taking on water. The *Martin* was rapidly losing power; coal to keep the boilers going had to be shoveled from three feet of water. As water continued rising on the tugboat, the captain, realizing he was in danger of sinking, cut the *Plymouth* free and sought refuge on the south side of Summer Island.

The barge floated helplessly. It carried a crew of seven men, six of them from the Marinette-Menominee area. Escape by lifeboat was impossible; no small boat could survive so terrible a sea. The only hope of survival laid in playing out enough anchor chain; then it might be possible to control the *Plymouth* and keep her from foundering on one of the many islands dotting the boundary between Green Bay and Lake Michigan. The chance was slim, but if the barge made it past the islands into Lake Michigan, a passing steamer might pick it up.

That chance never came. The *Martin* and other vessels searched all day on the 9th for signs of the *Plymouth*. None were found. The barge went down at the height of the storm with all hands. Its sinking added seven victims to the enormous death toll of this unprecedented November gale.

On Lake Superior, the steamer *Cornell* and its crew encountered a stormy nightmare similar to the one endured by the *Martin* and *Plymouth*. She passed out of the Sault the afternoon of the 7th, heading for Two Harbors, Minnesota. By early evening, the steamer rounded Whitefish Point. Captain Noble, the ship's master, expected to hit

The storm early on Saturday, November 8, 1913. Its winds had already taken down a barge on Lake Michigan and was menacing at least two other vessels on Lake Superior. (NOAA Central Library Data Imaging Project)

a southwest gale, but instead, noted a light southeast wind with overcast skies as the low-pressure system was still off to his southwest. By midnight the *Cornell* encountered a heavy northwest sea with a continued southeast breeze—an ominous sign that storm conditions were imminent.

A couple of hours later, with "the sea running so high that the propeller wheel was frequently out of the water," a sudden, violent wind shift to the north occurred accompanied by blinding snow. The primary low had moved east into the northern Lower Peninsula where it came to a virtual halt as the Georgia low began to take over. This atmospheric maneuvering brought the hapless crew of the steamer a three-day struggle for their lives.

On the west end of the lake, the ore carrier *L.C. Waldo* was blasted by northerly winds before they reached the *Cornell*. The vessel had loaded ore at Two Harbors on the 7th and was heading northeast into the lake when the gale hit. About midnight, a huge wave slammed into the *Waldo*, ripping off its pilothouse. The surge of water nearly killed the ship's captain, John Duddleston, who barely escaped to the lower wheelhouse.

With the steering gear severely damaged and the electrical system gone, Duddleston charted his course by oil lamp using a lifeboat compass. Gigantic seas continued pummeling the steamer and the zero visibility from the blizzard added to the danger. Duddleston had to get his vessel around hazardous Keweenaw Point, then he and his crew would have a chance at refuge on the east side of the Keweenaw Peninsula. Down below, amidst the violent pitching and swaying caused by the waves, the watchman courageously kept the engine fires stoked, which kept the propeller turning. A mountainous sea eventually broke into the cabin housing the rest of the crew. They all narrowly avoided getting washed away and sought refuge in the steel windlass house in the forward portion of the ship.

In the early hours of November 8, the beleaguered steamer rammed bow first into Gull Rock near the point. The force of the collision split the steamer in two, breaking the steam pipes in the engine room. The crew of 22 men and two women became stranded in the forward section of the steamer with no heat or access to warm clothing. They each did their best to come to grips with their circumstances—their ship was fatally wounded several miles off the mainland, while a furious blizzard continued unabated. Hypothermia and eventual death seemed inevitable.

Back on the eastern end of the lake, Captain Noble headed the *Cornell* "before the wind." At the time of the initial northerly blow, his ship was about 90 miles north of Whitefish Point, "completely covered with a thick coating of ice." After 12 hours of heavy rolling, despite the fact the engines were wide open, Noble was shocked to realize his ship was rapidly approaching the beach—the gale had moved her backwards nearly 90 miles toward the Upper Michigan shore!

Frantically, the crew sprang to action. Noble ordered one of the anchors out, then the other. All the while the vessel pitched wildly in the immense waves. With two anchors out and the engines fully stoked, Noble was able to "get her to wind" and avert a wreck on the beach. "She hung on for eleven solid hours, during which her engines never once stopped working at full speed," he recalled. "I estimate we were about a mile or mile and a half off the beach and probably five miles from the Deer River Lifesaving Station" (at Deer Park on the shore in Alger County).

The next afternoon, the wind let up a little. The crew hove up the anchors and Captain Noble headed northeast, seeking protection from the northerly gale on the north shore of Lake Superior. The lull in the winds occurred as the now primary Georgia low moved over the central Appalachians and intensified. This misleading period of relative calm led to one the great tragedies of the 1913 storm.

A view from on board the Henry B. Smith. *She was a newer, modern freighter when she hit the unforgettable storm of November 1913. (Courtesy of Superior View, Marquette)*

Jimmy Owen, captain of the 565-foot ore carrier *Henry B. Smith*, was in a hurry. This seasoned Great Lakes master usually proved easy to work with; his time was different. Rumors were flying that Owen was in the doghouse with the *Smith's* owners. Through circumstances out of his control, he had been running behind all season. He was reported to have been given the ultimatum—deliver the last load of the season on time or stay on shore next season.

So despite the stormy, cold weather, he demanded his steamer be loaded at the Lower Harbor ore dock in Marquette. The freezing, damp air caused the ore pellets to stick together and forced dock workers to crawl on hands and knees into the chute to loosen the frozen clumps. The dangerous work of loading the sleek, seven-year-old steamer with 10,000 tons of ore was finally completed late on the 9th. Owen, his confidence bolstered by the easing of the gale, decided to run for the Sault. Sailors on other boats at anchor noticed the crew members frantically rushing to finish battening down the hatches as the *Smith* pulled out of the harbor. Just as the boat left the safety of the breakwater, the second installment of the storm hit as the southern low moved due north toward Georgian Bay.

Observers on shore watched as the *Smith* heaved before the building seas. Captain Cleary, commander of the Lifesaving Station at Marquette, predicted the carrier would be back in Marquette Harbor within a few hours. Another lake captain swore that he saw the boat turn around less than a half hour after leaving the harbor. Surely Captain Owen decided to head for the relative shelter of the east side of the Keweenaw. That change in course was never confirmed; observers on shore lost sight of the *Smith* in a blinding snow squall.

Meanwhile, the *Cornell* had been chugging northeastward toward the east shore of Lake Superior when stage two of the Freshwater Fury began. The steamer was somewhere south of Caribou Island when a strong northeast wind hit the beleaguered vessel. The captain and crew battled the raging gale until early on the 10th "when a tremendous sea came over her aft." The wave, estimated at 40 feet high, flooded the dining room and the galley, breaking doors and smashing windows. The powerful surge of water pounded the dining room furniture "to kindling wood."

Back west, at the tip of Keewenaw Point on the bisected *L.C. Waldo*, the sailors broke up the interior of the cabin, the furniture and anything else wooden they could burn. One ingenious crew member devised a make-shift stove out of Captain Duddleston's bathtub and some fire buckets. The crew was divided into groups; one would take a turn warming themselves by the fire while the others would exercise to stay warm or gather more "firewood."

Amidst all the activity, one of the crew spotted a steamer. The *George Stephenson* passed relatively close to the wounded *Waldo*; close enough for its captain to get a good look at the ice-laden boat perched precariously on the rocky point of Gull Island. The *Stephenson* captain, despite his curiosity, dared not get too close to the wreck. Instead, he made his way to the comparative shelter of Bete Gris about 13 miles west of Gull Rock. This only darkened the emotional state of the stranded inhabitants of the *Waldo*; their only hope of rescue was from another boat, but the *Stephenson* passed by and kept going, leaving them to their fate.

On the exposed eastern end of the lake, the battered *Cornell* eventually found itself pushed back to the same vicinity it had been two days earlier. Desperately, Captain Noble turned the wheel "hard over to hard over" with one anchor out (the other's chain had broken and was lost) and the engines at full speed. He caught a glimpse of the beach off the Two Hearted River but kept his vessel from going aground.

Eventually, the wind let up enough to raise the anchor and move away from the beach. It also gradually backed to the northwest and the *Cornell* rode to safe port at Sault Ste. Marie. The smashed vessel with its exhausted crew limped back to the place it had left 78 hours earlier!

On the east side of the Keeweenaw, the *Stephenson* anchored in Bete Gris and a crew member was sent in a lifeboat to the mainland to report the wreck on Gull Rock. After the crew member rowed to shore, he waded through snow drifts and a driving blizzard eight miles to Delaware. There he phoned the lighthouse at Eagle Harbor, on the

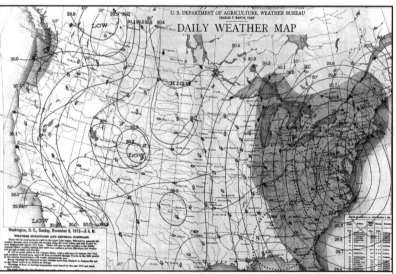

The second installment of the storm battered Lake Superior late on Sunday, November 9 when low pressure over Virginia in the morning headed north-northwestward. (NOAA Central Library Data Imaging Project)

west side of the Keweenaw, and told the lighthouse keeper about the wreck. The keeper then relayed the message to the Eagle Harbor Lifesaving Station.

The lifesaving crew took off around midnight the 9th in their big, gasoline-engine-powered surf boat. A short distance into their roughly 32-mile journey the engine sputtered and they had to put back for repairs. The motto of the Lifesaving Service stated that if a boat was in danger they had to go out. So the crew launched the smaller surf boat, powered by a tiny eight-horsepower motor. The small engine was no match against the 60-mile-an-hour gale. The crew resigned themselves to the futility of this attempt and returned to Eagle Harbor. Immediately, a couple of the more mechanically inclined crew members began working on the big surf boat engine.

Meanwhile, the Portage Lake Lifesaving Station got word of the wreck on Gull Rock. The shortest route to the *Waldo* was along the west shore of the Keweenaw; however, this way would expose the Portage Lake crew to the full fury of the northwesterly winds. Instead of this route, the station captain ordered his crew to take the long way to the Portage Entry, where they were met by the tug *Daniel Hebard*. The tugboat towed the lifeboat to Gull Rock. It took until the early morning hours of November 11 for the vessels to reach the vicinity of the wreck. The Portage crew could not risk groping in the dark for the *Waldo* so they took their boat to shelter behind Keweenaw Point until daylight.

The Annual Report of the Lifesaving Service described what the almost frozen survivors of the *Waldo* saw at the break of dawn: "They beheld in the early morning light of the 11th a grotesque, ghostly shape top a wave, poise on its crest for a moment, then sink out of sight as the wave slipped from under it and went racing on." The next time the shape came into view, the *Waldo* inmates recognized it as an ice-covered boat. One of them spotted the lifesaving emblem on its side. They were saved! A couple of the

Str. L. C. Waldo
Wrecked Nov. 8 - 11 - 1913
Manitou Island, Lake Superior.
Photo By A. F. Glaza.

The L.C. Waldo on her perch at Gull Rock, just off Keweenaw Point. (Courtesy of Superior View, Marquette)

men took axes and pounded on the ice-covered doors until they sprang open.

While the storm had moved on northeast into Canada, the lake was still rough, so it took some maneuvering but the crew managed to get 10 men off the *Waldo*. During all the excitement on board the remains of the *Waldo*, the Eagle Harbor lifesaving crew also arrived on the scene. They navigated into position as the Portage boat left and pulled the last dozen men and women off the rock. There was no hope for the *L.C. Waldo*; the mangled steamer was left to the mercy of Lake Superior.

The *Henry B. Smith* and her crew were also at its mercy once they pulled out of the breakwater. Back in Marquette, an uneasy feeling of apprehension settled over the marine community. Captain Cleary's prediction that the *Smith* would return to port did not come to pass. The storm reached its peak of violence just after the ship left. It seemed that no vessel could survive the near hurricane-force gusts that built mountainous waves and rendered the lake an awesome, frightening site.

The sailors in harbor held onto a shred of hope that the *Smith* had somehow pulled through. Cleary, interviewed by the local paper, said the *Smith* may have "forced her way much farther to the north than Keweenaw point" and sustained damage in fighting the waves. Just maybe Jimmy Owen brought his ship into some port for repairs and eventually the vessel and crew would turn up safe. He admitted there was only an outside chance this happened; most likely the *Henry B. Smith* foundered during the violent storm and went to the bottom.

Captain Jimmy Owen (far right) poses with a group of tourists at the pilothouse of the Henry B. Smith. *An easy-going, seasoned lake captain, he made an unfortunate decision to leave Marquette Harbor during one of the worst storms to ever hit the Great Lakes.*
(Courtesy of the Marquette Maritime Museum)

Communications on land finally returned to normal a couple of days later as telephone and telegraph wires brought down by the storm were repaired. *The Mining Journal* immediately received a telegram from Escanaba; a family of one of the crew members wanted to know the fate of the *Smith*. In Cleveland, the owners of the vessel sent messages asking for evidence of her demise after authorities at Sault Ste. Marie reported she had not passed through the locks.

Fears that the *Smith* was lost turned to certainty after a landlooker returned to Marquette from a nine-mile walk down the beach to the east of the city. He brought back an oar marked *Henry B. Smith*, "mute testimony" to her fate. Other wreckage, including a pike pole and pieces of the deck house, was also strewn along the deserted beach. The next spring, the body of the second engineer was found encased in a chunk of ice on Michipicoten Island, over 100 miles from where the *Smith* was presumed to have gone down. Despite several searches by marine interests over the years, including recent sweeps by a Navy plane equipped with a submarine detection device, the exact location of the *Henry B. Smith* remains a mystery.

After the worst of the blow was over, those lucky sailors who remained in port during the storm cast off and saw the shores of the Great Lakes littered with ships run aground—their wreckage strewn here and there along their way. One crew member on a Lake Superior steamer reported spotting a body floating face down with a life jacket on.

Bodies of sailors floated to shore along Lake Huron, which claimed the most casualties. The shift in wind from northwest to northeast on the 9th caught sailors by surprise. They had little room to maneuver their vessels on this relatively small lake and the result was an unmitigated disaster. Two hundred sailors perished on Lake Huron alone, making the storm of 1913 the greatest killer ever to strike the Great Lakes.

The Armistice Day Storm of 1940

"I don't remember anything as bad," declares Spar Sager of Escanaba when asked about the Armistice Day Storm of 1940. Sager, 28 years old at the time, worked for the forest service. He remembers vast tracts of eastern U.P. timber blown down during the gale. This unforgettable storm had a major impact from the Central Plains through the Upper Mississippi Valley into the Great Lakes.

The system developed and evolved in more traditional fashion than the "Freshwater Fury" of 1913. On November 10, low pressure was forming over southern Colorado, while a trough extended northeast from the low into the Upper Great Lakes. This trough cut the path that would be taken by this explosively deepening storm. The system

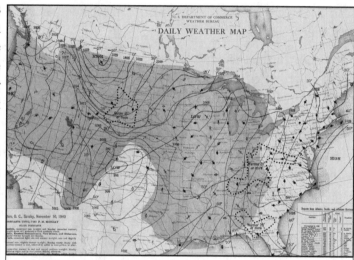

November 10, 1940: a weak low-pressure system over southeastern Minnesota was heading toward Upper Michigan, spreading a wide shield of rain across the Great Lakes. Bitter cold arctic air was pouring into the Northern Rockies, while the main storm formed over southern Colorado. (NOAA Central Library Data Imaging Project)

drifted east-southeastward into northern Oklahoma then "hooked" sharply northeastward, centering itself over central Iowa on Armistice Day morning. The southerly flow east of the low brought up warm, moisture-laden air. Meanwhile, bitter cold arctic air continued sinking into the Northern Rockies and northwestern High Plains, setting the stage for a monumental clash of air masses.

The southerly gale ahead of the storm created the most fury on the north-south oriented Lake Michigan. "The worst waves I

The top half of Jim Parent's home floated back into shore at Rapid River. A storm surge swept Parent and his home into Little Bay De Noc on November 11, 1940. (Courtesy of Delta County Historical Society)

have ever seen were on Lake Michigan during the 1940 Armistice Day storm," remembered one lake captain. "They ran all the way up from Chicago the whole length of the lake. Fifty-foot seas, I don't think anyone ever had that kind of experience." These mountainous waves, pushed over 300 miles by the wind, piled up along Upper Michigan's south-facing shore with devastating consequences.

"There was a guy by the name of Parent…that lived in a shack up at the head of the bay at Rapid River," remembers Sager. "He disappeared, shack and all." Sager goes on to explain that persistent southerly gales funneled water up into Little Bay De Noc until levels reached eight feet above normal. Jim Parent, who rented boats and worked as a fishing guide, did not have a chance; he was in his cabin as it was swept away at night during the height of the storm. The top half of the structure was washed back ashore the next day. No trace of Parent was ever found.

In Gladstone, considerable damage was inflicted by the gale. Many rowboats left in the harbor were piled together "in an ice-sheathed heap" at the conclusion of the storm. One fishing tug was pushed out of the harbor by the storm surge and left stranded on the adjacent roadway. Two other tugs were tossed almost 2,000 feet and left in the middle of a baseball diamond. A fish house, lifted from its pilings, collapsed in ruin when it was heaved on shore. Many other small boats were pounded to bits by the storm-driven waves. In town, hardware stores "did a land office business" the next several days, replacing windows blown in by the vicious winds.

Manistique had heavy rain all day Monday. A violent wind arose late in the day, while the rain turned to sleet, "then to a swirling blizzard of snow." Windows were smashed from one end of town to the other, including nine large plate glass windows at one area business. Flag poles snapped like matchsticks, and many trees were uprooted. One large maple tree smashed a car containing four passengers between Nahma Junction and Ensign; miraculously, no one was injured.

Nahma was exposed to the full fury of the southerly gale on Big Bay De Noc. Ferocious wind-driven waves battered shoreline businesses in the old lumbering settlement. Several hundred tons of coal fell into the bay after a dock collapsed. The Bay de Noquet Lumber Company was a mess after the storm. Wind and waves undermined a tramway and piles of lumber were scattered over the property. Large pine trees were blown down in the village parkway and a number of buildings sustained damage.

Farther east, the car ferry *City of Cheboygan* was pressed into service at Mackinaw City Deer hunting season was fast approaching and the vessel would be needed to alleviate traffic congestion; downstate deer hunters would soon be heading in droves across the Straits of Mackinac into Upper Michigan.

Dale Vinette of Escanaba was a self employed diver in 1940. He had just arrived home from a diving job when he got word that the *Cheboygan* needed help. He got a temporary job as wheelsman aboard the craft. "We were at the dock in Mackinaw City a couple of days," remembers Vinette. "Then they finally went into service, back and forth from Mackinaw City to St. Ignace."

The new ferry was only a couple of days into its assignment when the Armistice Day blow hit. "We came into Mackinaw City about 5:00 that afternoon," recalls Vinette. "It was blowing like hell. We started loading; we had about a half-a-dozen cars on our car deck." The ferry was so new to car transport that the railroad rails, used to transport railroad cars in a previous assignment, had not been removed.

Early morning of November 11, 1940: an already intense storm would strengthen further as it headed toward Upper Michigan, creating havoc along the Lake Michigan shore from Escanaba to the Straits. (NOAA Central Library Data Imaging Project)

As the ferry sat at the dock, the storm continued to worsen; soon the mooring lines parted. "The captain called a general alarm and said we were going to have to leave the dock," explains Vinette. "So we left the dock and went out into the Straits. We went to anchor between Bois Blanc Island and the shore just south of Mackinaw City. We put an anchor down, we're laying to the wind—the wind kept coming up and coming up and coming up." Finally, about 11:00 that night, a second anchor was put out to try and hold the beleaguered vessel in place.

Since the *City of Cheboygan* was new to car ferrying, it did not have tie downs for the automobiles onboard; that created a problem in the heaving sea. "Each car started rolling around," remembers Vinette with a chuckle. "There were only five cars, if I remember. They got smashed all to hell!"

Other ships came and anchored near the *Cheboygan*. One of them pulled within 200 feet of the ferry. It had a deck load of new automobiles on her. In 1940 and years prior, lake carriers would transport new cars on top of their cargo hatches. Even though these new autos had tie downs fastening them to the deck, the ferocious gale had its way with them. "The ship was rolling so bad," recounts Vinette, "she was rolling these cars off the deck into the water."

Lake Carriers transported new automobiles in 1940 and years prior. (Courtesy of Superior View, Marquette)

The *City of Cheboygan* waited out the storm and finally made her way back to Mackinaw City some 36 hours after escaping into the storm. The crew members were exhausted and

One of the fishermen involved in the heroic rescue of the Sinaloa *was Cecil Shawl. "Armistice Day 1940, it was about an 80-mile-an-hour wind and we were trying to keep our boats at the dock," he remembered. "They were getting crashed because the seas were coming right over the top of the dock and freezing. We lost one boat that went ashore."*

The 28-year-old Shawl and some other fishermen were warming themselves in the general store when the call for help came. A group of sailors on the stranded Sinaloa *was holed up at the back end of the ship and needed rescue. All they had to keep themselves warm was the wood they ripped from the cabin and burned in a five-gallon bucket.*

On shore, a number of people from the surrounding villages had gathered and were keeping vigil with a bonfire fueled, in part by the Sinaloa *herself. "Hatches were flying off the ship and coming ashore," recalled Shawl. "They were using the hatches to burn up in the bonfire."*

Shawl and his companions first bailed a boat that had flipped over. One of the fishermen then took that boat, while Shawl took his own and headed for the Sinaloa *through eight-foot waves. "We were in little open boats," said Shawl. "Fourteen-foot, wooden boats*

the cars on her deck destroyed. "They unloaded the cars.. that got flipped on their sides and back and forth and rolle all over the place," says Vinette. "They were all banged up They had wreckers come in and haul them away."

The *Cheboygan* then took on a full load of passengers deer hunters who had been waiting for over a day to cros the Straits. "Those hunters were lined up in their car for miles," remembers Vinette. "I think all the way t Cheboygan on the highway." The ferry limped into St Ignace and her injuries were assessed. "The ship had lot of damage to her gear. The owners noticed that th pilothouse windows had been broken. I think the captai put a stool through them because they got iced up and yo couldn't see through them," he explains.

The Coast Guard tied the *Cheboygan* up at St. Ignace It remained there until repairs were made. Vinette the got work on the car ferry *St. Marie*. He stayed on he until around November 20. Vinette would not be idle fo long; not far to the east another boat had succumbed to th Armistice Day Storm and a diver would be needed to chec her damage.

The Sinaloa, *beached in Sac Bay on the Garden Peninsula on November 12, 1940. (Courtesy of Superior View, Marquette)*

The 416-foot steamship *Sinaloa* had picked up a loac of sand on a Door Peninsula island when it encountered the gale. Captain William Fontaine decided to anchor a Death's Door Passage near Washington Island and wai out the storm. A powerful southwest gale pulled the boat helplessly northeastward after its engines failed. *Sinaloa* first went aground on the beach about a mile north of Fayette. It then broke loose and drifted until it rammed into a rock ledge at Sac Bay just off the Garden Peninsula.

Local residents gathered at the shore and kept vigil until all crewmembers were safely off the Sinaloa. *(Courtesy of J. Ervin Bates)*

Captain Fontaine and his crew of 41 men were stranded several hundred yards off the mainland in the raging storm. Fishermen from the Garden Peninsula sprang to action. Battling a treacherous sea, they took a line out to the ship and anchored the other end on a tree high up a limestone cliff on shore. On Tuesday afternoon, the first group of stranded sailors was taken off the boat. On the way back to shore, the small boat they were in capsized, but through hand-over-hand and wading, all aboard made it safely to shore. Twenty-two men were rescued in this way, while the rest were able to wait it out in a safe part of the craft until the Coast Guard arrived.

The Munising Coast Guard traveled overland and arrived at the scene about midnight the 12th. The guard set up a battery of lights, shot a line to the ship's deck and began rescue operations at about 3:00 a.m. One by one, the last of the men were taken off the vessel in a breeches buoy over the ship-to-shore line. Finally after three hours, the last man reached shore. One of the last to traverse the 600-foot line in the breeches buoy basket was the 250-pound Fontaine. He was a dead weight, pushed to near exhaustion after close to 48 hours fighting the storm. The line sagged as the skipper was pulled to shore, dragged under water much of the way. The rope held, and he along with the rest of the men, were taken to warm quarters in Garden. There they were treated for minor injuries and given food, warm clothing and "stimulating beverages."

Diver Dale Vinette was called into action as the *Sinaloa* remained marooned on her rocky perch. He was hired to inspect her for damages. "There wasn't much damage because she went up on a flat rock," he recalls. "So they got her out. It was a whole month later; they pumped her out and took her off for repairs."

that we use for setting nets and pulling nets—they have a lot of room on them."

Shawl and the other fisherman maneuvered the small vessels as close as they could to the beached sand carrier. The stranded sailors had gathered along the rail, waiting to be taken off. One by one, each sailor slid down a rope into the boats. "One of them had a wooden leg," remembered Shawl. "He had a little trouble sliding down that rope." They also had trouble navigating back safely to shore in the treacherous seas. The boat they had just bailed flipped over again. "The waves caught them and flipped it right over with all the men in it," recounted Shawl. "I'll say one thing, the state police were there and they weren't afraid to wade out in the water and help those guys reach shore."

Shawl kept his boat afloat with help from the sailors and the land-line that had been set up earlier. "I could see those big waves coming, so I'd tell the guys each time, 'hold tight—don't let this wave take us,'" he said. "So they'd all hold tight on the line. We made it in alright, and when we got to shore, the state police loaded the sailors in a boat and took them to the nearest store to warm up."

The late Cecil Shawl's family proudly displays the flag given to him and his fellow-fishermen by William Fontaine, captain of the Sinaloa, in appreciation for their heroic rescue. (Courtesy of J. Ervin Bates)

Later, the Sinaloa's captain, William Fontaine, presented Shawl and the other fishermen with the American flag that flew on the ship as a token of appreciation for their heroic rescue of his men that stormy November day.

Other vessels on storm-battered Lake Michigan were not as fortunate. A total of 59 sailors died in shipwrecks during the Armistice Day storm. On the west side of the system, a full-fledged blizzard raged. A weather forecast of flurries and colder temperatures was followed by nearly 17 inches of wind-whipped snow at the Twin Cities. Over two feet of snow piled up in the suburbs. Mild air before the storm led duck hunters into area rivers and marshes unprepared. A sudden drop in temperature accompanied by the quick-hitting blizzard created disaster. Forty-nine hunters died, many of them frozen to death in their blinds.

Wildlife and livestock also suffered. Thousands of cattle died of exposure in Iowa alone, while an estimated one million turkeys succumbed to the storm on farms from the Plains to the Upper Mississippi Valley. Near Gladstone, large numbers of fish brought up by the storm surge were left high and dry on land after the water receded. Area trappers had it easy after the gale. "The guys were trapping muskrats at the time," recalls Sager. "They were just picking up dead muskrats on the road. They got banged against those rocks and they got beaned among all the debris. You couldn't even drive that road [between Escanaba and Gladstone] for a couple of hours until they got it cleaned off."

The Armistice Day Storm of 1940 was designated as one

An unseasonably strong upper-air ridge dominated the country in early November 1975. (Courtesy of Plymouth State Weather Center NCEP/NCAR Reanalysis Map Generator)

of the major weather events of the 20th century in Minnesota. It ranked only behind the Dust Bowl years of the 1930s in terms of impact on the state. To the east, the gale remains one of the most memorable storms on the Great Lakes. The Armistice Day Storm was the last major killer until another system roared out of the southwest just one day shy of its 35th anniversary.

The Edmund Fitzgerald *Storm of 1975*

November 1975 began with record warmth across the Upper Midwest including the Great Lakes and Upper Michigan. The thermometer flirted with 70 degrees on several days during the first week of the month as a big, broad ridge of warm high pressure aloft centered itself over the mid-continent. The temperature averaged nearly 16 degrees above normal at Marquette during the first six days. Three of those days saw record highs, including the latest 70-degree reading on record—November 6.

The unseasonable warmth spread out over a large share of the country. Afternoon highs approached 80 in a wide arc from the Montana plains through the Mid-Mississippi Valley to the Mid-Atlantic. By November 7, the ridge was shoved to the East Coast as Pacific energy began working from the West Coast into the Great Plains. Colder air gradually seeped into the Rockies and spread eastward. At the same time, a strong disturbance shot southeastward out of the Gulf of Alaska toward the lower 48. It was this ripple in the flow that initiated Colorado low-pressure development late on the 8th.

The Colorado low centered itself over central Kansas the next morning. At the same time, the *Wilfred Sykes*, captained by Lake Master Dudley Paquette, was taking on a load of ore at Superior, Wisconsin. The *Sykes* was the flagship of Inland Steel Company. On the other side

The monstrous Edmund Fitzgerald *waiting to be launched in 1958. At 789 feet, she was the largest of the lake carriers at the time. (Courtesy of Superior View, Marquette)*

When it came time for the ship to be launched, she was side-launched away from the crowd. "When the Fitz started going, the whistles blew and horns blew," remembers Vinette. "She started sliding sideways. She went all the way across the slip and hit the wall on the other side. When she hit the wall, she bounced back. When she bounced back, she pushed a wall of water up over the dock. A wall of water four feet high wipes out the band. All you could see were horns and drums and folding chairs floating all over."

Vinette says the water even soaked the crowd sitting in the lower part of the bleachers. The sounds of whistles and boat horns were soon replaced by ambulance sirens. Some of the band members sustained injuries that required hospitalization. "That was quite an experience," says Vinette of the inauspicious launching of the Edmund Fitzgerald.

of the loading dock, opposite the 678-foot ore carrier wa the majestic *Edmund Fitzgerald*, the 729-foot pride of th Oglebay Norton fleet.

It was another beautiful morning, with a high, thickenin cloud cover and a light southeast wind. It looked, on th surface, like it would be another smooth down-bound tri but Paquette, who grew up in Marquette, knew better.

Author Hugh E. Bishop interviewed Paquette year after the disastrous storm. He told Bishop that weathe observation was important on his ship. "Ever since first made captain 11 years before, I had insisted that m mates monitor weather reports and record all the pertiner information on our running chart in the pilothouse," h said. His analysis of the weather situation on the mornin of November 9, 1975 told him something big was brewing "I could see from our charts that we had all the early sign that this was going to be a serious storm," he told Bishop "I saw no reason to challenge it."

The chart indicated to the weather-wise captain that th longer "north shore" route was his best and safest option. Thi detour from the usual course right across the lake followe Lake Superior's Minnesota shore through the 16-mile-wid passage between Isle Royale and the Ontario shore. Thi route would afford protection from the northeast gale h anticipated allowing hin to duck th *Sykes* behin Sleeping Giant the appendag of land tha extends nort to south int the lake nea Thunder Bay Ontario.

Paquette' analysis wa confirmed by private weathe forecasting company

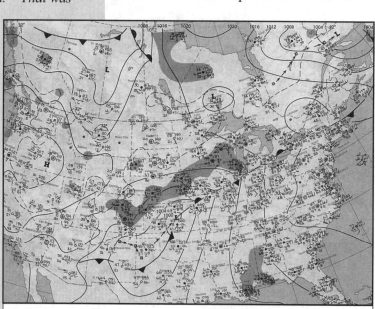

Low pressure, centered over Kansas would become a strong November gale 24 hours later. (NOAA Central Library Data Imaging Project)

tained by Inland Steel. "We really worked pretty directly with Mr. Block, the chairman of the board of Inland Steel," says Ontonagon resident John Murray. In 1975, Murray was part owner of Murray and Trettel, a weather consulting firm based in Chicago. "He called and we had put him on notice that there was a major storm brewing," he recalls. "We told him that when the *ykes* had loaded, it ought not ry to get across Lake Superior that particular day." Murray's company provided reassurance o Inland Steel that the captain

The Wilfred Sykes, *captained by Dud Paquette, was taken behind Isle Royale to wait out the storm. (Courtesy Superior View, Marquette)*

f their flagship was making the right decision in taking a route that would slow up delivery f the *Syke's* cargo. "That's a major thing for them to hold up a day—it costs them," explains Murray.

On the other hand, Captain Ernest McSorley, master of the *Fitzgerald*, had a reputation or always being in a hurry. This 40th trip of the 17-year-old vessel would be no exception; vith the last bit of the 26,000 tons of ore loaded, the boat quickly pulled away from the ock while the crew clambered to secure hatch covers. A while later, the *Sykes'* ship to hore radio picked up a conversation between McSorley and Bernie Cooper, captain of the *rthur M. Anderson*. Cooper had pulled out of Two Harbors, Minnesota, a little earlier. he two captains discussed the advisory the Weather Bureau had put out for gales on the ake. Despite the forecast and a rising wind, they decided to take the usual Lake Carriers Association down-bound route right across the lake. The men decided to travel closely just n case the storm got as bad as the forecast suggested. That way they could monitor each ther's progress and decide in tandem what to do if the seas got rough.

Paquette was not swayed by the other captains' decision. The *Sykes* was topped off and ulled out of Superior at about 4:15 p.m. The wind was just starting to pick up out of the northeast as the low-pressure storm system drifted closer.

Joe Warren, of Wakefield, was a 23-year-old deckhand on the *Arthur M. Anderson* in 1975. He remembers the northeast wind coming up as soon as they left Two Harbors. "I was the only one putting the boarding ladder away," he says. "It started blowing up in the air and I grabbed a hold of it and ended up about 10 or 15 feet off the deck. Like an idiot, I saved it nstead of just letting it go. I saved the ladder, putting myself at great risk."

As the night wore on, the storm intensified and pulled northeastward, positioning itself over central Wisconsin by midnight. As testimony to the system's intensity, severe thunderstorms

Waves crashing over the breakwater at Marquette on November 10, 1975.
(Photo by Tom Buchkoe)

broke out near the center of the storm. The *Fitzgerald* and the *Anderson* were now battling 50-knot northeast winds and mounting seas. On the lee of Isle Royale, Paquette was amazed at the size of the waves: "I've seen my share of big storms," he told Bishop. "But the seas still built to a size I couldn't believe. They materialized in giant waves that cleared the bow and washed the pilothouse windows with a gushing sound that I had never heard before."

Warren slept well in his cabin on the *Anderson* that night despite the rough weather. "always slept like a baby in rough weather," he says. "But I had never been on a ship before that went out in bad weather." He explains that he always sailed on older ships. When a big storm came up, the older ships went to anchor. He said this class of ship—steel freighters with diesel engines—did not go to anchor because it was believed they could not sink.

When Warren went to breakfast the next morning, he learned that one of the wheelsman barely escaped with his life the night before. "A wave came up over the observation deck. He went outside and if he hadn't grabbed onto the hand rail, he would have been washed overboard."

The storm worsened during the day and Captains McSorley and Cooper decided to head for protection from the northeaster on Canada's north and east shore. The decision would have been a good one had the storm passed to the south of Lake Superior; then the northeast wind would have gradually backed northerly and eventually northwesterly, giving the ore carriers a tail wind to Sault Ste. Marie. In reality, the decision was disastrous; the storm's actual path would eventually expose them to the worst this November gale had to offer.

Back on land, Jim Heikkila and his wife left Calumet bound for St. Paul, Minnesota. "left Calumet and it was fine," Heikkila remembers. "I probably had about normal time going over to Ironwood. From Ironwood to Duluth is where we had the problem." The problem was a heavy snowstorm on the northwest side, or cold sector, of the storm. "As we went across Wisconsin, we ended up with a flat tire...and I had to change it right there in the snow," says Heikkila. "Then my electrical system flooded out on me. By sitting there long enough the engine heat dried out the coil."

Heikkila finally made it to Duluth through snowpacked, drifted roads. "On the freeway from Duluth to St. Paul I only drove about 35 miles an hour," he remembers. "All you could see was from one delineator to another." He goes on to explain that highway delineators or markers are 250 feet apart; that is how poor the visibility was at the height of the storm.

Despite that and the snow-
filled roads, trucks kept
passing Heikkila. The truck
drivers probably felt their
added weight would help them
stay on the road; that plan did
not work well: "We counted
24 trucks in the ditch on our
way," recalls Heikkila. A trip
that normally took about three
hours took between six and
seven hours to complete.

The storm center passed near
Marquette early on Monday,
November 10 and kept a
steady northeast movement
while intensifying. The wind
shifted northwest, then west,

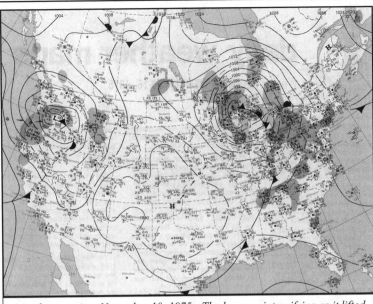

Monday morning, November 10, 1975: The low was intensifying as it lifted northeastward. (NOAA Central Library Data Imaging Project)

as the low lifted north of Lake Superior and headed toward James Bay. The wind shift
found Paquette and his ship tucked safely on the windward side of the lake. The *Fitzgerald*

and *Anderson*, however, were
in trouble; they were placed on
the leeward side with a couple
hundred miles of open water
for the wind to churn before
reaching them.

"At lunchtime, the wind
started picking the water off
the lake in sheets," recounts
Warren. "It was just literally
tearing the water off." A
while later, one of Warren's
shipmates took him up to
an observation point several
levels up to look out a porthole.
Warren couldn't believe what

*Waves washing over a freighter during a Great Lakes storm.
(Courtesy of Superior View, Marquette)*

he was seeing. "A wave was coming up over the observation deck—the deck just below
the pilothouse," he recalls. "It went over the deck crane, which was parked on the forward
end and came back, and when it hit the aft end, it shook the whole ship. You could hear the
lifeboats getting smashed to smithereens."

While Warren was watching the spectacle from his observation porthole, the ship
continued to pitch and roll violently. "It kept getting worse and worse," Warren recounts.
"The ship was making horrific noises. In the bowels, deep down in the ship it was just,

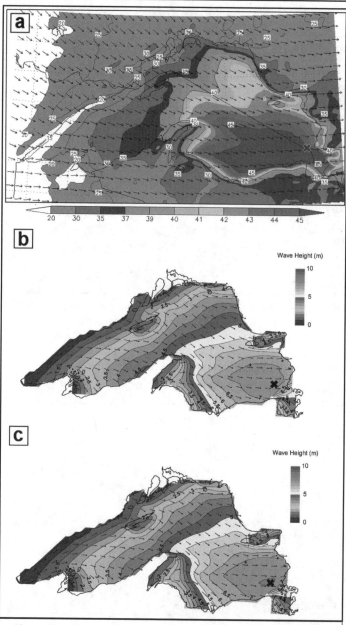

Charts depicting modern computer output using actual data from the Fitzgerald storm. All three pictures show an "x" where the boat sank. Figure (a) depicts winds at 7 p.m. The largest shaded area shows sustained winds at 45 knots (52 m.p.h.) or greater. Figure (b) and (c) shows wave heights in meters at 7 and 8 p.m. respectively. Note the 7.5 meter-wave (24+ feet) over the spot where the Edmund Fitzgerald sank. (Courtesy Tom Hultquist, National Weather Service, Marquette)

BRAAAAH, WRAAAAAH—was just the unbelievable sound of steel bending."

Later, the *Anderson's* chief engineer came up and just then, the *Fitzgerald* could be spotted going by on the *Anderson's* starboard side. "I will never, never forget what he said," says Warren. "He said, 'That old man [referring to McSorley] is either going to put 'er on the bottom or he's going to tear the engine out of 'er.' At least Cooper, my captain, checked down."

Warren explains that Cooper had slowed the *Anderson* down to the point where they were just maintaining headway, while McSorley blew by them. He says that slow and easy was the safest thing to do under those conditions. Even then, their ship was under tremendous stress. "I had never seen the flex and the bend or heard steel groan in such a horrific way. The waves had turned into mountains," he remembers. "The seas were running so big, if you're just running like in normal weather, you're taking on more water, you're doing a lot more twisting of your ship."

Modern computer models using actual data from the storm clearly show the *Edmund Fitzgerald's* perilous position. "It ended up in precisely the wrong place at the absolute worst time," explains Tom Hultquist, Science Operations Officer at the National Weather Service (NWS) in Marquette. Hultquist used a wind and wave model to show that the wind reached its peak of intensity while the waves reached their highest point on the eastern end of the lake at around 7:00 in the evening on November 10, the time McSorley was making a run to bring his crippled vessel into the relative shelter of Whitefish Bay.

arlier, the *Fitzgerald* had begun taking on water and developed a list. She had also lost her ıdar and sustained some top-side damage.

On land, as testimony to the severity of the blow, the NWS at Sault Ste. Marie had major roblems trying get off its weather balloon at the customary 7:00 p.m. launch time. A large, elium-filled balloon is sent up with an instrument called a radiosonde attached to it. This evice radios back information on wind, temperature, moisture and pressure at different :vels of the atmosphere.

John Wallis was in charge of the office at that time, but he was not at work. "November 10th ⁄as the last day of a ten-day vacation I took to help my wife with our newborn daughter," he :members. He was called into work anyway; the technicians back at the office were having roblems getting a launch off in the increasing wind.

Wallis worked with them in a second attempt but they were still unable to get the balloon p. "The third time we had this guy from Alaska," recalls Wallis. "He had experience with igh winds. He got it up, and as the balloon rises, the wind catches the instrument and blows : up into the balloon and POP!" The radiosonde punctured the balloon and the device came rashing to the ground. That night there were no upper-air measurements from Sault Ste. ⁄Iarie.

Back on the lake, Warren and his crewmates felt small. "We looked like a canoe on those nountains of water," he recalls. "When you'd go down those mountains, you wondered if we ⁄ere going to come up. It wasn't fun anymore. I talked to the Guy Upstairs. I said, 'Calm it ike you did way back when, anytime.'" After his prayer, the waves were still ferocious, but Varren felt a sense of peace and went down to his cabin, read a little and then actually fell sleep. When he woke up, he heard a commotion outside his cabin. "The guys were cursing ut in the companion way," he explains. "I went outside and said, 'What the hell's going ⁄n?' They said, 'The Fitzgerald sank and we're going back out to look for survivors.' The

guys were so upset because ve had made it around the ⁊oint into Whitefish Bay and ⁊ow we had to go back out in ough weather."

The seemingly impossible ⁊ad happened. A modern steel ⁊reighter, one of the largest on ⁊he lakes at the time, had gone ⁊own without a whimper. "I ⁊ut on every stitch of warm ⁊lothing I had," remembers Warren. "It was so cold, I ⁊ould only stay out for 10, ⁊5 minutes at a time." He ⁊nd another crewmember ⁊ook turns shining a light

A lifeboat, twisted and bent from the force of the sinking, washed up on the Canadian shore just east of the wreck. It is on display at Valley Camp Museum in Sault Ste. Marie. (Photo by E. Yelland)

onto the lake, looking for survivors or some sign of the ore carrier. "We found a lot of the wreckage—from life-ring buoys to different stuff, but that was it." There was no sign of the *Fitzgerald's* 29 crewmembers.

The next year, Gordon Lightfoot's song about the disaster became one of the top pop hits of the year. The haunting ballad etched the tragic last voyage of the ore boat into our collective memories and brought national attention to Lake Superior and its infamous "Gales of November."

As for Warren, he completed the 1975 boating season on the *Anderson*. This storm changed the way things were done. "After that, trust me, when a gale came up we dropped the hook," he says, explaining that they would go to anchor when there was a gale warning. "We dropped the hook because they found out the big ones could sink."

November 10, 1998: The Fitzgerald Storm Clone

Another mighty gale tore across the Upper Great Lakes 23 years to the day after the *Fitz* sank. This system was actually stronger than the Fitzgerald Storm and tracked farther west, similar to the Armistice Day Storm of 1940.

Like the days leading up to the 1975 gale, mild weather lingered during late fall of 1998. October averaged some 4 degrees above the long-term normal. November cooled down a little, but still came in close to the seasonal average. The lingering warmth waited for an energetic wave that dropped into the lower 48 from the Gulf of Alaska—a familiar breeding ground for November storms. The wave gradually deepened, as a building ridge aloft over the eastern Pacific dropped more energy into it. The wave emerged out onto the Southern Plains on November 9; here it met the last of fall's mild air and explosive deepening ensued.

The morning of November 10, 1998: Exactly 23 years after the loss of the Fitzgerald *another November gale had wound up over the Upper Midwest. It was already a stronger low-pressure system than the one that churned up Lake Superior the day the Fitz went down. (NOAA Central Library Data Imaging Project)*

Loren Graham remembers the storm well. Graham and his wife bought and renovated the lighthouse on Grand Island in Lake Superior, just off Munising. They maintain it as a primarily warm-season home. "Pat and I decided to spend Thanksgiving in the lighthouse," says Graham, "always a risky time of year to go to such a remote spot. I went first and Pat was to come later. As I pulled into the backyard of the lighthouse, I heard on the radio an announcer say, 'a storm of Biblical proportions is striking the U.P.'"

The storm, centered over northern Iowa early on Tuesday, November 10, displayed all the symptoms of a classic November gale. Heavy snow began falling on its western flank in the colder air, while rain and thunderstorms broke out in the warmer air to the system's east. As the

An aerial view of the north Lighthouse on Grand Island, the Graham's summer residence. (Photo by Bill Jorns)

pressure gradient around the low pressure increased, winds began to pick up over the Upper Great Lakes.

"The wind was howling," recounts Graham. "I ran outside and began closing the shutters. I thought, 'I am the only person on Grand Island, and it looks like I am going to die on it.'" Before he could close all the shutters, the wind blew out the glass on one of the windows. He closed the shutter over the shattered window and ran inside. Immediately, he noticed water coming in through the cracks in the shutter around the window—lots of water. He ran into the bathroom, ripped the shower curtain off the pole, and quickly nailed it up over the broken window.

Since there was no central heating system in the lighthouse, Graham decided to light a fire in the fireplace, which turned out to be a mistake. "The wind was blowing straight down the fireplace," remembers Graham, "and immediately the lighthouse began filling with smoke." He had no choice but to turn to the wood stove in the kitchen as his sole source of warmth. Graham survived, but spent an uncomfortable night sleeping in the kitchen, getting up every couple of

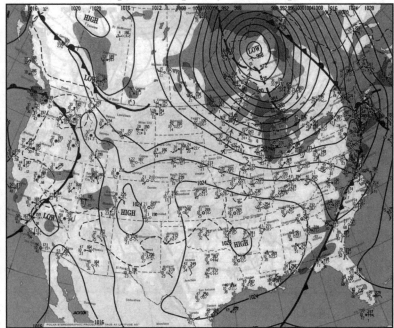

Early on November 11, 1998, the record-breaking storm was already weakening and heading for Hudson Bay. (NOAA Central Library Data Imaging Project)

hours to fill the stove with wood.

A number of other U.P. residents joined thousands downstate in spending Tuesday evening in the dark. High winds knocked out power to nearly 500,000 Michigan homes. Utility crews from as far away as Virginia were called in to help restore electricity. At least 144,000 residents remained in the dark 24 hours later.

As the storm lifted toward the west end of Lake Superior, the gale over Upper Michigan reached a crescendo. Sustained winds of 82 miles per hour were reported on Mackinac Island with a gust to 95. That gust was one of the highest ever recorded in the state of Michigan. In St. Ignace, a trooper reported that it felt like he was "in a hurricane." Trees and other debris were blowing around the southeast tip of Upper Michigan. Farther west significant beach erosion resulted from the strong southerly component to the wind. Areas from Manistique west were hardest hit.

This November gale meted out its worst punishment on the Lake Michigan side, similar to the Armistice Day 1940 blow. In contrast, while the *Fitzgerald* Storm was much weaker it lashed the Superior side, particularly the eastern end, the hardest. The '98 gale moved farther west, resulting in a more southwesterly component to the wind after the storm's passage. In 1975, the west-northwest wind after the storm's passage over the central portion of Lake Superior resulted in a funneling of wind over the ridges of the Huron Mountains and the Keweenaw Peninsula. This funneling effect brought ferocious wind and waves to the east end at the time the *Edmund Fitzgerald* was making a desperate attempt for the shelter of Whitefish Bay (*see "The* Edmund Fitzgerald *Storm of 1975" page 311*).

Nevertheless, the 1998 storm was a record breaker. The barometric pressure plunged to 28.55 inches at Duluth, while farther south, Austin registered 28.43 inches, a Minnesota record for lowest pressure. Record snowfall buried portions of the eastern Dakotas and Minnesota; however, this storm did not usher in true winter to Upper Michigan. Mild weather lingered through the balance of 1998. It would take until just before Christmas for serious winter cold and snow to set in.

No ships were caught on the Great Lakes during this record-breaking storm. The Lake Masters had learned their lesson 23 years earlier.

EPILOGUE

This book just scratched the surface of weather history in Upper Michigan over the last few hundred years. Many more weather events have slipped through the cracks—for now. I am waiting to hear about them. That is how this book was put together. For example, I gave a talk in Iron Mountain and afterward, a member of the audience, Myrna Ward, told me the story of her father and 19 other people who became stranded on a floating sheet of ice off Skanee in March 1941. I interviewed Larry Wanic and Lyn Veeser, long-time weather observers, about the events they remember and was led to Alvin and Claudia Lauren, who lost their home in one of the most violent tornadoes to ever hit the U.P.

What I have found in uncovering these events is the awesome variability in Upper Michigan weather from season to season and from year to year. One of the coldest winter periods of the 20th century occurred in 1936. It was immediately followed by the most intense heat wave on record that summer. What may be the harshest winter ever, in 1856-57, was followed by one of the mildest the next year.

As for trends, several stand out. The late 1800s, particularly the decades of the '60s through the '80s, were cold with the glaring exception of the snowless winter of 1877-78. The decade of the 1930s showed spastic variations, from very warm, to frigid. Upper Michigan endured a period of prolonged drought on the northeastern fringe of the Dust Bowl in the early portion of the decade and was buried under a legendary snowstorm near its close.

Two recent trends are noteworthy. First, snowfall, especially near Lake Superior, has increased. On the Keweenaw, the increase first appeared in the early '70s, reached a peak during the late-'70s into the mid-'80s, then showed a slow decline. The latter portion of the '80s through the first several years of the 21st century still showed higher snow totals than the years preceding the increase. In north-central Upper Michigan, record snow years occurred three times in seven years from the mid-'90s through the beginning of the new century. While old-timers might argue that there were bigger storms and deeper snow cover back in their day, looking at the record, there is no denying that more snow has fallen over recent years.

The second trend is also undeniable. "There's no question that we've been in a warming trend for the last 50 years," states Jon Davis, a Chicago-based long-range forecaster for energy concerns and commodities. "It kind of started in the fifties, then you cooled a little bit in the sixties and parts of the seventies, then you've really warmed up from that point on. Unquestionably, we've warmed, and not only here, but everywhere."

Davis uses this information when putting together a seasonal forecast. He catalogs the variables that he and his team feel will be keys in driving the weather over the season in question. One of the variables he now uses regularly is what forecasters call "trend." In this case, it is the warming trend over the last half century. "You have to add that warming component into a seasonal forecast," he explains. "If we think all the variables equal each other out, then trend would point us in the warm direction."

As to why we are warming, that question crosses the line into our greatest climate debate. "I don't think there is any question that human activity has caused some of this warming," says Davis. "The data is so overwhelming." But this does not answer the question to his satisfaction. Natural factors are responsible for warming, too. "Over the last ten years, there's been really sparse volcanic activity," he explains. Simply put, the earth's greatest polluters, volcanoes, have been quiet. "If you look at aerosol projection globally [the material volcanoes throw into the atmosphere], they're about as low as they've ever been," he explains. As we have seen, volcano debris, pushed high into the atmosphere, blocks sunlight and results in global cooling. Davis also says the ocean has put more warmth into the atmosphere over the last 20 years or so. "We've trended to an environment with more El Nino events [the warming of the equatorial eastern Pacific]. That means more warmth over the long haul."

When asked what he believes is the most important factor in this warming, he says he has to be honest. "I have no idea," he states candidly. "That's a question that nobody can answer. Is this human factor ten percent of the equation's influence or is it seventy?"

If you pay attention to the news, it would appear that man's activities are the main— possibly the only—catalyst in this warming and that the planet will continue to warm with catastrophic consequences. On the other hand, could it be that just like our ancestors in the Middle Ages who thought the sun rotated around the earth, we now think we are so important that we are the primary influence on this planet's climate?

Climate is a very complex phenomenon to observe, let alone forecast. A plot of temperatures over time, say thousands of years, goes up and down in irregular fashion. Many of these naturally occurring fluctuations are poorly understood. Furthermore, looking at just a 10-year or even a 50-year snapshot of the climate will not help answer the questions as to why we are warming and if we will continue to warm. One climatologist likens our observation of climate to an ant watching the hands of a clock, while perched on the hour hand. We cannot know exactly where we are, let alone where we are headed.

No matter where we are on the climate continuum, weather in Upper Michigan will continue to fascinate and frustrate us. Fascinate us because of its extraordinary variability over time and space, and frustrate those who expect the weather over this 16,500 square-mile peninsula nestled between the Great Lakes to behave a certain way. The weather will do what it wants to do, and continue to provide us with many more stories to tell.

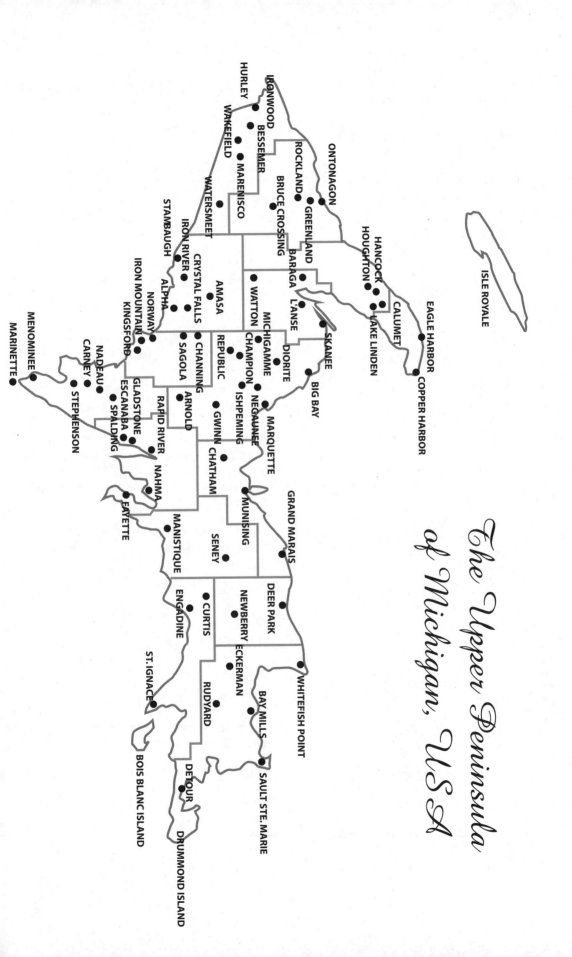

The Upper Peninsula
of Michigan, USA

BIBLIOGRAPHY

FIRST RECORDED STORIES OF WEATHER IN THE REGION

Thirty Years with the Indian Tribes on the American Frontier
With Brief Notices of Passing Events, Facts and Opinions
A.D. 1812 to A.D. 1842
Henry Rowe Schoolcraft
Philadelphia: Lippincott, Grambo & Co. 1850

Superior
Under the Shadow of the Gods
Barbara Chisholm, Andrea Gutshe, Russell Floren
Lynx Images Incorporated
Toronto, Canada 1999

PART I
CHAPTER 1 - FIRST EUROPEAN EXPLORERS IN THE LAKE SUPERIOR REGION

Jacques Marquette, S.J.
1637-1675
Joseph P. Donnelly, S.J.
Loyola University Press 1968

Marquette's Explorations
The Narratives Reexamined
Raphael N. Hamilton, S.J.

Missionary Labors of Father Marquette, Menard and Allouez in the Lake Superior Region
Rev. Chrysostom Verwyst, O. S. F.
Hoffman Brothers, 1886

Amasa, Michigan
1891-1991
Amasa-Hematite Centennial Corp.
Hematite Township, Amasa, Michigan 1992

Global Temperature Patterns in Past Centuries: An Interactive Presentation
Mann, M.E., E.P. Gille, R.S. Bradley, M.E. Hughes, et al
Earth Interactions: Vol. 4, Paper 4, November 2000

The Little Ice Age
How Climate Made History 1300-1850
Brian Fagan
Basic Books, New York 2000

Solar Forcing of Climate Through Changes in Atmospheric Circulation
Climate Change Institute, University of Maine
http://www.climatechange.umaine.edu/Research/Contrib/html/19.html

National Vital Statistics Reports, Vol. 51, No. 3; December 19, 2002
Table II

CHAPTER 2 - ALEXANDER HENRY'S ADVENTURES IN THE LAKE SUPERIOR REGION

Alexander Henry's Travels and Adventures in the Years 1760-1776
Edited with historical introduction and notes
By Milo Milton Quaife
The Lakeside Press, Chicago 1922
http://www.rootsweb.com/~wibayfie/michelcadotte.html
information on Jean Baptiste Cadot, fur trader

Massacre at Mackinac-1763
Alexander Henry's Travels and Adventures in Canada and the Indian Territories Between the Years 1760 and 1764
Edited by David A. Armour
Mackinac Island State Park Commission, Mackinac Island 1966

Mike McCollum, oral history interview, April 2004

CHAPTER 3 - WEATHER EVENTS OF THE EARLIEST AMERICAN SETTLEMENT: 1820s-1830s

Thirty Years with the Indian Tribes on the American Frontier
Henry Rowe Schoolcraft

State of Michigan Department of Military and Veteran Affairs
http://www.michigan.gov/dmva/0,1607,7-126-2360_3003_3009-16972--,00.html

Early American Winters
Volume II 1821 to 1870
David M. Ludlum
American Meteorological Society
Boston, Massachusetts 1968

Kitchi Gami
Life Among the Lake Superior Ojibway
Johann Georg Kohl
Originally published: London: Chapman and Hall, 1860
Minnesota Historical Society Press 1985

A Canoe Voyage up the Minnay Sotor; Vol. 1
G. W. Featherstonhaugh, F.R.S., F.G. S.
Richard Bentley
New Burlington Street, London 1847

CHAPTER 4 - WEATHER OF THE EARLY MINING BOOM: 1840s-1850s

Burt, William: Biography of William Austin Burt; Marquette County History Museum, "History of the Upper Peninsula of Michigan"
Chicago: The Western Historical Company, A. T. Andreas, Proprietor 1883

Call it North Country, The Story of Upper Michigan
John Bartlow Martin
Wayne State University Press Detroit
Alfred A. Knopf, Inc. 1944

Michigan State University
Department of Geography
http://www.geo.msu.edu/geo333/burt.html

This Ontonagon Country
James K. Jamison
Book Concern
Hancock, Michigan 1948

"Time by Moments Steals Away"
The 1848 Journal of Ruth Douglass
Robert L. Root
Great Lakes Books, Wayne State University Press Detroit 1998

The Honorable Peter White
A Biographical Sketch of the Lake Superior Iron Country
Ralph D. Williams
The Penton Publishing Co., Cleveland 1907

Great Lakes Shipwrecks and Survivors
William Ratigan
Wm. B. Eeardmans Publishing Company, Grand Rapids, Michigan 1960

Virtual American Biographies - Douglas Houghton
http://www.famousamericans.net/douglashoughton/

The Geological Report on the Copper Lands of Lake Superior Land District, Michigan
Foster and Whitney 1850

Massacre at Mackinac-1763
Alexander Henry's Travels and Adventures in Canada and the Indian Territories Between the Years 1760 and 1764
Edited by David A. Armour
Mackinac Island State Park Commission, Mackinac Island 1966

Historical Review: Lake Superior Copper Mining Industry
Horace J. Stevens
Houghton, Michigan 1899

Some Incidents of Pioneer Life in the Upper Peninsula of Michigan
John Harris Forster
From Michigan Pioneer and Historical Collections
Volume 17, 1890 Pages 1-14

Lake Superior: Its physical characteristic, vegetation and animals compared with those of other and similar regions.
Louis Agassiz with narrative of the tour by J. Elliot Cabot and contributions by other scientific gentlemen
Boston, Gould, Kendall and Lincoln 1850

Beyond the Boundaries
Life and Landscape at the Lake Superior Copper Mines, 1840-1875
Larry Lankton
Oxford University Press: Oxford New York 1997

J.M. Longyear Research Library
Marquette County History Museum
977.491 H26h Harvey, Charles, Thompson
re: Pioneer Railway Promoting

Early American Winters
Volume II 1821 to 1870
David M. Ludlum

CHAPTER 5 - THE SNOWSHOE PRIEST
The Diary of Bishop Frederic Baraga
First Bishop of Marquette, Michigan
Edited and Annotated by Regis M. Walling and Rev. N. Daniel Rupp,
Translated by Joseph Gregorich and Rev. Paul Prud'homme, S.J.
Great Lakes Books, Wayne State University Press Detroit 1990

The Apostle of the Chippewas
The Life of the Most Rev. Baraga, D.D.
Joseph Gregorich
The Bishop Baraga Association
Chicago, Illinois 1932

Historic Michigan
Michigan Pioneer and Historical Collections, XVII 332-345
John Harris Forster

Bishop Baraga Letters to the Leopoldine Society
Bishop Baraga Archives, Marquette, Michigan

American Catholic Quarterly
Volume XXII

History of the Diocese of Sault Ste. Marie and Marquette
A.J. Rezek, 1906

Kitchi Gami
Johann Georg Kohl

Early American Winters
Volume II 1821to1870
David M. Ludlum

PART II

CHAPTER 6 - COLD WAVES, COLD WINTERS

Historical Highlights, Radio Talks
Compiled by Kenyon Boyer
J.M. Longyear Research Library—Marquette County History Museum

The Mining Journal
Marquette, Michigan
January, February and March 1875
November, December 1883, Jan. - Mar. 1884

Ontonagon Lighthouse Journal
Firesteel Publications
Ontonagon, Michigan 2005

The Norway Current
Norway, Michigan
February and March 1885
January and February 1899

The Escanaba Daily Press
April 1885

The Iron Mountain Press
January and February 1899

DVI (Volcanic Dust Veil Indices)
Climatic Research Unit
University of East Anglia
Norwich, United Kingdom

The Iron Port
February 1899
Escanaba, Michigan
Courtesy: Delta County Historical Society

John Bohnak, oral history interview, April 2004

Richard Wright, correspondence, April 2004

Don Michelin, oral history, March 2004

Greg Albrecht, oral history, June 2004

Bud Clarke, oral history, August 2004

John Korhonen, oral history, June 2005

CHAPTER 7 - SNOWSTORMS, SNOWY WINTERS

Journal of the Lighthouse Station at Ontonagon, Lake Superior
Ontonagon Historical Society Archives
April-May 1857

Diary of Lewis Whitehead, Father of the Menominee Range 1833-1908
Mid-Peninsula Library Federation. Iron Mountain, MI 1970

The Mining Journal
Marquette, Michigan, November and December, 1869

The Escanaba Daily Press
Escanaba, Michigan
Courtesy: Delta County Historical Society
Jan. 1938, Mar. 1939, Apr. 1958

The Ironwood Daily Globe
Ironwood, Michigan

The Iron Mountain News
Iron Mountain, Michigan

The Herald-Leader
March 1959, April 1979, December 1995
Sault Ste. Marie, Michigan

The Evening News
Sault Ste. Marie, Michigan

The Daily Mining Gazette
Houghton, Michigan
Dec. 1979, Jan. 1979

Menominee Herald-Leader
Menominee, Michigan

The American Weather Book
David Ludlum

L'Anse Sentinel
Thursday, Mar. 20, 1941

"John is My American Name"
The Portrait of Our Grandfather
Lori Ward Hamm
1982

The Ice Flow
Edmund LeClaire
March 3, 1969

Arvon Township
1871-1971
The First One Hundred Years
Centennial Commemoration—Skanee, Michigan

Myrna Koski Ward, written reminiscence

Margaret Mullins, oral history interview, May 2004

Cliff (Kip) Waters, oral history interview, May 2004

Marguerite (Midge) Waters, oral history interview, May 2004

Kathy Lundin, oral history interview, May 2004

Fred Rydholm, oral history interview, October 1999

Marilyn Baker, correspondence, May 2004

ard Bess, oral history interview, October 2003

an McCollum, oral history interview, March 2004

Richard Wright, correspondence, April 2004

arry Wanic, oral history interview, March 2004

yn Veeser, oral history interview, March 2004

oe Freeman, oral history interview, April 2004

wen (Obie) O'Brien, oral history interview, October 2004

im Heikkila, oral history interview, October 2004

Paul Lehto, oral history interview, September 2004

arrett Ludlow, oral history interview, April 2005

om Boost, oral history interview, January 2005

3eth Hoy, oral history interview, September 2005

5teve Asplund, oral history interview, January 2005

om Buchkoe, oral history interview, April 2005

Mary Baginski, oral history interview, July 2005

om Ewing, oral history interview, August 2005

Ken Eagle, oral history interview, August 2005

John Wallis, oral history interview, August 2005

Jim Hutcheson, oral history interview, March 2005

5teve Brown, oral history interview, October 2003

Alek Bohnak, oral history interview, April 2005

an Bohnak, oral history interview, July 2005

Ken Michels, oral history interview, December 2004

Jeff Howell, oral history interview, May 2004

Judy Johnson, oral history interview, January 2006

CHAPTER 8 - LATE SEASON SNOWS

Escanaba Daily Press

Menominee Herald-Leader
May 1990

The Daily Mining Gazette
May 1954

The Mining Journal

June 1945, May 1947, May 1960
Cliff (Kip) Waters, oral history interview

Spar Sager, oral history interview, March 2004

Helen Lepola, history correspondence, May 2004

Steve Brown, oral history interview

Marguerite (Midge) Waters, oral history interview

CHAPTER 9 - FLOODS

The Ironwood Daily Globe
July 1909, June 1946

The Daily Mining Journal
Marquette, Michigan
September 1881

The Mining Journal
June 1939, July 1949, April 1960, May 1985,
May 2003
The Evening News
September 1916

Flood Descriptions
Ontonagon Historical Society Archives
Ontonagon, Michigan

Accounts of the Flood of 1920 in Manistique
Courtesy of the Schoolcraft County Historical Society

Ed Holmgren, oral history interview, May 2005

Gerry Gardner, oral history interview, May 2005

Margie Isaacson, oral history interview, May 2005

James Ghiardi, oral history interview, May 2005

Marko Movrich, oral history interview, June 2004

Joe Carlson, oral history interview, June 2004

Jim Ghiardi, oral history interview, June 2005

John Mullins, oral history interview, June 2005

Jeff Marshall, oral history interview, June 2005

Art Maki, oral history interview, June 2005

CHAPTER 10 - HEAT WAVES, HOT SUMMERS

A Fashionable Tour
Through the Great Lakes and Upper Mississippi
The 1852 Journal of Juliette Starr Dana
Edited by David T. Dana
Wayne State University Press Detroit 2004

Lake Superior Mining Journal

Sault Ste. Marie, Michigan 1852

Ironwood Daily Globe
July 1936

The Mining Journal
July 1936, May 1969

Journal at Light Station at Escanaba
Delta County Historical Society Archives

Iron Mountain Daily Press
July 1936
Marguerite Waters, oral history interview, June 2004

John Wallis, oral history interview

Jane Johns, oral history interview, March 2005

Larry Wanic, oral history interview

CHAPTER 11 - SEVERE WEATHER
Ontonagon Lighthouse Journal
Firesteel Publications
Ontonagon, Michigan 2005

Rockland Reporter
Rockland, Michigan
September 1899

I Married a Doctor-Life in Ontonagon, Michigan from 1900-1919
Alma Swinton
Marquette, Michigan December 1964

Daily Mining Gazette
April 1906

The Iron Port
Escanaba, Michigan
July 1906

The Ironwood Daily Globe
June 1908, July 1909, June 1939

Journal of Light Station at Escanaba
Delta County Historical Society Archives

The Daily Mining Journal
June 1878

The Mining Journal
June 1939, August 1988, July 1992

The Daily Press
July 1980

What is a Seiche?
University of Wisconsin Sea Grant Institute
http://www.seagrant.wisc.edu/communications/lakelevels/seiche.htm

City of Marquette
http://www.mqtcty.org/departments/parksrec/presque.htm

Spar Sager, oral history interview

Alvin and Claudia Lauren, oral history interview, April 2004

Dan Hornbogen, oral history interview, March 2005
Storm Observations, August 16, 1988
Written history

John Turausky, oral history interview, July 2004

Helen Micheau, oral history interview, May 2005

Lyn Veeser, oral history interview

Marv Taulbee, oral history interview, June 2005

Terry Soderman, oral history interview, March 2004

Greg Albrecht, oral history interview

Bruce Martin, oral history interview, May 2005

CHAPTER 12 - FIRE WEATHER
The Great Peshtigo Fire: An Eye Witness Account
Reverend Peter Pernin
State Historical Society of Wisconsin 1971

Michigan on Fire
Betty Sodders
Sam Speigel: Thunder Bay Press 1997

Light-House Establishment
Ontonagon Historical Society Archives

I Married a Doctor
Alma Swinton

The Daily Mining Journal
May 1896, May 1906, May 1908, May 1918

The Mining Journal
August, September 1933, August, September 1976, May 1986, May 1987, May 1999

Iron Mountain Daily Press
May 1906

Surveying Units and Terms
http://users.rcn.com/deeds/survey.htm

Seney Fire
Michigan Department of Natural Resources Publication

Forest fire terms
http://forestry.about.com/cs/glossary/g/wildfirec.htm?once=true&

Bruce Johanson, oral history interview, September 2004

Greg Lusk, oral history interview, May 2005

Robert Ziel, oral history interview, May 2005

Charlie Vallier, oral history interview, May 2005

Dan Holsworth, oral history interview, June 2005

Jeff Noble, oral history interview, May 2005

Gilbert Joy, oral history interview, May 2005

Barrett Ludlow, oral history interview

CHAPTER 13 - AUTUMN GALES

The Mining Journal
Marquette, Michigan, November and December, 1869

Historical Highlights, Radio Talks
Kenyon Boyer

Journal of Light Station at Escanaba
Delta County Historical Society Archives
November 8-10, 1913

Lore of the Lakes
Told in Story and Picture
Dana Thomas Bowen
Dana Thomas Bowen, Publisher
Daytona Beach, FL 1940

Freshwater Fury
Yarns and Reminiscences of the Greatest Storm in Inland Navigation
Frank Barcus
Wayne State University Press, 1960

Wreck Ashore
U. S. Lifesaving Service, Legendary Heroes of the Great Lakes
Frederick Stonehouse
Lake Superior Port Cities, Inc. 1994

Menominee Herald-Leader
November 10-12, 1913

The Mining Journal
November 8, 10, 12, 13 and 14, 1913

The Escanaba Daily Press
November 12-14, 1940

Spar Sager, oral history interview, March 2004

Dale Vinette, oral history interview, May 2005

Joe Warren, oral history interview, August 2005

The Night the Fitz Went Down
Hugh E. Bishop in cooperation with Dudley Paquette
Lake Superior Port Cities, Inc. 2000

Haunted Lake Superior
Ghostly Tales and Legends from the Mystical Inland Sea
Hugh E. Bishop
Lake Superior Port Cities, Inc. 2003

Minnesota Climate Journal
http://climate.umn.edu/doc/journal/981110.htm

Spar Sager, oral history interview

Dale Vinette, oral history interview, May 2005
John Wallis, oral history interview

Marv Taulbee, oral history interview, July 2005

Joe Warren, oral history interview, August 2005

John Murray, oral history interview, June 2005

Tom Hultquist, oral history interview, May 2005

Jim Heikkila, oral history interview

Loren Graham, correspondence, May 2005

EPILOGUE
The Earth's Fidgeting Climate
National Aeronautics and Space Administration
http://science.nasa.gov/headlines/y2000/ast20oct_1.htm

Here is an explanation of a few of the weather terms used frequently throughout the book.

Air: The mixture of gases forming the atmosphere. Dry air is composed mainly of nitrogen and oxygen with small amounts of carbon dioxide, hydrogen, ozone, and the inert gases. Moist air contains, in addition, varying amounts of water vapor.

Air mass: A body of air with similar properties of density, heat and moisture content throughout. An air mass will usually cover many thousands of square miles. It is at the interface or boundaries of differing air masses that stormy, unsettled weather occurs.

Anemometer: An instrument designed to measure wind speed.

Atmospheric pressure: The weight per unit area of the total mass of air above a given point; also called barometric pressure.

Blizzard: A snowstorm accompanied by winds in excess of 35 mph and visibilities of a ¼ mile or less for an extended period of time.

Circulation: The flow of air occurring within a somewhat circular wind system. There is the large scale flow that is the general circulation around semi-permanent features covering the entire earth. Secondary circulations occur around more transient, migratory systems moving through the general circulation.

Deepening: The decrease of pressure at the center of a low-pressure area or storm system.

Frost: Ice crystals formed on grass or other objects by the sublimation of water vapor from the air.

Gale: A wind speed from 32 to 63 mph or 28 to 55 knots. It is classified as a storm if wind speed is from 64 to 73 mph or 56 to 64 knots.

Gust: A sudden, brief increase in wind speed.

Jet stream: A band of strong winds concentrated in a narrow stream high in our weather-producing atmosphere. In the middle latitudes, this stream of high wind is associated with the main frontal boundary that separates cold air of the arctic from warm air of the tropics. In general, the stronger the temperature contrast across a frontal boundary, the stronger the winds will be aloft. As mentioned below, low pressure, or storm systems develop along these frontal boundaries. These systems are then pushed along by the jet-stream winds.

Front: A transition zone between air masses of differing density. Temperature is the most important determinant of density, so a front usually separates cold and warm air masses. There are different kinds of fronts, all with distinguishing characteristics. The main frontal boundaries are warm, cold, occluded and stationary fronts.

Low Pressure: An area of minimum atmospheric pressure. In the Northern Hemisphere, wind flows counter-clockwise around a low. These systems distribute heat from the tropics northward in the southerly flow ahead of them and cold air from the arctic southward in northerly flow behind them. On any given day, there are a number of low-pressure areas on the weather map across North America. The strongest of these systems turn into memorable storms that dump heavy rain and snow and bring gale-force winds to Upper Michigan.

A low often develops along a stalled frontal boundary. As the system matures, the boundary begins pin wheeling around the low. This action develops the familiar warm and cold fronts seen on weather maps. The structure of a low is such that the heaviest, steadiest precipitation falls to the north and northwest of the system in the cold air. A typical low will produce the heaviest snow from 100 to as much as 250 miles northwest of its track. The advancing cold front will usually produce more scattered, showery precipitation.

High Pressure: An area of maximum atmospheric pressure. In the Northern Hemisphere, air flows clockwise around a high. The largest of these systems sits over a region for days and takes on the characteristic heat and moisture content of the region. The high then becomes an air mass that can cover many thousand square miles. Highs often develop over the arctic regions of Canada, Alaska and Siberia. These house the bitterest air masses that drop southward into Upper Michigan during a typical winter. Another familiar spot for high-pressure development is the eastern Atlantic Ocean. This high becomes the "Bermuda High" that pumps heat and humidity toward Upper Michigan in the summer.

The air flow around a high promotes stable, fair weather. In Upper Michigan, the approach of a high-pressure system in the cold season often does just the opposite—the northerly component to the wind ahead of it blows across Lake Superior and results in cloud development and lake-effect snow.

Lake effect: In general, the effect of a lake in modifying the weather about it shores and for some distance downwind. Since Upper Michigan is a peninsula surrounded by water on all sides except its border with Wisconsin, lake effect plays a large role in the climate during all seasons. The U.P.'s most famous aspect of lake effect is snow. During the cold season, air flowing over the relatively warm water of Lake Superior causes evaporation, which leads to snow showers downwind over the Peninsula. Snow off Lake Michigan occurs less frequently because the predominant wind direction during the winter is northwest. The largest seasonal snowfalls in the United States outside of mountain locations occur over the snow belts of Upper Michigan and in some down-wind areas of upstate New York.

In the warm season, the Great Lakes are huge, natural air conditioners. Water warms much more slowly than land. This property of water means that the Great Lakes and the air just above them retains winter chill well into the warm season. This chilly air over the water is more dense than the warmer air over land. This means that the cold, lake-chilled air regularly moves inland as a lake breeze. This phenomenon gives rise to the familiar forecast phrase "cooler near the lake."

While evaporation occurs in the cold season, lake effect in the warm time of the year leads to condensation. Warm air with relatively high moisture content flows across Lakes Michigan, Superior and Huron and quickly saturates, forming great fog banks that roll inland along the shore. This effect is most pronounced in the spring and early summer when the water is the coldest. By late summer and early fall, the Great Lakes have finally reached their warmest levels of the season. This lingering warmth keeps the growing season going longer along the shoreline than in areas just a few miles inland. It also means an early inland snowstorm will likely be rain or a mixture of rain and sloppy snow within a few miles of the Great Lakes.

Millibar (mb): Is the metric unit of pressure. One millibar is 0.02953 inches of mercury (Hg). Average sea-level pressure is 1013.2 mb or 29.92 inches of mercury.

Precipitation: Falling products of condensation or sublimation such as rain, snow, sleet or drizzle. Precipitation elements are usually larger than 0.02 centimeters—particles smaller than this usually remain suspended in the air.

Radiosonde: A device attached to a weather balloon used to measure various constituents of the atmosphere. The most common constituents are wind, pressure, moisture and temperature measured at various altitudes and geographical positions. The radiosonde then transmits the information to a fixed receiver.

Severe Thunderstorm: A thunderstorm with winds of 50 knots (58 mph) or greater and/or hail of ¾ inches in diameter or greater.

Squall: A strong wind characterized by a sudden onset with duration on the order of minutes, and an equally sudden decrease in speed. An event is considered a squall only if the wind speed of 16 knots or higher is attained for at least two minutes. A squall line is a well-marked line of strong, gusty winds, turbulence and often heavy showers and/or thundershowers.

Straight-line winds: Winds blowing from the same direction. This term is usually used in distinguishing winds blowing in a straight line out of a thunderstorm from the circular winds of a tornado.

Tornado: A localized and violently destructive windstorm occurring over land characterized by a funnel-shaped cloud extending toward the ground.

Trough: An elongated area of low barometric pressure.

Upper Air: In this book, the term refers to the weather-producing atmosphere more than a mile above the ground.

Upper-air trough: A trough of low pressure in the upper atmosphere. Looking at a map, it appears to be a "dip" in the upper-level flow or jet stream. Surface low pressure often forms in the lower-right or southeast quadrant of an upper-air trough.

Upper-air ridge: This feature appears, literally, as a ridge or hill in the upper-level flow. Surface high pressure develops just downwind of the axis or peak in the ridge.

Troughs and ridges take up residence in any one location for a number of days, weeks and even a season. Their position in relation to Upper Michigan strongly influences the type of weather we receive.

Warm sector: The portion of a low-pressure area containing warm air, lying in advance of a cold front and to the rear of a warm front. The usual location of the warm sector in a low over the Northern Hemisphere is in its southeastern quadrant.

Wind: Is air in motion. This phenomenon occurs naturally in the atmosphere and is usually considered to be air moving parallel to the ground

INDEX

FOR ADDITIONAL COPIES OF "SO COLD A SKY"

Cold Sky Publishing

P.O. Box 228,
Negaunee, MI 49866

Email: kbohnak@chartermi.net

Web: www.upweatherhistory.com